The Anthropological Character of Theology

The Anthropological Character of Theology

Conditioning Theological Understanding

DAVID A. PAILIN

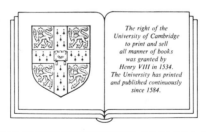

CAMBRIDGE UNIVERSITY PRESS

Cambridge

New York   Port Chester   Melbourne   Sydney

Published by the Press Syndicate of the University of Cambridge
The Pitt Building, Trumpington Street, Cambridge CB2 1RP
40 West 20th Street, New York, NY 10011 USA
10 Stamford Road, Oakleigh, Melbourne 3166, Australia

First published 1990

Printed in Great Britain at the University Press, Cambridge

British Library cataloguing in publication data
Pailin, David A. (David Arthur), 1936–
The anthropological character of theology.
1. Theology
I. Title
230

Library of Congress cataloguing in publication data
Pailin, David A. (David Arthur). 1936–
The anthropological character of theology: conditioning
theological understanding / David A. Pailin.
p.   cm.
Includes bibliographical references.
ISBN 0 521 39069 9
1. Theology – Methodology. 2. Cultural relativism.
3. Anthropomorphism. 4. Revelation.
I. Title
BR118.P26 1990
230'.01–dc20   89-29674   CIP

ISBN 0 521 39069 9

IVCVNDÆ
LAETÆ
CARISSIMÆ

Contents

Contents

Contents

Preface

During the long period of incubation which this study has under-
gone, I have come to realize that theology should be written in 'all-
inclusive' language. Accordingly, whereas in earlier drafts I
thoughtlessly used 'mankind' for 'humanity', normally spoke of a
person as 'he' and referred to God as 'he', I have tried in this text
to remove all such sexist implications. If at any point I have failed,
I apologize. Although most of the non-sexist usages should not be
obvious, I dislike such neologisms as 's/he'. Consequently, where a
singular personal pronoun is needed to refer to the God of theistic
belief (for 'it' is objectionably impersonal), I have, for want of
anything better, resorted to using phrases like 'the divine' and 'the
holy' as equivalents to a personal pronoun for God.

This study has benefited from the attention of various people to
whom thanks are due. Susan Smalley commented on the earliest
draft, Raymond Plant and John Harrod patiently and attentively
worked through later ones. Maurice Wiles has throughout shown
supportive interest, insight and friendship. Many of my students at
Manchester have, for several years, considered these issues and
several of them have provided me with genuine academic col-
leagueship in the quest for theological understanding. Jacqueline
Berry, Arnold Anderson and John Robertson have been percipient
critics of my ideas. My failures to take advantage of their advice
should not be blamed on them. To them all I am very grateful.

I

Introduction to a study of theology

Towards the end of the *Critique of Pure Reason*, Kant claims that he has provided a much needed assessment of 'our adventurous and self-reliant reason', which should help 'to prevent errors in its use' and thereby to secure 'general order and harmony' in human thought. So far as religion is concerned, his argument shows how metaphysics acts as 'a bulwark' for faith by defining the limits of human reason.[1] Whatever judgements may be made on Kant's own performance of this task, it is only by a self-critical investigation of the nature of its rationality that we can appreciate properly the nature and significance of theological understanding.

While, therefore, methodological investigations into a form of understanding may sometimes seem to be a way of avoiding the task of developing that understanding, they may also be a necessary preliminary if such development is to avoid pursuing illusory objectives by specious methods. The following study arises from the conviction that theology today needs such preliminary investigations if it is to establish its credibility as a mode of understanding. In particular, it considers what follows once we recognize that since theologians are human, their conclusions are conditioned by the nature of human thought.[2]

The scope of this study

Presupposing that theological understanding has not dropped from the skies nor been implanted in human minds by the miraculous provision of some *deus ex machina*, the following chapters investigate various ways in which theological conclusions are affected by the rationality of those who produce them. Although 'theology' is taken to be the attempt to understand the fundamental nature of reality in terms of the referent of religious faith, the investigation does not pretend to cover all forms of theological understanding. In order to keep its object within bounds, it is primarily concerned with those forms of understanding which are fundamentally theistic – that is, which attempt to understand reality in terms of a 'God' who is not only rationally, ontologically and valuatively ultimate, but is also most adequately understood in terms of a personal (i.e., self-aware, conscious, purposive) and agential mode of being. This personalistic view of theism and this theistic view of religion are not the only possible views of them, but they do express the dominant self-understanding of that major group of religious faiths constituted by Judaism, Christianity and Islam. The limitation of this study to such theisms, however, does not imply that what follows has no relevance to the thought of other, even non-theistic faiths. It only means that those attempts to grasp the ultimate nature and purpose of reality, and hence the answers to humanity's existential questions, are not the primary object of this study.

After some preliminary remarks in this chapter about the nature of this enquiry, chapter 2 clarifies what is meant by faith, belief, theology and reason, and how they are related to each other. The succeeding chapters identify six ways in which theological judgements are conditioned. Chapter 3 examines how the concept of God is a projection of human attributes, and chapter 4 how it is governed by our ideas of what would provide ultimate and self-explanatory completion for our search for understanding. The next two chapters consider the extent to which theological insights held to be derived from human experiences and from supposed revelations are conditioned by the culture and structure of thought of those who apprehend them. Chapter 7 investigates how our understanding of our deepest needs and of their remedy affects how we think of God, while chapter 8 examines how current thought about the world influences our understanding of God as the basis of the unity, harmony and meaning of all reality. The final chapter briefly mentions some further matters which need to be considered in determining the nature and status of theological understanding.

One major issue which this book does not attempt to investigate is that of the nature of claims to truth in theological understanding. This is not because such an investigation is either unimportant or unnecessary. Although theological understanding is conditioned by how we think, we must not forget that it purports to provide understanding of God as the ground of all reality and of the fundamental character of reality as grounded in the divine. As such it sees itself as determining what is true about God – and thereby truths which determine how everything else is finally to be correctly understood. The warrantability of its claims is a crucial and controversial matter in the pervading secular and sceptical culture of the contemporary Western world, but it is a matter which is outside the scope of this study.[3]

In this book, then, we shall examine six ways in which theological understanding is fundamentally conditioned. As a result of these factors theology must be seen to be inescapably tentative and changeable, not just because it is seeking understanding in relation to a living God and a processive reality, but also because it is produced by human beings.

Descriptive and revisionary

Since it is about theology, this study is illustrated by various references to theological judgements. It should not, however, be judged by the acceptability of those discussions but by its success in identifying the factors which condition theological judgements and in suggesting how in future they may be more adequately constructed. It aims, that is, to be a 'revisionary' as well as a 'descriptive' study of theology.[4]

Some theologians may not only reject the revisionary suggestions. They may also – and primarily – condemn the preliminary attempt to describe the structure of theological understanding as it is actually presented on the grounds that 'outsiders' cannot properly appreciate its character. In this way they may defend their position by means of an appeal to privileged status, but it is at the cost of restricting acceptable criticisms of it to the private circle of fellow believers.[5] Those who claim such immunity for their theology sterilize their capacity to produce an understanding which may reasonably claim to be generally credible.[6]

On the other hand, those who purport to describe theological understanding must take care that their analyses deal with what is actually maintained and not with inventions of their imagination. In recent years a number of professedly Wittgensteinian treatments of religious belief have appeared, which seem to some believers to reveal that their authors' philosophical competence is not matched by an acquaintance with (or even a memory of) authentic religious faith! While, therefore, assertions that theological understanding is immune from rational investigation are to be rejected, attempts to describe such understanding must take seriously claims that theology as a mode of understanding and, even more, religion itself is *sui generis*. Such claims do not rule out rational investigations of theology and religion. They warn those who undertake them that

3

they must ensure that the rational structures which they use are appropriate to what is being described.

Descriptions of how theologians reach their conclusions, both professedly and actually, raise questions about which of those ways is either traditionally acceptable or theologically preferable to any other. Such questions are not easy to answer. In certain respects it may be reasonable to consider that the proper answer to the question, 'What is the method of theology?', is given by describing the method or methods that respected theologians actually profess and employ. To ask of any method, however, 'But is it the correct one?', 'Is it rationally acceptable?' or even 'Is there a better way?', is to introduce questions of value, the basis of whose solution is not straightforward. In the case of theology, decisions about the 'right' way or about a 'better' way of reaching understanding have to be made by reference to what persons of sensitiveness and sense (and how they are to be identified cannot avoid begging the question to some extent) regard as providing satisfactory understanding of the relevant kind. To be satisfactory, such understanding must be credible according to generally accepted standards of rationality and appropriate to the object of theology as that which is ontologically, valuatively and rationally ultimate.

Fundamental problems arise when it becomes apparent that it is not at all clear how these criteria are to be satisfied. Attempts to find a solution by challenging the appeal to reason[7] are self-defeating. They demolish the possibility of any commonly agreed court of appeal and turn theological understanding into a matter of uncheckable private illumination. What is needed is, first, an elucidation of the various factors that seem to be essentially involved in theological understanding and, then, an investigation of whether they can be coherently combined and, if so, in what way. By such an approach it is to be hoped that theologians will be able to avoid the errors of the dogmatists whom Kant condemned for going beyond what was actually possible.[8] The resulting theological edifice may be a cottage and not a palace, but a cottage that is complete is better than a folly which never can be made habitable!

A form of human understanding

As has already been remarked, the basic presupposition of this study is that since theologians are human, theology is conditioned by the nature of human understanding. This may appear to be so obvious that it is trite to mention it. In practice, however, some theologians have apparently failed to appreciate that, while the object of their study may properly be regarded as being in certain respects absolute, their study of it is relative to their intellectual situation.

Karl Barth, for example, may seem to recognize this relativity when he says that the theologian has to speak 'from within his philosophical shell',[9] but it is questionable how far he accepts its implications since he goes on to hold that the true theologian must be 'ready to submit the coherence of his concepts and formulations to the coherence of the divine revelation and not conversely'.[10] In the first volume of *Church Dogmatics* Barth emphasizes the divine initiative in authentic theology to the point of asserting that in the event of Jesus Christ 'the proper content' of language about God becomes 'clear in a flash and in the highest perfection and certainty'. Although 'the event of human action' is needed to appropriate this knowledge, it is said to be 'frankly a second item as compared with the event proceeding from God'.[11] More recently this understanding of theology[12] has been put forward by T.F. Torrance. He states, for example, that 'Christian theology arises out of the actual knowledge of God' given by God 'in space and time'. It is 'positive knowledge' and our grasp of it does not 'begin with ourselves or our questions' but 'with the facts prescribed for us by the actuality of the object positively known'.[13]

These views of theological understanding challenge (and are in turn challenged by) the basic presupposition of this study. While acknowledging the 'creaturely form' of theological statements, Barth and Torrance apparently consider that theology can and must be primarily controlled by its object – 'God' – as given in divine self-revelation. In terms of the *ordo essendi* and of a desire to make concepts fit what they describe, they have the right priorities. In the *ordo cognoscendi* the situation is reversed. We cannot begin anywhere else than with ourselves[14] – with our questions and with our structures of understanding.[15] As will be argued later, even theological understanding which claims to be derived from God's self-revelation is importantly moulded by the intellectual character of those who claim to have apprehended it. The only apparent alternative to recognizing the human structuring of theological understanding is to regard theology as a miraculous activity in which God replaces the human intellect. Such a position is hardly tenable in view of the human conditioning that theological works display.[16]

Negatively, the recognition of the human basis of theological understanding means that theologians are always open to the criticism that they are only talking about themselves and about what makes sense to them, whereas the nature of ultimate reality may be quite – and unknowably – different.[17] The tradition of Western thought from Descartes and Locke which starts by investigating our ways of understanding may thus be held to prevent its followers from ever discerning the truth about God.[18] One purpose of this study is to investigate the significance of this criticism and of the counter-claim[19] that human self-understanding can only achieve completion if it is related to an understanding of God.[20]

Positively, the recognition of the human basis of theological understanding means that theologians are prevented from pretending that their utterances, if not God's own, at least have the support of God's unquestionable authority. If, as will be suggested later,[21] 'God' marks the limit of human understanding, they should not be surprised if their theology is troubled with loose ends, puzzles, perplexities, rough approximations and messily complex arguments. Such characteristics may indicate an honest attempt to apprehend what is intrinsically ultimate. Theologians, therefore, should proceed humbly, hoping that they are discerning truth rather than nonsense, and that what they claim to be cosmic insights are not in God's eyes hugely comical misunderstandings. If they wish to avoid being unwitting clowns, they need to follow Kant's example[22] in rejecting the dogmatism which refuses to determine its own competence, as well as the scepticism which refuses to entertain the possibility of theological understanding. Their primary task is to establish the conditions, limits and status of their understanding.

The point of studying theology

What is the point in studying theology? Once it was regarded as the queen of the sciences. Today it is haunted by the fear that it may be merely a subject for study in the history of ideas, like alchemy and astrology. Can it justify its claim to have a legitimate place in the contemporary search for understanding?

Theology is not to be regarded as simply another subject (dealing with 'God') directly comparable to physics (dealing with 'matter') or history (dealing with 'past personal activity'). This is not because its subject-matter is not directly observable (as if those of physics and history are), but because its subject-matter provides the final ground, coherence and point of all other forms of understanding. Theology is to be studied because it provides the keystone to the arch of understanding and, in this respect (but not in the sense of 'queening' it over others), it is properly regarded as the queen of the sciences.

It is also to be considered as a proper subject for study because it deals with people's attempts to find satisfying answers to the basic questions of human existence posed by its self-reflective, future-orientated, purpose-seeking character.[23] The notion of God is the notion of what is regarded in religious faith and theology as the self-explanatory foundation of all being, meaning and value. In spite of the crude ways in which 'God' has sometimes been understood, the notion thus refers to one way in which people have attempted to reach a fundamental understanding of themselves and of the reality of which they are part.

To recognize the importance of the questions which provoke theological enquiry does not, however, imply that theology is able to answer them. The study of theology may reveal that it is incapable of providing rationally satisfying answers. Whether or not this is the conclusion to be drawn from this study must wait until its investigations are completed. In the mean time, because human rationality makes us persist in asking questions about ulti-mate meaning and value, in spite of frequently being told that they are meaningless, pointless, confused or unanswerable questions, we cannot abandon the quest to understand the ultimate structure of reality without abandoning our basic self-understanding as reasoning persons. While, then, we may wonder about our com-petence to find answers to the questions of being, we cannot, with-out declaring the meaninglessness of life for us, abandon the search for answers to them. Theology may accordingly be held to be worth studying because, and so far as, the questions which give rise to it are basic, inescapable and important for human being.[24]

The relativity of this study

Egotism can be true humility in an author.[25] By continually pointing out that this and that assertion is what I think, I would make it clear that my claims express how things appear to me in my social, historical and intellectual situation. This would be tedious for the reader and might leave me with a disastrous sense of my own importance. Let me, therefore, simply state that when in future pages I discuss the relativity of thought, I do not exempt my own!

2

Faith, belief, theology and reason

Before we consider the factors conditioning theological understanding, it is important to clarify what is meant by the basic concepts of faith, belief, theology and reason, and to outline how they
are related to each other. It is not intended to present a comprehensive description of the variety of ways in which these notions are
used in practice but to indicate, by reference to a set of actual usages
appropriate to the theological position to be examined, how these
key concepts are understood in this study.

The nature of faith

'Faith' refers to the stance, understanding and disposition which
constitute a person's existential commitment. It includes assent to
a particular apprehension of the fundamental character of reality,
the acceptance of certain values contained within that apprehension
as normative, and the adoption of correspondingly appropriate
forms of activity. It embraces these different factors not as distinct
components but as interdependent facets of a single whole.

As a matter of commitment, faith involves risk. It is an affirmation of what can never, in its material content, be indisputably
demonstrated. This does not mean that those who have faith will
typically feel anxious or hesitant about it. As Tillich suggests, the
'doubt' that belongs to faith is 'not a permanent experience within
the act of faith' which is expressed in a specific psychological state.
It is rather to be regarded as a characteristic of the logical structure
of faith, which results from the tension between the relativity of
those who affirm it and 'its unconditional character'.[1] The 'courage'
of faith is hence the readiness to affirm faith in the consciousness
of this tension; the 'certainty' of faith is the certitude of conviction
in action, not the impossibility of intellectual error.[2]

In many cases people are largely unaware of the content of their
faith. Their commitment is not a matter of deliberate intellectual

assent, but a largely unconscious matter of belonging to some roughly defined group with only a vague awareness of its principal ideas. Through membership of the group, sharing its general ethos and observing its customs, its underlying faith comes to be imprinted upon them. Although, therefore, they live by that faith, they may become conscious of its elements only when its principles and practices are questioned. It is not unusual, furthermore, to find people who give allegiance to more than one group, and whose existential faith is consequently a matter of conformation to sets of ideas and practices that may not be wholly harmonious with each other.

Others manifestly live according to principles which conflict with the faith which they explicitly profess. Sometimes the distinction is due to ignorance or confusion, sometimes to weakness of the will, and sometimes to moral turpitude – 'hypocrisy'. As a result neither what people say nor what they do are straightforward guides to their actual faith. They may misunderstand what it involves or fail to live up to what they correctly appreciate to be its demands.[3]

On examination a self-consistent faith is found to have a structure that is far from simple. Among the components of a faith typical of religious believers are behaviour-patterns, value-principles, moral commitments, membership (formal or informal) of a community, social activities, ritual performances, specific attitudes towards the self and others, notions of corporate and private vocation, and expectations of experiences of numinous awe and of gracious support. Fundamental, however, to the type of theistic faith to be considered here is the entertainment of certain convictions about what is the case, in particular about the character of that reality which is ultimate ontologically, rationally and valuatively. If, therefore, the notion of 'fact' is not restricted to contingent states but is understood to refer to any state of affairs, whether a posteriori or a priori, contingent or necessary, empirical or metaphysical, another way of putting this point is to say that a factual element is basic to faith. Nevertheless, while the words 'fact' and 'factual' are widely used to refer to what is the case, whatever its modal status, etymology (*factum* is 'what has been made') implies they should strictly be confined to references to what is a posteriori and contingent. Hence, since the ultimate to which faith refers is in certain respects at least a priori and necessary, it is more appropriate to put it that a reference to what is mind-independently real is basic to faith.

Because the realist reference of faith is primarily to what in certain respects is necessary and a priori – to what is sometimes described as 'metaphysical reality' – it is not surprising that it has certain logical peculiarities. Attempts have, therefore, been made to avoid difficulties with theistic faith by holding that its apparently factual element is a somewhat misleading expression of something else.[4] 'God' has accordingly been treated as a value-term or as a cipher for some principle of behaviour. Braithwaite, for example, has suggested that 'God is love' is to be interpreted as the expression of 'an intention to follow an agapeistic way of life',[5] while Cupitt asserts that 'the doctrine of God is an encoded set of spiritual directives'.[6] Such views of theistic faith are fundamentally unsatisfactory. Their 'solution' to problems with that faith only works by converting it into something else. They either explicitly deny or merely overlook what is an essential part of the nature of theistic faith, namely, that it involves recognition of and responses to a reality that is ontologically independent of the believer's contingent existence.[7]

The nature of belief

While 'faith' refers to the whole understanding of reality and values and a corresponding way of life that constitutes a religion, 'belief' refers to the apprehension of and assent to the judgements about what is the case in being, value and rationality which are contained, at least implicitly, in a faith. 'Belief' in general thus refers to the conscious, intellectual aspect of faith, while 'a belief' is an expression of a particular constitutive judgement of a faith.

As in the case of behaviour which shows that in reality a person's existential commitment is not what they profess to be their faith, so in matters of belief discrepancies sometimes appear between what people declare to be their beliefs and what is implied by their actions, including other statements to which they clearly give assent. Where such discrepancies are not due to misunderstanding, weakness or hypocrisy, the expressions and perhaps the contents of their beliefs need to be revised if they are to provide an appropriate statement of what is genuinely believed to be the case.

Anselm's *Proslogion* illustrates the way in which beliefs may be affirmed which conflict with some aspects of the believer's practice. His statement in chapter 8 that God is impassible, for example, is strangely at odds with his passionate prayer to God for aid in chapter 1.[8] Either his prayer expresses a wish for which Anselm can expect no reciprocal response in God – in which case it seems to be a rather pointless expression of a feeling of inadequacy – or

Anselm's practice presupposes a responsiveness in God which his assertion of belief about God's impassibility cannot accommodate.[9] A similar contradiction appears in the *Book of Common Prayer*: its liturgies contain prayers asking God to 'have mercy', while the Articles of Religion state that God is 'without passions'. Although some theologians have tried to overcome the problem by arguing that God can be held consistently, if paradoxically, to be both impassible and compassionate, it seems more reasonable to regard these two beliefs about God[10] as basically incompatible. If, therefore, a credible solution to the problem is to be found, it must be by reconsidering the beliefs involved – for example, by rethinking how divine awareness and activity are to be understood, or by recognizing that the divine perfection does not entail unchangeability in every respect.

Another example of disagreement between theoretical assents and existential affirmations is highlighted by Ogden. Some radical theologians reject Christian theism because they identify it with its traditional formulations. (A generation ago a number of theologians of the 'death of God' movement followed Nietzsche in this respect.) At the same time, Ogden points out, they combine this denial with a commitment to the significance of life and to the obligation to love, which can reasonably be interpreted as an existential expression of the Christian faith.[11] In view of this not uncommon state of affairs, it is important in studying what people hold to be their beliefs to appreciate that, in spite of appearances, one person's assertion of belief and another's of unbelief may not be in conflict.[12] What the former in asserting their belief does not intend to imply, the other is explicitly denying in rejecting that statement of belief.[13]

The realist reference of faith and belief

Before we go on to discuss what is meant by theology and the functions of reason in theological thought, it is important to respond to an understanding of faith and belief which has some current vogue and which challenges the foundation of the treatment of them here. The claim that theistic faith and belief include reference to reality – and specifically to the reality of that which is ontologically, valuatively and rationally ultimate – does not enjoy universal consent. Although it would be hard to sustain the case that such an understanding of theism is unusual,[14] some argue that it is an understanding which arises from a naive appreciation of the use of language about God. They maintain, for example, that the grammatical structure and apparent reference of talk about God (e.g., 'God is . . .', 'God wills . . .') are different from its proper logical character. According to their interpretation 'God' is a predicative term ascribing a certain value, not the name of a mind-independent individual.[15] In order to meet this fundamental criticism of the view of faith investigated in this study, we shall first indicate the range of references to God as real at the heart of theistic faith, and then illustrate how such a reference is commonly, if not universally, regarded as an essential aspect of faith in the case of theistic religion.

What, then, do we discover if we follow Wittgenstein's advice, 'Don't ask for meaning, ask for use'? Does examination of those who use the term 'faith' (and who express the contents of their faith in beliefs) in connection with theistic religion justify the view that it includes a basic reference to what is independent of the believer's mind? When we consider how people speak about the contents and implications of their faith and its beliefs, we find that the picture which emerges is complex and inconsistent.

In some cases allegiance to a religious faith does appear to be wholly analysable in terms of the observance of a certain pattern of behaviour. To be a 'Christian' (or a Muslim or a Buddhist) is understood as a matter of acting as Christians (or Muslims or Buddhists) are commonly expected to act. There seems to be no significant reference to a transcendent reality in the content of such a faith. Any claims about 'God' included in its practices may be interpreted as rather puzzlingly empty ways by which the community identifies itself. Those whose faith is of this kind thus give some justification to those analyses which hold that faith does not include a cognitive reference to the being of an ontologically ultimate reality. It is arguable, however, that those who have such a faith are to be regarded as theists only so far as, by some kind of unconscious intellectual osmosis, they have come to adopt the intellectual attitudes of theists whose practices they share.

In many other cases, however, it is clear that religious faith and its beliefs involve assent, whether explicit or implicit, to claims about what is the case, as well as the observance of a way of life appropriate to those claims. The practice is not considered to be self-justifying. It is a response to judgements about the character of ultimate reality. As Whitehead suggests, what is expressed in these judgements is located within a triangle formed by the extremities of the doctrines of immanence, transcendence and monism.[16]

Sometimes the mind-independent reference to reality contained in faith and its beliefs merely identifies 'an impersonal order to which the world conforms'[17] but usually it is also understood to include or entail an important moral dimension. Matthew Arnold, for example, describes 'The Eternal' both as 'a real power' and as 'the *not ourselves* which makes for righteousness'.[18] Among the forms of such a faith are those which affirm that reality as a whole makes sense, that certain values are intrinsically obligatory, and that reality provides a fit, responsive and significant arena for their exercise. This type of faith and belief thus contradicts atheistic claims that reality is a purposeless and incoherent jumble of accidents produced by the haphazard interactions of chance and necessity, expressing no underlying purpose.[19] It also contradicts the view that there is nothing external to our individual or corporate decisions which provides a standard of good for us.

According to this interpretation of their basic nature, faith and belief refer to certain characteristics of reality which they consider to be finally and inescapably the case. References to 'God' are to these actual characteristics: they do not point to an element in reality which is intrinsically self-explanatory and in some purposive way responsible for the fundamental characteristics of the cosmos being what they are. Consequently, while faith and belief as so understood include references to reality, the use of the notion 'God' is only minimally theistic. It is, nevertheless, a position to which a number of contemporary theologians seem attracted, presumably because it releases them from having to make meaningful and credible assertions about God as an ultimate, agential and perhaps personal entity which (or who) is ontologically necessary.

Such assertions, however, are characteristic of what are generally – and properly – classed as fully theistic forms of faith and belief. According to this understanding of their nature, the references to reality basic to them is to the reality of that which is ontologically, valuatively and rationally ultimate, aware, purposive and agential. The basic characteristics of the cosmos are consequently held to have been determined by the agency of a purposively acting ultimate reality whose mode of being may most adequately be grasped by analogy with that of persons. For theism this entity, 'God', is either self-explanatory or the brute fact beyond which no explanation is possible.[20]

Matthew Arnold outlines such a view of theism in terms of 'A

Personal First Cause, the moral and intelligent Governor of the universe', although he himself considers that such an understanding of 'the not ourselves' goes far beyond what reason can justify.[21] According to Whitehead, one mode of this form of theism advances the concept of 'a definite personal individual entity, whose existence is the one ultimate metaphysical fact, absolute and underivative, and who decreed and ordered the derivative existence which we call the actual world'.[22] As Whitehead appreciates, however, this understanding of theism implies a view of divine transcendence which is problematic. On the other hand, the monistic (or pantheistic) alternative, according to which 'the actual world has the reality of being a partial description of what God is' while having no proper reality of its own, is equally unsatisfactory. The former so distinguishes and the latter so links God and the cosmos that in each case it is difficult to envisage the possibility of any significant relationship between them.

A large part of the difficulty lies in perceiving how we are to make sense of God's relationship to the rest of reality as its creative ground and the basis of its ultimate significance. It is a problem to which we will return in chapter 8.[23] Whitehead himself maintains that religious faith uncompromisingly affirms that human life has genuine value and permanent significance, because it 'contributes its quality as an immortal fact to the order which informs the world'.[24] This can be affirmed (and it can only be affirmed) because – and so far as – it is justifiable to consider that God, as the necessary, everlasting and ultimate reality, is conscious of, cares for and responds to what happens through human agency. Such a position presupposes that it is possible to conceive God as both transcendent and immanent, both ultimate and related, both necessary and contingent in appropriate respects.[25] It is the reality of such a God that theistic faith basically refers to and which constitutes the ground of its affirmation of the purposiveness, significance and value of the processes of reality.

It is important to note, then, that the theistic form of religious faith as well as the beliefs that express it, for all their puzzles, understand references to God as references to that ultimate reality which, while most adequately thought of as embracing the cosmos, is also to be distinguished from it.[26] Thus apprehended, 'God' is not a fictional construct serving as a theoretical representation of various claims about the basic characteristics of the world. 'God', rather, is the name for that mind-independent reality whose actuality, purposes and activity (even though our apprehensions of their nature may require much imaginative construction)[27] are the final and self-warranting ground for the world being rationally coherent, purposive and directed towards the creative achievement of aesthetic satisfaction.

The claim that theistic faith and belief are generally recognized to have a basic reference to what is real and ultimate may be illustrated by noting what a small but not unrepresentative selection of anti-theists and theists have said about them and their implications.[28] Many anti-theists, for example, clearly consider that they fully justify their position if they can decisively refute claims about the actual being of God. Thus La Mettrie repeats Holbach's view that 'if atheism . . . were generally accepted, all the forms of religion would be destroyed'.[29] Nietzsche, while rejoicing over 'the death of God' as the end of 'the enemy of life',[30] also recognizes that the values, goal and significance brought to life by religion disappear when the reality of God is no more: 'Are we not straying as through an infinite nothing?'[31] John Stuart Mill reports that his father found religious faith untenable because he judged the character of the world to be incompatible with the reality of the God of such a faith.[32] Mill himself, whatever his personal convictions,[33] held that the moral effectiveness of religion rests on 'the undoubting belief of the real existence' of 'a living Being' who incorporates 'our highest conceptions of . . . wisdom and goodness'.[34] Bertrand Russell condemns attempts to preserve religion merely because it is useful. While he is sure that they will not succeed, he considers that those who try to give 'reasons for supposing that there is a God' have properly appreciated what religion is about.[35] Ayer similarly points out that theistic faith will be irretrievably lost once it has been recognized that 'God exists' is not an intelligible proposition – for most believers religious doctrine is not acceptable simply as 'a useful myth'.[36]

On turning from atheists to self-confessed theists, we find that they too regard their understanding of ultimate value, significance and purpose as grounded upon their assent to the mind-independent reality of God. The long apologetic tradition which has sought arguments to justify claims about the existence of God witnesses to the centrality of those claims for theistic faith and belief.[37] Attempts by reductionists and revisionists to suggest that religious faith does not essentially involve belief in the reality of God are accordingly widely rejected as attempts to preserve a lifeless corpse. Barth, for example, sees Feuerbach's anthropological interpretation of Christianity as 'illusionism' contrary to authentic faith: genuine theistic understanding is grounded, for Barth, in the reality of God who gives it as an act of grace.[38] From a very different position John Wisdom suggests that attempts to defend religious belief by denying that it has 'to say something as to what in fact is so' will be seen by believers as presenting 'a blasphemous fable and a dangerous deceit'. It is a denial of what makes religious belief what it is.[39] Just over a generation later Küng made a similar protest against the attempt by 'some contemporary linguistic analysts, such as Norman Malcolm, G. E. Hughes, W. D. Hudson, P. Winch, D. Z. Phillips' to interpret religious language as 'an autonomous, irreducible language game' and to ignore 'the question of truth'.[40] The basic trust in the meaningfulness and value of all that is, which characterizes the life of faith, is justified for Küng by the existence of God.[41]

These views of religious faith are presupposed in many current theological studies. Richard Swinburne, for example, defines Christian faith as 'basically faith in a person or persons, God (or Christ) characterized as possessing certain properties and having done certain actions'.[42] Keith Ward begins *Rational Theology and the Creativity of God* by declaring that he wants to show that there are 'good reasons' for asserting God's reality as 'the foundation of all being and value'.[43] Karl Rahner recognizes that there is a mysterious elusiveness that belongs to our apprehension of the 'genuinely real' transcendent, but he regards it as 'the greatest misunderstanding' to explain the idea of God as a human creation.[44] John Cobb asserts that 'normally and properly' the word 'God' refers to 'a unitary actuality which is supremely worthy of worship and/or commitment'.[45] Finally, in this selection of contemporary writers on theistic faith, we may note Schubert Ogden's response to the view that theological utterances 'assert nothing whatever about God'. He retorts that whatever else Christians may do when they witness to their faith, they 'most surely' believe that somehow they are 'responding cognitively to a divine reality radically different from themselves, in whose gracious initiative and approach alone their witness has its basis and object'.[46]

Whereas, therefore, there are some non-cognitivist, non-objectivist, non-realist (or atheistic) interpretations of religious faith and belief, those who are properly considered to be theists definitively reject such analyses as fundamentally inadequate. They may appreciate that such interpretations are the product of attempts to salvage something morally, aesthetically or emotionally attractive from the supposed wreck of theism on the rocks of secularism, but they reject them for failing to preserve the foundations of religious faith, at least so far as it is genuinely theistic. Theists, in contrast, maintain that faith essentially refers to what is real and ultimate. It is the human awareness of and response to the mind-independent referent of such faith that is to be investigated in this study. Since what is being investigated is what faith in God is generally understood to be, this study may proceed without being embarrassed by non-cognitivist, non-objectivist, and non-realist views of what is meant by 'God' and by faith in God.

The nature of theology

Having considered 'faith' and 'belief', we come to consider what is meant by 'theology' and, in particular, to show why it is necessary to modify the view that theology is to be defined as the attempt to produce a rationally satisfactory account of the beliefs of a religious faith.

The traditional view of theology sees it as a matter of *fides quaerens intellectum* – of faith seeking understanding. As such it is a second-order activity which depends for its data upon faith's expression of its contents in the form of beliefs.[47] It seeks to produce a coherent and consistent statement of those beliefs, to investigate the grounds for holding them, and to explore their inter-relationships and implications for thought and practice. It is thus a deliberately rational attempt to understand a religious faith. In that it depends upon an actual religious faith, it is also held to be the product of a community of believers and to be judged by its appropriateness to the faith of that community.[48] This view of theology, however, does not entail that a theologian must be a *believing* member of the community of faith. Whether committed adherents or independent outsiders are in the better position to perceive the contents of faith, all that is required is that the resulting exposition express the faith held by a specific community of believers.

This traditional view of theology may appear to impose considerable restrictions on theologians by limiting them to a community's faith. In contrast, philosophers who are interested in the notion of 'God' may be thought to be limited only by the demands of the canon of reason. While, however, the distinction between theology and philosophy may be significant in some cases, it ought not to be exaggerated. On the one hand, philosophers work within and are influenced by an intellectual tradition. There is no supra-cultural stance available to them.[49] Since, for instance, any language that philosophers use is itself a value-loaded way of perceiving reality,[50] the conclusions which they reach will belong to an identifiable community, even if it may be a more extensive community than that to which the theologian is supposed to be committed. On the other hand, since the faith of a community is a tradition open to interpretation and development, theologians have not been noticeably constricted as they have attempted through that faith to determine the character of ultimate reality.

In *The Reality of God*, for example, Schubert Ogden describes the theologian as one who exists 'for the purpose of expressing as adequately as he can the faith of the historic Christian community'.[51] It is therefore interesting to note that when he comes to interpret 'The promise of faith' he maintains that the 'real reference' of such eschatological symbols as that of resurrection is to 'the abiding structure and meaning of our actual existence here and now'. The promise of faith does not essentially include claims about subjective immortality. Whether or not Ogden's views on immortality are correct, what is significant for our purposes here is the way in which his understanding of his commitment as a theologian to the community of faith clearly does not prevent him interpreting its faith in a way that opposes its 'commonly supposed' view of it.[52] In this respect Ogden's procedure is typical of most theologians.

In expounding the nature of a community's faith, theologians have generally not been purely descriptive. They have been prepared to be revisionary, not merely in putting that faith into rationally acceptable language, but also in defining what they consider to be its authentic form. Often with considerable hermeneutical ingenuity they have used the community's faith as a point of insight into what they consider to be the truth. Furthermore, if at times their exegeses have appeared forced to their contemporaries, later generations have primarily been concerned to test them according to whether or not they express the truth in terms of the traditional symbols of the faith, not according to whether they reiterate some supposed original understanding of the faith.[53] Indeed, as has been appreciated for some time, both faith itself and its theological expressions develop rather than are merely repeated in new forms in successive cultural periods.[54]

If, then, the supposed dependence of theology on the faith of a community does not in practice particularly hamper the development of theological thought, why should the traditional understanding of theology be regarded as unsatisfactory? There are four grounds for challenging the view that it is a second-order activity, parasitic on and finally to be judged by its conformity with the beliefs of an actual religious faith.

In the first place, there is the question of the identification of the data for theological study. If theology is wholly the product of rational reflection on the faith of a community, the limits of that community and of the authentic expressions of its faith cannot be determined by theological reflection, at least not without begging the question. Religious communities and the authentic forms of their faiths, however, are not clearly demarcated objects for study. Thus to define theology as essentially dependent on the faith of a community has the unfortunate consequence that it bars theology from attempting to answer crucial questions about what is to be included and what excluded from the community and its faith. While theologians may attempt to describe and systematize that faith, as such they have to accept that judgements about the limits of orthodoxy – that is, decisions about the proper extent of the community of faith – cannot be subject to theological determination, but must be presupposed by theological understanding. Furthermore, disputes between different communities about their faiths cannot be theological ones. These implications indicate that the traditional definition of theology needs to be revised if, as seems desirable, it is to be theologically legitimate for theologians to reflect on and to seek to establish the proper limits of the material which they seek to understand. Such a revised definition would not introduce something novel into theological practice for theologians have regularly regarded these tasks as coming within their purview.

Secondly, to define theology as the rational description of the actual faith of a community is likely, if followed strictly, to render theological understanding impossible. This is because rational description, simply because it seeks to be rational as well as descriptive, may be unable to avoid altering to some extent what it intends to comprehend. When, therefore, believers show themselves to be suspicious of theological expositions of what is supposed to be their faith, their hesitations may be the result, not only of unfamiliarity with the language that is used, but also of a justifiable suspicion that the faith has had to be altered somewhat in order to give it a conceptually coherent form.

Thirdly, the traditional definition of theology overlooks the contributions which rational reflection makes to the contents as well as to the form of its understanding. This is illustrated, for example, in those theological statements of the Christian faith which, while claiming to be expressing the faith found in the Bible and underlying the expectations and practices of believers, describe God's eternity as a mode of being without temporal successiveness. The notion of God's non-temporality does not come from the beliefs of the community and their formative biblical expressions. It comes from what theologians have considered (mistakenly according to some recent analyses)[55] to be entailed by the rationally necessary attribution of ultimacy and perfection to the divine. To judge that such a use of reason, deliberate or not, is untheological would be to withdraw the legitimacy of the description 'theological' from a great deal of what claims to be such and is commonly so regarded.

Fourthly, not everyone who seeks to grasp the truth about God considers that their activity is normatively controlled by the faith of a particular religious community. While the principles and structure of their thought cannot avoid being moulded to a large extent by the general community of understanding to which they belong (i.e., by the culture in which their thought has developed), some seek to perceive the character of ultimate reality through rational reflection on the experiences of humanity in general. In doing this they may take into account the claims of one or several religious faiths (or of none at all), but the norm for what they accept is what they judge to be rationally justified. Many who do theology in this way probably regard themselves as philosophers (or metaphysicians) rather than as theologians, but it is odd so to define 'theology' that the claims about God made by such as Herbert of Cherbury, Spinoza, Leibniz, Berkeley, Kant, Whitehead and Hartshorne[56] cannot be regarded as theological. Indeed, in spite of the illusion fostered by his 'credo ut intelligam', it is arguable that such a definition would entail that Anselm's *Proslogion* is not a theological study![57]

Although it would be a mistake to conclude from this last point that theology is (or should be) wholly a matter of speculative thought, the above four considerations, when taken together, indicate that theological understanding should not be seen as a purely descriptive activity. It is, rather, the product of a complex activity in which faith, beliefs, experience and rational reflection interact.[58] Even those theologians who want to be purely descriptive should recognize that the concepts which are chosen to apprehend faith, to express belief, and to structure theology to some extent interpret what is being described.[59] The relationship, however, is not all one way. There is a certain givenness about experiences which means that some conceptual structures appear to fit them better than others. It may be difficult or even impossible in many cases to show why one conceptual structure is preferable to another without begging the question, since any references to the underlying experience will be moulded by the concepts used to identify it. Nevertheless, the fittingness of some and the unfittingness of other concepts for a particular case is something that is felt and influences understanding. As a result, what is experienced, how the experience is apprehended, and the understanding of both the experience and its object reciprocally interact. Theology could never be a purely neutral descriptive activity even if it were considered desirable for it to be such.

How, then, should theology be understood? It cannot be a purely descriptive study of an actual religious faith, and it ought not to be restricted to a systematic, critical and revisionary study of such a faith.[60] It is most adequately understood as the attempt to answer the question, 'In what way and with what claims to truth does a religious perspective provide a rationally coherent understanding of the nature of ultimate reality?'

The reference to 'a religious perspective' distinguishes theology from metaphysical understanding in general. Although they seek the answer to what is basically the same question, theology is interested in only one possible range of answers to it – the religious one. Consequently, while theologians may claim that the correct answer to the metaphysical quest is to be found in their form of understanding,[61] metaphysicians as such are not restricted to the religious perspective in their search for it. Furthermore, as has already been mentioned, this study is primarily concerned with the theistic forms of the religious answer to the basic questions of human being. While, therefore, the following investigation into the conditioning of theological judgements may apply in many respects to the full range of religious perspectives, in practice the focus of its attention accords with Gordon Kaufman's view that at least 'an implicit concept of God must be present' if a study is 'properly to be regarded as *theo*logical' – and that what is meant by 'God' is not merely 'the ultimate point of reference', but also a reality who is most adequately regarded as 'personal or agential in character'.[62]

Theology's understanding of ultimate reality is produced by the interaction and mutual modification of various factors, often in a largely unconscious process of thought. The starting-point for such a process may be a religious faith whose contents are ordered and revised by rational reflection on their insights, or it may be some experiences or rationally acceptable principles which, either alone or in conjunction with other factors, lead to theological claims. These claims may then evoke considerations of other beliefs, experiences and principles which lead to modifications in the over-all understanding. The process of thought is more like the way in which mutually affective forces attain equilibrium than like the clear progress of a geometrical demonstration – or it may be compared to the way in which diverse pieces of evidence are interpreted and combined to produce a convincing solution to an historical problem.

The kind of reasoning process that is involved in reaching theo-logical understanding – though much more orderly than usually occurs in practice – may be illustrated by the following outline of the development of a doctrine of atonement. Four factors provide the starting-point: awareness of God as one who is primarily to be feared as a just and austere judge, a sense of oneness with God in place of previous experiences of alienation (though not necessarily apprehended in those terms), belief that the new experience is con-nected with the death of Jesus, and the conviction that the experi-ences express real states. Initially an attempt is made to combine these factors in a crude substitutionary theory of atonement. Reflection on its implications, using values which are considered to apply to God as perfect, then indicates that such a theory is unacceptable because it suggests that God is immoral or divided.[63] A revised understanding is advanced which suggests that the death of Jesus manifests the love of God: if it is to be seen as a sacrifice, it is a sacrifice of Godself to arrogant humanity. This understanding, however, implies that God is not to be feared but loved and trusted. Hence the initial awareness of God is now modified. Further changes may follow, such as the view that God is not as morally pernickety as was previously assumed,[64] or that experiences of alienation are not experiences of God's attitude to us but of our unhappiness with ourselves. The process of coming to understand-ing thus produces a radical reappraisal of the initial data and leads to the conclusion that the need for an atonement theory to combine them is fundamentally mistaken.

The above illustration – which does not pretend to be an historical study – indicates the complex way in which faith, beliefs and reason may interact in developing theological understanding. In practice the procedure may be very unorderly, with the possibly haphazard consideration of factors being controlled only teleologically by the desire to reach a rationally satisfying understanding of the ultimate nature of reality and of humanity's relationship to it.

The status of reason in theological understanding

Critics may argue that the view of theology developed in this study is flawed because reason has no status in matters of religious faith. The things of God are beyond the competence of rational reflection: faith and belief are autonomous. To give human reason authority in such matters is an illegitimate human intrusion into matters determined by God. Authentic theological understanding is attained by obedient acceptance of what God makes known to humanity. Torrance, for example, asserts that the knowledge of God must be through the 'disciplined obedience of our mind to God as He gives Himself to be known by us'. We should not begin by forming a theory about how God may be known and then seek to test it out. The knowledge of God 'must be determined from first to last' by the divine modes of self-disclosure.[65]

This view of theology is to be rejected. It not only depends on an unsatisfactory view of experience and revelation;[66] it also fails fundamentally to appreciate the significance of the fact that theology is a matter of human attempts to understand the nature of ultimate reality, not a transcription of divinely communicated propositions. To claim that faith, belief and theology are a-rational matters may seem to reflect a proper humility before God. In reality it is to abandon humanity's only way to responsible understanding and to misunderstand the role and nature of reason.

Reason is our way of judging what is so and of discerning what ought to be. It is not a devilish instrument by whose use we refuse to accept our limitations. Although it may be abused – as when people pretend to insights beyond their competence – this does not justify rejecting its use. In fact valid criticisms of reason's scope presuppose reason, for they appeal to a rational recognition of its proper power and methods. They may also – and justifiably – challenge a too narrow view of what is legitimate reasoning. Different subjects may require different procedures to reach valid conclusions.[67] Sometimes people are aware of how they reach their conclusions, but frequently the reasoning processes only become consciously recognized when their conclusions are questioned and investigations are set up into how they were reached.[68] Even then there can be no guarantee that the methods and arguments that are offered to explain the conclusions are the ones that were actually used to arrive at them.

Claims that reason has no place in theological understanding must be rejected. Rational reflection is necessarily involved both in reaching such understanding and in the prior task of determining its limits and status. John Baillie gives theological support to the view that faith and reason must be 'the best of friends'. Criticizing Barthian attacks on what is called 'human reason', Baillie maintains that reason is not what we actually find in people so much as what we 'desiderate for them'. Logic is the 'description of how God meant us to think, and hence is the reflected image of His own thought', while reason is defined as 'the ability to recognize the truth when it is presented to us'.[69] To deny reason any status in matters of faith, belief and theology is to leave believers and theologians with no way (except the notoriously unsatisfactory ones of private and corporate illumination) of distinguishing between justified understanding and unwarrantable credulity, between the proper and the improper implications of faith, and between sense and nonsense.

Even though it may seem arrogant to regard our minds as the touchstone for truth, such arrogance is preferable to parroting the unexaminable (and hence untestable and, in this sense, unjustifiable) claims of a religious supernaturalism.[70] For all its limited and conditioned character, reason is our only way to intellectually responsible understanding – including understanding in matters of faith. The history of modern philosophy – as constituted, for example, by the works of Descartes, Locke, Berkeley, Hume, Kant, Hamilton, Hegel and Wittgenstein – can be seen as the story of attempts to determine what humanity can legitimately claim to know. Although there have been some attempts to pursue this quest in relation to theological understanding – as in the works of Peter Browne, John Ellis, Søren Kierkegaard, H. L. Mansel, A. Ritschl, F. R. Tennant and today with G. D. Kaufman, E. Farley and T. W. Jennings – further investigations are needed. This study is a contribution to the task.

The internal and external roles of reason

Reason has what may be called external and internal roles in theological understanding. The former is concerned with justifying the truth-claims made for theological understanding; the latter with establishing the content, intrinsic coherence, mutual compatibility and implications of the various parts of a theological understanding of reality. We will consider the internal role first.

One function of reason in theology is to draw out the implications of what is being maintained. An example of this kind of reasoning is the (fallacious) argument that the perfection of God implies that temporal distinctions are only apparently real. This argument might begin from the premise that God is perfect to conclude that God must know everything without loss and error. From this it further concludes that our human experience of the lostness of past events and the not-yetness of future ones does not correspond to the nature of things from the perfect standpoint of the divine, and that all events must be immediately present to God as fully known. Consequently, in God temporal distinctions are unreal. Hence they are ultimately illusory. This argument illustrates, in an artificially neat form, how reasoning may elucidate the implications of a religious belief, and how it may lead to a reconsideration of that belief by showing that it has unacceptable but unavoidable consequences.

Another internal role of reason is to correct the thinking that has led to some theological assertions. In this respect rational reflection seeks to expose errors in previous thought, and to overcome conflicts between an existential faith and what is regarded as its theological expression. This activity of reason can be illustrated by a twofold argument which affirms the compatibility of divine perfection with the reality of temporal distinctions.

On the one hand, the argument holds that an analysis of existential faith shows that it presupposes that there is a relationship between the believer and God which makes it appropriate for the believer to pray to God to influence certain future events. Such activity would be pointless if there is for God no future open to influence but only an immediate awareness of all events as simultaneously and presently actual. Another form of this argument points out that existentially faith regards God as one who acts, but that there can be no activity where there is no distinction between present and future. In such ways, then, analyses of faith may be used to show that its notion of God's perfection does not (unless it is self-contradictory) include the concept of God as *actus purus*.

The other part of the argument claims that further reflection shows that it is fallacious to infer from God's perfect knowledge that future events must be presently determinate and so knowable by God. The fallacy lies in the failure to recognize that the future is essentially what is not yet determinate and so is not yet available to be known.[71] Even perfect knowledge cannot include knowledge of what is not knowable – such as the date of the good Samaritan's death, the name of the present Pope's father-in-law and the rate of acceleration of Jesus' body at the Ascension. Since, then, perfect knowledge cannot include knowledge of future events because as *future* events they are not determinate and so not (yet) knowable as such, there is no incompatibility between divine perfection, at least so far as it concerns divine knowledge, and the significance of the future as future. Although this twofold argument may be challenged,[72] it illustrates how rational reflection may lead to a reappraisal of theological understanding.

A third internal role of reason in theology is that of finding ways to reconcile apparently conflicting affirmations. Christian thought, for example, has traditionally faced the problem of making sense of the claim that Jesus is to be recognized as being fully human, fully God and one person. While some may be prepared to accept that the conjoint affirmation of these three doctrines is unavoidably a paradox, others are sensitive to the charge that it is self-contradictory. By means of rational reflection they seek either to find models which allow the claim to be upheld as self-consistent, or to modify the existing view of what has to be affirmed in order to render it less open to the charge of being incoherent and hence nonsense.

This aspect of the role of reason in theological understanding has produced some subtle distinctions in the search for coherence which are ingenious rather than ingenuous! Anselm, for example, attempts to hold that God is both compassionate and impassible, by suggesting that God is to be regarded as compassionate in terms of our experience and not in terms of God's own experience.[73] Aquinas is in similar trouble when he attempts to reconcile the belief that all creatures are related to God with the assertion that 'being related to creatures is not a reality in God', by holding that God does not change when creatures alter their relationship to God, just as a pillar does not change when people move so that it is now on their left whereas before it was on their right.[74]

Other attempts to use reason in this way have produced notable advances in theological understanding. Among important examples in this century are Bultmann's notion of demythologizing, Gadamer's model of the fusing of horizons and Hartshorne's dipolar conceptuality. The first two have opened up new insights into the interpretation of statements of belief which come from another culture. The third's distinction between essence, existence and actuality provides a self-consistent way of holding that God is *both* necessary, absolute, eternal and unchanging, *and* contingent, relative, temporal and changing in appropriate aspects of the divine being. It thus offers a way of talking about God as loving which threatens neither the godness of God nor the authenticity of divine love.

26

The fourth internal role of reason is found in the way that rational reflection itself produces and develops theological notions. This role is probably more influential than is yet generally appreciated, in spite of the many studies that have developed the seminal works of Harnack and Hatch on the formation of Christian theological understanding.[75] It is seen in action when certain views of God are regarded as self-evidently appropriate although there is no correlative element in the believers' existential faith. In spite of its supposed commitment to the biblical witness, Christian theology has traditionally been led astray by such reasoning into holding that God must be thought of as totally unchanging, without potentiality, beyond temporal distinctions, impassible and having all possible perfections.[76]

Nevertheless, while in some cases rational reflection may foist a theologian's individual and cultural prejudices onto the concept of God,[77] in other cases it leads to what are justifiably to be regarded as clearer insights into the content and significance of that concept. Hartshorne, for example, starting from the definition of God as the totally adequate object of worship,[78] has used the insights of his form of process philosophy to produce a much more satisfactory understanding of divine perfection than has traditionally been advanced.[79] Theologians who uphold the view that theology is only to express the existing faith of a community (and especially those who see that faith as canonically expressed in certain ancient documents which reflect the culture and understanding of a previous age) may deplore such contemporary contributions to the doctrine of God. Their views indicate that they have failed to recognize what is inescapable when attempts are made to apprehend the nature of ultimate reality. What is needed is not a retreat from reason but a more percipient use of it.

The external role of reason in theology is that of examining the justification of its claim to be a true understanding. In considering the grounds for holding that theology's judgements about ultimate reality correspond to what is actually the case, it probes the significance both of so-called 'natural theology' and of the arguments to authenticate claims to revelation. It is a role of reason which is important in a multi-faith, confused and uncertain age such as the present.

Some philosophers and theologians deny that theological claims ought to or can be verified. They maintain that the 'word of faith' has self-authenticating power and that its validity depends upon its recognition as such. Faith-statements and corresponding theological understanding are not to be verified by reason but asserted. Hearers will perceive their truth as they properly hear them – and, it is usually added, this happens through the grace of God.

Reliance upon the supposed self-authenticating character of faith-statements is, however, a most unsatisfactory guide to truth. There are many 'spirits' speaking in the world. The followers of each of them assert that theirs is the true one. If their claims are to be tested to discover which is from God,[80] they cannot be verified by reference to their intrinsic convincingness alone. Otherwise the faith of a Muslim, of a Pentecostalist, of a Jehovah's Witness, of a Methodist, of a student-converted Anglican, and any other faith that attracts committed believers will each have to be accepted as equally 'true'. In that case either truth becomes a subjective matter or the principle of non-contradiction cannot apply to theological understanding. Each option leads to an absurd situation. Consequently, it is far from clear that 'apologetic concern . . . is the death of serious theologizing'.[81] On the contrary, only such a concern to establish the truth will indicate, in a way that may hope for general consent, which call to faith is to be followed out of the many that are made.

Having indicated the importance of the external role of reason in theological understanding, we must leave it.[82] This study has other problems to tackle. I hope, however, to follow up this investigation of the conditioning of theological judgements with a study of the nature and discernment of truth in theological understanding.

Tentativeness in theological understanding

Although all forms of understanding are to some extent uncertain because they are human products, tentativeness is an especially appropriate characteristic of theological understanding at the present time. The foundations of such understanding are currently being questioned, and the great dogmatic structures of older theologians seem more like dinosaurian relics than convincing insights into the character of ultimate reality. In the optimism of the 1960s, when the overall mood was one of confidence, William Hamilton suggested that theologians should be content with presenting collections of 'fragments or images' which would speak to their contemporaries and leave the rest, the 'unsayable', unsaid.[83] Another theologian of that time, Alec Vidler, put it that the present is not a time for trying to produce 'major works of theological construction'. It is 'a time for making soundings, not charts or maps', and for 'candidly confessing where our perplexities lie'.[84] A generation later these remarks ring even more true. Faced with radical questions about the significance of the language which they use, the nature of their understanding and the warrants for their judgements, theologians need to be tentative about their claims to understanding.

The need for tentativeness, however, is not simply a characteristic of the present state of theological thought. Puzzles about its content and method seem to be an intrinsic characteristic of theological understanding. There are three reasons why claims to dogmatic finality in theology are absurd.

First, the ultimate nature of the object of theology means that it is grounded in mystery.[85] Confronted with God, Job did well to cease trying to comprehend. It is perhaps fitting that the mighty dogmatic systems of Aquinas and Barth were never completed.[86] Faith may demand understanding but the demand is an imperative that will never be finally satisfied.

Secondly, no theology which seeks to express truth about the living God ought to pretend to finality. As one who delights 'in making all things new', God is to be seen as continually provoking the tension and commotion which prevent a settled contentment with the established situation. The creator is a disturber whose consistency lies in the quest for the proliferation of values. Theologically this insight into the divine is reflected in William Dean's provocative comment that 'theology should not be concerned primarily with truth' – on the grounds that this leads it to endorse understanding which corresponds to current cultural beliefs – but with fostering 'interpretations of meaning that aesthetically contrast with common and accepted meanings'.[87] It might, however, be less misleading, even though less obviously disturbing, to say that theology is to seek the truth at all costs, while recognizing that the true understanding of God will involve continual reformation. Theologians who do not admit the tentativeness of their understanding comically presume to freeze the creating creator. They treat God as dead.

Thirdly, theology must be tentative in so far as it includes an attempt to discern the final fulfilment of things. This view of theology is not restricted to those future-orientated faiths which are particularly concerned about some eschatological fulfilment. It also agrees with metaphysical insights into the essentially processive character of reality and with anthropological understanding of human being as basically future-directed. Theologians, therefore, must not limit their aim to that of making sense of reality as it now appears to be; they must also recognize that they have the task of perceiving what is yet to be – and in light of that perception to recognize the changing nature of the present, including present perceptions of the character of the future. If Pannenberg is at least partly correct in asserting 'the future as the mode of God's being', and 'the ability to transcend one's own situation' as the characteristic of human being,[88] and if reality is in process and to live involves change, then theologians seeking to understand the nature of ultimate reality are working (and must work) from a non-ultimate situation. Their judgements, consequently, are to be seen as only tentative insights perceived from relative stances. In the following six chapters we shall consider how this relativity is actualized in the anthropological conditioning of theological understanding.

3

God as cosmic projection

Critics of theistic understanding have asserted that 'Man creates
God in his own image'! Sometimes the play on Genesis 1.26 is to
make the point that the way in which human beings perceive the
nature of God is derived from the ways in which they perceive their
own nature. Sometimes it is to claim that God is a human invention
and exists only as a figment of believers' imaginations. Although at
the end of the chapter we will comment on the latter charge, it is
the former one that will receive most attention as we consider this
aspect of the anthropological conditioning of theological understanding.

Claims that talk about God is talk about the human

Claims about the human source of notions of the divine are not
new. Just as modern Western portrayals of Jesus often lack Semitic
features, so in the ancient world Xenophanes pointed out that the
gods of the Ethiopians are 'black with snub noses' and 'those of the
Thracians are blond, with blue eyes and red hair'.[1] It has also long
been claimed that the nature of the gods is the product of human
attempts to make sense of what is disturbingly puzzling. Cicero
refers to Cleanthes' view that the 'awe' evoked by terrifying natural
phenomena and the desire to understand what happens in nature
has helped to produce the image of the divine.[2] Statius echoes
Lucretius when he bluntly states that 'Fear first made the gods'.[3]

During the past three centuries this kind of charge has had powerful advocates. Thomas Hobbes suggests that the 'seed of religion',
which is the 'fear of things invisible', comes to flower in creatures
of the imagination.[4] A century later David Hume finds the origin of
religion in the way that primitive people imagined that the unknown
forces controlling their fate were 'sensible, intelligent beings, like
mankind' – and, in addition, beings who could be bribed![5] In the
nineteenth century Friedrich Nietzsche adopts the projection

theory to argue that in worshipping God people worship an imaginary cause that reflects their situation: a confident people 'venerates the conditions through which it has prospered', and a threatened people find sanctified 'the virtues of submissiveness'. Jesus, as the representation of God, is likewise adjusted by his followers 'into an apologia of themselves'.[6] In the present century Sigmund Freud's version of this story adds the suggestion that the gods personify psychic forces internal to people as well as external, natural powers.[7] Furthermore, while Freud allows that an illusion is not necessarily false since it is defined as a belief predominantly motivated by desire, his treatment of religious beliefs presents them as both illusory and false. Belief in God as an omnipotent father, for example, is an illusion which arises from the desire for an invincible protector; it is a delusion because it has no correlate in reality.[8]

Freud maintains that how people perceive God's nature varies according to their relationships with their fathers.[9] Others link changes in the understanding of God with cultural and individual developments in the notion of what it is to be a full person. Parallel movements have occurred in Christian views of Jesus as the revelation of the character of the divine: from the Norsemen, who responded to the Jesus who came 'not to bring peace but a sword' to current presentations of Jesus as a freedom fighter; from Anselm's Jesus who satisfied God's honour to Abelard's great lover; the story of the quest for the so-called historical Jesus largely confirms Albert Schweitzer's conclusion that 'each epoch . . . found its reflection in Jesus' and 'each individual created Him in accordance with his own character'.[10] The object of faith is thus held by some to be a projection, perhaps idealized, of the believer's own personality and values.

Others find in talk about God personifications of social, political and economic realities. Engels described Calvinism, for example, as 'the true religious disguise of the interests of the bourgeoisie'.[11] While religion may have originated in misapprehensions about nature and about humanity, its developments have reflected 'the conditions of life' in each community.[12] Marx similarly sees 'the "religious sentiment" ' as a 'social product' and the reality of religion as 'the ensemble of the social relations',[13] a view developed at length in Durkheim's analysis of religion as 'the concentrated expression of the whole collective life' of a society. It is the character of society that is presented in the mythologies and theologies of religion.[14]

In various ways, then, it has long been maintained by critics of theism that the word 'God' refers to a reification, personification or projection of forces found in the external, internal and social worlds of human being. The classical statement of the view is given by Ludwig Feuerbach. He argues that 'theology is anthropology' since theism expresses humanity's cosmic projection of its nature: 'The divine being is nothing else than . . . the human nature purified, freed from the limits of the individual man, made objective.'[15] As the supposed totality of all perfections, 'God' is said both to combine what are perceived as all 'the attributes of the species'[16] and to manifest the secrets of the individual believer's 'inward nature'.[17] Although Feuerbach recognizes that his work will be condemned as 'atheistic', his own view is that he has uncovered the key to the true meaning of religion,[18] namely, that 'the consciousness of God is nothing else than the consciousness of the species' and that 'Man is the true God and Saviour of man'.[19]

Engels reflects the intention behind this analysis when he says that Feuerbach's wish is 'to perfect' religion. The bonds of love between persons will, in Feuerbach's view, only 'attain their full value' when 'consecrated by the name of religion'. While acknowledging, however, the liberating effect of the announcement of this 'new, true religion' of humanity, Engels rejects both the view that a religious crutch is needed to uphold these purely human relations and the assumption that religion can exist without God.[20]

In the twentieth century Karl Barth and Wolfhart Pannenberg have regarded Feuerbach's position as the one which theologians must answer if they are to preserve the integrity of their subject.[21] According to Barth, Feuerbach's work shows the impossibility of natural theology. A 'theology' which uses human reasoning about human experiences will never get beyond the human to the divine; the only way to avoid the Feuerbachian reduction of theology into anthropology is for theology to be derived wholly from divine revelation.[22]

The implications of the charge that God is a human product

For reasons that will be discussed in chapter 6, appeal to revelation does not provide the solution to the Feuerbachian problem which Barth claims for it. Unless the identification and authentication of a revelation is to be warranted by reference to some existing theistic understanding, the appeal to revelation, and especially the appeal to an allegedly self-authenticating revelation, gives a licence for the promotion of all kinds of credulity and nonsense. Theistic understanding will be credible only if a different answer can be found to the Feuerbachian critique.

The problem for this chapter, then, is to consider how a proper recognition of the humanity of the theologian's standpoint, materials and ways of thought is compatible with a theistic interpretation of theological understanding. It will be argued that although the concept of God found in faith and theology is in many respects to be seen as derived from a projection of human nature, this is the only way in which many of the characteristics of God as the object of theistic faith can be apprehended by human beings. Thus while, as Martin Buber puts it, 'Feuerbach follows the second creation story' in putting man at the centre,[23] it is not the Feuerbachian starting-point which is to be challenged, but the conclusions which Feuerbach holds to flow necessarily from it.

The remark that people create God in their own image covers two distinct charges. The first is that of anthropomorphism.[24] In itself this charge does not entail the non-existence of God. It merely maintains that the content of any material description of God is derived from and controlled by how people understand their own nature and responses. Those who press this charge, however, usually assume that whatever God may exist must be so utterly unlike human beings that any material descriptions of the divine in terms of human nature, even though greatly qualified, only present such distorted perceptions of God that they are worse than no descriptions of God at all.

The other charge is that of invention. Playing on the notion of creativity, it claims that the God of faith and theology is a human product. While there may be something that is the actual ground of reality, the God of religion is a fiction, ontologically dependent upon humanity. Believers therefore trust and theologians discuss what human beings have invented – a cosmic projection of their qualities. This second charge seeks to discredit theism by alleging that the relation between God and humanity is the opposite of what is presupposed in theistic faith.

The charge of anthropomorphism considered

The charge of anthropomorphism is a complex one. At one level of analysis anthropomorphism may be held to be the general character of all thought and expression. Whatever people are describing, their descriptions must be conditioned by their experi-

ences of their external and internal worlds, by their way of apprehending these experiences and by their structures of understanding.
They have no other standpoints for making descriptions and reaching understanding, whether the objects of their attention be real or
imaginary.

Applied to theism this means that any description of God that
can signify anything must use materials which belong to the universe
of human experience, apprehension and understanding.[25] If Xenophanes were correct in asserting of the highest God that 'in neither
his form nor his thought is he like unto mortals',[26] then that God is
inapprehensible and inexpressible. It is not at all clear how Xenophanes could even know of this reality sufficiently to be able to
justify his claims.

Theologians who follow this line of thought by declaring that God
is 'ineffable' sabotage their own work. What is properly ineffable
cannot be talked about. Those who state that God is 'utterly other'
similarly make it impossible to justify, and even to apprehend, the
meaning of their claim. How can they – or their readers – know
what is utterly other to be such? If the predicate be true, its subject
can have no determinate reference. Even if it could be shown that
there is a minimum sense in such an assertion (as, say, a way of
asserting the impossibility of describing what may nevertheless have
a known reference – a paradoxical situation), theologians who
make such remarks should immediately write 'Finis' and turn to
other activities. Otherwise they may be tempted to try to produce
what they have implied to be impossible, namely talk about God.
Since nothing can be known or expressed unless it has a place in or
is derivable from human experience and thought, at this level the
alternative to anthropomorphism is effectively no talk about God
at all.[27]

To say this, however, does not take us far in replying to Feuerbach. It merely reminds us that our modes of understanding are
inescapably conditioned by our humanity. In this respect, to say
that theological descriptions are anthropomorphic is to say little
more than that they are ones which human beings can apprehend.
Generalized in this way the charge of anthropomorphism is effectively evacuated of much of its significance.

Much more important is Feuerbach's specific charge that examination of its constituents shows that all talk about God is only talk
about the human. The hermeneutical principle underlying his claim
that 'the true sense of Theology is Anthropology' is that since 'there
is no distinction between the *predicates* of the divine and human

nature', there can consequently be 'no distinction between the divine and human *subject*'. Attempts to make distinctions between 'the
theological and anthropological predicates' are found on analysis
to collapse into absurdities.[28]

Feuerbach is here applying to statements about God what is often
referred to as Leibniz's principle of the identity of indiscernibles.[29]
In terms of Feuerbach's analysis of such statements, there is no
escape from his criticism by holding that he has failed to distinguish
between ways of discussing an object and the nature of that object
itself. The fact that an object 'A' is described in terms of a more
familiar object 'B' does not, of course, entail that 'A' is 'B' or even
is a type of 'B'. It only shows that those who describe 'A' consider
it advantageous to use descriptions directly applicable to the (more)
familiar 'B' as a way to communicate something about the (relatively) unfamiliar 'A'.[30] This point, however, is not sufficient to
rebut Feuerbach's analysis of language about God. This is because
those who so describe 'A' in terms of 'B' are presupposed to have,
prior to and independently of these descriptions, a way of distinguishing between 'A' and 'B'. Such a distinction is only possible if
there are predicates applicable to 'A' which are not applicable to
'B' and *vice versa*. Feuerbach's denial of the possibility of theistic
content in talk about God rests on the claim that there are no such
extra predicates which make it possible to distinguish between God
and the human. Since they cannot be distinguished, they must be
identical; and, since the human clearly exists, this, then, is what
God must represent!

Another attempt to reply to Feuerbach argues that the use of
human characteristics to describe God does not mean that God is
to be identified with the human, because the attribution applies
literally in the case of the human but only symbolically in the case
of God. Since, therefore, the application of the qualities used to
describe them differs, the two cases must have different references.
Paul Tillich's studies of the symbolic nature of talk about God shows
the flaw in this way of responding to Feuerbach. In his reply to his
critics in *The Theology of Paul Tillich*, he endorses Urban's point
that symbolic statements only make sense if they are delimited by
a non-symbolic statement.[31] Consequently, while he holds in the
first volume of his *Systematic Theology* that 'any concrete assertion
about God must be symbolic', he is careful to provide the most
abstract and unsymbolic statement about God that is possible –
'namely, that God is being itself or the absolute' – in order to show
the reference of the symbolic statements about God.[32]

It is not necessary here to go into Tillich's later attempts to revise his identification of the non-symbolic orientation of theological symbols. What is significant is the recognition that symbolic language about something is empty unless it is known what the symbols refer to. For this a non-symbolic statement is required. Feuerbach's point is that any such non-symbolic statement which uses predicates that are intrinsically coherent cannot avoid using predicates of God that are identical with those used of human beings. Consequently, the divine and the human are not distinguishable.

What, then, is to be done? Talk about God can only be shown to be theistically significant if predicates can be found which apply to God and not to human beings. One way of trying to do this is by pointing to the way in which anthropomorphic models (or metaphors) of causality, wisdom, goodness, purpose and love, for example, are 'qualified' when applied to God by words like 'first' (cf. 'first cause'), 'infinite' (cf. 'infinitely wise'), 'perfectly' (cf. 'perfectly good'), eternal (cf. 'eternal purpose') and 'all' (cf. 'all-loving'). As I. T. Ramsey suggests, the fact that these 'qualifiers' behave grammatically like words such as 'secondary', 'limitedly', 'moderately', 'temporary' and 'partially' should not mislead us into regarding them as having a similar logical function.[33] Their role, when properly apprehended, is to evoke the 'discernment–commitment . . . kind of situation characteristic of religion'.[34]

Although there are problems in defining what precisely is conveyed by these qualified models, it does not follow that they are either empty of content or merely disguised anthropomorphisms whose referent can only be the human. The intrinsic nature of the divine, it may be argued, forces us to use such elusive language and to depend upon 'disclosure-situations' to grasp its meaning. When Feuerbach protests against such procedures as converting talk about the human into 'an inexhaustible mine of falsehoods, illusions, contradictions, and sophisms',[35] it may be replied that he has failed to recognize that the 'qualifying' terms used to distinguish the referent of God-talk from the human are not straightforward descriptive terms, but 'operators'[36] which indicate how the material (and anthropomorphic) language of God is to be construed.

Ramsey's suggestions about 'disclosure-situations' may be criticized, however, on the grounds that they leave it unclear what the disclosures made in talk about God are 'of'. Such criticisms echo Urban's point about symbolic language. Is there any more straightforward way of showing that the qualified anthropomorphisms used to describe God refer to what is essentially other than the human in its reality? Both religious experience and philosophical concepts offer ways of satisfying this request.

The kinds of experience to which Otto and Buber draw attention indicate the 'other than human' nature of the divine. Whatever Otto's own position, his description of the experience of the numinous is not something which can be applied to the human, either as actual or as ideal. However much we may value human being, it would not seem appropriate to describe an experience of another person, no matter how respected, as one that properly evokes the sense of a 'mysterium tremendum et fascinans'.[37] The human, either in principle or in actuality, is not like this. Similarly, when Buber speaks of encountering 'unconditional exclusiveness and unconditional inclusiveness' in 'the Being . . . that may properly only be addressed, not expressed',[38] it is clear that it is not a human individual that is the object of the experience. Reference to the experience of worship provides another way of showing that the reality of the divine is essentially distinct from the human.[39] Hartshorne points out that God may be defined as the adequate object of worship.[40] Since, however, only 'the all-inclusive reality' is utterly worshipful,[41] it follows that 'non-theistic theories of worship fail' and, in particular, that 'humanity' cannot be the proper object of worship because ' "Humanity" leaves a vast world outside'.[42]

If, then, God is identified either as what is encountered in such religious experience or as what is unreservedly worshipful, talk about the divine is distinguishable from talk about the human. This is not to maintain that there exists a reality which does so encounter us or is to be so worshipped, but that Feuerbach is mistaken in holding that all coherent God-talk can be interpreted as being only about the human. His analysis is not adequate to the content of all aspects of religious experience.

Another way of establishing a distinction between God and the human is by showing that there are coherent concepts which are required to describe the divine reality but which are not applicable to human being. On the basis of his illuminating distinction between existence and actuality,[43] Hartshorne has shown that whereas human being is contingent, relative, temporary, finite and changing, the divine *existence* is definitively necessary, absolute, everlasting, infinite and unchanging. While, therefore, the divine *actuality* as loving, knowing, responding, acting, and so forth, is contingent upon, relative to, temporally ordered by, limited to and varying according to what there is in the world to be loved, known, responded to and acted upon, it is as the actualization of that whose *existence* is underived, omnitolerant and limitless. The distinctiveness of God can similarly be shown by analysing what is meant by divine perfection.[44] Such descriptions are not applicable to the human, individually, corporately or ideally. They identify a referent which is essentially other than the human and, thereby, provide predicates for God which distinguish the divine reality from human being.

In the second part of *The Essence of Christianity*, Feuerbach considers a number of 'supposed' ways of establishing a distinction 'between theological and anthropological predicates' and claims that they resolve themselves 'into an absurdity'.[45] His analyses make pertinent and often valid criticisms of some traditional theistic concepts. His argument, however, does not show that these concepts are the only possible ones, nor even that they are the appropriate ones for describing God. As has been suggested, references to religious experience and to a correct analysis of the defining characteristics of God indicate, contrary to Feuerbach's claim, that not all the predicates applicable to God are anthropomorphic. God and the human are coherently distinguishable. Accordingly, Feuerbach's hermeneutical objection to theistic utterances fails because discriminating predicates are available.[46]

Descriptions of God – 'not too little, not too much'

Within theology anthropomorphic descriptions of God range from the crudely literal to the highly sophisticated. Having, then, established the possibility of a coherent theistic reference for statements about God, the problem that arises is whether it is possible to produce acceptable descriptions of the material qualities of the divine being.[47] Theologians who want to make remarks about God which are more than purely formal and abstract face two dangers as they try to find a form of anthropomorphism which allows them to say something significant. The first is that they may make statements which imply a greater grasp of the divine than is justifiable. The other danger is that, in trying to avoid unsupportably crude anthropomorphisms, they may adopt ones that are too sophisticated to be able in practice to convey any apprehensible understanding of the divine nature.

Consider, for example, the notion of God's 'eye'.[48] A theologian who took this notion so crudely as to consider the question of the colour of the iris in God's eyeball would have difficulty in being taken seriously. Such a crude view of talk about God's 'eye' might initially be modified – and supposedly clarified – by holding that it is a pictorial way of talking about God as 'seeing'. This modification might then be qualified by holding that as God is non-material, this 'seeing' is not optical. It is, rather, a way of referring to the divine awareness of things. On reflection this may be further developed by pointing out that, whereas human awareness of things is by physical sense-perception from a relative standpoint, God's awareness is non-physical and absolute. The problem in that case is whether it is possible for human beings to envisage what it can mean when God is said to 'see' something.[49] Attempts to avoid unacceptably crude anthropomorphisms in talking about God may thus end up by making statements which are inapprehensible or contentless.[50]

There is no way of escaping from this difficulty by using terms which have no human correlate since they apply uniquely to God. No such language is available because a predicate must apply to a range of individuals if it is to be significant.[51] It is also not possible to avoid unacceptable anthropomorphisms by holding that the meanings of terms applied to God are quite different from their meanings when used in normal discourse. A passage in Hume's *Dialogues concerning Natural Religion* illuminates the unsatisfactoriness of such attempts.

At the end of Part III of the *Dialogues* Demea asserts that, since God is quite unlike the human, we should acknowledge that the meaning of any human quality which is applied to God is, in that use, 'totally incomprehensible'.[52] Cleanthes responds to this in Part IV by pointing out that, if Demea be correct, it is questionable whether theists (or 'Mystics') who 'maintain the absolute incomprehensibility of the Deity, differ from sceptics or atheists' who assert the unknowability and unintelligibility of the nature of ultimate reality. He reinforces his case by pointing out the implications of traditional views of the timeless eternity and simplicity of the divine for notions of God's understanding. A 'mind' which is 'wholly simple, and totally immutable' is one whose acts, sentiments and ideas cannot be 'distinct and successive'. In that case it is 'a mind which has no thought, no reason, no will, no sentiment, no love, no hatred; or in a word, is no mind at all.' It is 'an abuse of terms' to speak of it as a mind. While Philo points out that this implies that most orthodox divines are to be classed as atheists, Cleanthes' argument is a sound one.[53] A being who is totally other, unique in every respect, would be as unknowable and indescribable as a being whose apprehended attributes are mutually contradictory.[54]

Those who wish to make materially significant statements about God have thus to find their way along a ridge between the chasm of unacceptably crude anthropomorphisms, in which God is (mis)-treated as an enlarged human person, and the precipice of sophisticated qualifications which empty descriptions of God of all their content. This has long been recognized in discussions of the possibility of talk about God. For centuries the issue has been discussed in terms of studies of the nature of analogy; Tillich wrestles with the possibilities of symbolic expressions which both affirm and negate the reality which they employ; I. M. Crombie suggests that we can speak of God through authorized parables;[55] I. T. Ramsey sees theological language as composed by 'subtle selectivity' from a vast number of metaphors and models which are combined with 'qualifiers' that declare their inadequacy.[56] The list of possible examples is enormous. Critics of theology, in contrast, suspect that the ridge is too sharp to stand on. The theologians must fall to one side or the other – or be sliced in pieces!

It is not easy to envisage how the critics' suspicion is to be overcome. There is no possibility of defending the paradoxical character of some theistic statements by comparing the language used with observations of the reality of its referent. This way of showing that the oddness of the language is due to the nature of its referent[57] would require in the case of theology that God be an observable object. The God of theism is not such an object. Although it may be the genius of Christianity to point at the facts and then ask for their interpretation,[58] descriptions of God are not the product of attempts to find adequate ways of talking about a given object. Leaving aside the dubious records of theophanies, even those who claim to have direct awareness of God today do not claim to be confronted with a quasi-physical object but with something which they describe in such terms as experiences of 'deep joy', a 'sense of the presence of God'[59] or a 'mediated immediacy'.[60] While such experiences may be cognitively significant,[61] the descriptions of what is experienced therein are interpretations of the experiences, not a record of something directly given.[62] As a result, those who try to explain the nature of God-talk by reference to experiences of God find that they have to defend the legitimacy of their theistic interpretation of the experiences, although they want to use those experiences to show the necessity of talking about God in the way that they interpret them. Reference to experience does not provide a straightforward way of showing that talk about God is meaningful in spite of its oddities.

It is arguable, furthermore, that it is not only contingently true that God cannot be an immediately experienced object: the essence of the divine implies that it is necessarily true. The nature of God as the ground of being, the ultimate, the ontologically necessary and unbounded may, for instance, be held to make it impossible for God to be given as a describable object. By definition God is to be considered as 'beyond' or 'beneath' any given object – even of any real or imagined object that we wish to call God. Anselm's conclusion that 'that than which a greater cannot be conceived' must be 'greater than can be thought',[63] and Tillich's tortuous talk of God as being-itself 'which precedes the subject–object structure',[64] are thus reminders of the impossibility of experiencing God as a directly describable object, as well as of the profound difficulties facing any attempt to speak adequately of God.

Such remarks may be criticized on the grounds that they treat metaphysical compliments to God as significant descriptions. If, it may be asked, God is not given as an object, how are such remarks about the divine nature justified? The answer is that they are justified because they are formally implied by the concept of God. No self-conscious theism can be satisfied with concepts of God which do not represent the divine as ontologically, rationally and valuatively ultimate.[65] How in that case does talk about God develop and how may its referent be seen to justify its precarious character? To this topic we now turn.

Constructing the concept of God

Talk about God is best understood as the product of at least three factors. Its character is determined by a combination of the individual contributions of these factors and their interactions. It is established as the resultant is judged to present a coherent understanding of the divine.

The first factor is a type or quality of experience that is widely felt. Although such experience takes many forms and does not inescapably require theistic interpretation, a primary constituent of talk about God is what is variously described as a sense of utter joy and peace, as an awareness of all-inclusive wholeness, and as a consciousness of the infinite, the absolute, the transcendent, the sacred or the holy. Classically, the awarenesses of contingency, purpose and moral demand underlying the arguments for the existence of God have referred to modes of this experience. Schleiermacher gives a Romantic expression of it in his *Speeches on*

Religion,[66] while Otto's *Idea of the Holy* provides another seminal study in terms of the numinous. More recently works like Peter Berger's *Rumour of Angels* and Langdon Gilkey's *Naming the Whirlwind* have tried to show that 'within ordinary secular experience, that deeper range, which we have called that of ultimacy', does appear.[67] Whether these experiences are interpreted as disclosing another reality or as expressing 'dimensions' or 'depths' of present reality, they point to a factor in human experience of the world which indicates something fundamental 'beyond' the superficial and obvious.[68]

The second factor involved in producing a notion of God is the intellectual desire for understanding that is comprehensive, coherent and conclusive.[69] Explanations that tail off before everything is explained are unsatisfying. The quest for understanding thus leads to notions of ontological, rational and valuative ultimacy which formally indicate the final conclusions to questions about the ground of being, meaning and value. The desire for a single, all-embracing understanding of the nature and purpose of reality, which seems intrinsic to human rationality, leads to the concept of that which unifies these ultimates in itself.[70] Since reality would be judged to be absurd if it were held to arise from undirected energy or a mindless entity, the notion of God arises in part from people's desire to make sense of their world and their unconscious assumption that it does make sense in terms of meaning, purpose and value.

The third factor is a persistent and widespread presumption that the world is not only understandable but also basically good. The text 'and God saw all that he had made, and it was very good' expresses what many people basically trust, as well as hope, to be the case. Human beings are not only rational entities that want to understand; they are active beings who consider that there is justification for their confidence that they are accepted and that their efforts for good are not absurd performances in an ultimately valueless cosmos.[71] Despite how sometimes it appears to be, they are existentially convinced that reality is finally secure, ordered, trustworthy, even gracious and supportive of creativity. In the depths of their being, that is, they believe that life is worth living and that to be is in itself good. Talk about God arises partly from the desire to make sense of this basic human confidence.

The concept of God as the basis of the unity, meaningfulness and goodness of reality thus emerges as certain human experiences and the putative satisfaction of the search for understanding coalesce with a basic presumption about the goodness of reality. Is such a concept rationally justifiable? While certain experiences may point us beyond the superficial, on what grounds is it credible to hold that reality as a whole is, first, ultimately understandable and, secondly, has a particular meaningful character?

Answers to these questions cannot be found in the way that we find answers to questions about the nature of objects within the world. Whereas we can reach decisions about particular objects by comparing them with others, reality as a whole is not 'a thing' which can be examined in a similar way. Since it is doubtful whether we can imagine significantly different cosmic orders (as opposed to variants parasitic on our experiences of this world) to compare with the actual one, we can probably only engage in the problematic task of judging reality as a whole by comparing how it seems to us with some parts of it. Such judgements are further complicated by the fact that we are part of the whole we are trying to understand. In this respect, as Kierkegaard argued against the Hegelian system, no existentially universal judgement is possible because no system of understanding can completely include the one who produces it.[72] Finally, our judgements about the fundamental rationality and value of reality depend upon our structures of understanding and these too are part of what we are trying to understand. Consequently, decisions about the nature of reality are not only determined by norms which are directly or indirectly provided by the place of humanity in that reality;[73] they must also involve judgements about the rationality and value of the norms of rationality and value by which they are made!

Bearing in mind both the three factors involved in constituting the concept of God and the unavailability of God and of the fundamental character of reality as a whole as directly perceivable objects, how are we to arrive at a materially significant concept of God which offers a credible basis for understanding all reality? One answer is that a notion of God may be developed initially as the abstract idea of what is considered to have the formal characteristics of ontological, rational and valuative ultimacy.[74] The result is then combined with material attributes derived from our appreciation of concrete expressions of being, rationality and value. Those theists who maintain that our understanding of God's qualities should be derived wholly from direct acts of divine self-revelation are putting forward an unobtainable ideal. In practice, our conceptions of the material nature of the divine are predominantly constituted from and relative to our experiences and understanding within our cultural context. On the basis of the resulting concept of God, theists may then try to perceive the fundamental nature of reality.

While, however, this may be where the concept of God originates, attempts to absolutize values to make them applicable to God and to understand reality as a whole in terms of them, may lead to modifications both in the concept of God and in the understanding of values. The reasoning used in the process of developing and justifying a concept of God involves complex internal reciprocities. The concept of God is, therefore, not wholly a product of pre-existing understanding: its development is affected by continuing reappraisals of the notions of the divine and of the given character of reality as these mutually influence the perception of ultimate qualities. Whereas a concept of God is finally judged to be intellectually justifiable – and so as both significant and credible – if it is considered to describe that which might reasonably be regarded as the actual ground of reality, theologians develop such a concept by projecting their own understandings of being, rationality and value onto a supposed entity that has the characteristics of formal ultimacy.

Such intellectual activity may seem at first to be a case of human self-deification but, on reflection, it turns out to be far from an improper activity. Although human beings do not possess the highest qualities of being in every respect,[75] they may justifiably claim that their personal mode of being is the highest form of being which they can envisage.[76] The highest values for them (and hence the values most appropriate for them to ascribe to God as the definitively perfect being) are those that they recognize in their own understanding of themselves as persons. Barth remarks that when Feuerbach 'identifies God with the essence of man, he thereby pays God the highest honour that he can confer'.[77] In spite of Barth's attempt to derive theistic understanding from divine revelation, his comment not only describes what human beings do: it also reports, *pace* Barth, what they cannot avoid doing when they seek to understand God.

The cosmological argument illustrates this basic character of theistic thought, as it seeks to satisfy one aspect of the quest for understanding reality by tracing existence to a personal act of creativity.[78] The teleological argument, as F. R. Tennant points out, is not arrogantly exalting the human when it holds that the world is intelligible 'to the specifically anthropic intelligence possessed by us'. It is affirming that whereas 'no final purpose can be discerned' in less than human areas of reality, 'such purpose may be discerned in beings possessed of rationality, appreciation, self-determination, and morality'.[79] It is in terms of these qualities, furthermore, that the purpose is perceived. Theistic understanding is not simply following a current prejudice but taking up the results of more perceptive analyses when it regards the personal qualities of human being as superior to those of impersonal being for describing the divine. As for suggestions that the divine is to be described as supra-personal or supra-human, these are inapprehensible notions. There may be modes of being qualitatively higher than that of human being but we have no way to envisage them.

The cultural relativity of concepts of God

Once it is recognized that people construct their material concepts of God out of their appreciation of being, rationality and value, as conceived in principle and as exemplified in practice, it becomes clear why those concepts are culturally relative. Since their culture largely determines their ways of understanding, the distinctions and values that are fundamental to it are the distinctions and values by which they construct their notion of the divine nature.

We can see this happening most clearly in the case of those whose cultural presuppositions are importantly different from our own. Anselm, for example, holds that the impassibility of God follows from the recognition that God must be 'whatever it is better to be than not to be'.[80] That it is better to be passionless than not to be is so self-evident in his judgement that he does attempt to justify it. If, however, the perfection of the divine is considered to be more akin to that of a person than to that of an abstract ideal or an impersonal object, it is far from obvious that God, as perfect, must be thought to be impassible.[81] Why, then, does Anselm assume what he does? It is because his reasoning is governed, almost certainly unconsciously, by the cultural tradition in which he found himself. As a result he regards the conflict between what to him is the unquestionable impassibility of God and notions of the divine as loving, sympathizing and responding[82] as a paradox to be solved (or simply left as a paradox), and not as a contradiction which requires one or other conception to be abandoned if the contents of the terms are not to be so modified that they come to connote something different.

While, however, Anselm's view of what is self-evidently true of the divine reflects the prejudices of his culture, our situation in another cultural age leads us to regard some of those assumptions

46

as questionable. In spite of Barth's praise for his supposed method,[83] in practice Anselm deifies the values of his culture. Although Barth regards such a proceeding as a basic error in theology, it is largely unavoidable. We should not assume, therefore, that we are less prejudiced than Anselm, nor presume that our prejudices are necessarily preferable to his. More careful critical analyses may seem to establish the superiority of our position, but we must not forget that the criteria involved in such analyses, and the concepts which we consider appropriate to the material nature of the divine, are themselves likely to be culturally conditioned.

Another example is provided by Aquinas' view that God, as the 'first existent', must be 'sheerly actual and unalloyed with potentiality' and so 'altogether unchangeable'.[84] On the basis of this understanding of the divine, Aquinas holds that there are no reciprocal relations between God and creatures by which the latter can in any way affect the former.[85] God's activity (or perhaps, as the unchangeable, it ought to be spoken of as God's non-activity) is conceived as a final causality in a way that is incompatible with descriptions of God as deciding and acting, as well as with the implications of believers' trust that they are related to God as children to a loving parent. This concept of God is advanced because the prevalent (i.e., cultural) understanding of potentiality is in terms of lacking the completeness of perfection, and of change in terms of decay. Whatever may be suggested by the indications of the existential faith of Christian believers, cultural presuppositions rule out the attribution of potentiality and change to the divine.

During the present century various cultures – or, rather, subcultures – have emerged and each has had its theological correlate. Liberal Protestant theology embodied the optimism of the start of the century: God benevolently supervises a world which the prevailing culture saw as marked by progress and human solidarity. Barthian neo-orthodoxy, for all its claims about revelation, reflected the current sense of crisis as the foundations of Western civilization were shaken by the Great War, economic collapse, the growing power of the proletariat and the decline of traditional values in society, politics and morals. In the 1960s self-consciously radical theologies expressed, generally deliberately, the prevailing, if brief, mood of confidence in human ability to sort out the world. God's role was sometimes interpreted in terms of keeping out of the way so that human beings could get on with the job.[86] When the Vietnamese war, race riots and political and economic troubles changed the cultural scene, the change was partly reflected in the increasing prominence and popularity of reactionary affirmations of conservative attitudes and principles. They found religious expression in attempts to restore what were supposed to be the beliefs, values and practices of an earlier generation. Not all, however, shared this loss of nerve. Some reacted to the cultural situation with theologies of hope and interest in the God of the future. Others developed theologies concerned with humour and play. While the latter may only have been short-lived, it would be a mistake to dismiss them as defiant gestures which tried to camouflage basic despair in the face of widespread cynicism about values and the quest for meaning. They may be evaluated to some extent more positively as paradoxically serious gestures which affirm faithful living to the full, while recognizing the comic pretentiousness of theological understanding.[87]

In various ways, then, the understanding and values which are taken to be self-evidently valid in a culture are generally regarded as self-evidently valid for determining the nature of God and the relationship between God and humanity.[88] Nevertheless, what is 'generally' the case is not necessarily universally the case. The relationship between theological understanding and culture is not wholly in one direction. While the way in which theologians view the material nature of God is primarily influenced by their culture's values, reflection on those values in terms of God may lead to revised appreciations of them. Reflection on the claim that God is revealed in Jesus, for example, may lead to the recognition that impassibility is grossly inferior to the qualities of sympathy and awareness. On the whole, however, the strength of cultural presuppositions is such that the influence tends ('generally') to be in the other direction. Thus the presumption that impassibility is a necessary quality of the divine may lead to a shallower view of the significance of suffering than can be found in those who hold that God suffers, and this view of suffering to a more qualified view of the presence of God in Jesus.

The problem for theologians is that of finding a way by which they may become aware of their own culture's values sufficiently to be able to recognize how those values condition their theological understanding and critically to assess that conditioning. It is often easy to see the cultural relativity of theologies developed in other cultures and to admit in principle that our own must be similarly relative. What is difficult is to find ways of identifying and evaluating that relativity in our own understanding.

God as cosmic projection

The reply to the charge of anthropomorphism

A threefold response is therefore to be given to the charge that
theistic descriptions are anthropomorphic. First, the charge is to be
recognized to be largely correct: believers and theologians construct their material descriptions of God out of their image of
human nature. Secondly, anthropomorphism is unavoidable if
there are to be any significant notions of the material nature of
God since human nature is the highest mode of being that we can
envisage. Attempts to avoid anthropomorphisms produce concepts
of God that are either purely formal and empty, or constructed from
knowledge of parts of reality generally considered to be inferior to
the human mode of being. Thirdly, the role in theological descriptions of such formal terms as ultimate, necessary and eternal –
what Ramsey calls 'qualifiers' – is at least partly to indicate the
transcendent reference of the anthropomorphic material used to
describe God.

Theological descriptions are thus products of theologians'
humanity as members of particular cultures. They are relative to
the cultures that moulded them and open to revision. To this extent
theologians must take to heart Feuerbach's insight which, as Marx
puts it, 'consists in the dissolution of the religious world into its
secular basis'.[89] It would, however, be a mistake to conclude from
this that what theologians say about God cannot be proper and
adequate expressions of the truth about ultimate reality within their
particular cultural situations. On the contrary, if there be a God
and if faith in God is to be significant, understanding of God must
be related to current culture. Only so will the divine be recognized
as the God of people in that culture. The relativity that the charge
of anthropomorphism points to is the relativity of our apprehension
of the truth about reality, not the relativity of that truth itself.
Perhaps, nevertheless, theologians ought to acknowledge more
explicitly than they usually do the cultural relativity of (as well as
their individual responsibility for) what they advance as descriptions of God.

The charge of invention considered

Feuerbach's claim that talk of God is a projection of the idealized
qualities of human being not only charges theology with anthropomorphism. It also alleges that 'God' is a human creation or invention, having no ontological independence of the human. This

allegation threatens the foundations of theism. As a human idea 'God' would no longer be credible as the ground for the significance of life, the explanation of the contingency and purposiveness of reality, or as the source of the categorical demands of morality. The divine would cease to be that ultimate reality which, embracing all, stands over against human beings, correcting their understanding, commanding their respect, evoking their adoration, and eliciting their participation in the creative achievement of aesthetic joy. It would not be the reality that Job finally recognizes to be God (cf. Job 42. 1–6). The word 'God' might survive as a cipher for something like supreme value and serve as an indirect (and misleading) way of expressing convictions about the worthwhileness of life or about the sense of contingency, purposiveness and duty, but it would do no more than *express* these things. It would not refer to a ground for such experiences nor contain suggestions about the ultimate nature of reality.

According to Feuerbach such an understanding of theology makes clear its proper content and importance. While, however, this analysis shows that talk about God is important as an expression of human ideals, goals and desires, it radically alters its ontological basis. If it were accepted, theistic faith would lose its foundation in an ontologically prior ultimate and references to God would find their ground in human thought. Since we respond to what we believe to be the case, rather than to what is actually so from some absolute standpoint, theism might continue to persist for some time into the future as it has existed in the past – as a response to an unrecognized error. Once the Feuerbachian analysis was accepted as correct, however, such a response would become impossible. Theistic worship would be replaced by the celebration of human ideals.[90]

Feuerbach's claim that God is an imaginative invention cannot be dismissed simply on the grounds that to accept it would destroy theistic faith. It may be that such faith is based on error and so should be destroyed. Nor, furthermore, can we reject his claim by describing him as an outsider and a philosopher who, because he was not a believer, could not perceive the truth about God.[91] Sometimes it is the outsider who is in the best position to discern what is happening. If Feuerbach – and the tradition of Western thought from Descartes and Locke – is correct in holding that we must, even in religious understanding, start with ourselves, our world, our experiences and our structures of thought (and, *pace* such theologians as Barth and Torrance, it seems that there is in practice nowhere else for us to start from, whatever fictional realm might seem preferable), theism can only preserve its credibility by answering the charge of invention.[92]

The way to answer this charge is easier to specify than to carry out. In principle, the charge is rebutted by showing that the anthropomorphic conception of God is the most adequate way for human beings to grasp the nature of ultimate reality as it exists ontologically independently of them. Whereas, however, in the case of some apparently improbable objects like black swans and unilateral, three-dimensional figures, we can show that they are not merely imaginative projections by presenting doubters with a black swan and a Möbius strip, no such ostensive reference is possible in the case of God.

Nor can the charge of invention be rebutted simply by drawing attention to certain kinds of human experience. Schleiermacher's 'feeling of absolute dependence', Otto's sense of 'the numinous', Troeltsch's awareness of 'a power that is irresistibly transforming, profoundly moving, and binding in the highest degree',[93] and other such descriptions point to modes of human experience whose reality as experiences does not seem open to question. To infer from these experiences that they mediate a cognitive awareness of a theistic God is, in contrast, a controversial matter.[94] It can be justified only by showing that it is more plausible to interpret them in this way than as experiences of a dimension or quality in human life which has no correlate in reality other than the individual or social self. Since such an argument is not easy to sustain, references to religious experience tend not to answer the Feuerbachian charge so much as to raise the question of whether they should be interpreted in a Feuerbachian manner!

Can we, then, find convincing reasons for holding that the theistic conception of God describes something that exists ontologically independently of the human – where 'exists' is here used to refer to a mode of being appropriate to the ultimate? As was mentioned in chapter 2, the examination of this 'external' use of reason in theological understanding will have to wait for another occasion. There are, however, certain considerations which suggest that the Feuerbachian interpretation of the concept of God as a cosmic projection of human nature may be accepted by theists – and even affirmed by them as the only way in which the mind-independent reality of God can be apprehended.

In the first place, the fact that a straightforward 'No!' cannot be given to the charge that the concept of God is, in important respects at least, a human creation does not show that it does not significantly express the nature of a theistic reality. While we admit that concepts of God are culturally influenced products, we should also be aware of the 'genetic fallacy'.[95] Even if it could be shown that belief in God originated in human fears (cf. Hobbes and Hume), the projection of human ideals (cf. Feuerbach) or the personification of psychic forces (cf. Freud), this would not show that all theistic belief is necessarily false. Such intellectual processes, while not justifying the theistic conclusion, may have been the way that people initially arrived at true understanding.[96]

Secondly, the fact that we describe things materially in terms of our apprehension and interpretation of them does not mean that we are trapped in a form of epistemological solipsism. For all its superficial plausibility (which is not very much), solipsism is a false conclusion. Although what we consider ourselves to know as a result of our experiences is connected with our own being, it does not follow that all we can know is our awareness of our states of knowledge. We exist and we experience as persons in contexts. What we experience and come to hold as being known is largely of other selves and other things. Self-knowledge is not a primary awareness but a growing realization of our distinction from other things and persons. While, therefore, our structures of apprehension and of interpretation govern our thought, including our theological understanding, it does not follow that theological understanding is only understanding of those structures and of the human self which possesses them – any more that my present awareness of the berries on the Rowan only tells me about myself.

Thirdly, it is not self-evident that projective methods must always lead to invalid conclusions. Although they may sometimes lead us into error (as when human qualities are ascribed to inanimate objects – the car will not start because 'it is in a cussed mood'), it is arguable that we engage in projective ways of understanding because in many cases they seem to lead to insights into states and events which are pragmatically effective and, sometimes, also turn out to be rationally justifiable. It seems reasonable to try to understand other persons by projecting ourselves into their situation and trying to imagine what forces and considerations would have led them to act as they did. The problem is to determine how far this projective activity may be extended without unwarrantably intruding ourselves into the other whom we seek to understand. Interpreters can never prevent their own background and interests affecting their grasp of what they seek to interpret. Even when projective understanding is restricted to the understanding of fellow-members of the interpreter's culture, it is inevitably approximate. The degree to which such ways of understanding can be extended to persons of other cultures, animals, inanimate matter, sub-atomic particles, or even to reality as such is an increasingly controversial issue. In the end, projective ways of understanding are probably not to be justified generally but by their success in this or that particular case in producing understanding that is rationally satisfactory and superior to other views of the matter. Judgements of these characteristics are often somewhat circular but they need not be viciously so.[97]

Fourthly, the concept of God is used in correlation with the basic questions of human being. Pannenberg, for example, suggests that their experiences of finite reality lead people to see themselves as 'essentially referred to infinity'. As a result human subjectivity is finally 'conceivable only on the presupposition of a God'.[98] A similar kind of argument maintains that human beings want to find reality as making sense – and also good. The only way in which they can envisage it making sense and being good is in terms of its dependence upon some being with reason and values like their own but suitably qualified to reflect its ultimate status. If the meaning and value of reality cannot ultimately be grasped in this way, then reality is absurd and the basic human quest for understanding is doomed to be a confused hunt for a non-existent Woozle. Consequently, to affirm that the concept of God is a human construct which in no way corresponds to the fundamental nature of reality is to hold that human rationality, in spite of its technological successes, enters into a realm of nonsense when it seeks to answer metaphysical questions. This conclusion does not show that the concept of God significantly corresponds to the fundamental nature of reality. It does show that to deny any such correspondence is to affirm the final irrationality of the search for understanding, and the absurdity of human being as characteristically disturbed by the desire for it.

All that these points indicate is that the projective nature of the concept of God does not show that it must be regarded as a human invention with no mind-independent correlate in reality. What has still to be determined is whether this projection can be regarded as a credible view of the ultimate. Does it, for example, describe the regulative ideas of human understanding, or does it point to that which instantiates those ideas in its own reality? Although this is a crucial matter,[99] it lies beyond our remit here. What the present discussion suggests is that the Feuerbachian analysis of theological judgements does not succeed in demonstrating that descriptions of God can only tell us about the human. They can be interpreted as a way of expounding the epistemological significance of the religious claim that the human 'is made in the image of God': namely, as the claim that human beings, by considering their nature, are able to conceive the nature of ultimate reality. This response to Feuerbach is what Peter Berger has called the 'gigantic joke' of inverting Feuerbach's conclusion: what from one perspective may appear to be a human projection, from another 'may appear as a reflection of divine realities'.[100]

When 'theology as anthropology' is interpreted as referring to the cosmic projection of human nature, we are faced by charges that the concept of God is anthropomorphic and a human invention. To both charges theists may plead guilty and yet deny that their theism is false. They may justifiably claim that what the Feuerbachian analysis shows is that people construct the concept of God as, on the basis of what is highest for them, they develop the concept of an ontologically ultimate reality with values such that, if it does correspond to what actually is the case, it shows reality to be basically meaningful and good. Such projections are, of course, always culturally conditioned – but so, too, is the 'world' in which people find themselves.[101]

The theistic response to the Feuerbachian analysis, then, should be to accept its insights while denying the atheistic implications which Feuerbach finds in them. Since we cannot avoid making our concept of God in our own image, because there is nothing more adequate available to us by which to fashion it, the theistic question is whether it can be shown that the resulting concept describes what is ultimate. Contrary to what are generally regarded as the implications of philosophical investigations into religious language, the problem for theology is not how to find language adequate for talk about God (as if 'God' were a given subject and the problem were how to describe it), but how to find a way of establishing a significant correlation between the concept of God derived from a cosmic projection of human nature and the ultimate structure of reality.[102]

4

God as actualizing regulative ideas

In the *Monologion* Anselm argues that there must exist 'some one thing which alone exists most greatly and most highly of all'. This 'Supreme Being' is to be worshipped as it is 'the Supreme Good' and to be invoked because it is the supremely powerful origin of all else. It is properly called 'God'.[1]

The intrinsic ultimacy of God

Anselm's remarks remind us that the concept of God is the concept of what is prior and superior to all else. Questions such as, 'What caused God to exist?', 'From what do God's attributes derive their perfection?' and 'By what canons does God judge the goodness of divine actions?' are, in principle, either deeply confused, because they appear to treat as external to God what is intrinsic to the divine, or meaningless, because they presuppose in one way or another that God can be considered in relation to something superior in being or in value. Since the word 'God' properly denotes what is philosophically the ultimate and religiously the adequate object of worship, it refers to that entity which, if it exists, must satisfy the quest for total understanding.

Whereas in the *Monologion*, Anselm treats God as the highest in the hierarchy of actual entities, the *Proslogion* marks a fundamental development in his insight into theistic understanding since here he defines God as what it is logically (and not merely in fact) impossible to go beyond – as 'that than which nothing greater can be conceived'.[2] The supremacy of the divine is now seen to be such that it is incoherent to consider anything as even conceivably superior to it. It is not to be limited to the concept of the greatest that we can conceive, but must be regarded as 'something greater than can be thought'.[3] Although Anselm's argument on this point may not be strictly valid, and although its conclusion threatens to empty the concept of God of any significant material content, his comments point to the logical uniqueness and fundamental difficulty of the concept of God.

What Anselm establishes in the *Proslogion* is that if we think of God, then we must think of God as unqualifiedly perfect; and that if God exists, then the mode of divine being must, uniquely, be that of ontological necessity. This is no mean achievement.[4] For one thing it points out the logical error of maintaining that claims about God's existence can only be factually significant if we can specify what would falsify them. When properly analysed God's existence is seen not to be an empirical matter. It is such that either the whole of reality, both actual and possible, is theistically based or it is fundamentally non-theistic and hence absurd. Theistic verification is, accordingly, a matter of trying to discern whether theism's affirmation of the ultimate meaningfulness and rationality of reality is a credible understanding of the nature of all possible as well as of all actual reality.[5] Secondly, Anselm's argument, especially as developed by Hartshorne, reminds us that thought about God is thought about what is necessarily ultimate and perfect. If God can conceive the intrinsic character of the divine nature, it must be as that which only has limits as having self-identity. The divine existence[6] cannot be limited in practice or in principle by anything prior or superior to Godself.[7] Thirdly, the argument indicates that talk about God is such that 'the tendency toward ultimacy', which we recognize to be the proper reference of God-talk, 'continuously fights against the tendency toward concreteness' as we seek to grasp the material nature of God.[8] Hence, concepts of God must be seen to point beyond themselves to the reality of God which constitutes the ground and limit of understanding.

In this chapter we are to look at some of the implications of the ultimacy of God for theistic understanding. In particular we will consider the extent to which, since the concept of God is governed by our notion of what is ultimate, the perception of what gives direction and completion to our understanding may warrantably be held to provide insight into the intrinsic nature of God.

Some historic uses of God's ultimacy in philosophical thought

Whereas metaphysical and religious understanding in general is orientated by a notion of the unity of all the various elements of reality in a coherent whole, theistic understanding sees this unity as grounded in an actual, apparently personal, ultimate reality. The identification of the divine and the ultimate means, however, that as views on what is final in being, rationality and value change, so too does understanding of the nature of God. Accordingly, before we examine the significance of this aspect of the concept of God, we will briefly review some of the ways in which a concept of this kind has provided the basis for different systems of understanding. This will illustrate the range of ideas of the ultimate that have been entertained.

In Plato's thought it is not what he calls 'God' but 'the Form of the Good' or 'the Form of the Forms' which is most significant for theistic understanding of the ultimate. As a 'form', the 'Form of the Good' is that from which all the other forms are derived and in which reality has its unity;[9] as the 'good', it combines ultimate value with ultimate being and ultimate rationality. When, however, Plato comes to its description, he suggests that its nature as the origin of the unity, value and reality of all else means that it cannot itself be satisfactorily included among what is understood thereby: it is 'known' as what is beyond knowledge, and its being is 'superior' to reality 'in dignity and power'.[10]

While Aristotle criticizes these views on 'the Form of the Good',[11] the notion of the Unmoved Mover fulfils a parallel function in his own thought. Its characteristics as eternal, unchanging, necessary, good, separate from visible things and wholly actual are determined by what is needed to bring his metaphysical thought to completion.[12] It too shows itself on examination to be something that puts a limit on the quest for understanding rather than is itself understandable.[13] The endpoint of Aristotle's search for truth is similarly held to lie in 'the principles of eternal things' which are necessarily most true, the source of what is, and inexplicable.[14] Understanding reaches its completion when it discerns what is an essentially inexplicable brute state of affairs.

In the seventeenth century the dominant concern in Western philosophy came to be that of establishing the trustworthiness of human understanding. In place of the classical search for a metaphysical grasp of the nature of reality, attention was concentrated on the foundations of rationality. The ultimate, often identified as God, is accordingly seen in terms of being the final guarantor of the trustworthiness of human understanding.

Descartes, for example, invokes God's perfection in order to justify our confidence in our powers of understanding and, especially, the assumption that 'the things which we conceive very clearly and distinctly are all true'. Although it is on the basis of this assumption that he concludes that the existence of God as a perfect being is 'certain',[15] he is apparently untroubled by the circularity of his ensuing argument that our faculties must be trustworthy, if used correctly, since they have been given to us by God.[16] He thus maintains that God's perfection and trustworthiness free us to some extent from the crushing coils of doubt.[17]

According to Leibniz, God, as the 'ultimate reason of things' which has 'in itself the reason of its own existence', is alone able to provide our understanding with 'a sufficient reason with which we could stop'. The necessity of God's existence and perfection is accordingly inferred from the assumption that reality must satisfy the demands of the principle of sufficient reason.[18] Furthermore, as the origin of all,[19] God co-ordinates the monads of which reality is composed in 'a pre-established harmony' so that each of them represents 'one and the same universe'.[20] In this way affirmations about God provide the rational, ontological and epistemological bases for Leibniz's understanding of reality. They are justified, however, because they complete his system of understanding.

Hegel's metaphysical understanding finds its key insight in the identification of the Absolute as 'Mind' or 'Spirit'.[21] Frequently the Absolute is presented in terms of God as the unlimited and total, beyond any differentiation into individual qualities and objects,[22] and hence as a mystery which properly lies beyond our grasp.[23] Religion is the consciousness of this Absolute.[24] Theism describes it in pictorial – and imperfect – forms whereas philosophy (particularly Hegel's philosophy) gives it direct expression.[25] While, however, Hegel professes to be elucidating the authentic, if obscured, meaning of theistic notions, his interpretation of those notions is governed by the needs of his metaphysical understanding.[26] His exposition of the Absolute thus illustrates how theistic understanding may be modified in order to produce a credible understanding of the basis of reality.[27]

In this respect Hegel's views on the developing character of reality are particularly interesting. Since he holds that the real is the rational and necessary, it is possible to interpret his Absolute in a way that largely agrees with the traditional view that the perfection of the ultimate reality and value lies in its completeness and unalterability. A major contribution of his thought to the development of understanding, however, lies in the suggestion that the ultimate should be regarded as characterized by a self-initiated process of change.[28] While Engels was excited by the political implications of this suggestion,[29] it also has far-reaching significance for theism. If God is to be thought of as the active and conscious creator of a reality that is processive at all levels, then the divine nature must be compatible with appropriate modes of change and the purpose of divine activity orientated not by some fixed material goal but by the aesthetic satisfaction of creativity itself.

Maintaining that reality is inescapably in process through 'the immanence of the infinite in the finite', Whitehead condemns the view that 'changeless order' is 'the final perfection' as 'the outcome of tired decadence'.[30] The infinite, furthermore, is understood as an ultimate individual with universal relevance – God – whose primordial and consequent 'natures' are the ground of the creative novelty and personal unity of the process. God persistently affects the world to evoke novel expressions of beauty in it. This is 'the one aim which by its very nature is self-justifying'.[31]

Some of Whitehead's remarks[32] leave the impression that he considers creativity to be the primary reality (which is correct) and God to be derivative from it in all respects (which is a mistaken interpretation). It should be noted, therefore, that he also holds that 'God is the ultimate limitation' and that the divine existence is 'the ultimate irrationality . . . because that nature is the ground of rationality'.[33] In spite of some rather misleading ways of expressing his position, Whitehead does not regard the fundamental stimulus of creativity in reality as something which either produces God or is decided by God.[34] The metaphysical principles which describe this fundamental structure at the same time describe the essential nature of the divine.[35] God is neither prior nor posterior to 'the ultimate metaphysical ground', for that ground is necessarily what constitutes the divine nature. While, however, the creative ultimacy of the divine nature cannot be explained by reference to anything beyond itself, it is 'the ground of rationality' for Whitehead's metaphysics since its processive, rational and valuative reality both marks the limits of what is understandable and determines what it is finally to understand.

Hartshorne similarly[36] holds that the ultimate metaphysical principles are part of the essential nature of things for God as for everything else.[37] They constitute '*a priori* knowledge, valid "for all possible worlds" ' and so are contingent at no level, not even upon God.[38] In this respect 'God' represents the instantiation rather than some final arbiter of these ultimate principles, while the principles themselves are the basis of understanding rather than themselves explicable. They just are, even for God. To hold that they are analytic or intrinsically true is to presuppose rather than explain

their status. As embodied *a priori* in God these principles constitute, for Hartshorne's metaphysical thought, the ultimate limitation
of being, rationality and value and the final basis for all understanding.

Other contemporary writers employ the word 'God' to refer to
what is ultimate in their understanding. For Braithwaite reference
to God identifies a person's determinative behaviour policy;[39] for
Wisdom, van Buren, Evans and Hudson references to God describe
how believers view their world and seek to make sense of it;[40] for
Kaufman ' "God" ' is 'the key term in a complex of meaning which
is intended to grasp all experience and reality'.[41] Among those who
are committed to more clearly realist understanding of talk about
God, Ramsey suggests that 'God' serves as the apex of the metaphysical words by which we mark off the boundaries and co-ordi-
nate the 'maps' of the different ways in which we perceive our
world.[42] Lonergan finds the question of God arising when we investigate the possibility of fruitful enquiry into the intelligibility, conditionedness and worth of things, as well as into our religious
experience.[43] For Pannenberg the notion of God represents the
final solution to the question of human existence since it refers to
that future reality which already definitively decides the significance
of all individuals and events,[44] while Moltmann presents God as the
ground of the hope which determines the believer's thought and
action.[45] Ogden argues that the reality of the panentheistic God
provides the only final justification for the fundamental conviction
that human lives are significant.[46] In various ways – in terms of the
metaphysical ultimate, the guarantor of knowledge, the source of
process, the basis of understanding and the justification of human
confidence in the meaningfulness of life – the ultimacy essentially
involved in references to God is thus to be seen as referring to what
finally founds, directs and satisfies the quest for understanding.

Kant's treatment of regulative ideas

Before we consider how in any fully reflective theological understanding the concept of God not only moulds but, to a significant
extent, must also be moulded by what is considered to be ultimate
for understanding, it is important to note Kant's views on the regulative ideas of understanding. These provide the classic treatment
of this aspect of theistic thought. Since, however, Kant's discussions
of the subject are not as lucid and self-consistent as might be hoped,
and since our interest is not in Kant himself but in the insights

which his thought on regulative ideas provides into the nature of theological understanding, we shall proceed more systematically than the actual texts (if not Kant's intention) might justify.

According to Kant, our thought is not only determined by an inbuilt structure consisting of the forms of intuition and the categories of understanding. It is also governed by various fundamental ideas which are called 'regulative' because they present theoretical goals by which the different kinds of rational thought are orientated and given a systematic unity according to apparently necessary laws. Strawson points out that these ideas have four characteristics: they are absolute or unconditioned, they must inevitably be entertained by any appropriate systematic enquiry, they must transcend all possible experience, and they must have a regulative role in thinking.[47] Furthermore, as Ewing points out, these ideas do not simply function regulatively by providing 'some policy to organise our research'. They serve 'as an inspiration and encouragement', making us discontent with partial explanations and presenting us with the goal of a complete explanation. They also give the basis for a coherent use of the understanding by providing the ideas and the ideals by which reason is to judge.[48]

While Kant's remarks in the first *Critique* and the *Prolegomena*[49] suggest that there are only three regulative ideas, the psychological, the cosmological and the theological, inspection of his writings reveals that the latter two embrace several distinct ideas and that there are others which cannot be subsumed under these three heads.

The psychological idea is that of the mind (or soul). It refers to the ground of the transcendental unity of apperception which constitutes a person's identity – the 'I' of the individual self. While this subject 'I' is actualized in and through all the experiences and activities of the object 'me', it necessarily eludes all attempts to isolate it from forms of the 'me'.[50] The cosmological idea is the regulative idea of the natural sciences as they seek completion for their investigations into substances and processes in an unconditioned ground or 'First Cause'. This idea has various forms. Negatively the idea suggests that there is no end to the quest for a causal understanding. Each natural cause is itself the contingent effect of a prior cause.[51] Positively, the idea posits an unobtainable (rather than a necessarily non-existent) goal for the natural sciences. One form of it is the idea of a necessary first cause which is completely unconditioned and provides an absolute beginning to all series of appearances.[52] Another form, which governs the sciences' presupposition that nature is a rational whole, is the idea of 'a supreme intelligence' which orders all things 'in accordance with the wisest ends'.[53] This last form is also treated as a regulative idea in its own right as the idea of an ultimate purpose. It directs understanding both of organic nature and of history by positing the notion that processes ultimately make sense in terms of the rationally intended designs of an originating intelligence.[54] Another regulative idea is that of the supreme good – the state where the highest virtue is joined to the highest happiness. This idea is the unconditioned goal of practical (i.e., moral) reason.[55] Political science is governed by the idea of a perfect political state – a state, that is, in which the laws are in harmony with the natural rights and freedom of the citizens.[56]

It is the idea of pure reason – what Kant calls 'the theological idea' – that is the most significant for our purposes. The regulative principle for theological and metaphysical understanding is that of an *ens realissimum*, an ultimate and all-embracing reality, in terms of which it is possible completely to determine the character, connection, order and unity of all things in the cosmos.[57] There are several forms of this idea of an unconditionally necessary individual possessing all predicates;[58] as that from which all else is derived and by which all else is limited it is describable as the primordial being (*ens originarium*), as the highest being (*ens summum*), and as the being of all beings (*ens entium*).[59] In a footnote Kant suggests how this ideal is transformed into a theistic view of God by being objectified and then personified.[60] When, therefore, thought seeks ultimate and total understanding, it involves, according to Kant, the use of an ideal at least very like that of God to provide its regulative idea of the ground, coherence and bounds of all reality.[61]

Although Kant compares these ideas to Platonic ideas, the former do not have creative power. They only have practical power as guiding principles. Since coherent thought is intrinsically compelled to seek the unconditioned as its ground and goal,[62] the ideas provide the absolute goals which direct and organize our thought by offering it, in its different domains, orientation, completion[63] and final foundation. Where they are individuated as ideals, they provide reason with archetypes, that is, with representations of things which are entirely perfect in their kind and so act as standards for judgement.[64]

Since thought cannot avoid presupposing ideas even if it does not explicitly recognize them, Kant denies that they can be dismissed as mere 'figments of the brain'.[65] On the other hand, he also frequently denies that the ideas (and hence the ideals) are to be taken as referring to actual objects.[66] They are regulative and heuristic in function, not constitutive nor ostensive.[67] When we identify them, we identify the contents of the rational faith that is the necessary basis of our understanding; we do not perceive necessary constituents of the reality which we seek to understand by means of them.[68] Consideration of the ideas must therefore take care to avoid the 'dialectical illusion' of regarding 'the subjective conditions of our thought' as 'objective conditions of the things themselves'.[69]

In some passages Kant not merely holds that the ideas do not refer to objects. He argues that they could not be instantiated in any actual individuals.[70] Thought is lead into contradictions, according to the argument from the antinomies, when the ideas are treated as having constitutive significance.[71] An idea exists only as a theoretical construction. It directs thought to 'a *focus imaginarius*' which lies outside the bounds of all possible experience of reality.[72] In this respect, therefore, what Kant says about the ideas and, in particular, about the theological idea of a supreme being, suggests that theologians and believers may confuse the needs of their thought with the character of reality when they hold that such a being, God, must actually exist.

Other passages, however, imply that the illusion of holding that the theological ideal refers to a real object[73] is not the illusion of holding that such a being exists, but the illusion of holding that we could ever be in a position to know that it exists.[74] On different occasions in the first *Critique* Kant holds that the regulative principle of reason does not debar us from recognizing that the empirical order may rest on an unconditioned intelligible being,[75] and that the ideal of a supreme being is not incoherent but is '*an ideal without a flaw*'.[76] Nevertheless, even if such an object does exist, we could apprehend its attributes only so far as they are analogous to our limited structures of understanding, not as they are in themselves.[77] As for the belief that such a supreme being does exist, Kant suggests that it is confirmed in practice by the fruitfulness of the ideal of 'a wise Author of the world' in producing understanding.[78]

Kant himself thus seems uncertain about the actualization of the ideal of the supreme being. Probably we come closest to his own position when he states that we can neither satisfy our understanding by finding what has unconditional necessity, nor 'induce it to acquiesce in its incapacity'. Speculative reason can neither prove nor disprove the objective reality of this ideal.[79] What reason can do is to discern the origin of these ideas in the understanding, and their role in indicating both the limits of understanding and where it may find satisfaction.[80]

The necessarily regulative function of God

Although Kant himself was concerned to determine the nature of human reasoning, his views on regulative ideas, together with the other philosophical notions mentioned earlier in this chapter, point to a puzzling aspect of the nature of God in theistic thought. Since the concept of God refers to what is ultimate, God has to be understood in some way or other as that being whose reality determines the boundaries and provides the governing principles for all correct understanding, including thought about God.[81] If, then, the views of ultimacy which have been considered earlier are generally valid, a fully developed theistic understanding will have to show that God is properly to be conceived as an actual being which is the metaphysical ultimate, the foundation of knowledge, the ground of the processes of reality, the justification of faith in the meaningfulness of life and the utterly satisfying end-point for all quests for understanding.

It seems, that is, that a complete concept of God must include the recognition that God is the reality which instantiates regulative ideas, even though this apparently entails that the notion of God is logically odd in certain respects. Can this conclusion be avoided? It is possible, of course, to claim that thought should neither presuppose nor be directed by regulative ideas. Such a claim is not warranted when it is advanced by those who want thereby to avoid prejudgements in their considerations: all enquiries take place within some structure of understanding. It may possibly be justified in the case of those who maintain that reality is a pointless agglomeration of items, and that attempts to make sense of it are attempts to force meaningful patterns onto what is absurd. This, however, is not a position compatible with theistic understanding. Theists are committed as such to regarding reality as an intelligible whole whose fundamental meaningfulness is apprehensible to some extent in terms of God.

On the other hand, it should also be appreciated that those who recognize that their thought is grounded in and governed by regulative ideas are not on that account necessarily committed to a theistic way of understanding reality. They may be directed by totally profane regulative ideas in their search for understanding. The origin of all things may accordingly be viewed as an initial brute state of being,[82] the supreme value as an intrinsically absolute good, and the rationality of reality as structures pertaining to its chance persistence. The regulative ideas governing such non-theistic understanding have some features in common with their theistic counterparts. The distinguishing characteristic of theism in this respect is that it sees its own regulative ideas as instantiated in – and hence as expressing aspects of – the nature and purposes of God.

Since, then, thought may be directed by profane regulative ideas, theists must not be expected to have to include all the regulative ideas which may govern thinking in their notion of God. Not only are some regulative ideas which have a significant role in certain ways of understanding incompatible with a theistic understanding of the ultimate structure of reality,[83] others may justifiably be dismissed as wrong.[84] Still other regulative ideas are valid for certain domains of thought but are irrelevant to theistic understanding.[85] Such ideas are not to be incorporated into the theistic concept of the basic reality of the divine, even though it is arguable that they do indirectly involve God since they will be envisaged in the divine knowledge of human thought.

What theists have to present, if they wish to be taken seriously, is a concept of God which presents the divine as supreme and ultimate. Whereas there seems to be no valid argument from the concept to the existence of God, there is one from the theistic concept of God to the necessity of regarding God as the end-point of all appropriate forms of understanding. Theism entails that correct conclusions of investigations into the ultimate nature of reality (ontologically, valuatively and rationally) and correct views about God must cohere.[86]

The regulative role of God in thought may be illustrated by drawing a distinction between praise and adoration which shows that the latter rather than the former is the proper response to the divine. One way of developing this argument is to hold that praise is a form of judgement in which its object is assessed by reference to an independent standard by someone implicitly qualified to make such a judgement. Adoration, in contrast, is not so much an act of judgement as an act of recognition of the unqualified value of its object. Those who adore do not assess what they adore; they accept it as the standard by which they are to judge. Another form of the argument points to the different natures of what is praised and what is adored. Implicit in the notion of an object of praise is the judgement that while the object happens to be good (or even perfect), there is no necessity for it to be such; in contrast God, as the solely adequate object of worship (i.e., as the fit object of unqualified adoration), necessarily cannot be other than perfect. For theism God is not merely what happens to be the greatest at any time: at all times the divine is necessarily that than which a greater cannot (logically cannot) be conceived, and that by reference to which all is ultimately to be understood. Being, rationality and value derive from God. God alone, then, is properly and unreservedly to be adored.

The regulative ideas implied by theism

Although the concept of God involves regulative ideas, there is no universal agreement among theists about how the ultimacy and perfection of the divine are to be apprehended as constituting those ideas. Nevertheless, in spite of differences of detail and while poorly served by traditional attempts to express it in the categories of Greek philosophy, the Judaeo-Christian and Islamic form of theism does suggest certain general presuppositions for understanding.

The first of these is that things form a universe, an intrinsically coherent whole. Even though this may turn out on analysis to be a necessary presupposition for thinking about reality,[87] it is not self-evident from our experience. Bearing in mind the huge multiplicity of objects and series of events constituting our environment, many of them appearing to occur simultaneously in a disconnected manner, and the absence of any obvious over-riding factor linking them together, it may seem more plausible to suppose that we belong to a *multi*verse rather than to a *uni*verse. There is no manifest cohesion about the contents which unites them as a significant whole.[88] To hold that the physical contents constitute a whole because they interact according to the laws of natural forces is rather like saying that the buildings, vehicles and mass of dodging individuals in Trafalgar Square form a society because they affect each other. They interact because they are there but their interactions only signify their co-presence, not any overall meaning or purpose which renders them parts of a significant whole.[89]

Theism, however, maintains that the items in reality are linked together in a non-trivial way because they are all derived from, embraced in and influenced by a single being. While some have inferred from the unity of the world that it must be based on a single creator, it is arguable that the stronger case proceeds from belief in the reality of God as its ground to the unity of the world as a whole.[90] Similarly, the events of history are not considered by theists to be parts of a coherent whole as a result of observing those events[91] but because the divine is held, in one way or another, to give a (purposive) unity to the processes of history and, therefore, both a final significance to and a judgement upon its events. Natural and historical reality are thus presupposed by theism to form a universe, not because this is necessary for thought about it, nor because it is obvious from experience, but because of the primacy of God.

A second regulative idea which emerges from theistic understanding is that reality has a coherent, all-embracing meaning. Since the divine is valuatively and rationally as well as ontologically ultimate, theists do not only consider that reality forms one world because it has one source and goal; on the assumption that the divine would not act haphazardly, they presuppose that the world is derived from God for the fulfilment of a certain purpose. This gives it meaning and justifies attempts to understand it according to principles of value and rationality.[92]

A third presupposition for thought following from theistic understanding is that human personal being has significance because personal actions are appreciated by the divine. The doctrine of the *imago dei* status of humanity may accordingly be interpreted as affirming that each person is able to engage in creative activity, and the doctrine of judgement as an assertion that each individual's achievements make permanent contributions to the divine experience. God's perfect awareness entails that whatever occurs is noticed and for ever remembered. Whereas, then, the atheist considers that human attempts to impose temporary patches of value on a pointless agglomeration of states, however heroic,[93] eventually perish completely, the theist presupposes that human lives are significant because they are everlastingly embraced and valued in the divine.[94]

Theism implies, fourthly, the presupposition that the principles of being, value and rationality come together in one coherent understanding. Since God is the ground of all, we are not presented with several autonomous universes of thought but ultimately with only one. The different ways of understanding deal with different facets of one reality. They are complementary rather than independent modes of insight. Where their conclusions conflict, theists must assume that error is present. Unlike Kant they cannot allow the pure, the practical, the aesthetic and other forms of understanding to develop as isolated domains although, like Kant, they may consider it important to distinguish between the world as we perceive it and reality as it is in itself (and as it is perceived by God). Furthermore, unless some other way of maintaining the basic unity of being, rationality and value can be found, it is arguable that theism is presupposed by any metaphysical attempt to embrace all aspects of reality in a single story which unites what is, what could be and what ought to be.[95]

A fifth presupposition of understanding which arguably follows from theism is the principle of the objectivity of truth. It may be held that the divine perception, being perfect, provides a standard for truth-claims. While any claim which we make is conditioned by our situation, and while it is not possible for us directly to comprehend the contents of the divine mind, the knowledge that there is a divine judgement prevents theists from regarding all references to truth as merely expressions of cultural and personal perspectives. Attempts to understand are to be seen as governed by the aim to perceive what is the case as perceived by God.[96]

Some theists, as was noted earlier, have also held that theism justifies the presupposition of the reliability of our ways of knowing. In response to doubts about them, they have held that these capacities are to be trusted because God, as creator, would not have bestowed faulty tools on humankind. Unfortunately for those worried by basic scepticism, this supposed implication of theism is implausible. In the first place it attributes to our modes of understanding a God-given reliability which is at variance with our experience of the rest of our constitution. There seems to be no sound reason why we should consider that these aspects of our being are divinely protected from error when our hearts and brains, whose functioning is required by them, are clearly liable to malfunction physiologically. Secondly, the view that our modes of experience and reflection are 'God-given' implies a view of God's creative determination of the nature of things which is untenable in the light of post-Darwinian insights into the evolutionary process and investigations into the social conditioning of thought. Our trust in our ways of thought cannot rest on belief in God – especially if that belief is maintained because it is judged to be rationally credible. As was pointed out in the earlier reference to Descartes' views, this results in an unsatisfactorily circular argument. Instead we must be content to rely on our ways of thought because we have no other option in seeking to arrive at rationally credible understanding.

The preceding discussion has a certain oddity because it suggests that the regulative principles of understanding are based, for theism, on its understanding of the divine. Principles are usually regarded as their own basis, as self-evident and ultimate. Theistic understanding, however, holds that the principles of our understanding are not themselves its ultimate basis. The coherence, unity and meaningfulness of reality and the significance of human being are not, in its view, self-evident principles, absolute in themselves. They are principles which ought to regulate human thought because they are consequences of a proper recognition of the reality of God. The ultimate principle, the final regulative idea which explains the others, is the concept of God.

It is also odd to speak of God as the basis of the principles of understanding. If God is the *basis* of the *principles* of understanding, the concept of God has as its referent that which is in some sense prior to these principles and so not necessarily subject to understanding by them in every respect. It thus begins to appear why, in certain respects, it is hard to make sense of the notion of God. Since it stands for that which marks the absolute end of understanding, it is essentially puzzling and, at best, only partially understandable. It is that by which all else is understood; it is not itself open to understanding in the same way.

At this point, we begin to perceive why the ultimacy of God not only provides the limits for understanding but is itself understood in terms of what we regard as those limits. In other words, the concept of God not only conditions our understanding by establishing its limits. The content of that concept, because it is the concept of what is necessarily ultimate, is also conditioned by what we regard as the proper limits of understanding.[97] Formally, that is, the concept of God represents the bedrock where the spade of understanding is turned. Materially our identification of the constitution and character of this point is at least partially given by our perception of the limiting factors of our understanding in such matters.

The implications of the regulative role of God for theology

In what ways, then, does recognition of the regulative role of God throw light both on the peculiarities of the concept of God and on the nature of theological understanding?

If certain theological claims have a regulative function and express the presuppositions of our understanding, it follows that they cannot be verified by reference to that understanding without begging the question to some extent.[98] This does not mean that such claims have to be accepted or rejected on an arbitrary basis. What it does mean is that their justification involves more complex reasoning than the direct drawing of conclusions from evidence. The reasoning involved is more like that needed to justify a way of interpreting evidence which is not self-evident. In this respect theistic verification may be regarded as a matter of perceiving the overall fittingness and fruitfulness of the pattern of understanding given by a particular theistic story.

A second implication of the regulative role of God is that certain claims about God must express what the theist holds to be universally true. Here 'universally' does not merely refer to the trivial point that if something is true now, it will always be true that it was true now and be compatible with whatever else also happens to be true.[99] Propositions about God which are universally true express not only what must be true in all times and locations in the actual universe, but also what would have to be true in any possible universe. Since no state of being is possible which is incompatible with the reality of God,[100] no genuinely possible state of affairs could ever be conceived which would falsify the propositions which express the universal characteristics of God's existence.[101] Like the 'metaphysical first principles' which they incorporate, they can never fail of exemplification. Nor, since they are true whatever else may happen to be the case, can they be discerned by discrimination between states where they do and states where they do not obtain. One consequence of this, as Whitehead suggests, is that they can never be finally formulated.[102] They do not even report what merely happens to be the case with God – as if such statements about the divine were similar to statements about contingent facts in the world. They describe what necessarily constitutes the ultimate nature of all reality.[103]

This characteristic of claims about God is illustrated by the proper response to the criticism of the cosmological argument which asks, 'But what (or who) made God?' So far as a sequence of causes, temporal or ontological, is concerned, there is no reason to stop with any cause as the start of the series. The plausibility of holding that there is such a start and of announcing that it is 'God' arises from the fact that God is essentially a (and, more precisely, the only) being of whom the question, 'What (or who) made it?', cannot be coherently asked – and the 'cannot' here is a logical one. While this does not mean that the cosmological argument is valid as an argument for the existence of God, it indicates the oddity of the divine nature. Where, for example, causality acts as a category of understanding, God's mode of being cannot be so understood. It is the ultimate self-explanatory reality (or *the* brute inexplicable reality) which is the foundation of all total explanations. God thus instantiates the principle of explanation by being that *ne plus ultra* where all explanatory sequences end.[104]

Theologians have frequently misunderstood the aspect of the divine nature which is expressed in universal claims. In attempts to do it justice they have described God by such terms as absolute, necessary, eternal, unchanging and infinite. In that a being without these qualities would not be the divine, their descriptions are justified. Where they have erred is in considering that these qualities determine the divine in every respect, and so make it impossible to ascribe coherently to God any personal qualities which involve change, responsiveness or activity.[105] Often they have also made the mistake of treating terms such as absolute, necessary and eternal, which properly qualify the material attributes of God (e.g., attributes such as love, awareness and creativity), as if they described material attributes of the divine. What needs to be recognized is that terms such as absolute, necessary and eternal are formal qualifiers which elucidate the unique quality of the material attributes of the divine when considered abstractly (e.g., the divine love is in principle absolute, necessary and eternal), and that they need to be balanced by their opposites (such as relative, contingent and temporal) when the actualization of those material attributes is being described (e.g., in concrete practice the divine love is relative, contingent and temporal for it is a matter of specific expressions of love, for specific objects that happen to be there, with specific ends in view . . .). In terms of the material attribute of creativity and the formal attribute of unchangingness, this means that God is to be conceived as unchangingly creative (i.e., as unceasingly related to the world in the active relationship of being creative), not the nonsense of holding that God both creates and is unchanged.[106]

A third implication of the regulative role of the concept of God is that certain theistic claims do not themselves offer explanations and value-judgements, but rather describe what is to be regarded as an explanation and as a value.[107] In this respect the concept of God is the presupposition of the way in which theists understand life. It provides them with the terminus of all explanations by announcing the unexplicable reality where all explanations must end and from which, in theory, they must start.

Just as the regulative role of God means that God is to be considered ontologically as the ground of being and rationally as the

basis of explanation – and so as beyond causal and rational understanding – it also means that God, as the supreme value, is essentially not open to value-judgements. The divine embodies the
ultimate value and hence is not subject to judgement by reference
to any independent standard. If final value be understood in moral
terms, neither moral prescriptivism nor moral intuitionism provides
a satisfactory understanding of morality from a theistic perspective,
so far as the former suggests that the divine arbitrarily dictates what
is to be the good and the latter that there is a moral standard external to the divine.[108]

W. G. Maclagan has tried to solve the problem of the relationship
between the ultimacy of God and the ultimacy of moral values by
holding that talk about God is to be regarded in certain respects
as talk about what *is* the moral ultimate.[109] While differing from
Maclagan on some points, B. F. Porter similarly suggests that '*God
is good* is . . . an analytic proposition' which both expresses an
essential content of the concept of God and 'a necessary and metaphysical truth . . . about the universe'.[110] Classical theologians have
recognized this point when they have preferred to affirm that 'God
is goodness' rather than that 'God is good', for the former expression indicates that God is to be identified with the standard for
value-judgements, whereas the latter could be misinterpreted as
suggesting that God is subject to judgement by such a standard. If the
above analysis be accepted, it follows that the so-called naturalistic
fallacy is not applicable to the relationship between God and
morality. In this unique case ultimate being and ultimate value
coincide as two aspects of the one reality: the ultimacy of the divine,
when fully appreciated, means that neither God's goodness is contingent nor ultimate value is derivative. Both the intellectualist position which sees value as autonomous, and the voluntarist position
which sees it as dependent upon the divine will, are theistically
mistaken. Ultimate value is intrinsically part of God's being as God.

So far this discussion of God and value has largely accepted the
common view that the ultimate value is to be regarded as moral
value. Is this justified? It is arguable that the good which is the final
and all-sufficient goal is not to be identified as moral good.

Kant holds that the categorical imperative of morality must be
grounded in 'something the existence of which in itself [has] absolute worth' and so is 'an end in itself'. Since he finds this in 'rational
nature', he expresses the moral imperative as 'Act so that you treat
humanity . . . always as an end and never as a means only'.[111] His
exposition of morality thus asserts that people are to respect their

own and others' rational natures so as to allow them to flourish. But what are they to flourish for? To say that they flourish in order to respect their own and others' rational natures hardly seems to get anywhere. It makes the condition of flourishing its end.

One response to the question of the purpose of moral behaviour is to assert that moral values are not to be regarded as being 'for' anything. They are their own justification.[112] In so far, then, as God instantiates ultimate value, the divine being is to be held to instantiate moral values.

In spite of what some assume, such a response is not self-evidently correct. It does seem reasonable to question moral values (e.g., 'Why be generous?', 'Why care for others?', 'Why be honest?'). The fact that some supposed answers disvalue moral obligation (e.g., 'You should be generous so that people will admire you', 'You should care for others so that they will feel indebted to you', 'You should be honest since liars get found out'), does not show that the questions are improper, but that some answers reflect a poor appreciation of the goals that should guide conduct. Nor should the questions be ruled out because their formulation and responses to them cannot avoid being culturally relative. This only shows that our grasp of values in concrete terms is conditioned to some extent by our background. The basic issue is whether moral virtues must be regarded as self-justifying.

Consideration of what is meant by value suggests that a distinction needs to be drawn between values which are urged as means to ends, and values which are ends in themselves. The intrinsically valuable is that which is a final end in itself since it is wholly self-satisfying in its attainment. What in practice is concretely envisaged as constituting that state varies considerably.[113] Theistically this state has traditionally been described as 'the beatific vision' – a state in which individuals do not merely contemplate ('see') that which is ultimate value, but find its reality possessing their own being as in some way they sense themselves to be incorporated into it.[114] The identification of the material characteristics of the actual state, however, is not important for our present purposes. What is important is that some state is considered to be intrinsically valuable. Because 'beauty' in all its expressions is 'the one aim which by its very nature is self-justifying',[115] in principle this state may be said to be that of the aesthetically good. Whatever beneficial effects it may also have in cheering us or stimulating us or calming us, the aesthetically valuable is its own justification. It is self-evidently valuable because it provides intrinsic and unqualified satisfaction.

Moral values, in contrast, are values whose pursuit is intended to provide the conditions for realizing aesthetically satisfying states.

Theistic ethics, then, are to be regarded as a form of ideal utilitarianism.[116] Since, as Whitehead suggests, the world makes sense only as the locus for 'the attainment of value', its ground must be finally determined by 'aesthetic experience' rather than by cognitive or moral forms of experience.[117] The essential goodness of the divine, as instantiating the ultimately valuable, is thus not to be interpreted in moral terms. The absolute worth of God is as the perfection of that unselfregarding appreciation of beauty which gives every life satisfaction and makes it worth living. The divine is, therefore, to be thought of as a pure love which supremely incorporates the persistent urge for the permanent enjoyment of aesthetic values. The moral values which are grounded in the divine are those which lead to the realization of the highest forms of aesthetic satisfaction.

A fourth implication of the regulative role of God in theological understanding is that there can be no standards or reasons for God's actions which are other than what is constituted by the character of the divine being. To enquire why God chooses to act in one way rather than another is theologically mistaken if it presupposes that the activity can be explained by reference to standards other than God's own being. In the case of the ultimate metaphysical principles which govern what can possibly occur, it is a mistake to ask if they are *either* a result of some primordial divine decision *or* necessary for God as well as for the creation. Such a question seeks for reasons in the divine will or in the divine intellect where reasons cannot be given. The ultimate metaphysical principles express what God is. They are neither determined by the divine will in an initial and arbitrary act, nor perceived by the divine as self-evident principles. They are to be seen, rather, as a priori *for* creation but a priori *in* God.[118] Because, then, the principles governing divine activity are not themselves explicable, although they provide the basis for all explanations, no reasons can be given for them. God just necessarily is and acts so.[119]

The cultural relativity of our grasp of the regulative role of God

When we consider how the concept of God develops, it becomes apparent that, as with scientific thought,[120] much of our understanding is controlled by the intellectual conditions of our time. At the formal level it is clear that 'God' must represent what is ultimate both in reality and in thought. Problems emerge when attempts are made to identify the material content of the divine ultimacy. The more we try to determine what the concept of God contributes to the structure of our understanding by providing it with regulative ideas, the more our thought about God seems to be determined by that structure.

When, therefore, theologians consider the divine ultimacy, it can never be known for certain that they are describing God's own nature and not simply reflecting their entertainment, probably largely unconscious, of the prejudices of their culture. Critics from one cultural setting who discern cultural relativity in the thought of others belonging to a different one must not forget that their own judgements will be influenced to some extent by their situation. If, for example, God is held to be the uncaused cause of all, does this describe the nature of God as the absolutely first or our understanding's demand for completeness? Since, for some at least, the notion of an unending sequence is deeply unsatisfying, it is possible that elements in the idea of absolute ontological primacy have been projected onto God in order to make sense of reality in an apparently satisfying manner. If so, the description of God as 'first cause' may be the product of our intellectual unease with a genuine notion of infinity in relation to the ground of reality.[121] On the other hand, it may be that what is actually the case coincides with what gives us the satisfying sense of intellectual completeness. Since, however, the basic problem lies in the significance of our understanding, we cannot by using our understanding determine whether what satisfies it corresponds to the ontological status of God or imposes qualities upon it.[122]

The cultural relativity of thought about God is clearly displayed in treatments of the personal attributes of the divine as instantiating regulative ideas of ultimate value. What seem at one time or to one group of people to be self-evidently necessary characteristics of God as perfect appear from another point of view to express mistaken notions about the character of supreme value. The quality of impassibility is a case in point. In the case of Christian theology whose understanding of God's nature is held to be normatively formed by the biblical witness – a witness which frequently describes God as creating, loving, hearing, responding and saving – this may appear a strange attribute to apply to God. It is, nevertheless, an attribute which is persistently affirmed in a long tradition of Christian theology.

To return to an example which has been mentioned previously, Anselm, in spite of the invocation which opens the *Proslogion*, regards God's essential nature as unquestionably entailing that God experiences no compassion.[123] The reason for this is that Anselm, like many other theologians, understands perfection, according to its analysis in Greek thought, wholly in terms of what is complete and finished – and so as wholly unchanging and unchangeable: any change in what is perfect must be to some state of relative imperfection.[124] Anselm accordingly reflects the judgements of his cultural heritage when he interprets divine perfection as involving impassibility. Today, in a culture impressed by the values of life and creativity, this analysis of perfection is not self-evident. In some respects it is not changeability but unchangeability that is a mark of imperfection. To affirm that perfection involves the end of activity implies that a person would only be perfect by being totally inactive – and so, in effect, dead! Whereas, then, the perfection of a measure lies partly in its unchangeability, perfection in personal relationships is partly a matter of empathy and responsiveness and so of appropriate changeability. What was obvious to Anselm is not necessarily so to us.

The view that divine perfection involves unchangeability leads, furthermore, to the notion of the divine eternity as a state of the timeless presentness of all events, as well as to the notion of the divine awareness as a simultaneous awareness of all events, past, present and future. If that be the case, no verb that implies activity or receptivity can be coherently applied to the divine. God can never be surprised by joy since nothing truly novel can ever occur, nor be aware of changes in our situation so as to be able to respond to them in ways that take our temporal and contingent existence seriously. What may seem at first to be a proper analysis of the notion of perfection thus turns out to be theistically – and religiously – disastrous.

To the extent that the concept of divine perfection, which in principle determines our understanding of ultimate values, is likely to have its material content largely determined by our culturally formed view of such values, it is not surprising that the concept of God generally legitimates rather than criticizes prevailing value-judgements. Not all our perceptions of the ultimate values incorporated into God, however, are wholly the product of our culture. Reflection on the concept of God and consideration of what is ultimately valuable may, and on occasion do, interact to produce new insights into both which are critical of prevailing ways of under-

standing them. Furthermore, probably no culture has been so valuatively uniform and limited that its members could produce only
one consistent view of the divine as expressing its regulative values.
In practice different members of the same general culture can be
found to have been convinced of the ultimacy of different values,
and thus to have arrived at different views of God.

Anselm, for example, regards sin as a violation of God's honour
and so as something for which satisfaction must be paid. In reply
to Boso's query as to why God cannot forgive sin simply out of
compassion, he replies that 'it is not right' and 'fitting' for God 'to
cancel sin without compensation or punishment'.[125] By his references to what is 'right' and 'fitting', Anselm shows that in his
doctrine of atonement he is not simply taking a model from feudal
views of honour to express the doctrine in current terms. He sees
the reality of the divine–human relationship in feudal terms so that
it is evident to him that God's compassion cannot allow forgiveness
until divine honour has been satisfied.[126]

What was evident to Anselm, however, was not equally obvious
to all who shared his culture. Abelard, for example, regards love,
not honour, as the definitive quality of the divine. Commenting on
Romans 3. 19–26, he interprets God's justice in terms of love which
waits for sinners to repent so that they may be forgiven. The death
of Christ is not to satisfy divine honour, but to manifest divine grace
which binds human beings to God in love.[127] The treatments of
the doctrine of atonement by Anselm and Abelard illustrate how
personal preferences, influenced perhaps by personal experiences,
lead to different understandings of the divine and so of the values
which are to regulate human judgements.

A similar disagreement between theologians who were roughly
contemporary and belonged to what was generally the same culture[128] is that between McLeod Campbell and R. W. Dale. The
former considers that the supreme quality in God is that of self-
sacrificing love which, when recognized by us, gives us confidence
to regard ourselves as accepted by God. Salvation is through God's
revelation of that love.[129] According to Dale, however, salvation
can only be morally acceptable when sin has been duly punished.
In Christ's suffering the necessary penalties for sin are justly met.[130]
The source of the difference between these theologians is not that
they belong to different cultures, but that they regard different
elements within their largely common culture as indicative of the
determinative characteristics of God. The result is not unimportant;
how people understand their relationship with God affects how

they perceive the significance of their lives. Those who see God primarily in terms of moral exactions are hardly likely to approach life as creatively and openly as those who see themselves as accepted by God, whatever their errors.

What our thought presupposes as ultimate is, then, in fully reflective thought about God identified with some aspect of God's nature. If, for example, our understanding presupposes that reality has a necessary ground, that it coheres together as a unity with a purpose, and that values have some objective status, then God will only be adequately conceived when the divine is presented as the all-sufficient ground of all being, unity, meaning and value. Some of the resultant attributes of God will be a product of necessary principles of thought, but others will reflect the principles presupposed in a cultural group – or even by an individual. In terms of current views, however, it will not be easy or, in some cases, possible to distinguish between what is essential, because it is the product of the universal characteristics of thought, and what is culturally relative, and so of only temporary significance.[131] It is usually in a different culture or where there are incompatible views within a culture that what are claimed to be 'self-evidently' ultimate principles of understanding are recognized to be relative and questionable.

In principle it is easy to recognize that whether the regulative ideas constituting our concept of God are essential to all thought or in some cases basic only to a particular culture, the concept of God will not describe the reality of God unless it corresponds to the divine nature. Unfortunately, in practice, we cannot stand outside our situation to determine if and in what respects this correspondence obtains.

Oddity in language about God arising from its regulative role

Since talk about the regulative aspect of the divine is talk about what is ultimate, unique and beyond direct experience, it involves indirect modes of description. Notions derived from human experience of the contingent, dependent and derivative world are used as indicators, images, symbols and metaphors of what transcends it as its necessary, self-sufficient and ultimate ground.[132]

Besides the notion of 'qualifiers' which has previously been discussed, I. T. Ramsey suggests two other characteristics of language about God. The first is that it uses 'disclosure models' – notions taken from ordinary experience which are to be apprehended as revealing analogues (rather than as pictures) of the divine. The second is that the function of some language which is apparently about God – such as the doctrine of the Trinity – is to supply logical rules for the correct interpretation of disclosure models. In this way Ramsey applies to religious language Whitehead's view of religion as 'the vision of something' real which 'stands beyond, behind, and within, the passing flux of things'. He puts it that while religious language seeks to disclose that supreme reality which 'gives meaning to all that passes', and 'whose possession is the final good', it can express that reality only in 'inadequate, partial, and approximate' ways.[133] Ramsey's remarks are a reminder that attempts to grasp and express the material content of the regulative aspect of the divine stretch thought and language to their limits, since they attempt to grasp and express what all thought properly presupposes.

Its regulative status, furthermore, means that some theistic claims are about what is the case necessarily or a priori. The dogmas that whatever exists must be contingent, and that necessity can only be a quality of the relationship between propositions, are theistically unacceptable. For the theist some states of affairs (for example, some that constitute the existence of God) are necessary. They are the case whatever contingent state of affairs may or may not happen to be the case. Since propositions expressing them must be necessarily true in all genuinely possible states, they cannot and could not (logically cannot and could not) be falsified by any empirical test. Propositions which express what is the case a priori in God and a priori for the world unquestionably belong to this class of theistic propositions. It is also possible that there is another group of propositions which belongs to this class, namely those propositions which describe what is a priori for this world but a posteriori for God, because they describe what God chooses to create as the actual world. The possibility of the second group depends upon the justifiability of holding that some universal characteristics of the actual cosmos are (or have been) contingently chosen by the divine in creating the cosmos. In any event, whether there are in principle two kinds of a priori claims about God's relationship to the creation or only the first one, in practice the distinction is not significant. It may be interesting to speculate on how a perfect being (presumably making perfect choices) might choose to bring about one world rather than another (and, in view of some speculations by physicists, the one world might be made up of any number of non-interacting cosmoi), and why that being chose to create this actual one rather than a different one, but we have no reliable bases for developing and judging such imaginings. Consequently, the distinction between what has to be for any possible world, and what God may have chosen to be the necessary character of this actual one, seems not to be a distinction that can be significantly made. Does it matter? It hardly seems a severe limitation on theologians that they cannot discuss other possible worlds but have to confine their understanding to God's relationship to the process of reality in the actual world!

God as both regulative and actual

Since any comprehensive theological understanding must identify God with the regulative ideas of our thought, the question arises whether God can be coherently conceived as an actuality instantiating those ideas, or whether its regulative function means that the concept of God cannot refer to an actual being. Kant, as was noted earlier, generally considers that the regulative ideas 'never allow of any constitutive employment'.[134] Such a position is tenable for those who, like Kant in his *Critiques*, are concerned to identify the structures of understanding. It may be tenable for those who are prepared to divorce their religious faith from their appreciation of those structures. It is not a possible position for theists who wish their theological understanding to be rationally satisfying.[135] They have to find a way of showing that the concept of God combines regulative functions and a reference to what is actual. To do this they have to show first, that the concept of God is self-consistent and secondly, that its regulative role is compatible with thought of the divine as the 'living' God of faith.

The first problem arises from the non-compossibility of all values. If, for example, the *ens realissimum* is held to have 'all possible predicates',[136] no actual being can correspond to it because no actual being can embody at once incompatible qualities.[137] The incompatibility here is not that between a good quality and the deprivation of that quality – the incompatibility, for instance, between love and hate, or between compassion and cruelty. It is the serious incompatibility between qualities which can each be regarded as beneficial: the incompatibility, for example, between bliss and compassion, or between enjoying all values (granted that this be a coherent notion) and being creative.[138] Reference to the 'infinity' of the divine does not provide a way of overcoming the problem. The incompatibility between 'infinite' cases of contradictory qualities is, if anything, worse than that between their finite forms! The solution to this problem lies in recognizing that the valuative ultimacy of God is to be understood in aesthetic terms. Accordingly, God is not to be thought of as instantiating all possible values, but that combination of values which has the greatest potential for producing the maximum possible aesthetic satisfaction.

The second problem arises most acutely if theistic understanding is held to require that we conceive of the actuality of God most adequately in terms of a personal mode of being. Hartshorne's dipolar analysis of the concept of God, however, suggests a fruitful way of overcoming some of the conceptual difficulties that arise. As has been noted earlier, by distinguishing between abstract descriptions of divine *existence* and concrete descriptions of divine *actuality*, Hartshorne shows that God can be coherently conceived as in certain respects absolute, necessary, unchanging and eternal and, in other respects, as relative, contingent, changing and temporal.[139] On this basis it is possible to maintain that the regulative functions of the deity are incorporated in the characteristics of the abstract aspect of divine being, while the concrete actualization of this being is in a personal mode.[140]

One objection that may be raised against attempts to hold together the ultimacy of the divine with a personal mode of being is that it is difficult to reconcile the essential perfection of divine decisions with the freedom of personal living. If, as perfect, God's choices must always be determined by what will produce the maximum value, it may be claimed that the divine decisions must be more like the automatic responses of an impersonal calculus than the creatively free choices of a person. This problem disappears, however, when personal freedom is recognized to be the freedom to act according to one's desires, and that the divine may be thought to have no desire to choose other than the best. In that case God's conformity to what is perfect is no limitation on the divine freedom but a perfect expression of it.

The possibility of understanding the concept of God as having both regulative significance and a realist reference raises the question of whether the regulative content of the concept of God demands that God be thought of as an actual entity. Could 'God' be satisfactorily understood as an ideal which makes no claims about a state of affairs? In view of the difficulty of justifying claims about the existence of God, it has been suggested that religion does not require a realist reference, and that the crucial regulative element in the concept of God can be satisfactorily expressed as an abstract ideal rather than as a theistic notion.

At first sight it may seem that there is nothing incoherent in holding that there is no necessity to think of regulative ideas as actualized in some entity and hence no necessity to give the concept of God in its regulative role a theistic interpretation. If, for example, the traditional doctrine of divine impassibility is strictly maintained so that no responsiveness can be attributed to God,[141] there seems to be no significant difference between regarding the divine as an actual entity and as an idea with no actual correlate. Such an ideal, i.e., non-realist, interpretation of religion is presented by Vaihinger who argues that the regulative ideas of our thought must be regarded as 'heuristic fictions'.[142] Concepts like God are fictions which exert great influence but, nevertheless, they are illusions 'with which the psyche plays about'. Christ's teaching about a 'father in heaven' is correctly appreciated when it is seen as an instruction to behave '*as if*, just as though, he were your father and as if, just as though, he were . . . a constant observer of your actions'.[143]

In spite of the attractiveness of this position as a way to avoid the problems of justifying realist claims about God, this interpretation of religious talk about God is questionable, as has already been noted in the earlier discussion of the realist reference of faith and belief. There is a vast difference between thinking and acting in a certain way *because* God is held to exist as having a certain nature, and thinking and doing *as if* such a being existed while considering that no such being does exist. In the former case the behaviour is a response to what exists independently of human beings; in the latter case the source of the values represented by the concept of God is a matter of human thought, and commitment to them is a human attempt to impose them on a basically valueless reality.

The non-theistic position is clearly a possible stance towards the world. It resembles the brave commitment to values which Camus describes as rebellion.[144] In spite, however, of the non-theistic interpretation of religion presented by Feuerbach and currently popularized by Cupitt, it is not a satisfactory understanding of religion. It is incompatible with the basic religious attitude of worship and adoration as a response to that which is mind-independently real for the believer as well as ultimate. In the consciously 'as if' position, human being is what is ultimate as the source of meaning. In religion human beings, whether correctly or not, recognize themselves as non-ultimate and seek to understand themselves in the light of what they take to be ultimate. To interpret religion and its constitutive concept of God by an 'as if' way of understanding is in effect to transform it into something which is the antithesis of religion.

In religion, then, 'God' refers to ultimacy which stands over against the human. In some sense it is independent of and real apart from humanity, whether existing as some kind of Platonic form in a realm of values or, perhaps more intelligibly, as instantiated in a personal mode of being such as theism maintains. This view of the concept of God as referring to mind-independent reality is confirmed, for example, by its role as the regulative idea for ontological thought. It is incoherent to think of God as the origin of all being and as not real. This does not prove that 'God exists', but it does suggest that notions of an essentially fictitious God are self-contradictory. Similarly it may be argued that the role of God as the ground of meaning and rationality only makes sense when 'God' is thought of as an actual personal reality with a purposive and ordering mind. The concept of God in its regulative role thus appears to require us to regard it as referring to an actual entity and not simply as expressing an ideal.

On the other hand, does the regulative role of the concept of God provide any justification for holding that there is a God? Attempts to argue from the concept to the existence of God – the ontological argument – do not seem able to show more than that God must be thought of as having a non-contingent (i.e., necessary) mode of existence. The regulative role of God suggests, furthermore, that the traditional cosmological, teleological and moral arguments may beg the question in that they presuppose the concepts of endpoints to various ways of understanding, pursue those ways, and then arrive at those endpoints which they finally identify as 'God'. While the identification of those regulative endpoints with God is a legitimate understanding of the concept of God, the arguments do not show that God exists. They only show that certain ways of understanding presuppose such a concept.

It may be argued, however, that commitment to such ways of understanding involves an implicit affirmation of the existence of God if, as seems to be the case, there is no satisfactory non-theistic way of making sense of their presuppositions. The argument here is circular but not viciously so. What it suggests is that commitment to the meaningfulness of existence and to the correctness of certain ways of understanding may be fundamentally theistic. Furthermore, while it is not possible to demonstrate that reality is not essentially chaotic, and that attempts to make sense of it are not impositions of alien rationality, the apparent success of attempts at understanding suggests that there may be a strong pragmatic case for holding that its presuppositions significantly correspond to the nature of things. As we examine reality in terms of our ways of understanding, it does not appear that it is clearly a pointless absurdity produced by the chance interactions of mindless forces. On the other hand, it must also be admitted that no consistent, comprehensive, coherent and fruitful story of reality has yet been produced by using those presuppositions which makes it incredible to hold that God does not exist.[145]

The influence of regulative ideas on our understanding of God

Any fully developed concept of God must include elements which correspond to the regulative ideas of our thought. On the one hand, this means that theological insights into the nature of God may provide ideas which allow us to perceive in some respects what actually is the nature of the ultimate. Whereas sceptical theologians like Mansel hold that we are only given by God ideas which are to regulate our conduct,[146] others believe that we can attain thereby some knowledge of the divine nature which determines how we are to think correctly of ourselves. Augustine sees us as creatures made to find their satisfaction only in God, and Pannenberg holds that awareness of God, by disclosing the depths of human existence, makes possible a correct appreciation of it.[147] For such theologians, then, proper understanding of God produces the correct regulative ideas for thought about humanity and the world.

On the other hand, it is more likely that most of the influence on our understanding arising from the relationship between God and the regulative ideas of thought is in the other direction. The concept of God, that is, is determined to a large extent by the ultimate structures of our rational understanding and, in particular, by its presupposed regulative ideas. It is on the basis of such ideas, for example, that we decide the truth of claims about God and about claims to revelations of God. Since much theological understanding is fundamentally conditioned by the ultimate principles of our ways of thought, Feuerbach correctly perceived its character when he wrote that 'the fact is not that a quality is divine because God has it, but that God has it because it is in itself divine: because without it God would be a defective being'.[148] This, however, raises questions about the conditioning of theological understanding held to be derived from revelation, and to the prior issue of the significance of religious experience generally for theistic understanding. To these matters we turn in the next chapters.

Granted that God must be conceived of as embracing the basic presuppositions and regulative ideas of correct understanding, we can never decisively determine where our ways of understanding are correct in their appreciation of the divine ultimacy and where they should be amended. Theistic understanding is inescapably conditioned by the structures of the understanding that produces it.

5

Theology and religious experience

Although predominantly rational aspects of theological understanding have been the subject of the previous two chapters, the primary object of that understanding is not just an abstract idea or actualized ideal of ultimacy and perfection. It also – and crucially for religion – concerns what is held to be encountered in human experience. As Isaac Newton suggested, 'God is a word expressing a relation, and it refers to servants . . . for we say my God, your God, the God of Israel'.[1] More recently Martin Buber developed this kind of claim to the point of denying that God can be adequately treated as an object of thought: God is supremely the Thou 'that may properly only be addressed, not expressed'.[2] If, then, theism regards God as the perfect being who is apprehended in certain types or dimensions of experience, theological understanding is to be seen as partly an attempt to make sense of those forms of human experience and to draw out their implications. R. G. Collingwood, who views theology in this way,[3] thus emphasizes that the concept of God does not refer to 'a mere abstract unity' but is also, perhaps in its initial state totally, derived from religious experience.[4]

The apprehension of an experience, however, moulds its content as it finds and applies concepts to it. Even to identify certain experiences as having 'religious' significance, let alone to take them to be experiences of the divine, is to place them in a particular structure of interpretation. Nevertheless, although an experience, so far as we are aware of it, emerges through an interaction between our modes of awareness and our structures of understanding, this conditioning does not show that we must regard it as wholly the product of our ways of apprehension.[5] It is more credible to consider that in most cases it is something given that is moulded. Accordingly, while theology based on experience cannot claim to express an unmediated perception of ultimate reality, it need not be dismissed as nothing more than the explication of the contents of our minds. Although religious experience – and hence the theology which uses it – is conditioned, the conditioning does not rob it of all significance as a way to understanding.

Forms of religious experience

In various ways religious experience, which is the subject of this chapter, and revelation, which is discussed in the next, merge into each other. Revelation comes through experiences; religious experiences to some extent disclose the divine. John Macquarrie, however, suggests a useful way of distinguishing between them: religious experience designates those general aspects of the life of faith in which the divine is encountered as 'judging, assisting, renewing, and so on', whereas 'revelation' refers to those special situations in which paradigmatic disclosures of the divine are held to have occurred.[6] While, furthermore, in principle a revelation may be held to provide the standard by which the authenticity of supposed religious experiences is to be determined, claims to revelation may themselves be tested against the findings of general religious experience. The relationship between the two, as with other parts of theology, is reciprocal.

The phrase 'religious experience' is used to refer to a wide variety of experiences whose only common factor is the trivial one that they are taken to be in some way religiously significant – and in this context the notion of religion is itself very broad. Before, then, we consider how theological understanding is conditioned by the conditionedness of religious experience, we shall note some of the kinds of experience that may be regarded as relevant.

First, there is the experience of ecstasy, a state in which people consider that in some unusual way they stand 'outside' the normal world and are aware of themselves and of the world in a strange fashion.[7] Whether or not the experience involves a sense of unity with the divine, the individual feels overwhelmingly 'lost in wonder, love and praise' in deep and irresistible joy.

Another form of religious experience has the character of a fundamental sense of unity, wholeness or harmony. This may be presented as a monistic awareness of some neo-Platonic One or neo-Hegelian Absolute in which all things cohere and which alone is properly real.[8] A pluralistic form is found in an awareness of the integration of all things in an aesthetically satisfying pattern, and a feeling of oneness with reality. All is essentially well and we are well.[9] Those who have such an experience may not discern clearly the content of the pattern which unites all and shows it to be good. What they have is a profound sense of the reality of such a pattern.

According to a third view, religious experience is not a distinct type of experience so much as a dimension or quality which may be attached to ordinary experiences. It occurs, for example, when objects and events are 'seen' in 'a new light'. This does not deny their day-to-day characteristics but discloses otherwise unperceived depths of significance which are not apparent to superficial observation. Whitehead, for example, denies that there is 'a special religious sense'. He holds that religious awareness arises when 'our ordinary senses and intellectual operations are at their highest pitch of discipline' and discern the 'permanent side of the universe' as 'exemplified in particular instances'.[10]

A fourth view sees religious experience as a distinct mode of perception in which we become aware of the reality of God, of that 'Other' on whom all ultimately depends. John Baillie, for example, speaks of 'the sense of the presence of God' as a 'self-authenticating' and 'primary mode of apprehension' which belongs to 'a higher level' of awareness than our physical senses.[11] Although Baillie's description of this experience sometimes draws close to the previous view, at other times it is clear that he sees it as a direct and separate mode of perception. In one work he speaks of the ·'mediated immediacy' of 'God's presence to our soul' and, in his Gifford Lectures, of faith as 'an awareness of the divine Presence itself, however hidden behind the veil of sense'.[12]

Buber classically develops a fifth view of religious experience. This sees it as a direct and immediate person-to-person encounter with the divine. Faith – and so the theology derived from it – is based on experiences of being confronted with that 'Thou' who can never properly be an object of discussion.[13] Religious experience is a paradigm case of the givingness and openness of personal relationships.[14] This view has much influenced twentieth-century theology although there are serious problems with it, particularly because in the case of encounters at the human level there are identifying physical concomitants which are not obviously present in alleged encounters with the divine.[15]

A sixth view sees religious experience as an awareness of Being or of 'being-itself', as distinct from experiences of things whose reality depends upon and expresses it. Gabriel Marcel writes of God as that 'Absolute Being' which is 'rebellious to descriptions' but can be given 'as Absolute Presence in worship'.[16] Tillich holds that personal encounter with God is only fully appreciated when it is seen to be 'encounter with the God who is the ground of everything personal and as such is not *a* person'. God is 'Being itself, the ground and abyss of every being'.[17] Attempts to describe such experience fracture language since it seems to refer simultaneously to the most abstract (nothing is more general than 'being') and to the most concrete (for it is found in all that is).

A mode of feeling characterizes a seventh form of religious experience. In reacting against the rationalism of the Enlightenment and the biblicism of pietism Schleiermacher gives its classical exposition. In the early *Speeches on Religion*, religion is described as 'the immediate consciousness' or feeling that all 'being and living is a being and living in and through God'.[18] Later in a more systematic (and stolid) study, he locates the foundation of religion in 'the feeling of absolute dependence' which accompanies all our existence. The idea of God is the idea of the 'Whence' of this self-consciousness.[19] This basic 'feeling' is cognitive,[20] not only in making individuals sensible of their dependent status but also in bringing to awareness that on which they are dependent.[21]

An eighth view of religious experience holds that it is essentially of the 'holy'. Otto, for example, finds the identifying character of religion in the quality of numinousness. It is 'perfectly *sui generis* and irreducible to any other' but may be indirectly described by reference to a combination of experiences of creatureliness, mystery, otherness, overpoweringness, awe, fear, energy, urgency and fascination. The experience is dominantly of what has utter worth in itself.[22] A somewhat different view, as offered by Sam Keen,[23] suggests that the experience of the holy is of what gives worth to our existence.

Whereas Otto stresses that the holy is not primarily a moral category, others consider, ninthly, that religious experience is primarily a matter of moral sensibility. The popular view of conscience as the voice of God is expressed in Kant's statement that 'religion is (subjectively regarded) the recognition of all duties as divine commands'.[24] Together with awareness of the categorical demands of morality, however, religious experience includes, according to H. H. Farmer, a sense of divine aid to fulfil those demands.[25]

According to a tenth view, religious experience is distinctively expressed in a sense of freedom, creative inspiration, peace or joy. Whereas the moral demand has the negative effect of making people aware of sin and guilt (and as such may be regarded as the prolegomenon to religion), religious experience itself is marked by the positive qualities of unity, grace, certitude, creativity and vibrant expectation in the children of God.[26] For John Wesley persons under grace see 'the joyous light of heaven', have 'true peace . . . filling and ruling' their hearts, and enjoy 'true glorious liberty'[27] – experiences which his brother Charles celebrates in such hymns as,

> My God, I am Thine:
> What a comfort divine,
> What a blessing to know that my Jesus is mine!

and

> To him that in Thy name believes
> Eternal life with Thee is given;
> Into himself he all receives,
> Pardon, and holiness, and heaven.

Others see the experience in terms of intellectual or existential confidence, or in terms of the satisfying and stimulating experience of the beautiful. It is consequently describable as the multi-faceted experience of pure, all-embracing, joyful love.

A contrasting understanding of religious experience is that presented, eleventhly, by those who hold that currently its authentic form is the experience of the absence of God. Although those advancing this view are usually vague about what would constitute an experience of the presence of God, they are convinced that people today are aware of God's non-presence; it is like the positive absence of someone who is desired to be present and so is missed, not the vague non-presence of what, like a unicorn, has never been present. Buber writes of it as a sense of 'the eclipse of God', and William Hamilton as the 'deeply dissatisfying' experience which combines an awareness of God as withdrawn from the world with the sense of the divine as a disturbing pressure 'from which we would love to be free'.[28] The experience, however, is not novel. Mystics have long spoken of 'the dark night of the soul'.

Finally, in this catalogue of some of the variety of religious experiences, we must not forget claims to communications from God, including visions and auditions. Moses at the burning bush, Isaiah in the Temple, Paul on the road 'saw' and 'heard'. Samuel received a voice in the night, and Belshazzar the highest class of graffito. Joan of Arc had her voices, Bernadette Soubirous her visions, and John Wesley a 'strangely warmed' heart. The list of such experiences is vast, ranging from the bizarre to the almost humdrum, and from dramatic events which are as authentic for those experiencing them as normal sense perceptions to highly private modes of awareness in which the recipient becomes conscious of a 'word from the Lord'. Many believers, while holding that God is personal and benevolent, may not expect experiences of heard words, but they do expect that God will on occasion make known to them the divine will and promises – and they claim that this is what happens.

These different types of religious experience both overlap each other and may be further subdivided. Other, apparently more secular, forms of experience may also be held to have religious significance.[29] Nevertheless, in spite of the variety, there are certain basic issues which concern most, if not all, of them as they are used in developing theological understanding.

The importance of religious experience for theological understanding

The variety of the types as well as of the alleged contents of religious experience render a general appeal in theological thought to what 'experience indicates' confused and unconvincing. Some theologians, furthermore, seem to appeal to 'experience' to defend cherished positions when the argument is going against them or to check their reasoning when it is leading them towards undesired conclusions.[30] There is justification, therefore, for Hastings Rashdall's criticism that appeals to religious experience in theological thought are often spoilt by 'much deplorable vagueness', and that sometimes they amount to little more than 'the substitution of subjective emotion . . . for the honest effort to think rationally'.[31] Nevertheless , in spite of the unsatisfactory character of some references to it, it is not possible for a fully reflective theology to ignore religious experience.

So far as theology attempts to make sense of the actual faith of believers, it must refer to the experiences which constitute their consciousness of their faith. Atkinson Lee, for example, considers that just as philosophy is primarily reflection upon crude experience, so philosophy of religion 'assumes prior religious experience of a more naive unreflective kind'. Accordingly he holds that those who are 'largely insensitive' to the experience of faith will find discussions of it 'unintelligible'.[32] This claim may be generalized to apply to the wider issue of theological understanding. It does not entail that a theologian must personally entertain religious experiences in order to reflect intelligently upon them – an empathetic understanding of others' experiences would suffice – nor that those who claim to have religious experiences must be presupposed to have correctly apprehended them – they may have misinterpreted what they feel. What it does entail is that theology as reflection on religious experience must presuppose that some people actually have such experiences: if no one had them, there would be nothing to discuss. Some form of religious experience is thus 'an "a priori" of theological construction' of a certain kind.[33]

If theology, on the other hand, is held to be primarily a matter of rational reflection on the ultimate rather than narrowly derived from religious experiences, references to such experiences are still important. Without them theological understanding will appear to be of only theoretical interest. It will seem to be like the conclusion of the ontological argument – a fascinating abstract intellectual construction, but one which on its own has little or nothing to do with the reality in which people find themselves or with that actuality which commands their unreserved worship. Because of this John Henry Newman maintains that a living faith can only persist where there is a 'real' (as contrasted with a merely 'notional') apprehension of its object, while H. D. Lewis holds that genuine religion only occurs where individuals are aware of 'a totally mysterious reality' behind or beyond the 'facts of present existence'.[34] Reference to religious experience is thus essential if non-believers are to consider that religious beliefs may be existentially significant,[35] and believers that theological understanding is existentially relevant to the faith and practices by which they make sense of their lives.[36] It is this concern to connect theology with actual practice that Luther and Wesley restored to the study of doctrine and which Liberal Protestantism re-emphasized.[37] Such movements, varied as they may be, do not desert the cause of doctrine, but attempt to make the idea of true faith a living reality.

Another reason why religious experience is important for theological understanding is that some types of experience provide significant evidence about the credibility of certain doctrines. Buber's claim that God is encountered as the transcendent 'Thou', for example, will not arouse much interest unless there are a significant number of people who testify to having such experience. Similarly, Farmer's position will be undermined if there is no awareness of the moral demand and succour to which he refers. More broadly, religious affirmations about the personhood and benevolence of God are only likely to be regarded as more than pious hopes by people who consider that they have experiences of a personal and caring relationship with God.[38]

Not only specifically religious experience is significant in this respect. Ordinary secular experiences in general have a role, even if largely negative, in testing whether faith and its implications 'fit' the actual world. It may be easy to find numerous experiences which apparently confirm a particular belief. Experiences of beauty, harmony, creativity and moral awareness agree with claims about a benevolent God, while plague in Sennacherib's army, the gale that scattered the Armada and the calm at Dunkirk have been regarded (by those who benefited) as evidence of God's rule. As Popper has argued, however, the decisive experiences are not those which fit our theories, but those which do not conform with their expectations and so suggest that they may need to be modified or even scrapped. The so-called problem of evil – which designates a host of distinct problems – presents such a falsificatory challenge to theological understanding as it points to incompatibilities between experience and what is widely believed about the power, benevolence, creativity and providence of God.[39] Claims about the practical benevolence of God, for example, will only be considered factually significant if they can be shown to be compatible with the devastating experiences of suffering, loneliness and deep despair that occur. Affirmations about God as 'controller of history' and 'ruler of the nations' cease to be credible if they cannot be reconciled with the evidence of what has happened. One of the tasks of theology is consequently to find a way of harmonizing its understanding with the actual experiences of human living in order to show that it is a perception of the ultimate nature of reality and not merely a desirable fantasy.

A fourth reason for the importance of specifically religious experience is found in W. E. Hocking's suggestion that it makes people aware in the present of the reality of their future goal. Whereas, as has just been indicated, theological claims about what is now the case are only credible if they are perceived to fit what is experienced now, not all theological understanding is concerned with current states of affairs. Recognizing that reality is in process, some theological understanding is concerned about what ought to be, and about what ultimately will be, the fulfilment of that process. According to Hocking the arts see such a state as always future, but religious experience gives 'a present possession' and an 'anticipated attainment' of 'those objects which in the course of nature are reached only at the end of infinite progression'.[40] Religious experi-

ence can thus be held not merely to confirm that theological understanding fits the actual world, but also to be the occasion of that
'realizing light' in which, according to Charles Wesley, 'Whate'er
we hope, by faith we have, Future and past subsisting now'.
Although such experience may seem paradoxical, some believers
hold it to be real. It agrees with faith's character as an anticipatory
apprehension of what is unseen and future, and it makes real for
the believer what Pannenberg refers to when he writes of God as
'the coming God' who is proleptically revealed in Jesus.[41]

While religious experience – and experience generally – helps
to establish the significance and credibility of certain theological
claims, the relationship is not the straightforward one between, for
example, the claim that Lesley is wearing a red jacket and observation to see if this is so. The relationship between present experiences and theological understanding is complicated because the
latter refers in part to what is ultimately and universally true, to
what in other respects is yet to be, and to what is only puzzlingly
apprehended and conceived in terms of projections from our
experiences and understanding of this world. The basic difficulty,
however, is that the relationship between experience and understanding is not one way. What we apprehend as our experiences is
affected by our nature and existing ways of understanding. While
reference to experience, then, is important for theological understanding, it is also important to identify how that experience is
conditioned.

The cultural and conceptual conditioning of experience

The previous discussion applied to theological understanding
Kant's claim that concepts without percepts are 'empty'. We are
now to examine the implications for theology of the other part of
his claim, namely, that percepts without concepts are 'blind'.[42] We
are not able to identify what we experience except in a utterly
vague, confused and non-signifying manner unless we apprehend
it through the use of appropriate concepts. By these concepts we
initially express rather than describe the experience, for it is only
by being so grasped that the experience becomes something to be
described.

In familiar situations the gap between having sensations and
identifying them as particular sorts of experience is not noticed. As
I look up and 'see' a rose bush, I am not conscious of any process
of interpreting my visual perceptions although there is nothing in

them as such that informs me that it is a rose bush. Since, therefore, the apprehension of the content of what I immediately understand myself to be experiencing usually appears to be part of the experience, the term 'experience' is generally used to cover the amalgam of inchoate awareness and interpretative apprehension. When, however, we become aware of something unfamiliar or obscure, we may begin to appreciate the role of apprehension in identifying the contents of experience. On waking, for example, I may feel a vague sense of unease and then proceed to clarify it through increasingly precise classifications: mental, not physical; anxiety, not guilt; worry about tomorrow's paper, not career prospects in general; unhappiness at this particular argument in the paper, not its thesis as a whole. So the process of refinement goes on – though in practice there are usually far more than two possibilities to choose between – until I have grasped the feeling sufficiently to be able to respond to it.[43]

This process of identification, whether or not it is consciously recognized, is conditioned in each case by the available ways of understanding. Husserl's notion of a purely neutral phenomenological description of experiences is an unrealizable goal. As Feyerabend points out, 'experience arises *together* with theoretical assumptions *not* before them'. Observation and theory belong together and 'an experience without theory is . . . incomprehensible'.[44] Feyerabend's provocative study is primarily concerned with the natural sciences, but its epistemological conclusions apply also to the relationship between theology and religious experience. Where theology reflects on the supposed given of the experiences of existential faith, its data is influenced by the ontological, valuative and rational presuppositions of the framework of understanding by which that data is apprehended.

The moulding of experience includes what we decide to be its basic nature, whether it consists of units of sense data, or a blur of a continuum of consciousness, or perceived objects. This decision is a metaphysical one. It cannot be made simply by reference to the evidence of experience, though it must be compatible with it, because it involves a prior understanding of the nature of thought and of reality as determining the character of experience.[45] It is also a metaphysical decision that determines which experiences are acceptable as significant evidence and for what they are significant. Does, for example, an experience of joy (or of guilt) have external reference, or does it only record a subjective state? Though consideration of its apprehended character will influence the answer, in the end the decision will reflect an overall metaphysical understanding of the nature of reality in which apprehension and significance are reciprocally related.

What we apprehend as the content of our experiences is also formed by the ways of understanding available in our culture. Primarily this is a matter of language. Although the control is not absolute,[46] what we take to be our experiences is partly determined by the conceptual vocabulary available to us.

In *Philosophical Investigations* Wittgenstein makes the point that the distinctions which we observe have no intrinsic necessity. They express the conventions of a culture encapsulated in its language. What we identify as experiences of 'redness' and of 'pain' depends upon the language which we have learned.[47] If our language were different, what we apprehend as our experiences would be correspondingly affected. The English words 'snow' and 'rice', for example, cover a range of distinct concepts expressed by different words in Eskimo and Hindi respectively. More pertinent for theology is a concept like pain. English has a large number of words for states which people normally wish to avoid: pain, ache, sorrow, anxiety, guilt, fear, sin, evil, error, loss, and so on. It is imaginable that a culture might exist that had only one word for all these various states. In that case that word would have to be translated into English as 'a state to be avoided', and it would be difficult, perhaps impossible, to express in such a restricted language distinctions naturally made in English. Furthermore, because it would be necessary to use the same word to express both a father's sorrow at the death of his son and a murderer's guilt at having killed him, the impression would tend to be given that these are basically the same state. In a culture with such a limited vocabulary it is hard to envisage how our notions of moral sensibility could ever arise, and it would seem to be impossible to express traditional doctrines of salvation and atonement in it. Either there would be serious distortion of the doctrines (for salvation covers some but by no means all of what is to be avoided – guilt and anxiety but not pain and bankruptcy, for example), or the language (and so the culture which it encapsulated) would have to be modified in order to introduce previously unrecognized distinctions.

It is conceivable, therefore, that some ideas may not be immediately translatable into a particular language and culture because the latter lack the necessary concepts. They will find a place only when that culture's language, and hence its modes of understanding, have been modified.[48] Whether intended or not, the communication of ideas prevents the preservation of existing cultures. In the end what limits the emergence of a common global culture is not so much the fact that different phonemes are used for effectively the same concept in different languages. It is the differences in grammatical structure which ensure the non-equivalence of languages.

The illustration from the multivalency of 'a state to be avoided' is not as theologically irrelevant as might be thought. In English there has often been confusion in theological discussions because it is not recognized that 'evil' may be used of a number of distinct states: aesthetic, intellectual, moral, naturally produced physical and humanly produced physical evil. The 'problem of evil' thus refers to a range of difficulties for faith occasioned by such different matters as the stench of rotting flesh, mistakes, the human capacity to tell lies, drought in Africa and the torture of captives. These are distinct problems. To treat them as forms of a single problem for which a single solution is to be sought, because one word can be used for all of them, is to fall into linguistically inspired confusion.

The apprehension of experiences is influenced by culture's modes of understanding as well as by its language. People may observe the same object and yet, because of their different cultural backgrounds, appreciate its significance in distinct ways. A red flag has different valuative connotations for a Chinese youth (hopeful expectation) and a British railway worker (danger). The self-understanding of being a woman typically varies according to whether she is a member of a Dayak, Japanese, Omani, Italian or Texan culture, as well as according to any particular subgroup within that culture to which she may belong. What is an appropriate recognition of services to be rendered in one culture is bribery and corruption in another. Furthermore, as those acquainted with the cultures of England and America discover, cultures as ways of understanding are not coterminous with a language.

Not only how we evaluate our experiences, but even what we are aware of, is influenced by our background, heritage and interests. A child (unlike its culturally prejudiced parents) may simply not notice that its playmate is of a different race. Where one person sees a scarred slab of rock, another sees holds, belays and a challenge. One sees the outline of a duck's head, another that of a rabbit, and a third recognizes it as a psychological puzzle.[49] To move a little closer to theological understanding, the beaks which Captain FitzRoy saw as 'one of those admirable provisions of Infinite

Wisdom by which each created thing is adapted to the place for which it was intended', Charles Darwin found to be 'eminently curious' and deserving attention by 'the philosophical naturalist'.[50] For all they held in common, what they observed on the Galapagos Islands led one to give glory to God, and the other to begin to see a problem requiring a scientific solution.

Nevertheless, while the influence of cultural differences on human experiences is not negligible, it should not be exaggerated. There is no need to go to the extreme of holding with Blake that:

> Both read the Bible day and night,
> But thou read'st black where I read white.[51]

Languages and cultures, furthermore, are not static. The relationship between them and our experiences is a reciprocal one. To some extent they affect each other. Since, as Feyerabend notes, observation and theory arise together, we find ways of understanding being developed and new concepts invented, in order to cope with changes in our perception of our experience. Physicists develop notions of 'strangeness' and 'charm'; philosophers of history produce a distinction between 'Historie' and 'Geschichte' to clarify their thought; the philosophical theologian starts to talk of 'dipolar panentheism'. Some neologisms and new uses for existing terms are the product of a love of jargon, but others bring to consciousness a fresh way of understanding and, where applicable, a different way of apprehending experience. Sometimes, as with 'gazumping' and 'mugging', the new term attaches a moral valuation to a recognized practice; in other cases, as with Otto's use of the notion of the 'numinous', it identifies a characteristic which otherwise, for lack of a distinctive term, is likely to be overlooked. Experience may thus evoke developments in culture and language as well as be formed by them.

Novelty and change, however, are rarer than conformity. On the whole experience is moulded by existing ways of understanding. When we consider how experience is apprehended and interpreted for theological purposes, we find that the ways of thought contained in language and culture and metaphysical preferences have by far the dominant influence.

The influence of metaphysical preferences on the apprehended content and significance of experience may be illustrated by considering the report by Shackleton, Worsley and Crean, after their crossing of South Georgia, that they had 'each had a strange feeling that there had been a fourth in our party'.[52] While the description of the experience contains no explicitly theistic reference, preachers have used it as evidence of the benevolent presence of God. Others who are doubtful about such personalism may regard 'the fourth' as an anthropomorphic apprehension of the presence of 'the utterly other'. Those who deny the reality of the divine do not need to question the honesty of the report, but may interpret it according to their own frames of reference, as, for instance, an illusion produced by extreme conditions and the beliefs of the culture in which the men grew up. How fundamental intellectual commitments influence the apprehension of experience is also to be seen in the way that Farmer finds theistic content in moral experience of the categorical imperative whereas others do not, and in the way that Marghanita Laski finds no need to interpret ecstatic experience theistically whereas others do.

The case of the resurrection of Jesus illustrates how culture and language affect experience and theological understanding. Granted that statements about Jesus' resurrection refer to *something* in the disciples' experience, what was it that they experienced? The reports do not present a consistent picture. Sometimes the figure behaves like a resuscitated corpse, other times it suddenly appears and disappears; Luke writes of the apostles thinking that they saw a ghost, while Paul includes the event on the road to Damascus as a resurrection appearance. The evidence suggests that what the disciples experienced consolidated their faith in Jesus, but the inconsistencies in their attempts to express it suggest that they found it hard to apprehend. We may never be able to determine whether it was a physical, a psychical or an intellectual event that they describe as 'resurrection'. While we know that the metaphor of 'resurrection' was eventually accepted as the most adequate one available in their culture for reporting what happened, we have no way of telling how appropriate it was, nor the degree to which its adoption influenced both the description of the events and the disciples' own understanding of what it was that they had experienced.

Cultural influence on theological understanding is also clearly seen in the various doctrines of atonement that have been put forward. These use models, generally taken from current social practice, both to express and to understand the saving relationship between God and humanity. Although there is hardly any evidence to indicate why a particular model was initially adopted, what may well have happened was that believers felt that their experience of salvation resembled in some significant respect the experience found in a particular social relationship. Since the experiences were held to be similar, it then tended to be assumed that the relationships bringing them about would be similar. If, for instance, salvation felt like what it is to have been ransomed or manumitted or liberated, doctrines were produced which interpreted the divine work of salvation as the payment of a ransom or the gift of freedom or victory over invaders. The feudal sense of honour and its satisfaction, the converting power of love, substitutionary punishment where one person voluntarily pays the penalty due from another, and the transfer of credit whereby one person benefits from the capital accumulated by another are other social interactions whose effects have suggested them as ways of apprehending the experience of salvation.[53]

When, however, a social relationship was adopted as a way of apprehending the experience of 'being saved', the relationship did not remain as a way of expressing that experience. It soon tended to become a way of understanding the saving relationship between God and humanity, and of explaining how it came about. In the case of the ransom model, for instance, the experience of salvation was not just thought of as being *like* the feeling of liberation after ransom from captivity: salvation came to be thought of *as* a liberation through the payment of a ransom. As the theory was elaborated it was considered necessary to specify what the ransom was, to whom it was paid and why it was due. In this way models adopted from culture changed from being metaphorical ways of expressing an experience of salvation into being descriptions of the underlying state. The process is a theological form of what Frank Kermode finds in literature: 'Fictions . . . turn easily into myths; people will live by that which was designed only to know by.'[54] Heuristic devices thus petrify into monolithic structures and come to be mistaken for direct descriptions of reality itself.

Although theological reflection may modify how models of salvation are understood – leading, for example, to the rejection of immoral views of appeasement and substitution – both the nature of the primary awareness, and the understanding of what gives rise to it, are significantly moulded by the models used to apprehend it, especially when what was originally used figuratively comes to be taken literally. Doctrines of atonement, therefore, are not straightforward reflections on experience. They are the products of reflection on the results of interaction between primary awareness and models provided by current culture.[55] As a result apparently irreconcilable differences between doctrines may turn out not to be matters of substance, but due to the character of the models employed. Theologians must not forget the distinction between what they seek to describe and their ways of describing it. The fact that they can never evade such conditioning factors does not mean that they should forget about their influence.

Doctrines of the person of Christ reveal a similar situation. From the first attempts of the disciples to determine who it was that they followed through the Christologies of the Ecumenical Councils to debates today, the understanding is largely determined by the concepts available in the contemporary culture. The confessions of the early church, for example, are either misunderstood or meaningless if they are not seen in the context of the notions of Jewish and Hellenistic culture. It must also be appreciated that the situation is complicated by the fact that the character and fate of Jesus was not wholly congruent with popular understanding of the notions used. As a result both the reality to be understood and subsequent theological reflection modified the apprehension of the content of those notions. Nevertheless, the doctrines did not develop in a presuppositionless vacuum. Whether or not they were appropriate and adequate, current concepts largely governed what could be thought about the significance of Jesus. Modern studies into the formative influences on early Christian thought, however much they may raise questions about the continuing credibility of traditional doctrines, thus provide important insights into the way that Christian understanding has been, and still is, conditioned.[56]

The most noticeable way in which religious experience is conditioned by its cultural setting is found in reports about such exceptional experiences as visions and auditions. In the case of auditions, the words used are in the hearer's own language or, occasionally, in what the hearer regards as an appropriate religious language. To a French peasant the words are in French or Latin, never in Aramaic! As for visions, what is supposedly seen largely conforms to the current social, cultural and religious background. Anselm had a vision of the heavenly court which delightfully reflects the thoughts of 'a simple and innocent boy' who had been 'bred among the mountains' in the eleventh century. According to the vision, Anselm finds God alone with his steward since the household is out collecting the harvest; as a treat Anselm is given 'the whitest of bread' (no middle class prejudices for wholemeal in this court!) by which to refresh himself.[57] While Eadmer who reports the incident sees the vision as a dream conditioned by Anselm's upbringing, the story conforms to what generally occurs in reported visions. Appearances of the Virgin, for example, are recognized to be such because she looks like local icons of her. It is probably not an accident that Protestants tend to see nothing of this kind but to hear words, since their practice has less use of visual stimuli and lays more stress on words. On the other hand, if God be personal and wishes to communicate with persons in vivid ways, the resulting revelatory experiences would be as bafflingly uninformative as Ezekiel's vision of the wheels, unless they were in words and sights sufficiently familiar for their significance to be apprehensible.

The influence of individual personality on experience

What individuals experience is affected by their character and attitudes as well as by their cultural background. However much they may seek to be unprejudiced, their personality affects how they apprehend their experiences. They are *their* experiences. A painting does not change with its spectators, but what, for example, Lesley experiences as she looks at it depends not only upon her eyesight, but also upon her existing knowledge of art, her convictions about it, and the attitude in which she approaches it. If she approaches it annoyed because the authorities have spent money in acquiring it while refusing a grant for her research equipment, she is likely to have a different experience of it than if she goes to see it because Graham has told her how wonderful it is.

In *The Varieties of Religious Experience* William James suggests how our religious experiences may be affected by our temperaments. Taking up Francis Newman's distinction between 'the once-born' (healthy-minded optimists who feel that evil will go away if it is ignored) and 'the twice-born' (sick souls who feel that evil must be fought and natural life lost before spiritual happiness will be found), James holds that the result is 'two different experiences', as well as two different conceptions of the universe. They produce, among other things, contrasting views of the nature of salvation.[58] For one person the sense of health, happiness, wholeness and peace is what salvation is about; for another the crucial element is the experience of escape, rescue and change. James's response to the situation is to urge that we 'recognize that we live in partial systems' and, therefore, that we accept that different personality-types need different ways of understanding God and salvation.[59]

Whether or not James's attempt at theological comprehensiveness is intellectually satisfactory, it reminds us that when Wesley and Emerson, or Barth and Whitman, present conflicting positions, one important source of their theological disagreements may be their personalities. Similarly, from the time of the Gospel writers to the present, differences of tone and even content in presentations of 'Jesus' are to be attributed in part to the different characters of the presenters. What one person finds to be satisfying and convincing cannot be so regarded by another. Differences in their personalities render their experiences and understanding of the world significantly different. The recognition of these influences does not warrant the extreme conclusion that understanding in such matters is a wholly subjective invention. It does remind us that experience and understanding is conditioned by individuals as well as by their cultural setting.

Religious experience as being of the 'inexpressible'

In the discussion so far it has been assumed that religious experience has an apprehensible content. This assumption may be challenged on the grounds that the fundamental form of religious experience is of the inexpressible. What cannot be expressed, however, even to ourselves, cannot be apprehended.

Claims about inexpressibility are made in various ways. When Otto, for example, maintains that the holy is properly *sui generis*, his point is not that the experience of the holy is totally inexpressible in itself, but that it requires its own language since it involves 'beliefs and feelings qualitatively different' from what '"natural" sense-perception is capable of giving us'.[60] For the Wittgenstein of the *Tractatus*, no such language is available. Only the propositions of natural science are meaningful. Hence what is 'manifest' but 'cannot be put into words' we must regard as 'mystical', and recognize that 'what we cannot speak about we must pass over in silence'.[61] Reflecting on these two positions, Thomas McPherson suggests that the logical positivists in effect support religion by showing 'the absurdity of what theologians try to utter'. Since 'religion belongs to the sphere of the unutterable', the solution to problems with theological language is 'to retreat into silence'.[62]

Although theologians are unlikely to be happy with support for religion which holds that experiences of the divine cannot be apprehended and that theology is nonsensical, they should not forget the strong mystical tradition with some impeccable religious credentials which makes similar remarks. The author of *The Cloud of Unknowing*, for example, under the influence of the apophatic theology of

Dionysius the Areopagite, holds that authentic religious experience cannot be intellectually apprehended and described, although those who have it may be able to re-present it to themselves later as a remembered experience.[63]

Comments on the 'inexpressibility' of religious experiences may be taken seriously, however, without necessarily accepting that we should not try to apprehend and use them in theological understanding. In the first place, the claim that religious experience is inexpressible or of the inexpressible is strictly self-contradictory. To grasp an experience sufficiently to be able to perceive it as an experience of the 'inexpressible', let alone to recognize it as having religious significance, presupposes that it can be apprehended to some extent.

Most affirmations of inexpressibility, furthermore, are not to be taken so pedantically literally. Since religion deals with what is ultimate, experiences and discussions of its object stretch our conceptual frameworks to the limit. References to inexpressibility, like references to God as 'utterly other', can accordingly be understood as reminders that here we deal with what is intrinsically baffling and, in some respects, can only be described indirectly by using metaphorical, symbolic and parabolic forms of language. Collingwood, pointing out that religion needs theological language if it is not to be rejected as nonsensical, accordingly suggests that believers make two points when they assert the inexpressibility of religion. First, they warn against the common error of confusing what religion says with 'what it means'. Secondly, they indicate that when theological understanding distinguishes between the religious symbol and what it means, it passes outside religion and may even be seen as 'the negation of religion'.[64] Assertions about inexpressibility may thus be interpreted as reminders to theologians of the systematic elusiveness and oddity of God.[65]

Remarks about the inexpressibility of religion may also be seen as affirming that religion is not reducible or translatable without remainder into talk about something else, such as morality or aesthetics. They are protests against attempts by some philosophical analysts to develop such interpretations. Just as Moore argues that 'good' is a fundamental concept in morality, and Otto makes a similar claim for the 'holy' in its own sphere, so assertions of religion's inexpressibility may suggest that religion constitutes a language-game with its own subject-matter, concepts and rather odd logic.

So far as they are justified, then, assertions of the inexpressible nature of the object of religion and of religious experiences do not rule out theological studies of them, but they do draw attention to their limitations.

The cognitive significance of religious experience

While religious experience is important for theological understanding,[66] it is also conditioned. What, in that case, is its cognitive significance?

Some believers hold that their beliefs are validated, at least for themselves, because they have a sense of their certainty.[67] They may even claim to have the same feeling of unquestionability in the case of their religious convictions as they have for other matters which are generally accepted as being known and, as Newman points out, people 'are not commonly certain' of what is 'simply false'.[68] There are, however, enough cases of people claiming, apparently sincerely, to feel certain of judgements which turn out to be false or are mutually contradictory[69] to show that a sense of certitude by itself is not a safe indicator for what is true. While, therefore, John Wesley affirmed the believers' privilege of assurance of salvation, he was well aware of the need to counter the danger of resting our judgements upon the feeling of certainty alone. Accordingly, he holds that claims to this gift must be 'clearly and solidly distinguished, from the presumption of a natural mind, and from the delusion of the devil'[70] by reference, not to the qualities of the experience, but to the evidence of a corresponding change in behaviour.

The sense of certainty on its own may only indicate our ability to ignore objections or our success in fitting the evidence to our convictions. It may, on the other hand, be seen as witnessing to the truth of our convictions rather than just to the satisfaction of our intellect, if we assume that the ultimate character of reality significantly corresponds to what makes sense to human understanding. In that case, however, it is not the feeling of certainty itself but the conditions which produce it, namely the fit of the evidence with the understanding and the lack of worrying objections, which indicate that what we are certain about may be true.

More important than the question of the significance of the sense of certainty is the question of whether religious experiences can be used to support claims about the reality, nature and activity of God. Various critics of religious belief argue that such experiences tell us about those who have them, but provide no reliable information about any divine reality external to them.[71] Is there any way by which theistic interpretations and uses of religious experience may be justified?

The diversity of what is regarded as religious experience prevents any single answer to this question. Some forms of religious experience do seem to be predominantly self-referring. Other forms, however, seem to have a primary reference to states and objects independent of human being. The sense of the holy, for example, is apprehended by some as an awareness of what is itself holy and not as a quality of their feeling.

An initial problem facing attempts to show the external reference of supposedly objective forms of religious experience is that of identifying its referent. It is often unclear whether the experience is primarily of a state of affairs or of the entity which brings about that state. Is Schleiermacher's 'feeling of absolute dependence', for example, primarily an awareness of our contingency or an immediate awareness of the being on which (or on whom) we depend?

Simply to refer to descriptions of religious experiences does not provide the answer. When people report their experiences, they often adopt a theistic frame of reference without showing why such a conceptual structure is demanded by the experiences themselves.[72] H. D. Lewis, for example, in discussing religious experience, moves from talking about it as the perception of 'a totally mysterious reality on which all else depends' to speaking of it as experience of 'God'.[73] Marghanita Laski, on the other hand, in her study of ecstacy, rejects the equation of religious with theistic and argues that this kind of religious experience can be satisfactorily apprehended without any theistic content. As has been pointed out, the way in which an experience is apprehended and interpreted depends on the presuppositions of those considering it. Consequently, discussions of the cognitive value of religious experiences are always in danger of begging the question, because neutral phenomenological descriptions of them are unobtainable.[74]

Other sources of difficulty for attempts to evaluate religious experiences are the stretched language used to describe their content[75] and the dangers of delusion. In relation to the former problem, is it its secrecy or the inadequacies of language that constrains Paul's description of his vision?[76] Other reports of religious experiences suggest that the search for adequacy may cause their content to lose coherence.[77] As for the latter problem, mystics like Teresa and John of the Cross do not doubt that people can have awareness of the presence of God, but they also consider that visions can be produced by the devil. Where attempts are made to use such authorities as the church, orthodox doctrine or conscience to sift out genuine experiences, the result somewhat begs the question of their cognitive value. Such tests generally recognize as genuine only what conforms to an existing theological understanding which already affirms the reality of its object. The need for tests, however, is a reminder that the identification of authentic religious experiences poses problems.

For their recipients religious experiences are often of tremendous importance.[78] Taking them as manifestations of their ultimate situation, believers generally do not regard them as simply declaring their fundamental state of mind or bringing to life their existential self-understanding. They hold them to be perceptions of the divine reality which determines that situation. Is it, though, warrantable to claim that they justify theistic faith? Can the Schleiermacherian feeling of absolute dependence, for example, be shown to be an awareness of the absolute, or the Buberian encounter to be a confrontation by that which is self-existent? Although many theologians would like to be able to claim that clear, experiential confirmation of the reality of God is available, no unqualified 'Yes' to the above questions seems to be justified.

The character of the experiences is such that no straightforward comparison with our sense-experiences of external objects can be upheld. In the case of supposed encounters with a transcendent 'thou', for example, there are none of the accompanying physical experiences which characterize our meetings with other people. Again, when we meet other people we become aware of their personal being by the ways in which they are apparently affected by and respond to us. In the case of the divine 'thou', there is no obvious evidence of responsiveness by that 'thou'.[79] Religious experiences may thus have some characteristics which lead us to regard them as I–thou encounters, but they lack other characteristics which would allow us to claim that they demonstrate the reality of a personal being confronting us.

While, however, religious experiences do not prove the truth of theistic claims, it may be argued that they give them support because they fit theistic understanding of the divine as personal and non-manipulable. Such an argument depends on the possibility of maintaining that the experiences are not self-induced illusions.

Attempts have been made to rebut the illusion theory of religious experiences by reference to the character of such experiences.

James points out that many people certainly 'possess the objects of their belief' as directly apprehended 'quasi-sensible realities', and consider that their reality is 'as convincing . . . as any direct sensible experiences can be'.[80] Otto speaks of 'the creature-feeling' as 'indubitably' referring to 'an object outside the self'.[81] Nevertheless, no matter how finely the experiences themselves are analysed, they cannot by themselves show that their sense of being of an external reality is not imaginary or illusory. Any alleged consistency between the characteristics of such experiences, and what might be expected in experiences of the divine, only shows that they are consistent with their expected character. It does not show that they are not illusory, products of belief that the divine reality exists. Equally, it does not show that they are illusory.

Although Pannenberg agrees that 'deeper psychological understanding of religious consciousness' cannot by itself show that its 'intensive feeling of reality' is not 'completely erroneous', he argues that a study of 'the fundamental anthropological structures of human behaviour' can show that religious experience is not wholly deceptive. It does this by revealing that the structure of human existence both presupposes and finds its fulfilment in 'a mystery of reality transcending its finitude'. Religion is thus 'a necessary element' in human being. In religious experience people become aware of the reality towards which their existence is fundamentally directed. Its reality is confirmed for them by its 'happening' as power to bring wholeness to their current experience of existence.[82]

This argument only shows that religion has an essential place in human life. The object of religion could still be an idea, and religious experience the awareness of the effectiveness of that idea for human flourishing. It does not show that theistic understanding is correct in considering that the experience is an awareness of a reality which corresponds to that idea. To find reasons for holding this we need to move beyond 'philosophical anthropology' to a 'general ontology',[83] which can show that what makes sense of human existence may credibly be regarded as what is ultimately the case in reality.

A defence of a theistic interpretation of religious experience against the criticisms of Feuerbach ('projection') and Freud ('illusion') thus depends upon the justifiability of a metaphysical understanding of reality which is different from theirs. Our structures of understanding not only mould what we apprehend as our experiences; they also largely determine the significance of those experiences for us. Whether, then, we think of Samuel hearing the voice of the Lord,[84] or the sense of the holy, or the consciousness of unconditional moral demand and succour, or the awareness of encounter with a transcendent thou, or the feeling of gracious support, the experiences are recognized by theists to be experiences of God, because they are theists and not simply because of the character of the raw experience taken by itself.[85]

Since, therefore, the way in which we apprehend religious experiences is moulded by our metaphysical commitments, and their cognitive value is a product of the consideration of the experiences in the light of those commitments, it is not surprising to find that people claim that their experiences confirm their beliefs. On the other hand, it also becomes clear that theistic understanding cannot be justified directly by reference to religious experiences. Any such argument depends crucially upon a prior justification of the credibility of belief in the reality of God.[86]

Nevertheless, it would be a mistake to consider that this conclusion implies that religious experience has little cognitive value for theological understanding. In the first place, it has an important negative value. The absence of any correlative experiences would strongly suggest that theistic understanding is false and its concepts empty. Even though references to religious experiences cannot demonstrate the reality of God, and even though such experiences as theistically apprehended may be illusory, their occurrence stops the charge that theistic understanding is falsified by the fact that people do not have the kinds of experience that its truth would lead us to expect.

Secondly, although the apprehension and evaluation of these experiences is influenced by presupposed structures of understanding, the way in which understanding develops indicates that, in practice, even our basic thought is not completely closed. Experiences may lead us to revise our understanding, especially when they do not fit neatly into existing patterns. Since, then, the relationship between understanding and experience is to some extent reciprocal, religious experiences may contribute both to changes in and to confirmation of theological thought.

Thirdly, there is some significance in the intellectual experience that a position 'fits' or 'feels right' or 'makes sense'. Although the feeling of certainty by itself is an unsafe guide to truth, the situation is importantly different when that feeling is linked to the recognition that what we are certain about has a place in an overall pattern of understanding which we find generally credible.[87] The feeling may then express the sense that a particular thought coheres with what we already consider to be true. It may be, on the other hand, that the 'fit' is not *into* an existing pattern of understanding (like a piece into a jigsaw) but *of* a pattern as a whole. In this case the sense of certainty is the recognition that the pattern provides a 'story' which coherently, fruitfully and convincingly makes sense of what we are trying to understand. In either case the sense of fittingness may reasonably be regarded as an indication of truth. Where, then, theistic understanding is accompanied by a sense of intellectual satisfaction, the experience should not be regarded as having no cognitive significance.

Claims about the absence of experiences of God

In previous ages believers seem not only to have regarded experiences of God as possible but also, according to their testimony, to have had them. Although the evidence is not sufficient to be able to determine just how widespread such experiences might have been, what does exist gives the impression that sincere believers at least expected them to occur to some people.[88] In recent years, however, some theologians have claimed that people no longer have experiences of God as a mind-independent reality who encounters them as guide, judge and helper. This is a puzzling claim in that it suggests that those who make it know what it would be like to have such experiences, whereas this seems far from clear. The claim does, nevertheless, reflect a change in what some believers, at any rate, now expect as part of the life of faith.

The claim that God is not now experienced is presented in various ways. Bonhoeffer suggests that it is the will of God that we are to live maturely in the world 'without God': *'etsi deus non daretur.'*[89] While Buber speaks in *I and Thou* of the experience of 'remoteness from God', after the Holocaust he describes the present age as one of 'divine silence'.[90] William Hamilton puts it that religious experience is 'deeply dissatisfying', because God is felt both to be 'withdrawn from the world' when wanted and yet 'a pressure and a wounding' when not wanted.[91] In *The Secular City* Harvey Cox holds that the absence of God is a positive good since it is a necessary condition of human flourishing as creative and responsible being.[92] Gabriel Vahanian, in contrast, treats the non-experience of God as a cultural matter: since contemporary writers describe the world as 'a no God's land', self-consciously 'modern' people, influenced as well as represented by this culture, find nothing in their experience to correspond to the 'transcendental dimension' of human existence in earlier cultures.[93]

To some extent reports that God is not experienced today may act as self-fulfilling prophecies. Therefore the initial theistic response to them should be to check if they are correct. On closer inspection it may turn out that experiences of God are still to be found, although not generally recognized to be such. In that case it is not our situation but our way of apprehending it that has changed. Reports of the non-experience of God may thus provide further examples of the cultural conditioning of what we take to be our experiences. On the other hand, it may be that the human situation has significantly changed and that the divine was, but is no longer, to be experienced. It is, however, difficult to see how such a judgement could be substantiated in view of the cultural conditioning of past as well as of present reports about such experiences.

The theologians who have asserted that God is not an object of current experience have, on the whole, not considered that this shows that theistic understanding is fundamentally mistaken. They have found ways of incorporating the alleged non-experience of God in what they present as a theistic understanding of contemporary life. Bonhoeffer and Harvey Cox interpret God's absence as God's way of compelling people to accept their responsibility as members of a humanity come of age. William Hamilton presents the cross as the sign of the cost to God of the divine will that people should be responsible and free.[94] Buber suggests that the sense of the eclipse of God may not only be an effect of the Holocaust: it may also result from humanity's current obsession with manipulating and dominating that renders people 'unable to say Thou'. A time will come when these barriers between the human and the divine will be removed – by God's action.[95] Vahanian sees the cultural death of God as the means by which human understanding is cleared of its misconceptions and prepared for an authentic grasp of 'the reality of the living God'.[96]

It is interesting to note how such theologians assert the non-experience of God and yet find in the situation a perception of God's relationship with humanity. They interpret the experience so that it fits, as well as informs, their theistic understanding of reality.

The main significance of the alleged non-experience of the divine, however, may be that it points to the inadequacy and distortion of traditional views of religious experience. God is not to be experienced as one being among the others that we meet – like the lecturer in his study or the doctor in her laboratory. God is the necessary, omnipresent and ultimate ground of being. While the divine may be least inadequately thought of as personal (and so as an essentially open reality which can never be fully known), it is as a personal reality which embraces everything and influences everything. When, therefore, people say that they do not experience God, what they may be on the way to recognizing is that God is not an object which can be directly comprehended in any human experience. The divine is only to be experienced partially and indirectly through the creation and through the creator's relationships with it. In this way the supposed non-experience of God may turn out to reflect a proper appreciation of the transcendence of the divine.

Atheists may well be annoyed that theologians do not find reports that God is not experienced basically threatening, but rather manage to use them in their theistic understanding. These different evaluations of the same evidence are another illustration of the way in which the significance of experience is influenced by presupposed ways of thought. Our initial response to an experience is to try to fit it into our existing patterns. Only if we fail to do this is it likely to lead us to consider it as an indication that we should modify our position.

It is a mistake, therefore, to consider that religious experience by itself provides the basic materials for unprejudiced theological construction. While such experience is one of the factors which should be taken into account, its apprehension and evaluation are conditioned by our existing ways of understanding. Religious experience does not offer to theologians a way to evade the all-too-human limits and conditioning of their thought. Nevertheless, where it coheres with their thought it may be regarded as confirming it; and where it resists easy incorporation into existing patterns, it may contribute to the development of their understanding.

6

Theology and the apprehension of revelation

John Macquarrie describes revelation as 'the primary source of theology' and 'a basic category in theological thinking'. It has a gift-like character. Through 'the initiative of that towards which . . . faith is directed' people receive an understanding, both of themselves and of 'the wider being' within which they exist, which has hitherto been concealed from them.[1] In other words, revelation may be seen as God making Godself known to humanity and thereby providing a God-guaranteed basis for theological understanding. Where revelation is so understood, it may also be considered to provide a means by which theistic understanding may transcend the limits and cultural conditioning which normally influence human ways of thought. In revelation, that is, people receive a direct, unconditioned knowledge of the truth from the one who is unaffected by the distorting perspectives of the human situation.

This understanding of revelation is attractive because it allows those believers and theologians who accept it to claim the authority of God for some of their utterances. Unfortunately for these would-be oracles, it does not survive examination. Both in practice and in principle allegedly revealed knowledge of the divine is conditioned by the ways of understanding of those who grasp it. In order to show this, the following discussions of revelation will initially entertain the assumption that revelation comes from God. When it moves on to the relationship between supposedly revealed truths and events, however, it will be suggested that those truths are most adequately understood as insights evoked through particular ways of interpreting certain events rather than as direct divine communications to humanity.

The importance of revelation for theological understanding

Presupposing that God neither errs nor lies, those who believe that certain information has been revealed by God consider that what has thus been communicated must be true. Revelation accordingly provides theological understanding with information whose indubitability goes beyond what can be found in other modes of understanding. Nevertheless, while this may show the desirability of revelation where it has been given, it does not show that it is necessary for theological understanding to be possible. Why, then, do some theologians hold that revelation is essential? Why are the normal processes of rational reflection by which we achieve understanding in other matters not sufficient also in theology?

The last question assumes that our 'normal processes of rational reflection' do not involve revelation. This assumption may be challenged on two counts. In the first place, it may be pointed out that nothing can be known unless it manifests itself as available to be known and, in particular, that the deepest knowledge of other persons is only possible so far as they open themselves up to us. Theology, especially as it seeks understanding of a personal deity, may thus be held not to be distinctive in needing some form of revelation. On the other hand, as the discussion in the previous chapter indicates, claims to have experiences of God are very unlike claims to have become acquainted with other people.

Secondly, it may be argued that all understanding depends upon discoveries of key ideas by which we make sense of the data before us. While Whewell's view of scientific method in his classic treatise on the inductive sciences is now criticized, his recognition of the need to discern a 'connecting idea' by which we can perceive an order in the confused materials before us, and of the unpredictability of that discernment, still holds true. Certain preparations and particular qualities of mind may help but in the end the crucial insight just comes.[2] It is a happening which I. T. Ramsey calls a disclosure situation, an occasion which we describe as one in which 'the light dawns' or 'the penny drops'. Suddenly, 'out of the blue', we see that an idea, a theory or a story makes sense of an apparent jumble of observations, solves a puzzle, or opens the way to fruitful developments of our thought. It is something that happens to the scientist trying to sort out why the experiment does not give the predicted results, and to the theologian puzzling over a problem concerning our knowledge of God.[3]

There is, however, an essential difference between the perception of such key ideas and what is generally meant in theology by the notion of 'revelation'. While both forms of disclosure have in common the characteristic of being unpredictable and unmanipulable, the disclosure situation in our natural modes of understanding refers to something which just happens. Its causes may be unknowable and, in any case, are irrelevant to the significance of what is disclosed.[4] In religion, in contrast, claims to 'revelation' usually refer to insights which are considered to have been brought about by God's agency, and whose value depends upon their having that origin.[5]

Since, therefore, revelation as traditionally understood crucially differs from our normal reasoning processes, it is justifiable to take up the question of why it is deemed necessary for theological understanding. The standard answer is that deficiencies in human reasoning mean that revelation is needed to augment what reason can discover and, by acting as a divinely given standard of truth, to correct what reason considers that it has discovered. Aquinas, for example, maintains on two counts that our salvation requires that we should have teaching revealed by God as well as what we can determine by philosophical investigations.[6]

His first argument is that since 'God destines us for an end' which is beyond the grasp of our reason, that 'end' must be revealed if people are to secure salvation by directing their thoughts and actions towards it.[7] Other theologians, who have been unhappy at the notion that salvation is restricted to those who have encountered the revelation, nevertheless have agreed that revelation is necessary if people are to apprehend certain truths about God. Locke, for example, holds that it is only by revelation that we can know such matters as that 'part of the angels rebelled against God' because such things are beyond the competence of our rational powers.[8]

Aquinas' second argument is that revelation is needed even for those truths which in principle are within reason's powers. If it were left to human reasoning alone they would be known 'only to a few, and even so after a long time and mixed with many mistakes'.[9] As well as making known what otherwise must be hidden, revelation provides immediate and paradigmatically accurate disclosures of what reason may be able to ascertain. It is to divine revelation and not to 'the innate light of intelligence', then, that we are to look for the ultimate principles of Christian theology and for confirmation of the truth of what reason has discovered.[10] Many theologians share this diffidence about reason and compensating confidence in revelation as the source of clear and certain knowledge of the divine.[11] From the time of Locke, however, the canon of reason has increasingly been considered to be the self-evident basis of credible understanding in theology, as in other areas of thought. Among other things, this means that reason is held to provide the standards against which supposedly revealed knowledge is to be tested.[12] Those who assert that theologians and believers must prefer the disclosures of revelation to the findings of reason where the two conflict[13] have thus come to constitute a cognitive minority which is alienated from the dominant (though not necessarily correct) presupposition of modern thought.

Some theologians, nevertheless, battle against the tide of modern thought. They take a radically sceptical view of reason's competence and maintain that, whatever the status of the canon of reason in other disciplines, all authentic theistic thought must be wholly derived from revelation. According to this view, human reason working on human experiences in and of the world in which human beings find themselves can only tell us about the human. A genuine knowledge of God must come from God.

Ockham, for instance, maintains that unaided human reason cannot prove God's existence except by using an unsatisfactory notion of God: it is only by faith that we can hold that God exists as 'more noble and more perfect' than anything else.[14] In the eighteenth century John Ellis argued against Locke that, since human beings cannot 'ascend to Heaven' by their own powers, our basic ideas of the divine nature must have 'come down from thence' and been imparted to humanity according to its 'Capacities and Understanding' by divine 'Inspiration and Instruction'.[15] A century later Mansel, following Sir William Hamilton's thought, held that as reason cannot produce a coherent concept of God, we must be content to know how God 'wills that we should think of Him' through those self-manifestations which 'He has been pleased' to provide as best suited to our finite understanding.[16] In the twentieth century Barth declared that human attempts to apprehend the reality of God by reason are 'criminal arrogance'.[17] Dogmatics is 'possible only as an act of faith' in which we dutifully explicate what God chooses to make known.[18] More recently T. F. Torrance has written that the subject-matter of theology is 'the living God . . . who communicates Himself to us': unless theologians are 'obedient to the given . . . Word and Act of God', they will only produce 'a dumb idol' which reflects the character of its human makers.[19]

In various ways, then, a number of theologians have argued that revelation is the sole basis for valid theistic understanding. Their view of theology, however, is fundamentally misconceived. It fails to recognize that a 'word' from God can only be recognized and authenticated as such on the basis of some prior understanding of the reality and distinguishing marks of God as its divine revealer. This need to identify a revelation as being from God, however illuminating the contents of the revelation might be, means that revelation cannot satisfactorily be held to provide the basis, let alone be the sole source, of theological understanding. Furthermore, no revealed insights can avoid being conditioned by those who apprehend and use them. What Ellis, Mansel and Barth found as the revealed 'word' seems to readers at later times to have been noticeably influenced by their times. Whether or not it should be held that God reveals the divine nature and will in culturally relative ways so that the divine 'word' is relevant to the contemporary situation, it seems to be clear that even those who assert the revealed origin of all authentic theology show by what they produce that other factors contribute to it.

Revelation may, nevertheless, be held to be essential for theological understanding so far as God is held to have a personal mode of being. According to this argument, the active qualities of the divine can only be perceived a posteriori through some form of revelation. By a priori reasoning theologians may warrantably determine that God is to be thought of formally as intrinsically ultimate, although they must not forget in reaching such a conclusion that their cultural perspectives may significantly distort any a priori judgements which they go on to make about the material expressions of the divine ultimacy. Furthermore, by empirical investigations, theologians may discover some of the material content of God's passive actuality. Since, for example, everything is embraced by the divine experience, observing what in fact happens provides knowledge of a fragment of God's awareness. If we know that Jackie finished a report yesterday afternoon, for example, we also know that God knows this!

But while such knowledge of God may be interesting for certain purposes, it is not of primary and existential interest to believers and theologians. What they want to discover is how God actively responds to what happens. Those who consider that revelation is essential argue that the character determining God's creative responses to the human (and cosmic) situation can only be perceived by identifying events in which God's agency is revealingly displayed. Accordingly, they maintain that theological understanding of a personal God cannot be adequate unless it includes references to events which disclose the material qualities of the personal activity of the divine. This does not mean that the revealing events must have been deliberately intended by the divine to be self-revealing, but that some events are justifiably perceived as displaying the character of divine agency and hence to have this significance.

Six theological responses to the cultural conditioning of revelation

Whatever its importance for theological understanding revelation is limited to what human beings can apprehend. Just as a research worker can only reveal to me the significance of her investigations in terms of my capacity to understand such matters, so what is perceived through revelation, even if it comes from God, is conditioned by the state of those who receive it. Theologians respond to this limitation in various ways. In each case, how revelation is regarded is governed by how the theologian understands the potential of human beings as the receivers, as well as the nature of God as the giver of revelation.

Some theologians hold that divine power may overcome the limitations of human nature. But while God may be considered not to be restricted in what may be made known to individuals, such individuals, even with divine aid in discerning how to express what has been revealed to them, can only communicate it to others so far as those others have the capacity to apprehend what is expressed. Ibn Kaldun, for example, holds that at 'the moment of Revelation' God causes the prophets 'to shed their humanity'. Their task is then, with divine guidance as to its meaning, to translate the content of the revelation so as 'to make it intelligible to the common run of men'.[20] Even with the help of God, however, and even if God has chosen to give the revelation to those whose language is best suited for the purpose,[21] what has been revealed can only be communicated so far as it is communicable in some actual human language. It is a point which Locke emphasizes. Although God may reveal things to an individual which are utterly unknown to natural perception,[22] 'no man inspired by God can by any revelation communicate' anything of this to others except by using 'words and the ordinary ways of conveying our conceptions one to another'.[23] In this way, then, some theologians have tried to avoid limiting what God may present to an individual, while recognizing that the public significance of revelation is restricted to what is generally apprehensible.

Other theologians are more radical. They hold that there can be a significant revelation to an individual only if and so far as that person can grasp it and express it in ideas which are publicly apprehensible. For God to show inapprehensible things to an individual would be cognitively pointless. This position applies hermeneutical principles to divine activity in revelation and to the human grasp of revelation. These hermeneutical principles concern the apprehension of ideas and are at the heart of current debates about the possibility of cross-cultural communication and about the intra-cultural need for indirect language in talk about God. Some theologians in effect envisage God as having to decide which of the ideas already grasped by a people are the most satisfactory for the purpose of revealing to them an understanding of the divine. Revelation is thus held to be restricted at any time to the existing range of people's experience and thought.[24] To put it crudely, if hell be a snow-hole, God could not make it known to people in a culture which had no experience of a temperature of less than 22°C.

Revelation, according to this view, is not only restricted to the range of human ideas. The way in which its recipients grasp any revealed idea is influenced by their previous experience of such matters. If, for example, God is declared to us to be 'a loving Father', our grasp of the content of that revelation will be affected by our experience and appreciation of love and fatherhood, both individually and culturally, even though the revelation may also lead us to develop our notions of them.[25] Faced with the same disclosure, two individuals may vary considerably in grasping its significance because of differences in their experiences and maturity.

A third response to the limitations imposed on revelation by the nature of its recipients holds that it can point people beyond the range of their natural understanding by using items of their experience as symbols or analogies for God. The bounds on the information that can be conveyed by divine disclosure are thus not set by the range of natural understanding, but by the limits of what is available for use as indirect means of communication and of the possibilities of such usage.

Peter Browne, for example, considers that it is 'not reasonable' to expect revelation to include the provision of new faculties or the alteration of existing ones.[26] The suggestion that we might receive knowledge of God, who is utterly unlike all that we experience, by means of a *via negationis* is also rejected: 'if we *Abstract* entirely from *Material* . . . Properties', we are left with nothing by which to form a concept of the divine. The only way that we can conceive of God's nature is by means of the qualities of things with which we are acquainted.[27] Consequently, bearing in mind our 'Infirmity', God does not reveal the divine nature directly but, wishing to make known 'any thing entirely new concerning heavenly Things, he always does it by Analogy with the things of this World'.[28]

The unsatisfactoriness of attempts to use analogy to overcome the limits of human understanding is that the significance of what is revealed, so far as it is analogical, remains unclear. While the analogy ostensively informs us that there is something in God which in some way resembles a specific quality (say love or mercy or wisdom) in human experience, we cannot tell how far it is legitimate to draw inferences from that quality in God which correspond to its implications at the human level. Analogical usage, then, fails to be a means of significant communication if (and so far as) to qualify a predicate as analogical means that it is not possible to determine what follows from its contents in practice.[29] Analogies which have no application only appear to have significant content.

Another attempt to break out of the limits imposed by our natural understanding is by the use of symbolic reference. According to Tillich, God 'infinitely transcends that of which he is the ground'. As a result nothing that is known about finite things can be applied directly to the divine. The proper way to talk about God is symbolically since, while God is 'quite other' than the created world, 'the symbol participates in the reality which is symbolized'.[30] What Tillich means by 'participates' is not completely clear and, as in the case of analogy, the problem is how to determine the significance of religious symbols. We noted in chapter 3 how Urban argued that at least one non-symbolic statement is needed to locate the meaning of symbolic statements about God.[31] Although Tillich makes various attempts to identify such a statement,[32] none of them give a completely satisfactory solution to the problem. He accurately describes his basic position when he acknowledges that, while revelation may provide symbols of that which 'transcends the ordinary context of experience', the latter's essential mysteriousness is not lost 'even when it is revealed'.[33]

It seems, therefore, that the use of indirect means of expression does not provide a way by which revelation may make known information about God which goes beyond the contents of natural understanding. While analogical or symbolic use of a predicate may *point* to its referent being beyond what we can grasp, its available content is limited to what we can perceive of the meaning of that predicate in our understanding. God's wisdom, for example, may transcend all that we know as wisdom but, as such, it is unknowable and unrevealable: as a symbol for the divine nature, 'wisdom' is preserved from vacuity by being limited to what we know as wisdom.

A fourth response to the human restrictions on what can be revealed holds that revelation is not intended to provide information about God, but to instruct us about how we are to consider ourselves in relation to God and how, accordingly, we are to behave. Revelations of God as ruler and as faithful do not give insights into God's intrinsic nature, but tell us that we should regard ourselves as subjects and trust God without hesitation.

Mansel, for example, does not consider that theistic belief is made impossible by the discovery that three notions needed for an adequate concept of God – those of the Cause, the Absolute and the Infinite – are mutually contradictory 'as attributes of one and the same Being'.[34] He interprets our inability to produce a coherent concept of God as showing that we should be 'content with those *regulative* ideas' which God gives us to show 'how He wills that we should think of Him' and to guide our conduct.[35] In modern debates about religious language I. M. Crombie has argued that religion should not be disturbed by the discovery that we cannot know what God is like. Religious concern with God is correctly understood as the practical one of entering 'into relation with him', not a speculative one of gaining information about the divine nature. To meet this concern, revelation provides 'authorized' parables and images which, orientated by natural theology, guide our conduct in ways that are appropriately required of us by the reality of God.[36]

So long as people have some rudimentary idea of God as the ultimate who is to be obeyed, it may be possible to maintain that revelation only discloses principles of conduct which people are to follow as coming from God, although they have no clear understanding of the nature of the divine. Such a position, however, implies that people cannot know that the rules are not the pointless impositions of an arbitrary despot. In practice, most believers are not content to understand their faith in this way. They consider that a great deal of revelation is intended to provide direct information about God. They trust God as a parent, for example, because they interpret revelation as informing them that God is most adequately understood in certain respects as being parent-like. Furthermore, while they may be puzzled by some of the rules given by revelation, they consider that those rules as a whole indicate the kind of conduct that is a proper response to God and, hence, provide some indirect pointers to the divine nature. Mansel admits this: while revealed representations of God have a regulative function, these 'inadequate and human' images 'dimly indicate some corresponding reality in the Divine Nature'.[37] Crombie similarly allows that while revelation may not give a clear view of God, its images are regarded as significant because they are trusted to give 'such knowledge as we need to possess for the foundation of the religious life'.[38] So far, then, as revealed images of God serve as guides to conduct, it is parasitic upon their role as informants, even vague, puzzling and elusive informants, about the nature of God.

Another form of this 'practical' interpretation of revelation holds that, since people are incapable of apprehending the nature of God by their own rational powers, the otherwise unknown God provides models for it taken from human experience which indicate how they ought to relate themselves to the divine. Revelation is thus likened to the attempt of an 'expert' to guide others about what they should do in matters beyond their intellectual competence. Reflection on such situations, however, makes it clear that 'experts' are only identified and trusted to be such, because we have some grounds for judging that they have superior competence. When applied to the case of revelation, this suggests that it cannot credibly be regarded as presenting to us authoritative stories, images and rules, unless some independent knowledge warrants holding its source to be divine and hence trustworthy. Knowledge of God must, therefore, be available prior to any justifiable acceptance of a regulative revelation.

A fifth response to human limitations in matters of revelation claims that, while a revelation is apparently given in terms which human beings can apprehend, divine aid is required to understand its proper application. Grace, not intellectual capacity, determines whether or not we grasp what God wishes to communicate.

Barth, for example, asserts that authentic theological understanding is dependent on God's initiative in revelation to human beings. Maintaining that the theologian 'must always first proceed from God's relationship to man and only then continue with man's relationship to God',[39] he suggests that the correct way to express the nature of theology requires 'the more complex term "Theanthropology" '. Theological understanding is relational. An authentic doctrine of God can only be produced through a living relationship with God, not through abstract thought.[40] Barth does not accept, however, that the contents of what God reveals to human beings is restricted to the range of their natural understanding. Instead, he develops a doctrine of the 'analogia fidei' or 'analogia gratiae' which claims that God infuses fresh or deeper meaning into the ordinary language used in communicating a revelation. The knowledge of God is thus 'completely effected and determined' by God.[41] God controls both the revelation of Godself and also the power to grasp and interpret it correctly. Revelation, furthermore, is not restricted to perceptions of the divine–human relationship: our understanding of reality generally must finally be determined by what God reveals, not by what we discover by natural thought and reasoning.[42]

Revelation is thus treated by Barth as a miracle of illumination realized in and through the Holy Spirit for those chosen to receive it.[43] 'Human language as such' is not to be regarded as a means of revelation since it is not capable of expressing the divine nature: 'neither the object nor the intention converts man's language into hallowed language about God'.[44] On the other hand, divine power may make any natural language – or anything else[45] – a medium by which to convey truth which we could not otherwise grasp. It all depends upon God.

In order to find a way of combining the needs of understanding with adequacy to God, Barth thus holds that revelation is miraculous. Although ordinary words are used to express the 'Word', those to whom the 'Word' is given are enabled to perceive in the words a new content appropriate to the divine. This position is not satisfactory. In the first place, it implies that the existing language used for the supposed communication, by having new contents given to its words, has become a new language. Secondly, since the apprehension of this new language is the result of illumination given by God to chosen individuals, the content of a revelation only expressible in it could not be communicated to others without similar intervention by God. Nor would two persons claiming to have received a revelation expressed through a particular word – say 'mercy' – be able to determine whether what had been communicated to one through that word was the same as had been communicated by means of it to the other. This is to reduce words to ciphers whose contents may alter with each divine use of them. So understood, language in effect ceases to be describable as a means of communicating theological understanding.[46] It is arguable, indeed, that Barth's position on this point is basically incoherent. Where individuals cannot express to others what has been revealed to them because their apprehension of it involves private illumination, it is questionable whether they have apprehended anything in the first place. While percepts without concepts are blind, concepts can only have content, and not be mere labels which convey no information at all about what they label,[47] if they are applicable to a range of states or objects.[48] If they are applicable to only one thing, they do not enable us to grasp what that thing is. Consequently, either God must make the contents of a revelation publicly communicable or nothing is apprehended by anyone.

With his dialectical 'both-and' Barth oscillates between the demands of adequacy, which deny the appropriateness of normal language for expressing divine revelation, and the demands of understanding, which require the use of such language. Unfortunately, it is not possible to satisfy both demands in the way that he suggests. Since, furthermore, it is by language that we understand, the demand of adequacy can never be satisfied if it is correct that revelation cannot be adequately expressed in natural language. Whether or not it is correct, however, cannot be determined because there is no way of judging the inadequacy of language for what is not apprehensible! In spite of Barth's efforts to the contrary, revelation is limited to the range of human thought.

Pannenberg criticizes the Barthian view of revelation as arbitrary and subjective. It does not avoid the quality which it condemns in others.[49] Its presentation of the nature of authentic theological understanding involves a 'retreat into a supranaturalistic wildlife sanctuary'. To make talk about God dependent 'upon the decision of faith' is to presuppose rather than to replace 'Nietzsche's grounding of the truth upon the will'. Pannenberg's positive response is to hold that theologians must establish the significance of their talk about God by showing that it is important for 'the understanding of man',[50] and that as such it is not merely 'a mythological self-interpretation' of the human and of nothing but the human.[51] On the other hand, while Pannenberg does not deny the legitimacy of attempts to validate revelation,[52] he is unhappy with attempts to justify it by appeal to something 'prior to the biblical revelation'. This is held to be derogatory to God and to make the revelation redundant if it shows that what it discloses is independently knowable. Pannenberg therefore argues that God's self-revelation justifies itself by disclosing characteristics of human being and of the world which make sense of what otherwise would be incomprehensible.[53] In particular, the revealed reality of God is discovered to be alone capable of giving a comprehensive understanding of the 'real meaning' of 'the question of human existence' and of its 'definitive answer'.[54]

Pannenberg's view of theological insights derived from revelation illustrates a sixth way in which the limits of revelation may be understood. According to this position the reality of God is apprehensible only so far as it is interpretable as relevant to human existence. It is not just that God gives the definitive answer to the question of human existence: that existence, as perceived by human beings in the light of what revelation discloses about it, determines what can be apprehended of the God so revealed. The content and truth of revelation, as of theistic thought generally, are thus understood in terms of the questions which human being poses about itself.

Bultmann, for example, holds that what we discover through revelation is new understanding of ourselves and of our world. While he agrees with Barth that we cannot know God by natural reason,[55] he takes the unknowability of God radically, to the extent of denying that the divine nature can be revealed to us. God is apprehensible only as the inapprehensible ground and authority for faith.[56] Thus, whereas Barth sees theological understanding as revealed 'The-anthropology', Bultmann holds that what can be and is given by God in revelation is nothing more than the possibility of humanity's authentic self-understanding.[57] Theology is true anthropology and God is revealed only 'as the One who limits man and brings him to authenticity in his limitation'.[58] Properly speaking, revelation does not provide information about human nature: it directly addresses a person 'as an existing individual', producing the existential understanding of obedient response in the present moment.[59]

While Bultmann uses Heideggerian existentialist concepts to describe what faith realizes, he is convinced that, in practice at least, we can understand ourselves and our world correctly only when we view them in terms of a God-enabled relationship to

God.[60] What the transcendent otherness of God in his theism means is that we cannot know the reality of God except as the unknown ultimate 'that determines our existence' and offers us the possibility of authentic being if we respond in faith.[61] If we wish to speak of God, even after divine revelation, we must speak existentially of ourselves.

Bultmann thus considers that human limitations severely restrict what God may reveal. It may be questioned, however, whether a revelation, even if it be of the fundamental character of human existence, can be recognized to be such without some prior knowledge of God as its source and authority. Bultmann rejects such a question as religiously illegitimate. It treats faith and revelation in terms of theoretical knowledge. All we can have is an existential encounter with God to which we must first respond in obedience and only later discern what it means for our self-understanding. Nevertheless, whatever the satisfactoriness or otherwise of Bultmann's position (which in effect treats 'faith in' as prior to 'faith that' rather than as a response to it), it develops another way of responding to the limitations imposed on revelation by the nature of human understanding.

Reflection on revelation shows that its apprehension is conditioned by the intellectual structures of those to whom it is given. Although theologians disagree over the way in which such limitations affect its content, it is clear that revelation does not provide a means by which people may transcend their natural modes of understanding, even if it may disclose insights which they would not in practice have discovered by themselves. Theological understanding based on revelation is as anthropologically conditioned as any other way of understanding.

Revelation as conditioned by current experience

The human conditioning of a revelation does not cease with its initial apprehension. It continues to be communicable to others only to the extent that it can be linked to their current experiences and understanding. Macquarrie puts the point thus: 'the primordial revelation' given through the founder of a faith remains a paradigmatic disclosure of the holy so long as it is 'continually renewed in present experience' in the believing community. Otherwise it becomes a fossilized and 'unintelligible curiosity from the past'.[62] Claims about revelation, that is, lose their significance if and as people come to consider that they no longer can empathetically share in, or imaginatively reconstruct, the original revelatory experiences and find them credible. As a result, the current understanding of those who inherit traditions about revelation in the past affects what they perceive to have happened and how they judge its significance.

Revelatory situations are described by Macquarrie as having 'a gift-like character'. It is felt that in them 'the holy "breaks in" and the movement is from beyond man towards man'.[63] There is no shortage of classical reports of such experiences. Macquarrie cites Moses at the burning bush, the author of *Poimandres* and the theophany of Krishna to Arjuna. From Jacob at Bethel and Paul on the Damascus road to Muhammad receiving the Koran, revelatory insights are described as coming to individuals unexpectedly. References to such experiences, however, will only make sense to people today if they can imagine in terms of their own experiences what such a happening would have been like. They do not need to have experienced anything as dramatic or epochal as Paul or Muhammad, but if they live in an age of divine silence and can find nothing in their experience which significantly, even if faintly, links with the primordial revelation, they are likely either to dismiss references to it as unintelligible or to reinterpret them in terms of their own experiences.

I. T. Ramsey attempts to rehabilitate reports about revelation for a secular age by locating something akin to revelatory happenings in experiences of insight where we speak of 'the penny dropping' and 'the light dawning'. These experiences are not peculiar to religion but occur in a wide range of situations, as, for instance, when a person suddenly realizes why they keep meeting someone on their way to work, or when a scientist perceives the modification which will produce the desired results. What is significant for our purposes here is that Ramsey's attempt at rehabilitation occurs by interpreting revelatory experiences in terms of something which is widely experienced in the secular world and which has no theistic overtones. It replaces the 'given' aspect of revelation by the sense of 'discovery', and so shifts the basic emphasis from God as the 'giver' to people as the 'perceivers' of the insight. Ramsey's treatment of revelation may thus make sense to secular – even secularist – contemporaries, but it is arguably at the cost of losing essential theistic elements. On the other hand, it is also arguable that traditional theistic understanding of revelation no longer makes sense.

Another attempt to show that members of today's secular culture have experiences which allow them to appreciate reports about revelation uses Heidegger's discussion of 'primordial' or 'essential' thinking. This is neither a subject–object nor a subject–subject mode of knowing but a third mode in which, through the waiting and listening of meditation rather than through active enquiry, the self comes to be 'transcended, mastered' and 'known'. According to Macquarrie this 'philosophical thinking . . . which responds to the address of being' is a possibility for everyone. It provides those whose thought is largely formed by the secularism of today's culture with a way of understanding religious references to revelation, so far as these are experiences of being 'seized' in which the 'initiative' is with 'that which is known'.[64]

Macquarrie's case for the possibility of understanding records about revelation given in the past depends (as does Ramsey's) upon the acceptability of his identification of a similar type of experience in contemporary life. If, as may be the case with what he describes here, people do not recognize such experiences as occurring in their own lives, or they accept that the experiences occur but deny their similarity to religious revelations, they must either find other parallels or admit that they do not know how to make sense of reports about revelatory experiences. Furthermore, the authority that is held to belong to revelatory experiences will largely be determined by the authority that is considered to belong to the kind of experiences used to understand them – whether it is the scientific perception of a pattern, or the artistic awareness of depth of meaning, or the acceptance of the word of an expert – and be subject to similar testing procedures.[65] How, therefore, we understand a classical revelation, and what we recognize to be its authority, depends on what we take it to parallel in current experience. Otherwise it is absurd for our experience and its claim for significance an irrational intrusion into our thought. Here again revelation is conditioned by our experience and understanding.

The particularity of a revelation

Collingwood holds that a proposition is to be understood as an answer to a question, whether explicit or implicit, and its original meaning as accordingly governed by the question to which it offers an answer.[66] Applied to revelation this means that apprehension of the content of a revelatory disclosure, if it is to be true to its origin, must be related to the issue that provoked it. A revelation of the divine does not happen in general. While it manifests what is of ultimate concern, it does it to an individual or community with specific problems in a particular culture.[67] Even if what is revealed may be regarded as generally characteristic of the divine, its primary reference is correlative to a single situation and to what was then regarded as known.[68]

Since revelatory insights occur in and for particular situations, great care needs to be taken in referring to them and applying them at other times and places in order to avoid reading into them alien ideas. In cases like those of Jeremiah and Isaiah, it is clear that what was supposedly given was a 'word' for the people at that time.[69] The revelation of the Pentateuchal Law to Moses may claim, in contrast, to be of lasting significance, but examination of it shows at many places that it presupposes social and economic structures that no longer exist. As a result, it is only too easy to distort the original in order to find in it truths that apply to later times. Not infrequently preachers abuse what they hold to be revelatory in order to give it contemporary significance. They proclaim, for example, the destruction of the current enemy, whether Philip of Spain or Hitler or social injustice, by texts that refer to political squabbles in the ancient Near East.[70] It is easy to ridicule some of these uses of supposedly revealed texts, but the misapplications can have appalling results, as when, for instance, the phrase 'compel them to come in' is used to justify persecution of dissenters, and ancient texts about 'the promised land' are held to justify the modern displacement of a people. When, therefore, a revelation given in one age is applied to the situation in another, it must be borne in mind that the original setting both posed the problem to which it is a response, and fixed the structures of understanding in terms of which the response could be intelligibly delivered. Attempts to derive general principles and current applications from ancient revelations are not illegitimate in principle, but those who attempt it must be on the alert against distorting what they find so valuable.

The importance of the original context in determining the meaning of a revelation raises acute problems when theologians seek to determine the significance of the life and teaching of the founder of a faith – whether Moses, Zoroaster, Gotama, Jesus or Muhammad – for these are bound up with the conditions in which that person existed. Later theologians, who seek to perceive their current significance, have the tricky task of distinguishing the ephemeral from the continuingly valid.[71] Although we cannot go further into these fascinating hermeneutical problems, posing them is another reminder that revelation does not provide timeless truths by which understanding is freed from the relativities of past and present situations. What was supposedly given was conditioned by the questions which it was then intended to answer; what is currently regarded as the content of revelatory insights is similarly conditioned by the questions to which it is now seen as offering answers.

Revelation by verbal communication

Traditionally revelation has been thought of as predominantly verbal and aural. Although on occasion God might signify the divine will in other ways,[72] the standard formula is in terms of 'God spoke to . . . and said . . .' If, however, revelation is given in verbal form, its content will not only be limited by the vocabulary and grammar of the language used. What was said will be variously apprehended because of the open-textured character of language[73] and the changing interpretative capacities of those who hear it. This openness applies also, of course, to the texts of sacred scriptures which purport to record what has been revealed, whether or not their choice of words and grammatical structures is held to have been divinely guided.

Words do not have constant and precise meanings, particularly when they are not technical terms. 'Love', for example, covers a range of meanings, while the history of such words as 'democracy', 'liberation' and 'gay' shows that they have significantly changed their connotations. What is apprehended as the meaning of a word is also influenced by the background and education of the person reading it. Sentences and contexts limit the plausible reference-range of the words they use, but they cannot focus out all fuzziness. In the end, as Collingwood puts it, 'what we can get by reading any book is conditioned by what we bring to it'.[74] Even a verbally expressed revelation, then, can only provide a relatively clear means of communication because its apprehension is conditioned by the state of mind of its recipients – both originally and later.

The historical relativity of language also means that the original content of a revelation may not be communicated to another setting simply by repeating the terms in which it was first given. No matter how competent they were in the languages of the Bible, believers in plenary inspiration of its text would not escape the relativities of interpretation and application by reading the Bible in Hebrew and Greek rather than in a translation. To read with understanding is an art which is affected by the culture and development of the reader. It is not a mechanical transfer of equivalents.

Hermeneutical scepticism arising from the looseness of language must not be exaggerated. The fact of intellectual debate is evidence that a great degree of communication seems to be possible.[75] On the other hand, the relativities of language mean that even a verbally given revelation is not free from the conditioning characteristics of human understanding. The words of a command, for instance, may be regarded as divine and absolute in principle, but their significance for application in practice is a matter of human determination and so relative.[76] The history of theology provides many examples of the way in which words held to be divinely given have received different interpretations to make them fit different theological systems: the 'is' of 'This is my body' and the 'on this rock' of Jesus' remark to Peter are notoriously debated cases. The interpretation of other texts has been guided not by theological considerations so much as by what will render them culturally credible. The treatment of the creation narratives in Genesis during the past two centuries illustrates how their accepted meaning has changed to make it cohere with current scientific thought about the origin and development of the world.

Barth rejects such moulding of what is given in revelation. He holds that 'a free theologian' will not feel obliged to follow 'the latest prevailing philosophy', but will allow 'theology' to control 'ontology'.[77] Where the two conflict, as in the case of biblical references to angels, Barth admits that those who follow this approach may find that their theology spoils their philosophy – and *vice versa*.[78] Even then the result will not be free from culturally biassed interpretations. Instead of trying to make the revealed text harmonize with current thought, Barth's 'free' theologians will have used their freedom to employ medieval superstition or Hellenistic demonology as their basis for interpreting the words of revelation. Some culture will still affect their understanding and, as Barth's own theology indicates,[79] the dominant one will be the current one. Even a verbal revelation, then, is conditioned by the cultural situations of its hearers and its readers.

Revelation grasped through events

The view that revelation takes the form of verbal communication has largely been replaced in modern times by the view that it occurs in events. God's will is held to be encountered and perceived through things that happen rather than expressed through a 'word' that is heard or read. There seems, furthermore, to be no limits to the kinds of event in nature and in history that may be an occasion for a disclosure of the divine.[80] Revelation may also be held to be given through experiences in the privacy of an individual's mind. Theologians, however, are generally not very interested in reports about such private acts of awareness, whether they record inner convictions or, more dramatically, visions and auditions which are not publicly shared. There is little evidence by which to check their justifiability, especially in face of psychological studies of the apprehension and interpretation of inner experiences. What are much more interesting to theologians are claims to revelatory insight which arise out of what is publicly observable. In these cases believers discern the divine in or through objects, persons or events which anyone with natural senses may observe. While, however, a religious 'sixth sense' is not required to perceive the empirical locus of revelation, believers additionally see these things in 'a different way', at a different level of understanding, or as signifying 'more' than merely empirical observation notices. Macquarrie describes the revelatory experience as one of perceiving things 'in depth', or as noticing otherwise unnoticed features, or as seeing 'an extra dimension', or as becoming 'aware of the *being* that is *present* and *manifest* in, with, and through' particular persons or things.[81] In each case the grounding phenomenon of the revelation is something in the public world of secular people.

For Christianity the fundamental revelation of God is given in Jesus. In principle, the events of his life, including his teaching, were as open to observation and are as open to historical investigation as those of any other person. The fact that during the past two centuries attempts to write his biography have not reached a finally satisfying conclusion highlights the problematic nature of the evidence, but it does not show that his life was essentially different from that of any other person in the past. The Christian faith, however, does not stop there, for it maintains that through that life insight is gained into the nature and will of God.

Revelation that is considered to be given in and through events is more complex and more susceptible to cultural influences than one that is given in words. Since it is not clear what believers are supposed to find revealed in certain events, for example of the life of Jesus, it is not surprising to find that what they perceive through them largely reflects the intellectual and social commitments[82] with which they approach them. Consider the story of Jesus at the well at Sychar when, being tired, he asked a woman to give him a drink of water (John 4.4ff). Is anything revealed by these aspects of the incident? Presupposing that the divine nature is presented in Jesus, it might be argued that the story shows that Jesus experienced human weariness and thirst, and so the story could be used as evidence against the doctrine of divine impassibility. Or it might be suggested that the story shows God's need of human help: 'he has no hands but our hands.' Others, however, might judge that this part of the story has no revelatory value; it merely provides incidental background to a report of a significant conversation. How, then, are the details of Jesus' life, if they can be ascertained, to be used in Christian thought if that life is its foundational revelation? If all is background, nothing is revealed; if every detail is regarded as revelatory, the story of Jesus will be liable to become an incredible allegory; if only some details are revelatory, which are they and what do they reveal? What actually seems to happen in Christian thought is that revelatory significance is generally found in those parts of the story which can be used to illuminate or support the existing faith of those using it. As a result, theological understanding is not for the most part a product of the revelation so much as the determinant of what is held to be revelatory and of what is so revealed.

It could be objected that the above illustration deals with a trivial part of the Gospel record. The same type of problem, however, occurs with such a central event for Christian understanding as the death of Jesus. What is its revelatory significance? Some see it as the payment of penalties on behalf of others, others as the supreme revelation of divine love, others as a manifestation of God's condemnation of sin, others as an act of propitiation or of sacrifice, others as the revelation of God's patience and forgiveness, and others as the proof of the persistence and depth of Jesus' commitment to his mission. The last of these is compatible with each of the other five theological interpretations, but in its case alone is it possible to indicate how the interpretation may be justified by consideration of the historical records (granted that the Gospels can be treated as containing such material).[83] In contrast, there is no similar, clear procedure for deriving the theological significance of the event from the reports of what occurred. This not only makes it difficult to choose between inconsistent theological interpretations of it: it raises prior questions about why any event is held to reveal the divine, and about why this rather than another event (say, the death of Socrates or of John the Baptist) is to be held to be paradigmatically significant as revelation. Although there seems to be nothing intrinsic to the event which identifies it as revelatory, it is theologically uncomfortable to have to conclude that its revelatory status is something extrinsic which is read into it. As Lessing suggests, the movement from events and reports of events to the theistic insights which they evoke involves a logical type-jump which may only be justified, if it is justifiable at all, by using complex and controversial metaphysical arguments.[84]

The self-revealing activity of God does not occur as an agency in events which can be identified and analysed by differentiation from the other factors involved in them. Karl Rahner, for instance, suggests that the 'divine ground' is not to be apprehended as 'a function in a network of functions'. Instead, every special 'intervention of God in his world' is to be understood as the concrete historical expression of 'that "intervention" in which God . . . has from the outset embedded himself in this world as its self-communicating ground'. Some such view may be required if God is to be properly distinguished from the creation as that which is essentially ultimate. On the other hand, if God is 'not simply an element in the world', and yet is immanently related to it, how are we to discern God as revealed in, through or by events in the world? This problem comes to a climax with the claim that 'God's self-communication' is given 'in an absolute sense' in 'the corporeal, tangible and social dimension' of the event of Jesus.[85]

According to Rahner, it is through the resurrection that such a claim about Jesus is warranted.[86] The problem with this argument – and it is one that has persuaded theologians from Paul to Pannenberg[87] – is that the notion of resurrection (as an event due to God rather than a 'natural' event like the resuscitation of a corpse) does not solve the difficulty, but presents it in an acute form. Leaving aside baffling historical problems of what might have been observed, we are confronted with the puzzle of how a specific event or series of events is to be recognized as having been brought about by divine agency and as revealing the divine. The appeal to the resurrection as a 'miraculous' manifestation of divine agency is no help, unless we are given grounds for distinguishing between surprising events which are merely amazing, and surprising events which are to be attributed to divine agency. The more such grounds are sought, the more it seems that references to Jesus' resurrection are not to an event which proves his revelatory significance, but to an 'event' in which his status was recognized. While this act of recognition was an event, it was a disclosure event and it is misleading to describe it as an 'historical' event,[88] as if it were of the same order of reality as David emerging at En-gedi, or Richard Lionheart disclosing himself to Robin Hood. What is theologically important is not the historicity of events attending the body of the executed Jesus but, in Hans Küng's words, the declaration of 'the first, foundational witnesses . . . that the Crucified is not dead, but lives on and rules forever through and with God'.[89]

While, then, a revelation may be held to be given in this or that series of events, the events themselves, however unusual, do not justify the revelatory insights provoked by them. As Maurice Wiles suggests, people do not discover 'a sense of divine purpose' either in historical events or in patterns in nature because they perceive that their 'effective causation' is due to 'divine activity', but because they see in them clear expressions of 'God's purpose'.[90] How, in that case, do divine purposes come to be so recognized? Partly it happens because this is what our existing theological position predisposes us to discern, and partly (and most importantly in the case of novel insights) it happens because such a recognition of the divine leads us to alter, amend or develop that position in ways that make it a more coherent, comprehensive, adequate and fruitful understanding of the ultimate nature of reality.

If this analysis of revelation be correct, it follows that the traditional distinction between natural and revealed theology is a matter of a difference of source, not of kind: 'natural theology' largely finds its illuminating insights in the world of nature and 'revealed' in historical events. In both cases, however, the insight is evoked by a selection abstracted from nature or history. The resulting insight is then used to make sense of the whole of reality, natural and historical.[91] It should also be noted that according to this understanding of its nature, the justification of a revelatory insight lies in the credibility of the understanding which it produces, not of the claim that it has been directly disclosed by God.

In view of the way in which revelation is constituted, it is not surprising that what is taken to be revelatory more or less confirms existing understanding. It is identified as such in the context of presupposed values and beliefs. Even in those rare classical occurrences of revelation where strikingly novel ways of understanding are evoked, the basic changes come about through a gradual and often spasmodic transformation of thought. Although a paradigm shift may be revolutionary in a particular area, it occurs within a continuing context of overall understanding that is immediately affected by it only to a limited extent. Otherwise the shift would not make sense. Apparently dramatic switches do not mark the sudden emergence of a new pattern of understanding, but a change in allegiance from one more or less developed pattern to another. Revelations are predominantly apprehended on the basis of, and in response to, established ways of understanding and are accordingly conditioned by them.

The cultural and theological conditioning of revelation becomes even less surprising when it is recognized that no identification of an event as revelatory is possible without some prior knowledge of the God who is revealed thereby, whether that knowledge comes from arguments of natural theology or expresses the received wisdom in a community. This is still the case if the evidence used to develop fundamental theology is itself partly provided by the events that, on its basis, are judged to be revelatory. Just as an embassy can be entertained as such only if it is accepted that there is a government who sent it, so Moses could consider the incident at the burning bush to be a divine revelation only because he already believed that there was a God. What happened may have led him to revise his thought about God, but it was only possible for him to apprehend the happening in terms of God's self-manifestation because the notion of God's reality already had some meaning for him.

There is, then, a reciprocal relationship between revelatory insights and existing thought. Although the former may lead to new ways of understanding, existing ways provide the structure of thought which the revelation confirms, amends or replaces. In the first place, while revelation may give fresh, even revolutionary, views of God's nature, it presupposes the reality of God and so cannot demonstrate it. Secondly, existing beliefs play a large part in determining which events are revelatory, what in them is revelatory and how their revelatory content is to be interpreted. What we find disclosed by the Exodus, the fall of Jerusalem, the execution of Jesus and the rise of Islam is affected by the beliefs with which we approach them. Thirdly, however, some events are considered to be revelatory, even paradigmatically so, because they provoke insights which lead to rationally justifiable developments in current beliefs and values. While existing understanding provides the basis for their initial interpretation, they are significantly revelatory because they correct, modify or augment that understanding. Events like the fall of Jerusalem and the death of Jesus, for example, led some to revise their views on what it is to be God's chosen people and the Messiah.

The influence of existing values and beliefs on the apprehension of revelatory events continues so long as they are used in the development of understanding. It is notorious how in the history of Christian thought theologians have interpreted the same reports to support a variety of conflicting theological positions. To some extent the variations result from personal characteristics of the theologians concerned. Just as religious differences between Amos and Hosea may reflect differences in temperament, so personality differences between Wesley and Butler may be partly responsible for their different appreciations of the Christian revelation. Differences in cultural background and presuppositions, however, are the dominant source of variations in the use of what are acknowledged to be revelatory events. And as culture changes, so also does the significance that is found in such events.

The treatment of Jesus in Christian thought illustrates how the same Gospel material has been used to support a wide range of faiths. Some Norsemen were converted to a Christ who brought fire and the sword and whose loyal followers were richly rewarded hereafter.[92] We have already mentioned how Anselm's Christ reflects feudal notions of honour. Luther's Christ belongs to a culture deeply concerned about sin and forgiveness, while Calvin's seems to respond more to the rational mind of the Renaissance. In the eighteenth century Jesus is frequently presented as a teacher of reasonable beliefs and high morality. Harnack's Jesus fits the liberal optimism of the beginning of this century as he stands for righteousness, community and the coming kingdom. Schweitzer's use of eschatological ideas in his presentation of Jesus was more in accord with the sense of impending doom found in other quarters at that time. Teilhard de Chardin found in Christ a cosmic figure appropriate to a scientific age; political radicals have interpreted Jesus as a revolutionary figure; and social radicals have seen him as an exemplar of the life of creative freedom which renounces the inhibitions of tradition. And there are many more images, each of which is presented as the 'true' Jesus and the model for humanity's proper self-understanding.

It is easy to be cynical about the variety of figures of the allegedly historical Jesus, and to hold that they show how theologians mould the reports to produce a Christ which suits them. In reply it may be pointed out that Jesus will only be the Christ figure for each generation, if the records about him can be shown to meet its fundamental needs and understanding. The cultural relativity of portraits of Jesus as the Christ may thus be held to be a mark of his reality as the Christ and not to falsify claims about his revelatory status. At the same time, it has to be admitted that how Jesus is and must be understood as the Christ is strongly conditioned by current culture. The problem for theologians is how to distinguish between a proper apprehension of the reality of God revealed in Jesus as the Christ and an attractive, but basically fictitious, cultural invention.

The effectiveness and human conditioning of revelation

All revelatory insights, then, are culturally conditioned to some extent. Their identification depends upon existing theological thought; their exposition depends upon the situation to which they are to be applied. Nevertheless, in the end what is apprehended as a revelation is what is encountered as making known the character of ultimate reality and as meeting the ultimate questions of human existence. It is a point which Coleridge makes. He says of the inspiration (and so of the revelatory value) of the Bible that 'whatever *finds* me, bears witness for itself that it has proceeded from a Holy Spirit'. The words of the Bible prove themselves to Coleridge because they find him 'at greater depths' of his being than anything else manages to do.[93] Similarly, Pannenberg's remarks about 'the reality of God or of divine power' are particularly true of revelation: it 'can be proven only by its *happening* [*Widerfahrnis*], namely, in that it proves itself powerful within the horizon of current experience of existence'.[94] Here again, however, we find that revelation is not free from human conditioning because it is revelatory for people only as it brings them in their actual situation into an awareness of what is ultimate.

The recognition of the human conditioning of theological understanding derived from revelation is not new. In the seventeenth century Spinoza maintained that revelations were given to the prophets according to their 'individual dispositions and temperament' and existing opinions.[95] To recognize this, however, is not to show that revelatory insights are completely the product of existing values and beliefs. The more important of them contain novel views, even if their novelty is limited by the positions which modify. A revelation may thus challenge existing patterns of thought, although it is unlikely to be taken seriously if it claims to do more than modify them. A purported revelation which totally threatened existing understanding would not seem credible since it would deny all the bases by which its credibility could be assessed. As Jesus reportedly recognized,[96] even with the aid of divine revelation people may only gradually and spasmodically alter their beliefs and arrive at a knowledge of the truth, whatever that may be.[97] The human conditioning of revelation does not prevent new understanding being gained thereby, but it does influence whatever is perceived. Revelation is not a way by which theologians are enabled to prevent their understanding being limited and conditioned by existing structures of thought.

7

Theology and human need

According to 'that Learned and Judicious Divine, Dr Sibs', we may 'be comforted in the certainty of our salvation'. This is because it rests on the unfailing 'grace, and love, and favour' of God and not on our own qualities. The attributes of God are held by him to have practical significance for human destiny. Just as each malady has its corresponding remedy, so God is to be recognized to be 'larger in his helps, than we can be in our diseases and distresses'.[1] These remarks are typical of many sermons and much religious apologetic. They remind us that for most believers the basic role of religion is to provide concrete enhancement and security for their lives. So far as its ideas are concerned, they are important for those believers for whom intellectual satisfaction is a basic need; they are of little concern for those others who are not personally worried about matters of thought.

God and religion perceived as salvific

In a sermon on 'The need of the nineteenth century', preached in 1885, Edwin Hatch emphasizes the difference between a philosophical faith and a religion. In classical times Greek philosophy and literature provided people with a set of beliefs for which they 'might be content to die'. Some of 'the philosophical divines who knew not Christ' developed majestic intellectual systems. But they were a tremendous failure. Their failure showed that 'the soul had a thirst which philosophy could not satisfy'. That thirst is 'the need of God' as one whom people can love and on whom they can lean in their troubles.[2]

Religion is essentially concerned with attempts to secure whole and full lives – 'salvation' – in place of the distorted and threatened existence which people currently find to be theirs. Accordingly, theological understanding, so far as it deals with religion, is not wholly a matter of solving intellectual puzzles about the ultimate nature of reality. Although pinpoint choreography may fascinate theologians who are more interested in ideas than in people, the primary concern of those seeking to understand the object of religious faith is to perceive the character of that which is fundamental to the fullness and wholeness of actual living. Van Der Leeuw thus holds that, while the numinous is important in religion, the varieties of religious practice are united in being quests for power. People look for contact with 'something that is superior' through which they hope 'to elevate life, to enhance its value, to gain for it some deeper and wider meaning'. Religion is about 'deliverance'. It is never directed solely 'towards life as it is given'.[3]

When religion is examined from this point of view, some of the varieties of belief and practice may be seen to be conditioned by different understandings of basic human needs and of their proper satisfactions. This may be illustrated by reference to a number of different perceptions of the nature of God. Luther, as Feuerbach puts it, holds that all the 'divine powers and attributes are for our benefit and welfare; they all abound for us'.[4] Just as Van Der Leeuw sees religion as a response to the human sense of powerlessness, so Hume and Freud, as has been mentioned earlier, see it as humanity's way of dealing with forces that threaten life: God is conceived as a personal power who can be bribed or trusted to be a protector. Others are troubled by guilt and alienation: they regard God as the source of forgiveness and reconciliation. Thus Tillich, influenced by psychological analyses of existential anxiety, presents God as the ground of being that grasps people in their despair about death, meaninglessness and condemnation.[5] For Pannenberg, God is the coming God of the future who provides 'the definitive answer' to the questions posed by the openness and future-orientation of human being.[6] God is interpreted by Harvey Cox in terms of an unconquerable power, 'which inspires and supports the endless struggle for liberation' and healing, and is concerned that people should be free from the chains of the past, the bondages of the present and the fear of the future.[7] Current struggles for social, economic, sexual and political justice have evoked presentations of God as the deliverer of the oppressed, the champion of rights and the promoter of revolution. James Cone describes Black rebellion as a present-day manifestation of divine activity.[8] Mary Daly has called for patriarchal models of God to be replaced by androgynous conceptions which promote the wholeness of human being, while Rosemary Radford Ruether points out that 'a masculinist Christ' is an inadequate image of the saving God who offers 'full human redemption' to all.[9]

These diverse examples illustrate the way in which theistic understanding partly varies according to people's perceptions of their needs.[10] For many, God is only real if the divine is significant for their lives; how they conceive God is likewise affected by their perceptions of what the divine effectively does (or should do) for them. In this respect, religion turns out not to be a wholly disinterested quest for the ultimate truth about reality. To some extent it is conditioned by human self-interest linked to the presumption that the ultimate reality is for human well-being.

As summarized by Feuerbach, Luther finds 'the essence of faith' in the belief that God exists '*for us*' and that 'it is only for our benefit that God is good'.[11] Consciously or unconsciously, this conviction lies at the heart of most theistic faith. God is not only understood from the human standpoint: the primary concern of the divine is assumed to be human flourishing. Although Copernicus expelled the earth from the physical centre of God's universe, theists generally remain confident that human well-being, individually and corporately, is at the centre of God's attention.[12]

The justification of holding that God seeks human well-being

Put baldly, this aspect of theistic belief seems open to question. Is it legitimate for human beings to assume that God is concerned about their welfare? Kierkegaard emphasizes the apparent foolishness of this conviction when he points out that 'Christianity teaches' that each individual 'exists before God, can talk with God any moment he will, sure to be heard by Him'. To compound the absurdity it also claims that God came to the world, suffered and died 'for this man's sake' and 'almost begs and entreats this man to accept the help which is offered him!'[13] On reflection it hardly seems credible to hold that God, properly regarded as God, is intimately interested in the welfare of each of us.

The justifiability of claims about God's salvific concern raises questions about the appropriate models by which to understand the divine–human relationship. Why, for example, is God's relationship to human beings thought to be more akin to a mother's care for her children than to her concern for their pets, or to her interest in the plants in her garden? The values of a person who was as devoted to a hamster or to a rose (sacrificing for its welfare, grieving deeply over its death) as to a child would generally be regarded as unbalanced. If this is so, are people being presumptuous when they regard themselves as more valuable to God than hamsters and roses are to them?[14]

A common reply is that human beings are intrinsically more valuable than pets and plants[15] because they alone are able to have personal relationships with each other and with God. The problem with this argument is the credibility of maintaining that the personal relationships which human beings have with God, granted that they occur, are in comparison decisively more valuable for God than the value for us of our relationships with our pets and plants. It does not seem possible to justify such a claim without begging the question, either by presupposing the special value of human beings to God, or by holding that personal relationships give special significance and then defining such relationships as ones that are peculiar to human beings and to God.

Another defence of claims about God's care for humanity's well-being holds that it follows from the divine ultimacy. This argument leaves open the question of God's attitude to the non-human and does not involve claims about the superiority of the human. It affirms (with Anselm, Descartes and Hartshorne) that God, as ultimate in value, must be thought of as essentially perfect, and then holds that such perfection entails concern for human flourishing. This inference, however, may be disputed. Some (although wrongly) hold that divine perfection is an absolutely impassible state of contemplation of the divine essence. Simply to assert in reply that God's perfection must involve a favourable interest in human flourishing is to beg the question at issue. What would make the argument work is an a priori analysis of the meaning of divine perfection which shows that it has this implication. As was suggested in chapter 4, however, our ability to do this simply by reflecting on the notion of perfection is open to question.

A different argument for the benevolence of God towards humanity claims that only such a concept of the divine satisfies what is meant by 'God'. According to Gordon Kaufman, for example, the concept of God is an imaginative construction of that which both relativizes the world and has 'a humanized and humanizing quality'. This means that the concept of God is 'formulated to a considerable extent in terms of human needs and desires' for what promotes humane values.[16] In defending this position, Kaufman acknowledges that it replaces the traditional view that theology has 'ultimate utility and significance', because it deals with what is ultimately the case by the view that the criterion for theological understanding is 'what is necessary . . . to build a humane order in this world'. The 'true God' is to be conceived as 'the one who truly brings fulfilment to humanity'.[17] Nevertheless, while Kaufman thus produces a criterion for the concept of God which is close to what believers have widely considered (or hoped) to be the case with the divine, he has not succeeded in showing (at least in his writings to date) that the concept significantly corresponds to the ultimate nature of reality. When 'God' is in effect benevolent by definition, the question remains whether what is ultimate is like this.

Although beliefs about a malevolent deity (either as solely supreme or as dualistically in tension with a benevolent deity) do occur,[18] more important intellectually are metaphysically formed beliefs such as neo-Platonism and some of the diverse collection of beliefs referred to as 'deist'. These doubt whether either good-will or evil-will is properly attributable to the ultimate. Beliefs that affirm the practical non-significance of God, however, usually coincide with and probably express a decline in living theistic faith. Where such faith is found, God is almost always assumed to be favourably diposed to humanity,[19] even though it may be difficult to find arguments to defend the claim against critics.

For some being salvific is a contingent quality of the divine, for others it is a necessary quality. Troeltsch suggests that one of the differences between the Protestantism of the Reformation and that of the modern world is the change from the former belief to the latter.[20] Either way, theistic belief is so linked to the saving efficacy of God that it would collapse if it were found that the ultimate reality is indifferent or hostile to human flourishing. As a result, theistic understanding harbours a potential conflict between what is the case and what people hope to be the case.

Nevertheless, whether or not the ultimate actually offers satisfaction to the human desire for wholeness, the concept of God is conditioned by what is held to be salvific. We are now to consider what this means for theological understanding.

The cultural relativity of views of salvation

How people understand their basic needs affects how they conceive of God and salvation. Engels holds that Christianity first established itself and then changed according to the dominant structures of the societies in which it found itself.[21] A similar claim can be made for views of salvation in all religions. Harvey Cox suggests that since primitive people were afraid of the forces of nature, they saw salvation in terms of establishing harmonious relationships with those forces; later the 'compelling concerns' for humanity were connected with death, guilt and history, and accordingly salvation was regarded in terms of 'choice and destiny, rebellion and reconciliation'; today, the primary need for urban people in a technologically dominated world is to find significance for their lives, and so they seek a salvation which deals with the problems of control, 'power, institutional corruption and corporate greed'.[22] Although evidence may be found to show that people of every period have been concerned about all the factors which Cox mentions,[23] his historical generalities have broad credibility. They cohere with the view that the survival, modification or disappearance of a religious faith is not simply the result of investigations into its truth. A more potent influence is its pragmatic relevance and effectiveness for the current condition of humanity. Preachers and apologists soon discover that it is not what is merely true, but the truth that is significant for living today which arouses most people's interest.

According to Tillich, religious symbols cannot be produced or sustained at will. They come to life 'when the situation is ripe for them', and they die when it so changes that they no longer establish an effective correlation between the ultimate and the existential situation of humanity.[24] His position is illustrated by his own exposition of the meaning of salvation. Holding that people seek salvation from three basic types of anxiety – ontic (fate and death), moral (guilt and condemnation) and spiritual (emptiness and meaninglessness) – he argues that the Christian gospel will only be effectively proclaimed when it is shown to answer these fundamental needs. He further suggests that while these different forms of anxiety are always present, the first predominated at the end of ancient civilization, the second at the end of the Middle Ages, and the third in the present at the end of the modern period.[25] This implies that people today are now more likely to respond to a faith which affirms the significance of their lives, than to one that assures them of the remission of their sins. It presumably is the reason for the way that many recent liturgies, in comparison to what Harry Williams has called Cranmer's 'incomparably unchristian liturgy',[26] do not revolve round the issue of confession and absolution. If it be correct that people today are generally not deeply troubled by the question of death,[27] nor by a deep sense of personal guilt,[28] symbols of salvation which refer to such problems are dying, or dead, for them. The 'saviour' that does arouse their interest is the one who meets their actual existential fears about the ultimate pointlessness and valuelessness of human being.

The cultural relativity of people's views of salvation can also be illustrated by comparing Paul's letter to the Colossians with John Wesley's sermon on 'Salvation by faith'. Paul writes to a community which apparently considers that the fundamental problems for their existence are due to demonic forces. Accordingly, he proclaims that the Christian gospel is the message that these terrifying powers have been conquered, and that ultimate control belongs to Christ.[29] This message may still be appropriate in parts of the world where people fear the power of such spirits, but it is not one that may be expected to achieve existential reality for 'enlightened' suburbanites who have benefited from a 'scientific' education. It may only become significant for them when it has been interpreted into another way of thought to such an extent that it has lost its original content. Salvation from demonic control is only important for those who believe in demons.

For Wesley the substance of the gospel is God's offer of salvation 'from original and actual, past and present sin', and so from guilt and fear. Although his remarks do not appear to have made much impact in the University of Oxford, his presentation of the gospel evoked powerful and emotional responses elsewhere in England. When he spoke of 'the propitiation made by the blood' of Christ,[30] it seems that people understood what he was talking about and recognized it as important for their lives. Today this would be much less likely to happen, not just because of unfamiliarity with his language, but even more because of the strangeness of his ideas. On the whole people do not now fear God's wrath towards them as sinners, nor see themselves as needing to be 'rightwised'[31] with an affronted God. Consequently worries about 'righteousness' and 'justification' which were so important to Wesley do not evoke a corresponding concern in them, even when put into supposedly modern terminology.

The view that what is to be understood as salvation differs in essence from culture to culture is rejected by many theologians. They maintain that while the emphases and forms of expression may vary, basically human being does not change. It always has the same needs and is made whole by the same remedy. Barth, for example, holds that twentieth-century people can learn from first-century Paul because the problems and answers in matters of 'grave importance' are the same for both. Barth's hermeneutical concern, therefore, is 'to see through and beyond history' into 'the Eternal

Spirit' of the Bible.[32] Similarly Bultmann, who is sensitive to the different ways in which cultures apprehend and express human existence, considers it legitimate to speak of human existence and its relationship to God in a way that applies to all people. The reality of salvation, as the realization of authentic being, has the same structure in all ages even though the ways of perceiving and expressing its character may change.[33]

Underlying such claims is the hermeneutical principle that all people share a common humanity, and that this provides a bridge across cultural divides. When, therefore, theologians who use this principle, whether consciously or not, affirm that salvation does not essentially differ from culture to culture, they have not proved their point but have presupposed it in their interpretations of the evidence of what people say about salvation. If this principle is questioned, as Gadamer's work suggests that it should be, it becomes more reasonable to consider that different views of salvation may sometimes reflect essentially different perceptions of human nature and its needs.

The way, for example, that ideas of salvation in some cultures are largely to do with answering the problem of death suggests that the fact of death posed an existential problem for people in them. Today this seems not to be the case for a number of people. They accept death as a natural event – regrettable, maybe, but not requiring a salvific solution.[34] For them the major problem of natural life is not that persons may be destroyed in their prime, but that they may remain alive long after their capacity for creative fulfilment has disappeared. What they want is not salvation from death but salvation from the mess of senile decay. If this analysis be correct, the way in which some people perceive the natural basis and needs of human life, and hence the existential situation from which they seek salvation, has essentially, not merely superficially, changed.

When, therefore, theologians hold that all people seek the same salvation, they are probably correct at the purely formal level of holding that all people want to escape whatever prevents their lives from being significant, from flourishing and from being fulfilled. All theists may thus agree in regarding God as saviour as the answer to the basic questions of human existence.[35] Real differences, however, may arise when the nature of those questions is put in material terms. What is meant by significance, flourishing and fulfilment is seen differently in different cultures. As a result, people may disagree about the concrete nature of salvation, and so about the nature and activity of God as saviour. Here again theological understanding is found to be subject to conditioning by the culture in which it appears.[36]

The interaction between 'needs' and 'remedies' in understanding

How people perceive their need of salvation is influenced by the descriptions of salvation which faith offers them as well as by their culturally conditioned self-understanding. This accords with the triadic character of 'needs': 'x' needs 'y' in order to achieve 'z'. In this relationship the goal or purpose ('z') enables us to identify the need ('y'), to see that it is intelligible as a need (because without it we would not achieve 'z'), and to judge that it is morally justifiable (because 'z' is a proper goal to be sought).[37] Accordingly, through its view of God as the ultimate in value, as well as through its view of the goal of human being as that of contributing to the divine experience, theological understanding may lead to revisions of human self-understanding as well as be affected by it. In particular what theologians hold to be the state of salvation – that is, the state which the divine seeks to establish as that in which the ends of human being are fully satisfied – may lead them to modify their view of the proper goals for human being.[38] The relationship between theological understanding of salvation and general human self-understanding is thus reciprocal. By presenting God as the answer, theology may be considered to indicate our real needs in contrast to what we think that they are.

The reciprocal relationship between needs and remedies is not without its dangers. It is possible to promote illusory needs under the pretence of identifying genuine ones. Advertisers are well aware of ways in which illusions about 'needs' can be created by presenting what answers them. In religion 'evangelists' may seek to convict us of sin or to convince us of our insecurity or to appal us at the aimlessness of our lives, whether we are aware of these problems or not, so that they may bring us the glad relief of the message that all is forgiven or is ultimately well or has a point. Sometimes such efforts seem demonic in that the advocates appear more interested in persuading us of their diagnosis and treatment, than in discerning the actual human situation and the divine response to it. We should not, on the other hand, cynically reject everything which is offered to us. Occasionally, by showing us what they have to offer, advertisers identify a real need and a genuine remedy. Accordingly, it is conceivable that in religion we become properly conscious of our condition only as we perceive the character of divine salvation.

Barth, for example, holds that we can only discover the real question posed by our existence when we are confronted by God's answer to it: 'Men call upon God, because, and only because, He has answered before they call.' What evokes 'the tribulation of our existence', though we may not be aware of it, are 'the riches of divine salvation and divine healing' for which we long.[39]

Bultmann similarly holds that through faith a person becomes aware that the ultimate question of human existence contains its own answer, since 'it is only God who can *so* question him'. In knowing the question correctly, an individual becomes aware that 'the answer is primary'.[40] On the other hand, whereas Barth holds that people can only become aware of the correct question of human existence through knowing the answer to it given by revelation, Bultmann considers that it is possible for people to become aware of that question, to some extent, by using their natural understanding.[41] What, in his view, they cannot become aware of apart from God's revelation is the reality of God as the authentic answer to that question. Furthermore, even though natural understanding by itself can achieve a partial grasp of the fundamental question, a full and accurate perception of it depends on revelation.

Those who hold that a correct understanding of the human situation is only obtainable through perceiving the nature of the salvation which God offers may consider that what is thereby apprehended, both about the nature of human being and about the salvific activity of God, will be free from cultural conditioning. If so they are mistaken. Divine indications of the nature of salvation are not able to liberate any resulting understanding from such conditioning.

First, as was noted in the previous chapter, the apprehension of any alleged revelation is not free from cultural conditioning. In the case of salvation what we perceive as God's offer will initially be interpreted in terms of our existing awareness of our needs, even though subsequent reflection on the character of the offer may interact with our self-awareness to modify our appreciation of both. Secondly, the view that our perception of our needs is a product of God's answer may be used to impose mistaken perceptions of that answer and inauthentic needs upon us. Theologians are no more immune than evangelists and advertisers from trying to force their clients into predetermined moulds. Having, for example, decided that salvation is a matter of divine pardon, they may charge those who do not feel guilty with failing to identify their real situation.

At professedly 'evangelical' rallies attempts are thus made to cajole healthy teenagers into feeling guilty about the tensions natural to growing up so as to prepare them to receive the pardon which 'God' thrusts upon them. Thirdly, attempts to determine people's needs by extrapolation from the salvation allegedly offered to them by God may be too abstract and formal to speak significantly to any particular individual. If people are to take seriously the claim that they must have offended God because God offers them reconciliation, they need to know how and where they have caused offence and why God was properly offended at the behaviour. The message of salvation, that is, is effectively grasped when individuals consider concrete aspects of their lives in the light of their understanding of God, not when they are told about salvation in general terms. The way in which they apprehend these concrete aspects, however, will be conditioned to some extent by their culturally moulded values and expectations for human being.

Our apprehension of the nature of the answer of salvation appears, then, to be at least partly conditioned in its material content by our prior grasp of the questions to which it is seen as providing an answer. On the other hand, to conclude that the understanding of the divine answer is wholly determined by the antecedent grasp of the question would render theological understanding open to the charge that characteristics are being foisted onto God in order to meet our supposed needs. Instead of inventing either needs to suit the remedy or a remedy to suit the needs, theologians need to recognize that in the case of God and humanity, the provision of the solution helps to disclose the nature of the question, and the understanding of the question clarifies the content of the answer.

This interdependence of question and answer is used by Tillich as the basis for developing a systematic theology according to what he calls the method of correlation. Rejecting both the attempt of 'self-defying apologetic theology' to derive the answers from the questions posed by the human condition, and that of 'self-defying kerygmatic theology' to elaborate the answer of the gospel message without reference to those existential questions, he seeks to correlate 'questions and answers, situation and message, human existence and divine manifestation'.[42] His theology is thus a working out of the reciprocity between 'the questions implied in human existence' and 'the answers implied in the event of revelation' to the point where question and answer cannot be separated. Each is only properly understood in correlation with the other.[43]

In his writings Tillich accordingly considers the existential problems highlighted in a wide range of contemporary culture and seeks to show how the Christian message is to be interpreted as meeting them. At the same time he indicates how that message gives further insight into those problems. In his judgement theologians produce more penetrating analyses of human existence than is to be found in most philosophies because they use the materials of faith as well as of culture.[44]

Tillich thus resolves the problem of whether the question posed by the human condition, or the answer given by the divine response, has priority for theological understanding by holding that the two are reciprocally related. This accords with our understanding generally. We do not properly grasp a question until we perceive what kind of answer it requires, nor do we properly understand what someone is stating until we recognize what question they are answering.

It must not be overlooked, however, that the divine offer of salvation is necessarily determined by the actual situation of human beings. It is the expression of the divine will for real people. God presumably does not seek to remedy non-existent defects, to restore unbroken relationships, or to pardon offences which have not been committed. So far as it deals with religion as an actual saving faith, theology is therefore anthropologically conditioned in two ways. First, it is conditioned by the human condition as God perceives it and responds to it. This is the authentic reality of the divine–human relationship. Secondly, it is in practice also conditioned by what people consider to be their situation, for it is in terms of this that they expect and interpret salvation.

These two factors may not agree with each other. Theologians, for example, having decided that basically the human role is to obey God, may accordingly regard salvation as primarily a matter of forgiveness for disobedience, whereas it may be that in reality the divine will for humanity is more appropriately to be thought of in terms of creative activity and aesthetic fulfilment and, hence, salvation as a matter of energizing the slothful and stimulating the dull. The human conditioning of theological understanding of salvation is consequently complicated by a third factor. While the divine response is to the actual needs of humanity but our apprehension of it is influenced by our perceptions of those needs, part of the divine response will presumably take into account human self-understanding, including its erroneous views of the human and the divine! It is out of this mix that theological understanding of the relation between God and humanity arises.

Reality and illusion in understanding salvation

Tillich rightly rejects any theological method which seeks to 'derive the answers from the questions'.[45] Such an approach may develop a concept of God which suits human desires but at the cost of losing contact with the reality of God. Since, however, the way in which the human situation is apprehended inescapably influences how salvation is understood, the possibility of such an error raises the question of whether it is possible to establish that claims about God as saviour are not merely wishful projections from that apprehension.

Behind this problem is the perception that a question fixes the reference-range of the answers that can properly be given to it.[46] In the case, for example, of the question 'Will the candidate make a good research-associate?', we can only answer it properly when we know the qualities for being 'a good research-associate' as well as the characteristics of the candidate. Some questions are so open-textured that they cannot be clearly answered until they have been made more precise. To answer, 'Is Llanfairfechan a good place for a holiday?', I need to know what the questioner looks for in a holiday. Other questions can only be satisfactorily answered by correcting their presuppositions – as in the case of, 'Why did you say that in your lecture?', when I never said it. In the case of salvation, theologians are faced with the problem of whether they can recognize the saving activity of God if God provides the kind of salvation which they are not expecting, and with the problem of whether they can distinguish an illusion projected as the answer to existential needs from the real activity of God.

Some views of salvation seem to be basically invented by extrapolating from what people consider will meet their needs. Such critics of religion as Hobbes, Hume and Freud have pointed out how certain notions of God may be regarded as products of a desire for security. Numerous passages in the Old Testament express the belief that God is the defender of the nation, while others call on God for individual protection against assault.[47] In some cases, what is alleged to be the divinely ordained structure of the believing community appears to reflect the sociological needs of the believers,[48] or the political needs of those who govern them. The question that arises is, Are all notions of divine salvations wish-fulfilments? Must the forgiving God be an invention of those who feel guilty, and the God who makes whole a fictitious product of those who feel that their lives are disintegrating? If so, religion is the grand illusion. It may still give considerable comfort so long as its real character is not discovered, but once its nature is recognized its effectiveness will deflate like a punctured tyre.[49]

In considering whether claims about salvation are illusory, it is important to bear in mind that unless a religion offers some form of salvation, it is likely to be largely ignored as irrelevant,[50] or treated merely as a topic for idle thought. Furthermore, because a religious faith may claim to have real value for actual life, it does not follow that in every case it must be an illusion which has no effectiveness besides that induced by belief in it. There are quack remedies whose power depends on faith in them, but there are other drugs which have definite physiological effects whatever the attitude of the person taking them. While, then, testimonies about salvation may only record the self-induced effects of faith in God, they may express what God actually does for, with and in human beings. The problem is how to distinguish which is which, and so how to justify claims about the reality of salvation.

Attempts to find a solution to this problem have to be made on two levels. Initially, it needs to be shown that in practice people do feel forgiven, or liberated, or made whole, as a result of what they take to be divine activity. While, however, such feelings may be genuine experiences, they may be the product of trust in an illusion rather than due to salvific activity by God.[51] The problem of determining which is the case is aggravated by the fact that divine saving activity is not directly perceivable. It is only discernible as a theistic interpretation of certain patterns in events or states of mind, and as an interpretation which non-theists find no persuasive reason to adopt.

At a second level, therefore, those who want to establish the non-illusory basis of claims about salvation are faced with the need to find ways of showing that experiences of salvation are awarenesses of actual changes brought about by God. It is bizarre in this respect to try to conceive of a theological equivalent of the blind test procedures used for checking on the effectiveness of a drug in the treatment of a disease. Most references to salvation concern states of individual self-awareness. It is not at all clear how those involved could distinguish between illusion and reality. The sense of being forgiven, for example, is likely to feel the same whether the individual having the experience is or is not actually forgiven.

Empirical observation may show that individuals act as if they feel forgiven: it cannot show that the feeling is objectively justified. Where, in comparison, references to salvation concern a publicly observable event, its occurrence can be ascertained (e.g., that Robert survived the avalanche, or that the library survived the fire), but there seem to be no tests available which will show that the outcome was due to divine activity rather than to natural causes. Theologians, furthermore, have no way of conducting blind tests. They cannot give true faith to some and false faith to others in order to compare the effects! Divine activity is not open to manipulation by our experimental strategies. How God deals with people and their situations is determined by the divine nature and will, not by their merits, faith or requests. According to Paul that nature is one of unlimited and unlimitable grace;[52] it is also universal in its activity. If, therefore, the divine saving activity follows from the divine nature, it will not be possible to contrast cases where God acts in a saving way with other cases where such activity is withheld. It will only be possible to distinguish between cases where the divine activity is apprehended in faith and those where it is not so apprehended.[53]

Claims about the reality of salvation cannot, therefore, be justified by reference to experience alone. They may be defended, however, as inferences from beliefs about the nature and personal agency of God. On the basis of such beliefs, allegedly falsifying incidents may be interpreted away as only appearing to be such because of a faithlessness which either fails to perceive God's activity or misunderstands its nature. Sceptics may point out that this means that if salvation is an illusion, its illusory nature can never be demonstrated to those who believe that it is a reality. On the other hand, sceptics who deny its reality can equally be charged with seeking immunity from falsification, in the way that they hold that all theistic interpretations of events read into them factors which are not present. In the end no neutral analysis of evidence about the reality of salvation is possible. All assessments to some extent beg the question, both because of the need to interpret the evidence theistically or non-theistically, and because of the essential universality of the divine.

The impossibility of showing the reality of God's saving activity by direct inference from experience means that any significant conclusions about it can only be reached as implications from a general understanding of God's reality, and of the divine relationship to humanity as one of concern for human flourishing and fulfilment.

If such arguments be feasible, they will use references to human experiences only in combination with other considerations that make it reasonable (or not, as the case may be) to hold that the ultimate is savingly effective. While there is no manifestly conclusive way of rebutting the charge that notions of salvation are comforting illusions, produced by people to cope with needs that seem beyond human remedy, the fact that divine answers to some of our needs can be envisaged does not prove they are (all) illusory. Not all needs are never to be really satisfied! If there is a God such as theism conceives, it may well be justifiable to hold that divine activity is salvifically directed towards actualizing values in humanity. Whatever its reality, however, our perception of its concrete nature will never avoid being conditioned to some extent by our understanding of our situation, since it is this that determines what we take to be real, and it is to this that we conceive God as responding.

Doctrinal revisions suggested by the understanding of salvation

The human conditioning of theological understanding is also to be seen in the way that certain doctrines are criticized because they seem to be contrary to the satisfaction of basic human needs. Some theologians, for example, regard doctrines which imply that God may not always act in the best interests of all people as shown thereby to be erroneous. Although they may not explicitly acknowledge it,[54] the intention behind their consequent proposals to revise theological understanding is to make it cohere with what they consider to be the self-evident criterion of human flourishing and fulfilment. Insights into what people are supposed to need from God are thus used to indicate how thought about God should be developed.

Herbert of Cherbury, for example, describes as 'mean, base, and unworthy' of God any doctrine that condemns 'the far greater part' of humanity to 'Eternal Perdition' because it is outside the scope of Christ's redemptive death. Such doctrine contradicts the nature of the *'Universal Divine Providence'*. Accordingly, he identifies a means of salvation – repentance, a good life and worship – by which all may 'come to God'.[55] As a corollary, he rejects various doctrines of atonement on the grounds that their particularism is incompatible with the necessarily universal scope of God's benevolence. Herbert's view that all people need, and that a truly worshipful God will unquestionably provide, means of salvation is thus a norm for his theological understanding.

A similar presupposition lies behind Matthew Tindal's view that the Gospel must be 'a republication of the religion of nature' and so as 'old as the creation'. He considers it impossible to believe that a God who has given to animals 'sufficient means to act for their own preservation' will not have provided all human beings with 'sufficient means to provide for their eternal happiness'. It is equally absurd to suppose that 'an infinitely good & gracious Being', who has given people the ability to perceive 'what does good or hurt to their bodies', will not have given them the power to understand what 'makes for the good of their Souls'.[56] Consequently, if Christianity is the true religion, it must express what God has made available to all from the beginning.[57] The role of the gospel revelation was to re-present this religion in a pure form, uncorrupted by priestcraft. Tindal's classic statement of the so-called 'deist heresy' is thus partly an attempt to work out the significance of the Christian faith, without denying the universality of God's saving activity.

In *The Natural History of Religion* David Hume attacks Christian beliefs on the grounds that they inculcate as moral virtues qualities which are contrary to the best interests of human being. Monotheism is unfavourably compared to polytheism because it advocates 'mortification, penance, humility, and passive suffering' as acceptable to God, whereas the latter favours qualities like 'activity, spirit, courage, magnanimity' and 'love of liberty'.[58] Hume's remarks clearly imply that, while polytheism may be intellectually unacceptable, its practical implications make it preferable to monotheism.

The use of human flourishing as a criterion for criticizing doctrine is stridently employed by Friedrich Nietzsche. He rejoices over the 'death' of the God who poses an overwhelming threat to the freedom and significance of human being. The all-sufficient God of traditional Christian thought, to whom all are deemed accountable, makes human creativity either pointless or impossibly threatened. It is therefore by denying God that 'we redeem the world'.[59] Here again theistic doctrines are condemned because they fail to present God as a real saviour, even though in Nietzsche 'salvation' is envisaged as abundantly creative life in the present world, rather than as harmony with the ultimate hereafter.[60]

Herbert of Cherbury, Tindal, Hume and Nietzsche are not the more obvious advocates of Christian theism! Some reputedly more orthodox Christian theologians, however, similarly argue that ideas about God need to be modified in order to fit what they assume must be the character of God's saving purposes. John Oman, for example, seeks to understand God's relationship to humanity in terms of an all-embracing grace that fosters personal development. God does not act as an irresistible force but by patient persuasion that succours moral growth.[61] A similar concern is expressed in some of Bonhoeffer's later letters when he suggests that God is teaching humanity that it has 'come of age'. Conceptions of God as a powerful *deus ex machina* who may intervene in the world's affairs are mistaken: God helps by the powerlessness and suffering through which humanity learns that its management of its destiny is the fulfilment of God's will.[62] Bonhoeffer thus suggests revisions in theistic understanding to make it conform to his appreciation of the significance of human powers. In the 1960s Harvey Cox's *Secular City* provided a widely read development of this line of thought. Cox interprets the secular culture and autonomy of contemporary urban society as an expression of the divine will for humanity. Talk about God is revised so that it frees people from the 'prejudice of immaturity' and makes them ready 'to accept a larger and freer role in fashioning' human society.[63] Cox's book is a deliberate attempt to understand the divine nature and will in a way which fosters the significance of human achievements.

A similar concern has partly been responsible for leading other contemporary theologians, notably those influenced by process thought, to oppose traditional doctrines of divine impassibility and timelessness. These doctrines are rejected on the grounds that they deny any genuine significance to human existence and are incompatible with notions of God as loving and creative. A 'God' who is in all respects timeless and impassible, so it is argued, could neither be aware of human achievements nor enter into any reciprocal personal relationships with human beings. The concept of God is thus modified on the basis of the presupposition that human existence must be understood as significant and, in particular, as significant for God.[64] William Beardslee has extended the argument to the notion of a future state. On the grounds that it is in creative activity which never ends that human existence both finds its worth and participates in the divine nature, he holds that hope is not to be directed towards a final heavenly state of eternal rest in timeless bliss, but towards the excitement of unceasing creativity. It is to this that human beings are called by God and for which God acts as saviour.[65]

John Hick's advocacy of a 'Copernican revolution' in theology is another example of the way in which the human need of salvation is used as a basis for revising doctrine. Following in the spirit of Herbert of Cherbury and Tindal – and not the less 'Christian' for doing so – Hick holds that while Christianity properly sees itself as 'a way of life and salvation', it should not regard itself as the only possible way. Its self-understanding should take radically seriously the conviction that God is the centre of faith and, as 'universal love, . . . wills the ultimate good . . . of all men'.[66] Hence the different religions of humanity should be regarded as responses to different perceptions of the divine and each as justified so far as it develops the appropriate perception for its cultural situation.[67] Hick thus uses the acceptability of claims about the universality of divine grace to call for a reappraisal of Christian attitudes to other religions.

Attempts to revise theological understanding in order to make it fit what is perceived to be the best interests of humanity raise the question of whether they are applying a legitimate principle of theistic criticism. If it be accepted that this is a proper method, critics of theistic understanding may argue that the concept of God is being shaped according to human needs. As has already been noted, this is not an easy charge to rebut. On the other hand, if this method is held to be an improper one for determining the nature of God, it is implied that God may not be salvific – that the ultimacy of the divine in being, rationality and value does not entail any concern to promote human welfare. What people are likely to find most disturbing about this conclusion is not that it regards salvation as contingent upon divine goodwill, but that it suggests that goodwill towards humanity is not a necessary characteristic of ultimacy in value. While initially this suggestion may seem to follow from a proper recognition of God's autonomy, it raises the question of the possibility of any theological understanding. It does this because it implies that it may not be justifiable to use the human point of view to draw out the material significance of God's ultimacy. To suggest that God should not be assumed to be well disposed towards humanity also threatens the fundamental security sought in religious faith.

Consideration of the notion of God as saviour thus reveals that theological understanding contains, at least potentially, a fundamental tension between the status of God as ultimate reality and the role of God as ultimate remedy. This may be seen as a tension between the metaphysical aspect of theology as an *understanding* of the truth about ultimate reality, and its religious aspect as having to do with *faith* and *hope* by which people may live. Theistic faith, however, rests on the conviction that the two are in principle compatible with each other and in fact coincide. As a result, the salvific aspect of the anthropological conditioning of theological judgements is theistically appropriate. The problem to which we return is that of whether this conviction can be justified, especially since it seems that the material development of the concept of God largely depends upon its acceptance.

One way of putting the problem is to ask if it is incoherent to say either, 'God exists but does not save', or 'A saving God exists but is not ultimate'? There seems to be nothing intrinsically incoherent in the former statement. It holds that the word 'God' refers to something regulatively ultimate, but that so far as its referent is to be envisaged as having purposes, these do not include human flourishing. The concept of God as the unmoved mover whose bliss is to contemplate the divine essence, if taken strictly, appears to describe such a being. While, however, such a God is compatible with a religion that meets certain intellectual and aesthetic needs through the contemplation of ultimate reality and the worship of ultimate values, it is inadequate for those forms of theistic faith which include trust in God as personally active for human good.

The statement that 'A saving God exists but is not ultimate' is much less theologically satisfactory, although not necessarily incoherent. It uses the word 'God' to refer to some power which seeks human flourishing, but which is not the ground of all reality. With such a notion of God it would be possible to develop a henotheistic or a polytheistic theology in which different persons, societies or cultures apply the label 'God' to different realities because they have different perceptions of what is savingly effective. 'God' could thus be identified with the forces that enabled a captive race to be liberated, a nation to attain dominion, an individual to prosper and a religion to survive. If we think of the Exodus, the conquest of Palestine, Solomon and Judaism, we might consider that these forces are mutually compatible – indeed, are monotheistic expressions of one force; if we think of Jews and Muslims, we may well conclude that conflicting powers are identified as 'God'. This illustrates the point that the use of salvation as the primary identifying characteristic of God is theistically unsatisfactory. It contradicts theism's basic self-understanding that theism refers to what is ultimate and regulative – to what Anselm defines as 'that than which a greater cannot be conceived'.

Ultimacy, then, is definitive for theism but salvific characteristics are also generally assumed to be essential qualities of the divine nature. Here again the humanity of believers and theologians is seen to condition their understanding. Unwilling to consider that human being might have no ultimate significance, they bind the notion of God to what saves, while at the same time asserting that what truly saves must be ultimate.

This basic connection between divinity and being salvific can be seen in the identification of Jesus as the Christ in Christian thought. Jesus is recognized to be the Christ (and so as the one in whom God's activity is present), because of his saving efficacy in the experiences of those who encounter him.[68] The recognition of who Jesus is thus depends upon what he does, linked to the presupposition that God is essentially identifiable in events by their saving effectiveness. This mode of recognition not only highlights the way in which religious faith regards God as both ultimate and salvific. It also means that Christian thought does not have to identify the Christ with the Jesus tradition in an exclusive manner. God may, in principle, be perceived in other events that are salvific.[69] Here again it is the human situation and the meeting of its needs which determines where theologians find God and how they understand the divine nature.

Is divine salvation needed today?

It is claimed by some that religious faith and theological understanding are now redundant because people today, especially the self-conscious members of modern Western culture, have no need of God. Humanity is self-sufficient. Whereas, in the past, beliefs about salvation may have given comfort, illusions of divine aid are no longer required. If they manage to do anything significant, it is to distract humanity from finding its own authentic remedies to its problems.

The confidence underlying such claims is largely the result of successes in the natural and human sciences and their technological applications, combined with the spread of moral and educational views which emphasize that individuals and societies are responsible for their future. Particularly in the technologically advanced areas of the world, it is widely considered that salvation is to be sought in the power and potentialities of human beings. Accompanying this belief is a profound loss of interest in God. Power is to be sought from physicists, health from doctors, forgiveness from psychiatrists, social improvements from social scientists, while intellectual puzzles about ultimate reality are 'solved' by 'scientifically' orientated philosophers who attempt to demonstrate that they are nonsensical.[70] The saving God of old is redundant.[71]

Some contemporary theologians, however, have taken up the challenge of these claims. They argue that human beings do not have the resources to meet certain basic needs. Either they find salvation from beyond themselves – in God – or those needs will never be satisfied. Pannenberg, for example, insists that human being has a 'limit-transcending openness' which can find satisfaction only in the infinity of God as the coming 'Lord of the future'.[72] Ogden maintains that human self-understanding fundamentally affirms the worth of individual lives in a way that can only be satisfied in a God who embraces all in the divine being.[73] Classically the view is presented in Augustine's 'Thou hast formed us for Thyself, and our hearts are restless till they find rest in Thee',[74] and in Jesus' response to temptation, 'Man cannot live on bread alone; he lives on every word that God utters'.[75]

Is salvation that comes from God needed? Secular humanity tends to consider that those needs which are answerable are those which can be met by humanity's efforts. Theists, in contrast, argue that human beings are not competent to satisfy their most basic needs by themselves, but that they may find satisfaction in God. The difference between these positions is not a matter of disagreement over the analysis of human nature which can be settled by getting the protagonists to reconsider the evidence from which they reach their conclusions. The difference here is a matter of whole world-views. For one, everything is derived from and its significance is determined by God. For the other, nothing at all has this nature. What this means is that any understanding of God, including the role of being saviour, influences as well as is influenced by the whole world-view in which it is developed. It is not possible to show that human beings need God as saviour simply by examining their nature in an unprejudiced way. What is found to be that nature partly depends on whether or not the examination presupposes that human beings – and their world – have a genuine reference to God. The reference to God is thus implicit in any approach to questions about the need and nature of a saving God, as well as being a possible answer to those questions. On the other hand, what is found when human being is considered is one of the factors which have to be taken into account in deciding whether it is credible to affirm the reality of God as the one to whom all being is referred. Here, as elsewhere in theology, how the evidence is

perceived and what conclusions are drawn from it reciprocally interact.

Reflection on the notion of salvation thus provides further insight
into the nature of theological understanding as both being anthropologically conditioned and reaching its conclusions through complex reasoning processes. On the one hand, human self-
understanding guides how God is understood as saviour; on the
other hand, it is how God is understood as saviour that guides
human self-understanding. Each influences the other. It is not possible to determine which, if either, came first. They mutually and
persistently interact. As a result theological understanding of
salvation is inescapably conditioned by the human nature of those
who produce it.

8

Theology and the completion of understanding

Theology has traditionally been described as 'the queen of the sciences'. For Thomas Stackhouse this meant that it is 'the Perfection of all other Knowledge', and, consequently, that those who study it need to be competent in practically all aspects of 'human learning'.[1] It was a forbidding agenda for a would-be theologian in his day. Today the growth of knowledge makes it impossible for any one person to satisfy it. On the other hand, as we are to consider in this chapter, the current state of knowledge conditions any theology which is intended to be taken seriously as a way of understanding, since it provides data which it must take account of, if not actually incorporate.

The 'queen of the sciences', God and the world

Stackhouse defends the superiority and certainty of theology by the traditional argument. This is based on two premises, that theology expresses what God reveals and that God cannot err.[2] Although the second of these premises, affirmation of the infallibility of divine knowledge, seems unquestionable, the first one, that theology expresses what God reveals, is not convincing. As has been discussed previously, in practice both the identification and the apprehension of the contents of alleged revelations are conditioned by our present ways of thought. Hence references to revelation have to be justified by reasoned arguments rather than accepted as standards for true understanding.

Theology's claim to be the highest form of understanding may, however, be justified on the grounds that its primary object is the ultimate in being, rationality and value.[3] It is concerned with what is final, even though its discussions of it are conditioned and provisional. Furthermore, as Whitehead puts it, religion (and so theology) endeavours to find in 'something permanent and intelligible' that by which it may 'interpret' and order all the details of the experienced world.[4]

The reality of God as ultimate means that theism regards all the different forms of knowledge as partial insights into a coherent, intelligible and purposive whole. Accordingly, it does not only share the general metaphysical view that reality forms a universe rather than a chaotic collection of entities. It also holds that the observable universe neither is an inexplicable brute fact, nor provides an adequate explanation of itself. The reality of God implies that the universe makes sense in terms of a ground and purpose outside itself.[5] Whereas, for example, Russell claims that the word 'universe' does not stand for anything that has a meaning and for which a total explanation can be sought, Copleston as a theist maintains both that it is possible to speak significantly about the universe as a whole, and that it is 'intrinsically unintelligible, apart from the existence of God'. God, as 'His own sufficient reason', is the self-explanatory being in terms of which all else makes sense.[6] Kaufman similarly holds that the concept of God entails that God is creator, that the world receives 'its fundamental forms of order from a source outside of or beyond itself', and that the world is essentially hospitable to the meaning and value of human being.[7]

The ultimacy of God does not mean that theism is a rag-bag aggregate of unconnected principles belonging to autonomous domains of thought. The idea of the divine refers to that which integrates all valid modes of understanding in an intelligible way. While formally, therefore, it corresponds to the metaphysical presupposition of the principle of rationality, theism also maintains that this regulative idea of thought is instantiated in a particular actuality. Belief in the reality of God is accordingly misunderstood when it is regarded as merely belief that a particular personal entity with exceptional powers exists.[8] Properly understood it is seen to be belief in the reality of that which determines the final unity, harmony and meaning of all.[9]

The study of God has consequently to treat God both as an object of investigation, albeit a peculiar one,[10] and as the ground and final goal of all understanding. And since God constitutes the actuality which is the ideal end of all studies as well as something to be studied, these two ways of thinking about God are mutually dependent. Each deals with an aspect of the total reality of God which is affected by and needs to be compatible with how we understand the other. In particular, the way in which God is understood as an actual individual needs to cohere with the status of the divine as the ground of the meaning of reality. This in turn implies that claims about God will only be credible if they are appropriate to the character of what exists. The liberal axiom of the simplicity of religious truth is an illusion.[11]

Granted that the understanding of God and of the world as creation must cohere, it may be argued that the best point to start from is the nature and will of God. Having first discovered 'the mind of the Maker', we may then determine the nature of the creation as the expression of the divine purposes. There is in that case no need to worry about reconciling our view of the world with our understanding of God. Our knowledge of the latter must show what is really the case, whatever may appear to be so. This was the position of those who rejected the empirical observations of Galileo: on the basis of revelation and self-evident principles of the intellect, they 'knew' what must be so and did not see why they should give way to the suspect evidence of the senses.[12] Similarly, John Hutchinson opposed the post-Newtonian views of the natural scientists. On the grounds that only the creator was present at the creation, he argues that we should accept the divine word about what happened. Hence God's revelation through Moses recorded in Genesis is 'the Fountain of all . . . real Knowledge' of what is called 'Nature', and in particular of the 'truth' about 'the Creation and Formation of Matter'.[13]

However desirable in prospect, such a way of understanding is not available to theologians. They are not given a set of unchallengeable judgements about God from which they may deduce what they wish to know about nature and humanity.[14] On the contrary, as they try to perceive the material attributes of God as creator, they need to take into account the empirical character of the world as experienced. In doing this they must bear in mind that what they take to be the nature and significance of what they experience may differ considerably according to the perspectives from which they are assessed. Nevertheless, if their conclusions do not manifestly cohere with a rationally appropriate[15] appreciation of what is generally accepted to be the case in the world,[16] those conclusions will be liable to be rejected as attractive fantasies rather than accepted as a serious way of understanding reality. Because, therefore, the credibility of theology partly depends on its compatibility with reality, and because that reality is widely taken to be a 'given', theological understanding is to be seen as conditioned by how people make sense of their world.[17]

The nature of understanding

The recognition that theologians' judgements are influenced by their understanding of reality must not lead us to overlook the way in which the content of that understanding is itself conditioned by its cultural setting, as well as by the theologians' intellectual development. What, however, is it to 'understand'? The concept may well be a primary one whose meaning is to be grasped through studies of its use. The word itself – like 'substance' – suggests a situation in which a person regards something 'from below' and is able to discern its fundamental structure. But while to understand something is to perceive what it is, it is more than a matter of identification or recognition. We understand objects when we grasp what brought them into being, their relationships with other objects and, where appropriate, the purposes which influenced their production and the uses to which they may be put.[18]

Complete understanding is an unattainable ideal. When we talk of achieving understanding, we normally refer to a situation in which we grasp the intrinsic and extrinsic nature of an object or event in a way that satisfies us: it makes sense to us and there are no serious questions about it which still niggle us.[19] Understanding consequently varies according to the persons involved – their interests, abilities and intellectual development – as well as according to the questions which occur to them. The possible range of these questions and of acceptable answers to them is also relative to the cultural context. What puzzles and what satisfies at one time may not at another.

We can properly understand only what is essentially intelligible. Although in the case of a brute fact (which either is its own justification or 'just is what is so') intelligibility may be limited to identifying the pattern and nature of its constituents and its relations to other objects, in the case of most intelligible objects it includes reasons for their structure and relations being what they are and the identification of the forces that produced them. In some instances these latter aspects of intelligibility warrant the search for intentionality and value which have guided the operation of those forces. Where this is so, things are intelligible because their structure, relations, causes and purposes are determinable. There is, however, a danger that some patterns of apparent intelligibility may be imposed upon what is in those respects unintelligible. Critics of theism, for example, accuse it of intruding personal factors into its explanation of reality as a whole. At less esoteric levels some of the patterns discerned in nature and in history appear to be the result of patterning activity in the minds of their 'discoverers', rather than insights into what is actually the case. In seeking to understand, therefore, investigators must be careful to seek intelligibility that is intrinsic to their objects, as well as intelligibility that properly satisfies their questions.

While intellectual enquiry may initially be stimulated by practical problems, its ultimate aim is the discovery of intelligibility in the form of coherent patterns and orderly connections.[20] Physicists, for example, look for the ordered relationships that make sense of the behaviour of natural processes; historians seek the stories that make sense of sequences of events. Such activity presupposes that its objects are at least internally coherent. This is the minimum requirement of the principle of rationality.[21] What is more significant for this study of the conditioning of theological judgements is that the understanding which is reached is largely determined by the patterns of intelligibility with which its objects are approached. What makes sense to physicists depends upon the mathematical and material models conceivable by them, while historical understanding reflects what historians consider to be the appropriate interpretive structures for events. As a result, what different people take to be an entity or an event that is a proper object for understanding, as well as the ways in which they make sense of it, may vary widely because they approach it with different interests and explanatory commitments.[22]

Understanding, then, is a form of interpretation.[23] It is conditioned by the frames of reference and structures of thought that are available and considered to be appropriate. Things are not given as making sense: they become intelligible as they are apprehended according to what is accepted as a rationally coherent pattern. In this respect the story-form is important. Not only does it enable us to make sense of processes whose patterns are temporally as well as spatially extensive; it also allows us to incorporate ideas of value and purpose. In many cases understanding is finally a matter of being convinced by a story because it seems to tell a coherent, comprehensive and rationally significant tale about the matter under review.[24]

Metaphysicians and theologians are concerned with understanding the fundamental and universal characteristics of reality. Nevertheless, while they presuppose that reality as a whole is a unity with intelligible internal coherence, they have to try to make sense of it in terms of the models of intelligible structures which are available to them. These models are largely derived from their experience and interpretation of things within the universe. Thus they also have to presuppose that the nature of the whole, particularly in its material characteristics, is not utterly unlike that of some of its parts. In view of the way that nature and history seem to be composed of a flux of largely independent sets of objects and events, it is easy to be sceptical about the way in which metaphysicians and theologians thus attempt to combine everything into a coherent pattern or a story. On the other hand, there seems to be no way of showing that the presupposition of an intelligible whole is wrong because things constitute a random and meaningless chaos. Any attempt to prove this would require us so to understand the universe that we could show that it could not possibly have any overall intelligibility. It would not be sufficient to point out that we cannot perceive its intelligibility, because this situation might be due to our intellectual incompetence and not to the intrinsic unintelligibility of the universe. Such a task seems beyond our competence. If, however, atheism (which affirms a negative conclusion about the intelligibility of the totality of things) cannot be proved to be true, neither can theism (which affirms its ultimate intelligibility) be established beyond the challenge of significant doubts. Any attempt to demonstrate the intelligibility of reality will to some extent beg the question by applying rational thought to it.[25] Furthermore, the processiveness of reality renders questionable any claim to grasp its final nature through the evidence of some of its previous and present states.[26]

Success in finding an intelligible story for reality as a whole might, then, be judged only to be a tribute to the imaginative powers of those who produce it. There are, however, grounds for regarding the achievement as having more significance. By showing that reality is amenable to such understanding, its attainment might be held to justify the metaphysical enterprise. Nevertheless, so far as secular metaphysics is concerned, such a story could at best only be held to be a probable discernment of the ultimate nature of things. In practice, the conflicting constituents and complexities of reality make it unlikely that a coherent pattern which fits all that is known and which is fruitful of further insights will be discerned.

Theism, in contrast, does not have in principle to show how every item of the observable character of reality can be seen to fit its story. It may maintain that reality must be finally intelligible, even though in some respects we may be unable to discern its intelligibility, because it derives from the ultimate, personal and rational activity of God.[27] Indeed, the fact that theistic belief in the reality of God guarantees that the universe is essentially intelligible does not entail that that intelligibility must be even partly perceptible by human beings.[28] When, however, theologians seek to avoid problems by thus asserting that the intelligibility of the universe is beyond our grasp, they pay metaphysical compliments to divine transcendence at the cost of undermining the significance of theism. If they are correct, there may be no point in affirming God's being as the ground of all reality. On the other hand, if humanity's duty is to obey God and not to worry about metaphysical insights, the fulfilment of this duty cannot avoid some understanding of the world and of God's creative purposes for it.

Four consequences follow from the theistic view of the relationship between God and the world. The first is that if the concept of God as the ground of the meaning and unity of reality is to be a serious way of understanding reality, it must be compatible with its observable nature. Secondly, arguments for theism from the rational orderliness of the world may presuppose God in their view of the data,[29] although they do show that the theistic interpretation of reality is possible since it fits a way of apprehending its observable character. Thirdly, if theism be correct, God is the integrating apex of all valid ways of understanding reality, and at least some claims about God are fundamental and universal. Fourthly, whatever is held about the purposes and activity of God in and for the world must agree with what actually occurs in it, if they are not to be dismissed as idle fantasies.

'God' as the explanation of reality

Theism maintains that to hold that the cosmos is just what happens to be the case is intellectually unsatisfying. Its reality as a whole does not contain its own sufficient reason. It can only be satisfyingly understood when it is seen to be derived from something that is ontologically prior to and responsible for it. If this 'something' is not itself to demand similar explanation, it must be self-explanatory as that whose existence is 'necessary' – in the sense that the nature of its being is such that it 'it must exist and cannot not-exist'.[30] In that case, it is rationally legitimate to ask for an explanation of the world, but it is not legitimate to ask in the same way for an explanation of the existence of God. Properly understood, that 'God is' is its own explanation whereas all else is ultimately explicable only by reference to God.

Does theism thereby offer a satisfying and adequate explanation of the cosmos or does it merely impose an unintelligible limit on the search for understanding? This is the question of whether the theistic search for ultimate understanding has an attainable goal or is merely a regulative idea. When the nature of explanation is considered, it may seem that only in cases where the lines of explanation lead back to analytically true propositions can we find an explanation which is not and cannot itself be the object of further explanations.[31] In the case of reality, however, it seems that any satisfying explanation has to be in the form of a synthetic proposition describing a prior state of reality of which similar questions may then be asked.[32] The sequence can only finally be ended by discerning a material state of affairs that is *understandable* as intrinsically self-explanatory and an adequate explanation of all else, and is not simply *said* to have this character. Theism can thus justify its claim to provide an ultimate explanation of reality only to the extent that the claim that God's existence is 'necessary' (i.e., that the divine essence entails that the divine existence is underived and indestructible) is an understandable claim.

One attempt to defend the significance of theism as an explanation of reality takes up the point that when questions about some events are answered by such a statement as 'I did it', we are satisfied that there is nothing more to explain. Similarly, it is suggested, when an 'I did it my way' is attributable to God as creator, we have a totally adequate and intelligible explanation of reality which contains its own sufficient reason. This defence collapses once it is realized that an 'I did it' is not necessarily a satisfying end-point of a search for explanation: this reply may instead provoke further lines of questions, for example, questions about 'why' one did it which expect answers in moral and in natural (e.g., physiological and psychological) terms. Such further questioning comes to an end only when we get tired, bored or baffled, rather than because we have reached a point where no further questions can be meaningfully asked. In the case of God, in contrast, we are dealing with that which logically must end all trails for understanding. Hence, reference to God is essentially different from all other modes of explanation, including that of the 'I did it' of human personal actions.

Furthermore, even if we were to be satisfied with an 'I did it' mode of explanation in the case of human personal actions, differences between the human and the divine raise doubts about the usefulness of this explanation for understanding God's relationship to the world. The human 'I' is contingent, limited in power and duration, and only partially aware of its situation and of the consequences of its actions: God is necessary, limited only to what is possible, and aware of all that is knowable. In so far, then, as we grasp the meaning of 'I did it' in terms of our experiences as human persons, it is questionable how far that understanding allows us to apprehend the actions of the necessarily existing 'I', whose sphere of influence is unlimited and whose activity constitutes the final ground of all reality.

Talk about God, then, is logically peculiar. As Whitehead points out,[33] we cannot find anything explanatory of the world simply by considering its totality of actual fact, but neither can we apprehend any such explanation except by reflection on our experiences of constituents of that totality. Explanation, furthermore, finally has to end in the 'ultimate arbitrariness'[34] of a 'That's how it is'. In view of this it may be maintained that theism does not offer more than a formal, but materially empty, 'explanation' of reality when it asserts that God is the self-explanatory explanation of all that is. Unless some material significance can be apprehended in God's ultimacy, the claim that God provides a satisfying explanation for reality turns out to be a formal assertion that whatever is the nature of that which ultimately explains reality, God must have that nature.

Some thinkers have attempted to identify characteristics of the divine which show that theistic explanation of reality is not materially empty. Schelling, for example, holds that the 'primal ground' is 'groundless', 'before all existence' and, as preceding 'all antitheses', absolutely indifferent to them.[35] While difficult to understand, these views had a profound influence on Tillich. He accordingly holds that God, as the ground of being, is prior to the division between subject and object and, as 'beyond essence and existence', is not to be said to 'exist'.[36] As 'the power of being', God is not beside things nor above them but is 'their creative ground, here and now, always and everywhere'.[37] In spite of being elusive and much criticized, Tillich's views on this point are a formidable attempt to make sense of God's ultimacy. More widely known (that is, in theological and philosophical circles) is Aquinas' description of God's reality as one in which 'essence does not differ from existence'. Since God's nature, as 'the primary existent', is 'to exist',[38] God is held to be simple and complete, without parts or accidents.[39] The

'five ways' indicate how God is to be understood as the unchangeable cause of change, the efficient cause which is not an effect, the
being which has its own necessity, the origin of all qualities, and
the ultimate source of order.[40] Although Hartshorne has frequently
expressed unhappiness with much of Aquinas' thought about God's
nature as the ultimate explanation, he acknowledges that Aquinas
is correct in holding, with Aristotle, that 'there is a one-way dependence of worldly things upon God'. This dependence means that
while 'God could have existed though every detail in the world had
been otherwise', nothing could exist 'without God'.[41] God is the
'supreme and indispensable aspect' of creativity whose 'flexibility
is coincident with possibility itself' and whose 'infinite capacity to
respond' means that the divine can 'experience, know, or deal
adequately with quite literally anything'.[42]

Attempts such as these to grasp the nature of the divine as the
ultimate explanation make the point that God is to be conceived as
the ontological, valuative and rational ground of all. It is questionable, however, whether their descriptions of God's necessity, primacy and non-objectivity say little, if anything, more than that God
is not to be regarded as contingent, secondary or a finite object. As
such they have a negative and limiting significance for our understanding of the divine nature, rather than provide a materially significant explanation of reality. When, for example, Tillich holds
that God precedes the division of subject and object, he reminds
his readers that to treat God as an object alongside other objects
will lead to mistaken questions about the divine nature. On the
other hand, no matter how sophisticated our language may appear
to be, we can envisage what lies beyond the distinction of subject
and object only as an object – even if a uniquely peculiar object. In
the end all we can do, granted that Tillich's perception of the divine
ultimacy be correct, is to oscillate between thinking of God as an
object and pointing out that such a way of thinking is in important
respects inappropriate to this mode of being. Similarly, when Hartshorne declares that God is necessary, all-tolerant, omnicapable
and infinitely flexible, we are not given a materially significant conception of God's nature as an adequate explanation of reality, so
much as a declaration of the formal qualities which that nature
must have in order to provide such an explanation, together with a
warning against thinking of God as contingent, subject to destruction and having a limited capacity to respond. These qualities of
the divine are determined by our view of what would satisfy our
search for explanation. Extrapolated from and conditioned by our

basic structures of understanding, they indicate how we are compelled to conceive of God's ultimacy. They may or may not, however, describe its actual nature.[43]

Theology as incorporating all other ways of understanding

Since the concept of God is the concept of that which combines all
ways of understanding reality as parts of a single whole, theism is
not simply another way of interpreting a specific aspect of reality
alongside and of the same logical status as pharmacology, history,
economics, physics and other intellectual disciplines. While it is a
mode of perception which claims, like those others, to give understanding, a fully self-conscious theism also sees itself as the mode
of perception which integrates what is valid in all the others.
Accordingly, it must in principle be understood to comprehend
within its grasp of the all-embracing nature of the divine the insights
perceived by all other, limited ways of perception.

The way in which theistic understanding incorporates the insights
of other disciplines does not only depend upon the structures of
thought available to it which seem appropriate to conceiving the
reality of the divine; it also depends upon what are judged to be
correct insights into the nature of reality. If, therefore, God's
relation to all that is not God is to be materially apprehended and
credible, theological understanding will be conditioned both by the
patterns of thought which we regard as intrinsically intelligible,
and by how we make sense of contingent reality, both natural and
historical.

God as the ground of the being and character of the observable world

As the essentially ultimate ground and final explanation of reality,
God is to be conceived as its creative origin, the focus of its unity
and the source of its meaning. Questions such as 'Why is there
something rather than nothing?' and 'What is the point of it all?',
if answerable at all, are to be answered, according to theism, in
terms of the nature and purposes of the divine.

The notion of God as creator raises problems at a formal level as
well as in relation to the empirical character of reality. If, for
example, the divine perfection is considered to be a state of completion or fulfilment (cf. the Greek τελος, 'telos') which 'lacks no
excellence of any sort',[44] it is in effect a state of being dead, since

there is nothing more to be achieved. In that case, divine creativity seems at best to be an unnecessary and superfluous activity. The solution to this problem lies in recognizing that the notion of an absolute maximum of actual enjoyable value is incoherent (just as is the notion of an actual number which cannot be surpassed), and hence that the divine perfection is partly to be seen in terms of unceasing activity for the attainment and enjoyment of further value.[45]

Another formal problem is whether it makes sense to talk of God as creating 'out of nothing'. The doctrine of *creatio ex nihilo* affirms that even though creatures may use their freedom in ways contrary to the divine will, primarily the divine is not limited in its creative activity by recalcitrant 'stuff' whose bare existence is independent of the divine. While the doctrine is also widely considered to refer to an initial – and incomprehensible – act in which God produced something out of nothing, reflection suggests that just as it is incoherent to think of divine activity as ceasing, since there is no end to the possibility of further achievements of value, so it is incoherent to think of the divine activity – and hence of creativity as its result – as ever having had a beginning. As essentially creative, the divine is to be conceived as always having a creation with which to interact, and divine creativity as an endless process of 'the adjustment of the present' for the sake of novel 'value in the future, immediately or remotely'.[46] In that case, the puzzle for our intellectual imagination is not to conceive how 'something' once appeared out of absolutely 'nothing' at all besides God; it is to conceive how contingent reality is without a beginning although ontologically dependent upon God.

Our main interest in this chapter, however, is not with problems of a formal nature in the concept of God as creator. It is with ways in which empirical considerations influence the concept of God. Whatever the *ordo essendi*, theism will only present a credible understanding of God as the ground and meaning of the real world if its concept of God is compatible with what we discover by experience and reflection to be its actual character. Can theistic understanding satisfy this requirement? Is it possible to conceive the material content of the divine in a way which is appropriate for God's status as the ground and goal of the world as it is found to be?

Initially, the threat posed to theism by modern scientific thought may seem to be one that arises from the amount of material to be considered. Since it is no longer possible to be an omnicompetent polymath, it may be asked whether it is reasonable to expect a theologian to conceive of God as the creative ground of all. In reply it may be pointed out, first, that theologians only have to ensure that their concept of God is compatible with what is the case in reality; secondly, that theology may be undertaken as a corporate activity to which different people contribute their expertise; and, thirdly, that theologians are only concerned with the overall picture of reality developed by scientific understanding. When, for example, theologians consider divine creativity in relation to cosmogenesis, what matters is not whether astro-physicists currently consider that the universe contains millions or billions of galaxies, but that their notion of God's activity is of an appropriate order.

The basic threat to theism posed by scientific understanding lies in its assertion of well-established findings which cannot easily be reconciled with materially significant views of God as creator. Contrary to popular belief, this is not because the findings of the empirical sciences can be used to determine the question of the *existence* of God. In spite of attempts by such as Ray, Newton and Derham, Paley and the authors of the Bridgewater Treatises to use scientific discoveries to prove the reality of God and of counter-arguments from Hume and La Mettrie onwards to use that evidence to disprove it, the existence of God is not an empirical question.[47] Where science does threaten theism is in its mind-boggling claims about the nature of the universe, and in its perception of ways in which the world fails to conform to traditional conceptions of God's activity as its creator. These raise doubts about the possibility of imagining a credible notion of God as creator, and hence about the significance of theism as a way of understanding reality.

If scientific and theistic ways of understanding apparently conflict, it does not necessarily follow that the scientific view must be correct. The story of science contains many examples of apparently well-established views turning out to be mistaken.[48] Theologians, however, need to be cautious before using the possibility of such errors in defence of their own views. Although scientists may tend to prefer established orthodoxies to new insights, the story of theology in the past two centuries contains many embarrassing examples of cases where it now seems clear that the current scientific view was far closer to the truth than the passionately defended view of traditional theology. In 1834, for example, Henry Cole attacked Adam Sedgwick for suggesting in a sermon that the earth was created 'many thousands of years before man'. This 'scripture-prostrating doctrine' is condemned for preferring the evidence of 'little-understood . . . specimens of organic remains' to what scripture declares.[49] Such a defence of theistic understanding is now a curiosity. While geological studies since then have massively revised Sedgwick's theories, they have only increased the implausibility of Cole's objections to them. Scientists may sometimes misunderstand things, but theologians must take seriously what are currently widely accepted hypotheses if their views are to be credible to their contemporaries. The fossils in the rocks may expose the theologian's credulity rather than be a test of the scientist's faith.[50] On the other hand, neither scientists nor theologians must forget that their insights are culturally relative steps along an interesting, but apparently endless, route of revisions. This is the humbling moral of the history of ideas.[51]

Scientific understanding and theological understanding

'Genesis v. Geology' and 'Creation v. Evolution' contests properly belong to a past era. Underlying them, however, was a still unresolved question about the proper extent of scientific knowledge. When, for example, the presuppositions of scientific thought are assumed to apply to all valid ways of understanding, theological claims about purpose, providence and personal freedom may find themselves contradicted by scientific attempts to make sense of the world as a closed, causal nexus governed by physical forces acting according to natural laws (taking into account, where appropriate, the randomness in events in the quantum domain). We are then apparently confronted with incompatible views about the ultimate nature of reality.

According to John Stuart Mill, for example, the 'Law of Causation' applies universally and deterministically: 'invariability of succession' connects 'every consequent' to an antecedent state. From this it follows that if we could know exactly all the forces in the universe at one moment, we could predict all that would subsequently happen, including all personal conduct.[52] Is, however, the causal nexus as universal as Mill here maintains? If it is, then it seems that theistic claims about providential influences and moral claims about personal responsibility refer to what does not exist. What in that case needs to be challenged in order to justify such theistic and moral claims is Mill's assertion that we find 'by observation' that the causal nexus applies 'to every fact in nature'.[53] This is not something which is discovered by scientific investigations: it is the presupposition which directs them. The success of the scientific method indicates that it is an important way to understanding, but it does not show, without begging the question, that it is the only proper way to a complete understanding of reality.[54]

What Mill expresses is the classical self-understanding of the natural sciences. In the twentieth century it has been profoundly modified by the development of quantum theory. According to this development, individual future states at subatomic levels can never be precisely predicted. This is not merely because we are unable in principle to determine precisely the state of all particles at one moment. That this is the case, while correct, may be regarded as a methodological limitation which arises from the fact that any physical investigation into this domain of reality cannot avoid introducing forces, no matter how small, which significantly affect what is being studied. The fundamental reason why the classical view of reality as a total causal nexus has to be revised is that, according to quantum theory, individual subatomic events are significantly anarchic. How each of them will behave is indeterminate because it is random to some degree. Nevertheless, in spite of widespread misconceptions to the contrary, this development of quantum theory does not basically alter the problem of finding a way of understanding the ultimate nature of reality that embraces the valid insights of scientific thought and the legitimate claims of theological thought. That at a certain level of reality physical events are indeterminate according to scientific understanding does not mean that it makes sense to ascribe what happens at any level to divine influence or to the exercise of moral freedom. It just means that what is to be made sense of in a total understanding of reality is more complicated than was previously envisaged.

Conflict between theological understanding and the materialistic determinism of the natural sciences, even when the latter has been modified by quantum theory, is not to be resolved simply by further examination of the 'facts'. While consideration of what thereby appears to be the case will be relevant, the basic issue concerns presuppositions about what constitutes a 'fact' and about how 'events' are to be understood. This discussion is complex and controversial. Theological understanding is under no obligation to submit to imperialistic claims about the universality of the scientific method. It is, however, obliged to show that it presents a valid way of understanding which takes due account of what is discovered by using that method.

Apart from this fundamental methodological problem, the challenge to theistic understanding posed by science arises from the way in which it seems to require a rethinking of parts of that understanding. In the past such challenges have led to changes which, though at first strenuously resisted, are now recognized as valuable advances. Thus, in the case of the interpretation of Genesis, for most of Christian history it was generally accepted without question that the first two chapters, in spite of internal problems,[55] give a literal account of what occurred.[56] When scientific studies began to question this interpretation, many believers felt obliged to affirm the traditional view. In 1827 Bishop George Gleig, for example, condemned 'a sect of philosophical divines' who were using 'fashionable geological theories' as a reason for treating 'the Mosaic account of the Cosmogony' as 'allegorical history, or a mere *mythos*'.[57] Such a rejection of current thought is now seen to have been more likely to have hindered than to have helped those seeking to discern the religious significance of the creation stories.

The problem for theologians today, however, is that developments in scientific understanding seem to have so altered our view of the natural world that a theistic interpretation of it has become implausible. What Gleig and Cole feared from the geology of their time may now have happened. Is it possible to present a credible belief in God as creator in view of the scale and complexity of current scientific understanding of the cosmos? The current problem is not one of biblical interpretation. It concerns the fundamental possibility of an adequate and significant concept of God. As essentially ultimate God must be thought of as creator. Although it is relatively easy to specify what is meant formally by this notion (namely, that God is the purposeful ground of all that is), great difficulties arise when attempts are made to envisage materially what is *actually* referred to when God is described in this way.

Consider, for example, the vastness of the observed cosmos. The psalmist had difficulty in making sense of theism when contemplating the heavens.[58] The cosmos as then perceived was minute compared with the one which astro-physicists now describe. When they write about the numbers of the stars and galaxies, the distances between them, the amounts of energy in them, the significance of the 'red shift' and the ages involved, their statements make formal sense in that the noughts in their figures are countable! On the other hand, what they signify often seems unimaginable – at least I find it impossible to comprehend the material content of such statements as that the observable universe contains approximately a hundred billion (10^{11}) galaxies and 10^{80} particles – and I am not clear what difference 'approximately' makes in such matters. At the other end of the physical scale, the story seems as baffling. When physicists talk about hadrons and leptons, quarks with different 'flavours' and the 'colours' of those flavours, gluons and gravitons, the words fascinate but the reality which they seek to make sense of becomes increasingly elusive. The mysteries of the fundamental particles indicate that even our most familiar objects are basically puzzling.

If, then, we leave aside questions about how anything might be created 'out of nothing' and consider the immensity and complexity of the cosmos, it is questionable if we can envisage what it would be to be the 'creator' of it. It may be comforting to sing, 'He has the whole world in his hands', but there seems to be no way of giving material content to the symbol of having it 'in his hands' which is adequate to the cosmic extent of 'the whole'. On the other hand, if the symbols of creativity are materially empty, it follows that talk about God, except that which is purely formal, is essentially beyond us.[59] In that case theism collapses as a significant way of understanding.

F. R. Tennant suggests that this problem loses its force once it is recognized that theistic understanding is concerned with values and purposes, and that 'magnitude and worth are incommensurable'.[60] In principle this is correct. Consequently, it may be maintained that the significance of the universe in terms of values and purposes is neither enhanced nor diminished because it consists of billions of galaxies rather than a few concentric spheres. On reflection, however, it seems that distinguishing between size and value is unable to overcome the problem posed by scale in establishing the material significance of talk about God as creator. Apart from the questionableness (pointed to, for example, by Hume) of using characteristics observed in one fragment of the universe as a clue to the meaning of the whole, the fundamental difficulty is that of envisaging notions of purpose and value appropriate to the cosmos which would make sense of its being 'created' as an intentional activity, whether this activity is the result of a contingent choice by God or is a necessary (and endless) expression of God's nature. Even if formally we hold that its point is the aesthetic enrichment of the divine experience,[61] the magnitude of the whole makes it impossible to conceive of a mind that would desire and enjoy its overwhelming profusion. While, therefore, Tennant rightly recognizes that the notion of divine creativity is unimaginable,[62] it is also the case that a material grasp of its purpose seems beyond us.

Doubts about the material significance of talk about God as creator also arise from investigations into how the present state of affairs has emerged. The concept of 'creating' is usually held to refer to deliberate activities in which agents produce things which more or less conform to their original intentions. Even if creating involves positing creatures which have their own (limited) freedom, with the result that ensuing productions will be affected by the exercise of that freedom, the concept implies that the purposes and activity of the creator play an important – and generally a decisive – role in determining what eventually appears. In view, however, of the ways in which scientists now consider that things have developed to produce the present state in nature, it is hard to envisage what could be the material significance of talk about God as the 'creator' of what is now the case.

Consider, for example, the fascinating tale which geologists tell about the formation of the present geography of the globe through the effects of great plates drifting across it, volcanoes bursting through its crust, glaciers gouging its surface and slow erosion by the weather. Although the time taken is presumably no problem for God, it is hard to see how these processes, which are explicable in terms of physical laws, are influenced by the divine. In terms of geology the notion of God's creative function is empty. While theists may sing Isaac Watts' lines in praise of God's power 'that made the mountains rise' and 'spread the flowing seas abroad', they are unable to give them any material content which is compatible with the geological evidence.

The study of biology is equally unhappy for attempts to give material content to talk about God as creator. Watts writes of 'the goodness of the Lord' that 'filled the earth with food' and 'formed the creatures', but the way in which evolutionary developments apparently led to the present organic order does not give support to claims that it was guided by an underlying benevolent (or even rational) purpose. By taking a broad view, it is perhaps plausible to regard God as ensuring that the process eventually led from the first protoplasms to beings aware of moral and aesthetic values. Such a view meets our desire to believe that the appearance of human beings was not an accident, but the result of a divine plan. When, however, we consider the details of the process that led to that appearance, the notion of divine creative involvement becomes problematic.

Although the evolutionary process, which has produced the Baluchitherium as well as fleas and human beings, may display an overall movement towards increasing complexity and sensitivity of response, the individual twists and turns composing it do not indicate the consistent working-out of a preconceived purpose. From the perspective of future states, the changes that occurred in it include aberrations and dead-ends, as well as those (relatively very few) which would turn out to be fruitful modifications. The latter are least contentiously perceived as the results of accidental and haphazard alterations, sometimes combined with the affects of a changing environment. So far, then, as it may be possible to affirm any control by a divine creator, it must be seen as compatible with considerable autonomy and chance in the natural order of things.

Furthermore, when the current state of affairs in nature is examined, it is hard to make sense of it as the expression of a benevolent purpose. Although Darwin's theory helped to bring home to people the amoral harshness of a great deal of the natural order, it was not needed to make it evident. Theologians had long puzzled over the presence of 'natural' evil in what they took to be the world which God had made. Mill had suggested that 'men are hanged or imprisoned for doing to one another' what nature does 'every day',[63] and Tennyson had pointed out that the rocks provide evidence of the destruction of types as well as of single lives.[64] Today, reports about shortages of food and fuel, droughts and floods, overpopulation and the spread of disease, the mutation of viruses and the emergence of cancerous tumours support Hume's suggestion that the natural world in which we find ourselves is best understood as the 'rude essay of some infant Deity' or the product of one in dotage.[65]

The problem for theism is that it seems able to affirm the goodness and purposiveness of God as creator only by divorcing the divine from the details of the actual processes of organic development. Suggestions that natural evil is the unintended result of the combination of autonomous laws with accidental coincidences provide theodicies which cast doubt on God's continuing control over developments in nature, whatever the divine responsibility may be for the original pattern. God's benevolence is thereby reconciled with the observed character of the world at the cost of greatly reducing, if not totally eradicating, any material significance in the notion of current divine creativity.

Whitehead, on the other hand, holds that God is intimately involved in every event that comes to be. This is because God influences each concrescing event by presenting it with possibilities between which it decides in its act of partial self-determination. Whitehead consequently holds that where evil is not the result of accidental encounters and non-compossible values, it is the product of creaturely freedom. Furthermore, he considers that evil 'promotes its own elimination by degradation, . . . or by elevation' into something better.[66] Heaven is where what is evil is transmuted into good through the realization of the 'ideal vision' which God has of it.[67] Even if it be possible to entertain Whitehead's basic notion of each concrescing event being influenced by God in making its self-determining decision, his picture of the relation between God and the world is much more attractive when it is viewed from a theocentric position, than when it is considered from the perspective of those who are experiencing evil. It is not obvious that the possibility of future enrichments of aesthetic satisfaction is the ultimate good which justifies the present experiences of agonies which may bring about the dissolution of personal being.

In view of the need to make their understanding compatible with what natural scientists have apparently discovered about the processes of reality, theists face serious problems when they seek to make sense of the notion of God as creator. As amassed and interpreted, the empirical evidence of the character of the natural world not only provides little or no positive indication of God's creative activity; it also makes it difficult to give any significant material content to such a notion. Although this does not show that theism is invalid, it does suggest that traditional views of God as the active ground of reality may need considerable modification if theological understanding is to be adequate and credible.

The humanities and theological understanding

Investigations into the human aspects of reality also produce insights which theists need to take into account if they are to present a credible way of understanding reality as a whole. What, for example, theological understanding affirms about the nature and destiny of human being needs to accord with what anthropological studies discover about that being. If theologians hold that humanity is made 'in the image of God', how they understand that doctrine needs to be compatible with what psychologists and philosophers, as well as common sense, find to be its character. If they maintain that all people recognize the binding force of certain moral values, they must be able to show that this fits what is observed. If they make claims about a universal 'natural religion', their descriptions must agree with what happens in practice – or they will be liable to be judged as unconvincing as eighteenth-century fantasies about 'the noble savage'.[68]

At present the greatest impact of anthropological studies upon theistic understanding probably comes from the study of other religions. For most of its existence each tradition in Jewish-Christian-Islamic theism has largely been content to prove, to its own satisfaction, its superiority to the other two while agreeing with them in dismissing all other religions as largely unworthy of notice.[69] Today, the cultural isolation and imperialism which encouraged such views no longer exist. Having emerged from the *de facto* henotheisms of tribe, nation and culture, theistic understanding has now to come to terms with the implications of monotheism in its appreciation of other faiths. This not only means abandoning the grosser forms of religious imperialism,[70] it also involves taking radically seriously the possibility that the universality of God's benevolent concern for humanity may mean that other faiths contain authentic insights into the divine. As anthropological studies make known the contents of other faiths and show how they give security, understanding and orientation to their adherents, theists need to find ways of evaluating those contents without either presuming an unwarrantable finality for their own beliefs,[71] or ignoring the question of truth by assuming that all beliefs can be combined in some religious Chop Suey – a recipe for an unholy mess![72]

Hermeneutics is another intellectual discipline whose findings must be taken seriously by theologians, especially by those who refer to what they regard as sacred scriptures and authoritative credal formulae.[73] Claims about the meaning of such texts will only be credible if they are in harmony with what is discovered to be the nature of interpretation appropriate to such materials. Although historical and literary studies in the past three centuries have undermined the classical view of the Bible's divine status,[74] most Christians still consider that theological understanding must be at least consistent with,[75] if not actually derived from, the Bible if it is to be authentically Christian.[76] Schubert Ogden, for example, states that the canon of Scripture has a unique place among the normative elements in the Christian tradition. In particular, in spite of the difficulties of applying it, 'agreement with the witness of the apostles that is contained in the New Testament is still the primary test of the appropriateness of theological statements'.[77] The problem with this view of the criterion for theological understanding is that some hermeneutical studies suggest that texts may not have the kind of independence which allows them to serve as satisfactory norms for theological judgements.

The basic problem does not lie in the fact that biblical studies have shown the human origin and quality of the canonical texts. This has not deterred theologians from continuing to regard the materials as fundamental for their understanding.[78] It lies in the hermeneutical claim that what is discerned as the content of a text is significantly affected by the standpoint, presuppositions and problems of its readers. The meaning of a passage is not a constant which can serve as an objective doctrinal standard. It varies according to who is reading it and for what purposes. Thus George Steiner reminds his readers that no two people ever mean 'exactly the same thing when they use the same words',[79] while Hans-Georg Gadamer stresses the need to recognize the historical conditionedness of all understanding.[80] E. D. Hirsch, on the other hand, challenges what he regards as the extreme historicism of Gadamer's position. He holds that an act of interpretation is to be and can be distinguished from an act of authorship by taking into account the author's original perspective as well as that of the interpreter.[81] Paul Ricoeur, however, while agreeing that it is possible to defend the superiority of one interpretation to another,[82] denies that either the intentions of the author or the state of the original addressee of the text provide norms for governing its interpretation: it is the form of the text as discerned by structural analysis that justifies claims to an objective grasp of its meaning.[83]

This hermeneutical debate, whose resolution is far from settled (as debates about deconstructionism indicate), raises fundamental questions about the nature of understanding, as well as about the significance of texts. What is clear is that theological views on the interpretation, use and authority of texts, and especially of canonical texts such as the Bible, must come to terms with its established insights. Theologians who scorn Joseph Smith's claim to magic spectacles for reading the Book of Mormon should be careful that their uses of the Bible and other documents do not presuppose a similarly unconvincing pretence to be able to avoid the conditions of understanding revealed by hermeneutical studies.

The study of history is another discipline whose findings condition credible theistic understanding of reality. Even though historical reality is a product of an interaction between the examined evidence and the historian's point of view, historical investigations into what happened in the past provide theologians with materials which test the practical significance of theistic understanding. The evidence of the past may reveal, for example, that what theologians have considered, perhaps for sound reasons, to be the case does not correspond with what actually occurs. Where this is so, their understanding must be revised to make it compatible with reality.

Historical studies, for example, limit what may reasonably be held about authorities for faith and belief. If authority is located in the teaching of Jesus, what is claimed on the basis of that teaching needs to agree with what historical investigations discover to have been its contents,[84] and to take account of such discrepancies as may be established between what Jesus taught, say, about the imminent end of history and the fact that it did not thus end. Whatever is maintained about the inspiration and authority of the Bible likewise needs to be compatible with what the evidence indicates about the construction, selection and transmission of its contents.

In a similar way, claims about the authority of the church and of its ministry will only be credible if they accord with how those bodies have actually behaved. It is not easy, for instance, to regard the credal decisions of Councils of the Church as divinely inspired guides to orthodoxy when the skullduggery involved in reaching those decisions is disclosed.[85] In some cases the ecclesiastical mafia may have acted subtly, but at Ephesus in 449 the agreement of many bishops was apparently extorted by the use of threats and actual physical violence.[86] It may be that God's will is done and truth established by such methods – or that closer inspection of the evidence supports a different view of what occurred – but theological claims about the authority of the decisions reached by ecclesiastical assemblies must not be divorced from the evidence of their procedures.

Likewise, whatever is maintained about the authority of individuals holding certain positions within the church, such as popes and bishops, must be consistent with what they have actually said and done. Newman, for example, upset the Roman hierarchy when he showed that historical evidence indicates that what happened on certain occasions does not wholly accord with some beliefs about the divinely guided role of the bishops and, supremely, of the bishop of Rome.[87] Nevertheless, however unpalatable the evidence, what has happened cannot be changed. Either, then, those beliefs must be amended to make them accord with the evidence, or it must be admitted that they do not entail anything about the actual conduct of bishops and so are in practice empty. As for non-episcopal churches, the evidence of history seems not so much to have falsified as to have prevented the birth of parallel doctrines. The behaviour of congregational assemblies and of connexional conferences has meant that most theologians have not been tempted to claim for them the divine superintendence that may seem possible at first sight in the case of august prelates!

All doctrines which claim to have empirical significance are open to empirical falsification. When Manning asserts the harmonious continuity of doctrine as it has developed in the church,[88] his claim must be authenticated by *historians* of thought, not determined a priori by theologians, if it is to be credible. Beliefs about divine activity in the world, about God as 'Lord of History', about the effectiveness of prayer and about the saving interventions and retributive justice of God must be reconciled with what has actually happened in the past, if they are to be taken seriously. Affirmations about the gifts of the Spirit need to be squared with the obtuseness of theologians!

In the end, that is, theological understanding can only justify its claim to present an understanding of reality if that understanding coheres with the evidence of what is the case. Otherwise it will seem to be a matter of escapist fantasizing.

The relativity of theological understanding

The view that theological understanding should be influenced by what has been discovered about the world may be criticized on the grounds that theism deals with God, and that the insights into the character of the world which are appropriate to it follow from its understanding of God as creator. As has already been noted, this argument is unconvincing. God is not given as a reality from which truths about the world may be extrapolated. On the contrary, apprehension of God's material qualities depends to a large extent on how the divine may be understood as that in terms of which all things make sense and, hence, as conditioned by our knowledge of them.

Where current views about the world clash with existing theistic beliefs, theologians may try to defend the latter by pointing out that what is currently held to be the nature of reality is moulded by our standpoints and structures of understanding. As Walgrave puts it, 'human thought is always thought and not reality' and 'the "perspectiveness" of human thinking is incurable'.[89] Accordingly, it may be argued that where supposed knowledge apparently contradicts a particular theistic belief, it may be discountable since from a different perspective reality might appear compatible with that belief. Alternatively, the supposed knowledge may be simply incorrect – human judgements are fallible.

These points are valid in principle. It is equally true, however, that what we understand to be the nature of God is similarly relative and corrigible. To assert the relativity of our knowledge of the world in order to preserve a theological doctrine which clashes with it is to treat one piece of our understanding as absolute and another as relative. This is not a justifiable procedure, especially when it is recognized that what is being protected in this way is itself partly the product of moulding by previous states of knowledge. It is unwarrantable to give absolute status to the forms of understanding which conditioned our inherited doctrines. Such an attitude destroys rather than preserves theism. It divorces the way in which we understand God from our apprehension of the world in which we find ourselves. Theism will only be credible when it is conditioned by, and hence relative to, our understanding of everything else.

Some theologians, on the other hand, are too uncritical in their readiness to espouse the latest movements in thought. Theistic understanding also ceases to be credible if it appears to alter with every ephemeral change in intellectual fashion. Modern classics like Barth's *Epistle to the Romans* and Bonhoeffer's *Letters and Papers from Prison* may have been more conditioned by their immediate context than later reflection would approve. In recent decades the frenetic desire of some theologians to be 'with it' has spawned secular theologies, urban theologies, folk theologies, liberation theologies, black theologies, third-world theologies, theologies of hope, feminist theologies, theologies of humour, carnal theologies, aesthetic theologies, and doubtless more. As a result it is not surprising that doubts have been expressed about whether theology should be taken seriously. Nevertheless, while it is easy to ridicule theological bandwaggonery, these movements have shown that inherited forms of theological thought are not to be regarded as permanently binding. Even the foundations of theistic understanding are subject to critical inspection, alteration and possible replacement. What must also be appreciated is that the current views which are found so stimulating are also relative and may be quickly superseded.

Theologians should, therefore, neither be too quick to adopt novel forms of thought nor too ready to ignore them. Existing theories and novel ones should be probed to determine which offer the more credible forms of understanding. Whichever are adopted, the theology that is conditioned by them will be inescapably relative. This is the price of appropriateness to the currently real world. Because it attempts to make sense of God as the ground and goal of reality, theological understanding cannot avoid being both relative to what makes sense for human thought and provisional with respect to the current state of knowledge.

Theological understanding is also conditioned by the currently available structures of coherent combination which provide ways of linking together in a fruitful manner what are perceived to be the formal characteristics of deity and the material qualities of the world. Although theologians may occasionally be able to imagine new modes of combination, these structures of combination are generally limited to the range of models provided by their culture. From this range they select those that seem most suitable for the matters in hand. The criteria for 'suitability' are fittingness and illuminating power: the ideal model is one which copes with all the materials neatly (cf. the quality of 'elegance' in mathematical proofs), and which opens up new insights by the way in which it relates them to each other.

Developments in theological understanding in this respect have generally been through the transference and adaptation of structures developed elsewhere. Donald Schon has explored how insights may occur through using ways of understanding developed in one realm as metaphors to illuminate problematic situations in other realms. [90] I. T. Ramsey and I. G. Barbour have explored how this may happen in theology by considering the role of models in thought.[91]

Ever since the seminal studies of Edwin Hatch and Adolf Harnack, theologians have had to recognize the way in which current culture moulds the formulation of beliefs. Whether or not this influence has been considered beneficial, it has primarily been seen in terms of the effects of specific concepts on the contents of individual beliefs.[92] What needs to be recognized is that the influence extends to the whole pattern of faith. As Hatch puts it, 'the religion of a given race at a given time is relative to the whole mental attitude of that time'.[93] This perception forms the crucial insight behind Bultmann's demythologizing programme and Gadamer's questions about the possibility of understanding the products of another culture. In attempting to make sense of the whole of reality, theistic understanding is conditioned by the fundamental notions in contemporary culture which determine what may be regarded as 'making sense'.

Theistic understanding is thus conditioned in one respect by the way in which certain ideas are considered to identify what is ultimate for thought. As was suggested in chapter 4, however, at least some of the ideas which offer completion to understanding may themselves be culturally relative. In the self-consciously culturally diverse world of today, theists have therefore not only to try to perceive how theism makes sense of reality as a whole. They also have to select, consciously or unconsciously, the metaphysical principles which are to structure their understanding.

The way in which this basic choice affects theological understanding can be seen in some recent presentations of the Christian faith. While most theologians are somewhat eclectic in their use of such principles, it can on the whole be held that F. R. Tennant indicates how belief in God may look from an empirical standpoint and R. B. Braithwaite from an empiricist one; Paul van Buren, Harvey Cox and Don Cupitt have offered different versions of a secular interpretation of Christianity; Fritz Buri presents an existentialist view of it; John Cobb expounds it from the perspective of process thought; and Gordon Kaufman works out a constructionist view of it. The list of varieties is not endless, but such surveys as Macquarrie's *Twentieth-Century Religious Thought* show that it is considerable. Many of the important differences between theologians arise primarily because their thought is governed by different appreciations of what constitutes ultimacy in the case of theological understanding, not because they are dealing with different faiths.

Theistic understanding is also conditioned by what are acceptable as coherent structures and by what, in contrast, are dismissed as mutually incompatible combinations of concepts. It is in this respect that, as has been noted, Hartshorne's perception of the dipolar structure of the concept of God may be judged to provide a major advance in the appreciation of the logic of talk about God. According to traditional analyses of the concepts involved, it is self-contradictory to speak of an absolute God as creating, a necessary God as merciful, an eternal God as acting and an unchanging God as caring. By carefully distinguishing, however, between the abstract qualities of divine 'existence' and the concrete qualities of divine 'actuality', Hartshorne shows that theologians may not have been perverse in persisting to speak of God in these ways. A more adequate ('dipolar') analysis of the concepts indicates that it is possible to conceive coherently of God as both properly divine and personally agential.[94]

In many cases these two forms of cultural conditioning affect understanding unconsciously. People think as their culture teaches them to think and regard its limits and structures as self-evident. Nevertheless, if theologians are to avoid being culturally blinkered – and expressing their thought in a culturally imperialistic way – they must try to become conscious of the basically different ways in which people understand reality. Whereas such attempts will reveal the difficulties of inter-cultural communication, they will also make possible the richer understanding that comes from the extension of intellectual horizons.

The character of decisions about structures of understanding

Faced with different possible structures of understanding, can theologians choose rationally which to use? This is a critical question. The selection determines what makes sense to them, their conceptions of divine ultimacy, and the ways in which their theological understanding will be affected by their knowledge of the world.

In most cases any such 'choice' is basically determined by the plausibility structures inherent in the theologian's culture. These provide criteria of intellectual acceptability which strongly bias decisions in favour of that culture's way of understanding. As a result thinkers cannot avoid reflecting to some extent the basic views of the society in which they have been brought up, and most of them are not aware of any need to examine this conditioning. The alternative for them seems to be to convert to another culture. By replacing their previous plausibility structures with those of another culture, they may undergo 'a radical transformation . . . on all levels of living' as a result of which they apprehend, value and relate to things in a new way.[95]

Such a conversion may be regarded as an essentially arational decision. Because all warrants must be internal to some system of understanding, it may be maintained that there can be no reasons to justify replacing one fundamental and overall way of understanding by another. H. A. Hodges, for example, holds that since each of the 'alternative patterns of life and thought' is 'unintelligible from the standpoint of the others', there can be 'no logical road' from one to another. In his view people only begin to accept the views of another structure of understanding because they have already, albeit unconsciously, begun to adopt its standpoint.[96]

The situation, however, may not be as intellectually bleak as the above remarks suggest. It is arguable that all attempts at understanding presuppose certain criteria which are not wholly culturally relative. One criterion is that of conceptual coherence. A structure of understanding that uses contradictory notions is not merely inferior to one that does not have such problems: so far as the contradictory elements are concerned it appears to be meaningless. Another criterion is that of self-consistency: a structure of understanding that is at least consistent according to its own rules is to be judged superior to one that is not.[97] A third test is that of universal applicability. Although each structure of understanding may seem to make itself universal by determining what its adherents can acknowledge as being the case, in practice some appear to be unable to cope adequately with certain matters. Hodges himself suggests an 'existential' test: that structure is to be preferred which opens up new 'possibilities of life, experience, and activity'.[98] Two other possible tests are fittingness (or elegance) and pragmatic effectiveness. A structure of understanding which involves fewer eccentricities and which 'produces the goods' is generally deemed superior to one that does not.

As materially understood and applied in practice, these criteria for selecting and justifying a structure of understanding are likely to be culturally conditioned. Furthermore, any choice of a structure of understanding will be limited to a choice among the options that are known. This fundamental conditioning of all thought, however, does not mean that we should be deeply sceptical about all claims to understanding. The existence of at least formal agreement about the criteria suggests that the choice of a structure of understanding, so far as it is a matter of choice, may be rationally justifiable to a significant extent. Even if judgements about structures and about understanding based on those structures are conditioned by their perspectives, they may still provide valuable perceptions of aspects of their objects. What their conditionality implies is not that genuine understanding is unobtainable, but that assumptions about its incorrigibility and absoluteness are unwarranted. Consequently, just as Engels recognizes the revolutionary significance of the Hegelian view that 'all acquired knowledge . . . is conditioned by the circumstances in which it was acquired', so theologians should recognize that in their understanding nothing is to be treated as 'final, absolute, sacred'.[99] What for good reasons may be held to be true about God, at the same time must be recognized to be relative to the context in which it is perceived.

Attempts to show the rational justifiability of theistic understanding may, however, be criticized as fundamentally mistaken. Under the influence of existentialist thought, it may be argued that theism is about the meaning of life, and that choice here is a matter of decision rather than of intellectual evaluation. The 'meaning' of reality is the meaning that we give to it by our decisions about it.[100]

In reply it is to be pointed out that we cannot simply choose what reality is like. Otherwise every infant would have the moon. Certain things in reality are given. We may choose so far as we have freedom concerning them and how we choose may affect our appreciation of them, but we cannot choose concerning their givenness for us. Karl Britton argues that this includes the intrinsic values which determine the meaning of life. We can only decide whether or not we shall act according to what is discovered to be the case, valuatively as well as factually.[101] Similarly Rudolf Bultmann, while stressing the role of responsible decision, holds that Christian existence is a matter of faithful response to the address of Christ as 'the ever-present Lord'.[102] Such a decision, however, is only possible for those who have first understood the nature and significance of Christ's address as given to them.

Our decisions, then, may produce results which develop and revise our understanding but they do not fundamentally constitute it. Understanding both is a prerequisite (and in this sense a 'condition') of our decisions and conditions them. It is itself a product of the interaction between reality as we apprehend it through structures of understanding, whether culturally inherited or chosen, and those structures themselves. Furthermore, our acceptance or choice of those structures is itself influenced by the raw givenness of what is there. When, therefore, we seek to analyse how understanding happens, we find that it involves a reciprocal interplay of choices made in response to apparent facts, and those facts as themselves perceived in the light of the choices. What emerges thus seems to be on the whole self-evidently valid: the choices affect what are taken to be reasons, and the reasons what are to be seen as proper choices. In this way a culture develops an apparently coherent and comprehensive way of understanding that moulds our judgements about everything, including about God and the world.

Theological understanding and hope for the future

Finally, in this discussion of theology as understanding, it should be noted that some theologians maintain that expressions of theistic faith are misunderstood when they are treated as matters of understanding what is the case. In their view the proper role of faith is to provide inspiring descriptions of what might be the case, ought to be the case and perhaps will be the case. These descriptions are to provoke discontent with the present and to evoke hope for the future.

The advocates of this view of theological understanding present it in various ways. William Dean asserts that theology is to produce 'intellectual commotion' by giving an interpretation of life which contrasts 'aesthetically' with the commonly accepted notions of its present reality.[103] It should, therefore, prefer the stance of wonder and play to that of the manipulating technologist.[104] Harvey Cox has emphasized the roles of festivity (in celebrating the past) and fantasy (in anticipating the future) in the images presented in theology.[105] José Míguez Bonino speaks of the revolutionary function of theology in 'kindling imagination' as it talks of a love which opens up new human possibilities and acts as a horizon of hope.[106]

The principle behind this view of theological understanding has some validity. Faith in a personally caring and active God cannot allow the present state of affairs to be the end of the story. If the current world is all that God offers, theism may be the way to understand the ultimate nature of things but it will not evoke a faith. The brave will protest: they will 'curse God and die'.[107] In the face of how things now are, theistic faith must include a future dimension. It must tell stories that give hope[108] by showing that the reality of the divine as the ultimate in value is practically significant for what will eventually come to be.

Nevertheless, while theism is more than a synthesis of our notions of God with our present knowledge of the world, its understanding will give a genuine basis for hope and creativity only if it is grounded in the ultimate structure of reality as it actually exists. Otherwise it will be open to rejection as a collection of day-dreams, and its thought as a travesty of understanding. In order to justify its claim to express a genuine basis for hope, it needs to relate its apprehension of the divine to the world as we now find it to be, and only then to infer from that understanding what the world is to become. In this way it will establish its credibility and warrant the hopes that are derived from it.

At the same time it also needs to be recognized that theism is seeking ultimate understanding from insights established in a realm which is not the final state of things. As Wolfhart Pannenberg and Jürgen Moltmann have pointed out, in certain important respects God is the coming God of the future.[109] Even so, that God cannot be known except through understanding the God of the world's past and present states. Only by studying what has happened and is happening will Christian theologians, for example, be able to justify the claim that there is 'a principle of creative transformation everywhere at work' whose image, as John Cobb puts it, is best perceived in the image of Christ as the Logos of God.[110]

Theological understanding, then, is both properly described as 'the queen of the sciences' and is conditioned by the various ways of understanding which it is to integrate and make sense of in a meaningful whole. Lest, however, this role should tempt theologians to pride, we should remember Voltaire's comment on their activity. After describing the many things which a certain 'real theologian' had to know and arrange, Voltaire said that the difficulty of 'throwing a little light into so much obscurity often discouraged him'. Nevertheless the theologian persisted; finally he 'arrived at knowledge unknown to most of his confrères'. The result was that 'the more he grew truly learned, the more he distrusted everything he knew . . and at his death, he confessed he had squandered his life uselessly'.[111] The 'queen of the sciences' may be a temptress who makes fools of those who fall for her!

9

Conclusion

Although this study has attempted to probe a number of the fundamental characteristics of theological understanding, I do not pretend that it is comprehensive. Among the issues which remain to be investigated are the ways in which sacred texts, historical reports and tradition are used as sources for the discernment, formulation and development of that understanding. Such studies need to consider the aims and canons of interpretation, the justifiability of seeking insights into the nature and will of God from such sources, and the criteria for distinguishing authentic from inauthentic developments in the cumulative tradition which constitutes a religious faith. Enquiries also need to be made into the relationship between religious belief and morality. Furthermore, since religious faith is a public as well as a private matter, a comprehensive view of theological understanding should examine the social dynamics involved in the processes of thought within religious groups, and the ways in which faith expresses a society's fundamental presuppositions as well as an individual's self-understanding. Another factor in understanding which deserves attention is the role of imagination in the production and development of thought, as well as in the inspiration of creatively novel insights. Without imagination rationality may be confined to dull, mechanical routines; with it rationality may share in the creativity of the divine.

Theological understanding, however, is not a matter of inventing fictions, whether comforting, challenging, entertaining or harmonizing. It is a matter of 'understanding' – of apprehending the ultimate truth about reality. Accordingly, a complete survey of theology must consider the possibility, necessity, nature and appropriate forms of truth-testing in such matters. Such investigations will involve consideration of the relationship between the actual character of reality and the theistic story or stories by which we seek, from our human and culturally conditioned perspectives, to make sense of that character. If, furthermore, God is to be held to be essentially – and so persistently – creative, any such considerations will need to take into account the implications of divine activity for reality as a dynamically creative process which neither has been nor ever will be completed. Truth-testing in such processive, elusive and fundamental matters is not easy nor uncomplicated.

Readers who start with this final chapter to discover what the book is about may now wonder what has been achieved if so much remains to be done! Leaving, then, the agenda for future studies, what have the previous chapters established? Basically they have sought to illuminate six ways in which theological understanding is unavoidably conditioned by the human nature and cultural setting of those who undertake it.

The first two chapters having indicated the scope and basic concepts of the study, chapter 3 considers how the notion of God is in some respects a cosmic projection of human nature. The problem for theologians is how to find ways of speaking significantly of God in an anthropomorphic and relative manner which is not unacceptably crude and inappropriate to the divine. The following chapter investigates how the ultimacy of the divine means that it must be presented as that which actualizes in its own being the regulative ideas of thought. As such, God's nature is more that in terms of which we understand than that which is understandable. It must be recognized, however, that what is considered to be regulative and what is properly so may not be identical.

Chapters 5 and 6 discuss the significance of references to experience and revelation in theology. What is experienced and what is apprehended as revealed are conditioned both by the cultural context and by individual personal characteristics. While, therefore, such references may be regarded as ways to grasp the nature of the divine, the insights that are found thereby are the product of the interaction of human, culturally relative ways of perceiving and conceiving with what may be 'given' to us.

The following chapter considers how theological understanding is influenced by what people consider to be their fundamental needs, and by how the divine is envisaged as able to provide 'salvation' as a remedy for those needs. Here again the understanding is conditioned by the human and the socio-historical situations of those who seek to identify the human question and the divine answer. Finally, chapter 8 investigates how theology seeks completion in understanding and, as a result, is affected by the current state of the different forms of knowledge as it attempts to unite them in a coherent whole. As a result, while theological understanding aims to identify the nature of the ultimate which makes sense of all reality, what in practice it is able to achieve is relative to the ways in which the sciences and the humanities currently understand the structure and constituents of reality.

Unexpectedly, the long period during which this study has been maturing has made it more rather than less appropriate to the current debate about Christian belief. What started off as a personal interest in discovering how theologians reached their conclusions, and what developed as an attempt to interest students in such matters, has ceased to appear to be a rather old-fashioned form of philosophical theology. In the heady atmosphere of the radical and liberation theologies, when 'praxis' was acclaimed as the dominant concern, investigations into the foundations of theological understanding and, in particular, attempts to discover the possibility of authentic claims about God seemed to many to be dull, impractical and unexcitingly metaphysical. In the past few years, however, the theological scene in Western Christendom has been marked by a conservative backlash against attempts to develop theological understanding in ways that will reduce its 'credibility gap' with modern thought.

In Roman Catholicism official disapproval has been indicated in the case of Hans Küng – a rather old-fashioned liberal to some Protestant eyes – and, to a lesser extent, that of Edward Schillebeeckx. In Britain theologians such as Maurice Wiles, John Hick, Dennis Nineham and David Jenkins have been the targets of widespread and prolonged (and often what may be kindly described as 'uninformed' but more accurately as 'obscurantist') criticisms. Elsewhere in the world attempts by theological conservatives (who fail to recognize that what they seek to preserve is a stage in a living tradition which has long left it behind) to turn back the intellectual clock in theology (or to prevent it moving forward synchronously with the secular world) have had some success. In the USA the Moral Majority movement has been wound up by its founder on the grounds that its work has been done; 'creationism' is presented in schools, colleges and the media as a credible idea of God's relation to the world.

The result, however, is that the faith and theological understanding represented by these movements, no matter how strong they may be within the circle of fellow-believers, appear – with good reason – incredible to those aware of the world described by modern thought and lived in by self-consciously contemporary people. The result is that faith and theological understanding are increasingly taken seriously only in the self-imposed ghettos of blinkered believers. It is a situation which Bultmann described in his programmatic essay in 1941 when he wrote that, 'We cannot use electric light and radios and . . . avail ourselves of modern medical and clinical means and at the same time believe in the spirit and wonder world of the New Testament. And if we suppose that we can do so ourselves, we must be clear that we can represent this as the attitude of Christian faith only by making the Christian proclamation unintelligible and impossible for our contemporaries'.[1] Half a century later it is even more important that those interested in theistic faith and theological understanding should recognize the truth of Bultmann's warning.

The critics of modern developments in theological understanding typically display an awesome confidence in their perception of the nature and will of God and of the content of true doctrine. They seem to find the heart of theological understanding clear, definite and unproblematic. Their comments leave the impression that the history of theological thought since the Enlightenment has never happened, and remind me of the text, 'They have the answers because they have not understood the problem'!

It cannot be pretended that this study provides many, if any, answers to the question of the contents of a rationally credible theistic faith.[2] What it tries to do is to identify and investigate some of the basic problems for theological understanding which arise from the anthropological factors that condition it. Thereby it shows the fundamental implausibility of the view of theology apparently assumed by many of the critics of its recent developments. Theological understanding – whether at the level of the religious 'man in the street' or in a sophisticated, self-critical system – is conditioned by the human, social, cultural and individual setting of those who produce it. It is not surprising, therefore, that those who are struggling to make sense of theism today find their task difficult and complicated.

Some hold that because theological understanding is found to be such a decidedly human activity, it ought to be abandoned, at least so far as it professes to be theistic in its basic reference. While, therefore, 'believing' critics of recent developments talk as if their theological understanding is divinely given and protected, unbelieving critics suggest that its basic theistic references offer only confused, confusing and unwarrantable expressions of human fantasies. What, then, is to be done? If we are unwilling to be

credulous in our acceptance of theological understanding, is it possible to avoid dismissing its theistic concerns as incredible? This is
our final question. It is the question of the propriety of theology so
far as it seeks to be basically theistic, and a question which is most
effectively answered by pointing to the problem posed by the
character of human being to which theism is presented as an answer.

To those who argue that recognition of 'the anthropological
character of theology' indicates that we should give up the misleading obscurities of the pseudo-subject 'theology' and concentrate
on the study of 'anthropology' as such, it may be replied that no
anthropology will be finally satisfying which does not include a
theistic reference. Human being is such that its fundamental self-
understanding cannot make sense unless we perceive that it finds
its ground and goal in the divine. Karl Rahner, for example,
suggests that human being is to be perceived as orientated 'towards
the absolute mystery' which is God: 'at this point theology and
anthropology necessarily become one'.[3] H. Richard Niebuhr maintains that 'without belief in something that makes life worth living
men cannot exist', and that the conviction of 'the infinite worth of
persons' only makes sense in terms of 'some infinite being to whom
they are valuable'.[4] Schubert Ogden similarly argues that our fundamental 'confidence in the final worth of our existence' only makes
sense in terms of the reality of God who is 'the ground' of this
'confidence'.[5] According to Hans Küng, human being is characterized by 'a *fundamental trust*, a basic confidence' in reality as 'in
principle meaningful, valuable, actual', in spite of its uncertainties
and ambiguities. Belief in God is thus to be understood as belief
in the being of that which provides 'an ultimate reason, support,
meaning' for reality as a whole.[6]

These analyses of human being may be mistaken, or there may
be nothing which grounds the human confidence in the significance
of being. If so, reality will be finally absurd and affirmations of its
meaning pious delusions. Nevertheless, whatever the final outcome
may be (an outcome which is unlikely ever to be finally determined), the questions posed by human being cannot be dismissed
as non-existent or trivial. So far as attempts are made to establish
adequate answers to them, theological understanding will have a
legitimate – and important – place among the topics for human
enquiry. Those who embark on such an enquiry, however, must
take into account its unavoidable limitations. The recognition of its

proper character does not make theistic understanding impossible or pointless, but it does make clear that it is human understanding and unavoidably conditioned by its anthropological character.

Notes

1 Introduction to a study of theology

1 Immanuel Kant, *Critique of Pure Reason*, translated by N. K. Smith, London: Macmillan, 1933, pp. 664f; cf. p. 29: 'I have therefore found it necessary to deny *knowledge*, in order to make room for *faith*.'

2 Cf. 'No science can escape from the conditions imposed by the constitution of the thinking mind which gives it birth': E. Troeltsch, *Protestantism and Progress*, translated by W. Montgomery, London: Williams and Norgate, 1912, p. 1.

3 I have considered aspects of the question of the truth of theological judgements in 'Can the theologian legitimately try to answer the question: is the Christian faith true?', *The Expository Times*, August 1973, pp. 325–9; 'Theistic verification' in D. Kirkpatrick (ed.), *The Living God*, Nashville: Abingdon Press, 1971, pp. 47–75; ' "Credo ut intelligam" as the method of theology and of its verification' in *Die Wirkungsgeschichte Anselms von Canterbury*, *Analecta Anselmiana*, Frankfurt-on-Main: Minerva, 1975, volume IV part 1, pp. 111–29; 'Lessing's ditch revisited' in R. H. Preston (ed.), *Theology and Change*, London: SCM Press, 1975, pp. 78–103.

4 P. F. Strawson outlines this distinction in relation to metaphysics thus: 'Descriptive metaphysics is content to describe the actual structure of our thought about the world, revisionary metaphysics is concerned to produce a better structure.' He adds that probably no metaphysician has been 'both in intention and effect, wholly the one thing or the other'. *Individuals*, London: Methuen, 1964, p. 9.

5 Note that in this case both the 'circle' and the 'legitimacy' of the criticism are determined by their agreement with the views of the theologians concerned.

6 As Wolfhart Pannenberg puts it, they will have made the threat of rational examination 'an occasion to retreat into a supranaturalistic wildlife sanctuary': *Basic Questions in Theology*, 3 vols., London: SCM Press, 1970, 1971, 1973, volume II, p. 192.

7 C. Gunton, for example, has criticized two contemporary theological thinkers for their 'confidence in the power of reason alone' and their failure to recognize 'the need for grace' in theological work: 'The knowledge of God according to two process theologians: a twentieth-century agnosticism', *Religious Studies*, 11, 1, March 1975, p. 96.

201

8 See Kant, *Critique of Pure Reason*, p. 32; cf. also Luke 14. 28ff.
9 Karl Barth, 'The gift of freedom' in *The Humanity of God*, London: Collins, 1967, p. 90; cf. *Church Dogmatics*, I/1, translated by G. T. Thomson, Edinburgh: T. and T. Clark, 1936, p. 1.
10 Barth, 'The gift of freedom', p. 91.
11 Barth, *Church Dogmatics*, I/1, p. 12; cf. 'we can attain to an *intelligere* worthy of the name only if we give to the *credere* our full and exclusive attention and confidence . . . And faith relates to the witness of Holy Scripture. It is the willingness and readiness to be taught from this source, referring all the concern for *intelligere* to what is said there, because there we have to do with the origin and object of faith . . . And faith is the confidence that what we are told there is grounded in itself, i.e., in the matter attested': *Church Dogmatics*, III/3, translated by G. W. Bromiley and R. J. Ehrlich, Edinburgh: T. and T. Clark, 1961, p. 403; cf. pp. 372f, 379ff.
12 Contrary to what is often maintained, this view does not coincide with Anselm's own use of the Augustinian principle of 'credo ut intelligam': see Pailin, ' "Credo ut intelligam" as the method of theology.'
13 Thomas F. Torrance, *Theological Science*, Oxford: Oxford University Press, 1969, pp. 26f; cf. also *Space, Time and Incarnation*, Oxford: Oxford University Press, 1969, pp. 1, 17, 19ff.
14 Cf. the protests of Torrance in *Theological Science*, pp. viiiff, xivff.
15 Although some existentialists may seem to deny it, we cannot choose where to begin. Our starting-point is given as ourselves with the capacities, structures and limitations of our understanding as determined by our nature and its cultural setting. Any existential commitment has to be made from that basis.
16 Barth's commentary on Romans illustrates this. The exposition is dominantly influenced by Barth's culturally influenced reactions to the supposed ineffectiveness of Liberal Protestantism and to the seeming collapse of Western civilization as a result of the 1914–18 war.
17 Just as Kant's critical philosophy maintains that the only possible a priori synthetic judgements are those which express the fundamental structures of our understanding, so Barth's theology rejects all attempts to reach a theological understanding which starts from the human situation. Barth maintains that Feuerbach is correct in holding that thought which starts with the human will never get beyond the human.
18 The only use of reason likely to be regarded as theologically acceptable by those who share this position is that which uses rational investigations of human understanding to show reason's incompetence in theological matters and, consequently, the dependence of theological understanding upon revelation. Such a view of the role of reason in theological understanding was put forward by John Ellis, *The Knowledge of Divine Things from Revelation, not from Reason or Nature*,

London, 1747, and H. L. Mansel, *The Limits of Religious Thought*, Oxford, 1858.

19 In different ways S. M. Ogden, W. Pannenberg, H. Küng and K. Rahner maintain that human self-understanding can never achieve intellectual completion unless it is related to an understanding of God.

20 This, of course, leaves open the question of whether the intellectual completeness produced by such an understanding (granted that it does provide it) expresses a true insight into the ultimate nature of reality.

21 See chapter 4.

22 See Kant, *Critique of Pure Reason*, p. 32.

23 Cf. Pannenberg, *Basic Questions*, volume II, pp. 216f: it is 'the ability to transcend one's own situation, which characterizes man . . . In questioning the reality he encounters and going beyond its currently given aspects to its very essence through this enquiry, thus disclosing *its* questionableness, man is in the last analysis asking about himself, about his own destination. Thus it makes good sense to describe man as a question that continually pushes him further into the open.'

24 Cf. ibid., pp. 220ff.

25 Cf. John Henry Newman, 'in these provinces of enquiry egotism is true modesty. In religious enquiry each of us can speak only for himself': *An Essay in Aid of a Grammar of Assent*, edited by I. T. Ker, Oxford: Clarendon Press, 1985, p. 248; cf. also Sam Keen, *To A Dancing God*, London: Collins, 1971, p. 3, and John Oman's comment (*Honest Religion*, Cambridge: Cambridge University Press, 1941, p. 1) that: 'Strictly speaking no book was ever written except in the first person, and it is not modesty to say "This is merely my opinion on my limited experience," for no human verdict on anything was ever more.'

2 *Faith, belief, theology and reason*

1 Paul Tillich, *The Dynamics of Faith*, New York: Harper Torchbooks, 1958, pp. 21f; cf. Søren Kierkegaard, *Concluding Unscientific Postscript*, translated by D. F. Swenson and W. Lowrie, Princeton: Princeton University Press, 1941, p. 182: 'Without risk there is no faith. Faith is precisely the contradiction between the infinite passion of the individual's inwardness and the objective uncertainty.'

2 Cf. F. R. Tennant, *The Nature of Belief*, London: Centenary Press, 1943.

3 Cf. what R. Hare says about 'weakness of will' in *Freedom and Reason*, Oxford: Oxford University Press, 1965, pp. 67ff. Because of the weakness of will it is not safe to identify practice with assent. R. B. Braithwaite seems not to be fully aware of this problem in his Eddington lecture when, after suggesting that 'the primary use of a moral assertion' is to express 'the intention of the asserter to act in a particular way', he goes on to claim that 'whether or not a man has the intention

of pursuing a particular behaviour policy can be empirically tested, both by observing what he does and by hearing what he replies when he is questioned about his intentions': 'An empiricist's view of the nature of religious belief' reprinted in I. T. Ramsey (ed.), *Christian Ethics and Contemporary Philosophy*, London: SCM Press, 1966, p. 60.

4 D. Z. Phillips, for example, claims that 'the prayer of petition is best understood, not as an attempt at influencing the way things go, but as an expression of, and a request for devotion to God through the way things go' (*The Concept of Prayer*, London: Routledge and Kegan Paul, 1965, pp. 120f), and that belief in immortality is not about an individual's survival of death as a subject but about a relationship to 'the unchanging reality of God' (*Death and Immortality*, London: Macmillan, 1970, p. 50; cf. p. 60). Although Phillips' analyses may present intellectually attractive interpretations of petitionary prayer and of belief in immortality, it is arguable that they do not represent what examination shows that religious believers in these matters actually 'do and say' (*Concept of Prayer*, p. 1).

5 Braithwaite, 'An empiricist's view' in Ramsey, *Christian Ethics*, p. 63. While Braithwaite may be correct in holding that this is the only meaning for 'God is love' within the criterion of meaning which he is using, this may show that that criterion of meaning is unsuitable for a fully adequate appreciation of what is meant by the assertion: cf. Braithwaite's response to discussions of his paper in pp. 88f.

6 See Don Cupitt, *Taking Leave of God*, London: SCM Press, 1980, p. 101.

7 This pre-understanding of faith as containing a reference to what is real distinguishes this study of theological understanding from those in which religion is treated solely as a *sui generis* mode of experience, which is not appropriately apprehended in terms of having relationships with or experiences of anything other than the believer.

8 In *Proslogion*, chapter 8, Anselm says of God, 'You experience no compassion for misery', but in chapter 1 he has prayed, 'How long will You turn away Your face from us? . . . Have compassion upon the efforts and attempts which we direct toward You': *Anselm of Canterbury*, edited and translated by J. Hopkins and H. W. Richardson, London: SCM Press, 1974, volume 1, pp. 98, 92.

9 Even if chapter 1 of *Proslogion* is held to be a smoke-screen added by Anselm to obscure the rationalism of his argument, the contradiction is still present in Anselm, both because chapter 1 is in keeping with his devotional practice and because its effectiveness as a smoke-screen depends upon its agreement with an authentic attitude of faith.

10 Cf. E. L. Mascall who argues that the denial of this compossibility in the unique case of God 'rests upon an implicit denial of the absolute infinity of God'. It needs, however, more than Mascall's assertion that

it is so to show that even in the case of an infinite being it is coherent to hold both that our states 'affect' God, and that they can 'neither augment nor diminish' his beatitude: *He Who Is*, London: Green and Co., 1943, p. 111.

11 See Schubert S. M. Ogden, 'The strange witness of unbelief' in *The Reality of God*, London: SCM Press, 1967, pp. 120–43; David A. Pailin, 'A Christian possibility of proclaiming the "death of God" ', *The Church Quarterly*, 1, 3, January 1969, pp. 216–32.

12 Schubert M. Ogden, 'The Christian proclamation of God to men of the so-called "Atheistic Age" ', *Concilium*, 6, 2, June 1966, p. 47: the distinction between the faith that is practised and the beliefs that are professed makes it 'clear why not everyone who gives theoretical assent to the Christian proclamation of God necessarily trusts God existentially; and why theoretical dissent from this proclamation may or may not betoken existential distrust of the God so proclaimed'. Cf. also John Baillie, *Our Knowledge of God*, London: Oxford University Press, 1939, pp. 47ff, where he distinguishes between consciousness and self-consciousness and, following Cook Wilson, holds that people may 'have an awareness' of the reality of God 'without being aware of that awareness'. God may thus be 'directly present' to the consciousness of people who 'in all good faith' deny belief in God's existence.

13 Along these lines it is possible for Christian theists to accept at least part of Nietzsche's proclamation of the 'death of God' as a proper condemnation of pietistic misunderstanding of the divine nature.

14 That it is a basic component of the notion of theistic faith is indicated, for example, when those who have this type of faith are questioned about their practices, and consider that they justify them not by holding that they are self-justifying but by asserting something about God's nature and will to be the case.

15 Cf. Ludwig Feuerbach's claim that 'the fact is not that a quality is divine because God has it, but that God has it because it is in itself divine': *The Essence of Christianity*, translated by G. Eliot, New York: Harper and Brothers, 1957, p. 21; H. M. Schulweis, *Evil and the Morality of God*, Cincinnati: Hebrew Union College Press, 1984, pp. 115ff, takes up Feuerbach's methodology ('that which in religion is the predicate we must make the subject, and that which in religion is a subject we must make a predicate', p. 60) as the basis of his response to the problem of evil, in which he interprets descriptions of God as affirmations of the godliness of the attributes ascribed to God.

16 A. N. Whitehead, *Religion in the Making*, Cambridge: Cambridge University Press, 1926, pp. 56f.

17 Ibid.

18 Matthew Arnold, *Literature and Dogma*, London: Smith, Elder and Co., 1876, pp. 31, 42, 44; cf. p. 44: 'To please God, to serve God, to obey God's will, means to follow a law of things which is found in

conscience, and which is an indication, irrespective of our arbitrary wish and fancy, of what we ought to do. There *is*, then, a real power which makes for righteousness; and it is the greatest of realities for us.'

19 The fact that events in the world are the products of the interactions of chance and necessity would not by itself show that reality is atheistic. Contrary to Jacques Monod's conclusion in *Chance and Necessity* (London: Collins, 1972, cf. p. 160), it is arguable that a creator delighting in the play of creativity might choose to express the divine creative purpose through such a kind of universe (cf. Arthur R. Peacocke, *Creation and the World of Science*, Oxford: Clarendon Press, 1979, and David Bartholomew, *God of Chance*, London: SCM Press, 1984). What would make it atheistic would be if the nature of its processes, as the interaction of chance and necessity, were not to be the result of some ultimate purpose.

20 Cf. F. C. Copleston, 'An adequate explanation must ultimately be a total explanation, to which nothing further can be added': 'The existence of God, a debate between Bertrand Russell and Father F. C. Copleston, SJ' in Bertrand Russell, *Why I am not a Christian and Other Essays*, London: George Allen and Unwin, 1975, p. 138.

21 See Arnold, *Literature and Dogma*, p. 42. Arnold himself holds that such claims exceed what can be regarded as 'certain and verifiable'.

22 Whitehead, *Religion in the Making*, p. 57.

23 Among the problems that arise is whether the divine should be held to be free as creator and yet always to have a creation. Attempts may be made to develop a satisfactory notion of God as creator by holding that while the existence of *some* created order is necessary for God, which possible order is actualized is subject to divine choice. This solution, however, gives rise to further puzzles, such as how the divine as essentially perfect may be envisaged as having freedom to choose, and the relationship between the creative determinations of the divine and the contingent acts of the created: for further discussion of these issues see David A. Pailin, *God and the Processes of Reality: Foundations of a Credible Theism*, London: Routledge, 1989, pp. 96ff.

24 Whitehead, *Religion in the Making*, p. 68; cf. A. N. Whitehead, *Process and Reality: An Essay in Cosmology*, corrected edition edited by D. R. Griffin and D. W. Sherburne, New York: The Free Press, 1978, pp. 345ff, on 'the consequent nature of God'.

25 It is a 'dipolar' concept which has been worked out in some detail in the works of Charles Hartshorne: see *Man's Vision of God and the Logic of Theism*, Chicago: Willett, Clark and Co., 1941; *The Divine Relativity*, New Haven: Yale University Press, 1948; *Reality as Social Process*, Glencoe: The Free Press and Boston: Beacon Press, 1953; *Creative Synthesis and Philosophic Method*, London: SCM Press, 1970; see also Ogden, *The Reality of God*, and Pailin, *God and the Processes of Reality*, pp. 57ff.

26 Cf. Hartshorne's 'panentheistic' concept of God which seeks to avoid both the problems of a pantheism which fails satisfactorily to distinguish God and the world, and the problems of those forms of theism which fail satisfactorily to relate them: cf. Pailin, *God and the Processes of Reality*, pp. 76ff.

27 Cf. Gordon D. Kaufman, *An Essay on Theological Method*, Missoula: Scholars Press for American Academy of Religion, 1975, and *The Theological Imagination: Constructing the Concept of God*, Philadelphia: Westminster Press, 1981. Just as the fact that a historian is involved in constructive activity in discerning the character of John Wesley does not imply the basic fictionality of John Wesley so, conversely, the fact that God is held to be a reality does not mean that imaginative construction is not required to grasp the divine nature. It is not constructivity in theology but the fictionality of its products that is denied by affirming the reality of God.

28 In the following discussion what people have written is basically accepted at its face-value. It does not seem reasonable to follow certain modern interpreters of theism in that wholesale hermeneutical suspicion of God-talk which makes out that what people say about God's reality is radically different from what they mean.

29 Julien Offray de la Mettrie, *Man a Machine*, La Salle, Ill.: Open Court, 1912, p. 127.

30 See Friedrich Nietzsche, *Twilight of the Idols*, paras. 4 and 8 in W. Kaufmann (ed.), *The Portable Nietzsche*, New York: Viking Press, 1954, pp. 490, 500f.

31 See Nietzsche, *The Gay Science* in Kaufmann, *The Portable Nietzsche*, p. 95.

32 See John Stuart Mill, *Autobiography*, New York: Columbia University Press, 1924, p. 28.

33 See John Stuart Mill, *Three Essays on Religion*, London: Longmans, Green, Reader and Dyer, 1874, p. 242.

34 Ibid., pp. 250ff.

35 Russell, 'Can religion cure our troubles?' in *Why I am not a Christian*, p. 157.

36 Alfred J. Ayer, *The Central Questions of Philosophy*, Harmondsworth: Penguin Books, 1976, pp. 234f; cf. pp. 211ff; and *Language, Truth and Logic*, 2nd edition, New York: Dover, n.d., pp. 114ff.

37 Not all believers regard such arguments as an aid to faith. Søren Kierkegaard, for example, argues that a conclusive demonstration of the existence of God would prevent rather than foster authentic faith: *Philosophical Fragments*, translated by D. F. Swenson, Princeton: Princeton University Press, 1936, pp. 31f, 33f; cf. *Concluding Unscientific Postscript*, p. 182: 'If I am capable of grasping God objectively, I do not believe, but precisely because I cannot do this I must believe';

cf. also Martin Buber, *I and Thou*, translated by R. Gregor Smith, Edinburgh: T. and T. Clark, 1937, pp. 8of.

38 Karl Barth, *Protestant Theology in the Nineteenth Century*, London: SCM Press, 1972, pp. 536, 539; cf. Barth, 'An introductory essay' in Feuerbach, *Essence of Christianity*, pp. xxviiif.

39 J. O. Wisdom, 'Religious belief', *The Cambridge Review*, 77, June 1956, p. 668.

40 Hans Küng, *Does God Exist?*, translated by E. Quinn, London: Collins, 1980, pp. 504f; cf. p. 334, where he points out that 'committed atheists are understandably irritated when theologians defend a completely vague, overstretched, *eroded concept of God* and blur the frontiers between belief in God and atheism'.

41 See Hans Küng, *On Being a Christian*, translated by E. Quinn, London: Collins, 1977, pp. 70ff.

42 Richard Swinburne, *Faith and Reason*, Oxford: Clarendon Press, 1981, p. 104; *The Coherence of Theism* Oxford: Clarendon Press, 1977, p. 1.

43 Keith Ward, *Rational Theology and the Creativity of God*, Oxford: Basil Blackwell, 1982, p. 1.

44 Karl Rahner, *Foundations of Christian Faith*, translated by W. V. Dych, New York: Seabury Press, 1978, p. 67; cf. pp. 21f, 42ff, 83f.

45 John B. Cobb, Jr., *God and the World*, Philadelphia: Westminster Press, 1969, p. 20.

46 Ogden, *The Reality of God*, pp. 86f; cf. p. 14.

47 It is, indeed, possible to argue that it is a third-order activity on the grounds that faith is the primary activity, its expression in beliefs is the second-order activity, and the systematization of beliefs in theology is a third-order activity. It seems more plausible, however, to regard faith as the primary and theology as the secondary activity, with belief as the material that they have in common, although it should be noted in this respect that the more reason is involved in formulating beliefs, the more the expression of those beliefs is a matter of theology and the less they are a direct expression of the primary faith.

48 John Macquarrie, *Principles of Christian Theology*, London: SCM Press, 1966, p. 2: 'It is some specific faith that expresses itself in theology, not just faith in general but the faith of an historic community . . . [Theology] implies participation in a community . . . [Theologians] are not expressing a private faith, but have become spokesmen for their community, charged with a special responsibility within it.'

49 Some even argue that what are regarded as purely formal, self-evident truths may be culturally relative: cf. Gordon D. Kaufman, *Relativism, Knowledge and Truth*, Chicago: University of Chicago Press, 1960, pp. 95, 104.

50 Cf. George Steiner, *After Babel*, Oxford: Oxford University Press, 1975, for illustrations of the value-loaded character of language.

51 Ogden, 'What does it mean to affirm "Jesus Christ is Lord"?' in *The Reality of God*, p. 188.

52 Ogden, 'The promise of faith' in ibid., pp. 210, 220, 229. It should be noted, however, that in 'What is theology?', *Perkins Journal*, 26, Winter 1973 (reprinted from *The Journal of Religion*, 52, January 1972), Ogden holds that theological statements have to satisfy the twin criteria of 'appropriateness and understandability' (p. 2). In *The Point of Christology*, London: SCM Press, 1982, he clarifies what he means by the latter criterion by changing the terminology to that of 'appropriateness' and 'credibility' (p. 4), and he uses these terms in the version of 'What is theology?' printed in his *On Theology* (San Francisco: Harper and Row, 1986). His treatment of the 'promise of faith' presumably varies from the commonly supposed view of human destiny in the Christian tradition because of the need to satisfy the criterion of credibility (or understandability).

53 What, for example, is today an acceptable understanding in Christian theology of the notion of God as 'creator' is not determined by precise agreement (even if it could be ascertained) with how Paul, Augustine, Aquinas and Paley understood the notion (presuming that they agreed!). It is determined by how the general approach to understanding the basis of reality found within the cumulative tradition of the Christian community can be developed in a way that is now credible.

54 Cf. David A. Pailin, 'Authenticity in the interpretation of Christianity' in M. Pye and R. Morgan (eds.), *The Cardinal Meaning*, The Hague: Mouton, 1973, pp. 127–59.

55 Cf. David A. Pailin, 'The genuinely active God', *The Modern Churchman*, 27, 1985, pp. 16–32.

56 Hartshorne is an example not only of a theologian whose understanding arises out of rational reflection, but also of a person whose religious faith is similarly the product of rational investigations. According to his own account, he decided 'about the age of seventeen' to 'trust reason to the end' and to make his 'thinking about metaphysical and religious thinking good thinking, good by the proper criteria of thinking' (*The Logic of Perfection and other Essays in Neoclassical Metaphysics*, La Salle, Ill.: Open Court, 1962, pp. viiif). Acquaintance with Hartshorne makes it clear that these remarks describe his existential understanding of, and response to, the nature of reality. This does not make him a dessicated rationalist or an apathetic theist.

57 See David A. Pailin, ' "Credo ut intelligam" as the method of theology and of its verification' in *Die Wirkungsgeschichte Anselms von Canterbury, Analecta Anselmiana*, Frankfurt-on-Main: Minerva, 1975, volume IV, part 1.

58 For suggestions about the kind of reasoning involved in this interaction, see Pailin, ibid, and 'Theistic verification' in D. Kirkpatrick (ed.), *The Living God*, Nashville: Abingdon Press, 1971.

59 Consider, for example, how the prior selection of appropriate concepts by a Methodist, a Russian orthodox, a Quaker, a Muslim, an atheistic sociologist and a Marxist psychologist for describing the experience of being part of the community of faith will influence how it is perceived.

60 Cf. Schubert M. Ogden, 'The task of philosophical theology' in R. A. Evans (ed.), *The Future of Philosophical Theology*, Philadelphia: Westminster Press, 1971, p. 73, where he speaks of theology as 'the more sustained, deliberate, and, therefore, specialized reflection whereby the primary expression of religion is subjected to critical analysis and interpretation'. Although religion in itself is 'the primary and most direct reflection of the basic existential faith by which we all live simply as men', it is always expressed as 'a religion which has its origin in some particular occasion of insight or special revelation' and which is actualized as 'a particular form of faith'.

61 Cf. ibid., pp. 69 (with reference to Hartshorne), 74.

62 Kaufman, *Essay on Theological Method*, pp. 10, 13f; cf. also *Theological Imagination*. Although in considerable sympathy with Kaufman's remarks on the way in which we produce a concept of God, I find his work to date deficient in relation to the problems of the logical status and verification of theological statements.

63 The theory implies that God is *immoral* since one person is being punished for the sins of another, and *divided* since one person of the Trinity is sacrificed to satisfy the needs of another.

64 Cf. Whitehead, *Process and Reality*, p. 343: 'Love neither rules, nor is it unmoved; also it is a little oblivious as to morals.'

65 Torrance, *Theological Science*, p. 9.

66 See chapters 5 and 6.

67 The inferential methods of syllogistic logic and mathematical demonstration are not the only ways of reaching justified conclusions. Significant reasoning may, in appropriate circumstances, also be by the accumulation and convergence of probabilities, by analogical comparison, by statistical induction, by non-disconfirmation, by *reductio ad absurdum*, and by perceiving the overall fittingness of an explanatory hypothesis.

68 Cf. Gilbert Ryle, *The Concept of Mind*, London: Hutchinson, 1949, p. 30: 'Rules of correct reasoning were first extracted by Aristotle, yet men knew how to avoid and detect fallacies before they learned his lessons, just as men since Aristotle, and including Aristotle, ordinarily conduct their arguments without making any internal reference to his formulae' Further investigations into the methods of reasoning, however, have shown that the forms of the syllogism recognized by Aristotle are not the only significant forms of reasoning: cf. John Locke, *Essay Concerning Human Understanding*, London, 1690, Book IV, chapter 17; John Henry Newman, *An Essay in Aid of a Grammar of Assent*, London Burns and Oates, 1870; edited by I. T.

Ker, Oxford: Oxford University Press, 1985, especially chapters 8 and 9; and Stephen Toulmin, *The Uses of Argument*, Cambridge: Cambridge University Press, 1958, and *Human Understanding*, Oxford: Clarendon Press, 1972, volume I; cf. also David A. Pailin, *The Way to Faith*, London: Epworth Press, 1969, pp. 136ff.

69 John Baillie, *Invitation to Pilgrimage*, Harmondsworth: Penguin Books, 1960, pp. 41f. On Baillie's remark that logic describes how we *ought* to think, cf. P. F. Strawson, *Introduction to Logical Theory*, London: Methuen, 1952, p. 1: 'The words "logical" and "illogical" are themselves among the words of logical appraisal. If you call a discourse logical, you are in some degree commending it.'

70 Cf. W. G. de Burgh, *From Morality to Religion*, London: MacDonald and Evans, 1938, p. 286.

71 Cf. Charles Hartshorne, *A Natural Theology for Our Time*, La Salle, Ill.: Open Court, 1967, p. 73: 'As Peirce insisted, possibility is in principle general rather than particular, determinable rather than determinate. It is in some degree indefinite . . .' What is future is not the 'what' of a determinate thing that is knowable as such but the 'what' of ranges of possibilities. It is a basic error to consider, because the noun 'the future' acts in many ways like the noun 'the past', that they refer to things with basically the same properties. Whatever the ontological status of 'the past', 'the future' is not yet some *thing*. To reify it is to fail to understand its meaning. Furthermore, the relations of the past to present and of the present to the future are asymmetrical.

72 Cf. Mascall, *He Who Is*, pp. 119f. Mascall attempts to solve the problem of God's knowledge today of future events by arguing that if God's existence is outside time, it is meaningless to talk about God as knowing anything *today*. In the end, however, he admits that this solution in effect leaves the material significance of God's omniscience 'a mystery beyond our power to unravel'. It is thus hardly a solution!

73 Anselm, *Proslogion*, chapter 8. Here Anselm's dialectical skill seems to have led him astray. His position, in effect, either is self-contradictory (since it affirms that God is compassionate but denies the quality of compassion to be in God), or denies that God is compassionate (since it affirms that while our experience of God suggests that God is compassionate, in fact there is no such quality in God). Both interpretations conflict with what he affirms earlier (cf. chapters 5 and 6) about the nature of God's essential perfection.

74 Thomas Aquinas, *Summa Theologiae*, Ia, 13, 7, translated by H. McCabe, London: Eyre and Spottiswoode, 1964, volume III. Rational reflection on the conflict between the belief that God is unchangeable and the belief that God is related to the creatures produces here a model which in effect denies the substance of the faith underlying the second belief.

75 See Adolf Harnack, *History of Dogma*, the first volume of which

appeared in Germany in 1886; Edwin Hatch, *The Influence of Greek Ideas and Usages upon the Christian Church* (Hibbert Lectures for 1888), London: Williams and Norgate, 1890. For a recent discussion of the issues, cf. Pannenberg, *Basic Questions*, volume II, pp. 119–83.

76 Anselm's *Proslogion* is a good example of this use of reason (as well as of the subtleties needed to try to avoid contradictions at certain points), as it unfolds what Anselm considers to be entailed by the self-evidently correct insight that God, as 'that than which a greater cannot be conceived', must be 'whatever it is better to be than not to be': *Proslogion*, chapter 5; cf. *Monologion*, chapter 15, and *Reply to Gaunilo*, section 10. This kind of thinking is exemplified from a Thomist perspective in modern theology by E. L. Mascall's treatment of some of the divine attributes in *He Who Is*, and in *Existence and Analogy*, London: Longmans, Green and Co., 1949.

77 Cf. Pailin, ' "Credo ut Intelligam" as the method of theology' in *Analecta Anselmiana*, volume IV, part 1.

78 And so from a similar starting-point to that of Anselm in the *Proslogion*.

79 See Hartshorne, *The Logic of Perfection* pp. 40–4; and 'The principle of dual transcendence and its basis in ordinary language' in *Creative Synthesis and Philosophic Method*, pp. 227–43.

80 Cf. I John 4.1.

81 Donald M. MacKinnon, *Borderlands of Theology*, London: Lutterworth Press, p. 54. On being asked about this remark, however, MacKinnon said in conversation that he did not always agree with it!

82 Cf. papers mentioned in note 3, chapter 1.

83 William Hamilton, *The New Essence of Christianity*, London: Darton, Longman and Todd, 1966, p. 13.

84 A. R. Vidler (ed.), *Soundings: Essays Concerning Christian Understanding*, Cambridge: Cambridge University Press, 1962, p. ix.

85 Cf. I. T. Ramsey, *Models for Divine Activity*, London: SCM Press, 1973, p. 53.

86 Aquinas stopped writing his *Summa Theologiae* after a mystical experience; Barth was stopped by the weakness of old age: see his comments on this in his *Church Dogmatics*, IV/4, translated by G. W. Bromiley, Edinburgh: T. and T. Clark, 1969, pp. viiff.

87 William D. Dean, *Coming To: A Theology of Beauty*, Philadelphia: Westminster Press, 1972, p. 153.

88 Pannenberg, *Basic Questions*, volume II, pp. 242, 216.

3   God as cosmic projection

1 Quoted from Clement of Alexandria in W. Jaeger, *The Theology of the Early Greek Philosophers*, Oxford: Oxford University Press, 1967, p. 47.

2 Cicero, *The Nature of the Gods*, translated by H. C. P. MacGregor, Harmondsworth: Penguin Books, 1972, pp. 128f.
3 Statius, *Thebais*, III, 360; cf. Lucretius, *The Nature of the Universe*, translated by R. E. Latham, Harmondsworth: Penguin Books, 1951, pp. 218f, where he argues that fear due to 'ignorance of the causes of phenomena' drives people to superstitious 'terror of the gods', although in reality 'things are created and occasioned without the aid of the gods'.
4 Thomas Hobbes, *Leviathan*, edited by M. Oakeshott, Oxford: Basil Blackwell, n.d., p. 69: Hobbes makes out that he is particularly referring to 'the many gods of the Gentiles' when he suggests that 'from the innumerable variety of fancy, men have created in the world innumerable sorts of gods' (pp. 69f).
5 David Hume, *The Natural History of Religion*, edited by H. E. Root, London: A. and C. Black, 1956, p. 47.
6 Friedrich Nietzsche, *The Anti-Christ*, paras. 15f, 31, in *Twilight of the Idols and the Anti-Christ*, translated by R. J. Hollingdale, Harmondsworth: Penguin Books, 1968, pp. 125ff, 142f; cf. para. 40, pp. 152f.
7 Sigmund Freud, *Totem and Taboo*, London: Routledge and Kegan Paul, 1960, p. 92: 'Spirits and demons . . . are only projections of man's own emotional impulses.' In the figures of their religion, therefore, people meet their 'internal mental processes again outside' themselves; cf. also p. 64.
8 Cf. abid., pp. 147ff; S. Freud, *The Future of an Illusion*, London: Hogarth Press, pp. 13ff and 26f, where Freud defines an illusion as 'not necessarily . . . false' but as characterized by being 'derived from human wishes': 'we call a belief an illusion when a wish-fulfilment is a prominent factor in its motivation, and in doing so we disregard its relation to reality.'
9 Freud, *Totem and Taboo*, p. 147: 'The god of each of them is formed in the likeness of his father . . . his personal relation to God depends on his relation to his father in the flesh and oscillates and changes along with that relation . . .'
10 Albert Schweitzer, *The Quest of the Historical Jesus*, 3rd edition, London: A. and C. Black, London, 1954, p. 4: 'There is no historical task which so reveals a man's true self as the writing of a Life of Jesus.'
11 F. Engels, 'Ludwig Feuerbach and the end of classical German philosophy' in K. Marx and F. Engels, *On Religion*, Moscow: Foreign Languages Publishing House, 1957, p. 264; cf. p. 262.
12 Ibid., p. 261.
13 K. Marx, 'Theses on Feuerbach' in Marx and Engels, *On Religion*, p. 71.
14 E. Durkheim, *The Elementary Forms of the Religious Life*, translated by J. W. Swain, London: George Allen and Unwin, 1951, pp. 418f; cf. pp. 421ff; on theology as a socially constructed understanding of

reality, cf. Robin Gill, *The Social Context of Theology. A Methodological Enquiry*, London and Oxford: Mowbrays, 1975, and *Theology and Social Structure*, London and Oxford: Mowbrays, 1977.

15 Ludwig Feuerbach, *The Essence of Christianity*, translated by G. Eliot, New York: Harper and Brothers, 1957, p. 14; cf. p. 26 and p. 273: 'Love is not holy because it is a predicate of God, but it is a predicate of God because it is in itself divine.'

16 Ludwig Feuerbach, *Principles of the Philosophy of the Future*, translated by M. F. Vogel, Indianapolis: Bobbs-Merrill, 1966, p. 17: 'man's conception of God is the human individual's conception of his own species . . .'

17 Feuerbach, *Essence of Christianity*, pp. 12f: 'By his God thou knowest the man, and by the man his God; the two are identical. Whatever is God to a man, that is his heart and soul; and conversely, God is the manifested inward nature, the expressed self of a man – religion is the solemn unveiling of a man's hidden treasures, the revelation of his intimate thoughts, the open confession of his love-secrets.'

18 See ibid., pp. xxxviff.

19 Ibid., pp. 270, 277.

20 Engels, 'Ludwig Feuerbach' in Marx and Engels, *On Religion*, pp. 236ff. Engels also speaks of 'the liberating effect' of Feuerbach's *Essence of Christianity* and of the way in which Marx, in spite of some reservations, 'enthusiastically greeted the new conception'.

21 Cf. K. Barth, 'An introductory essay' in Feuerbach, *The Essence of Christianity*, p. x: 'No philosopher of his time penetrated the contemporary theological situation as effectually' and as pertinently as Feuerbach; cf. p. xxv; cf. also Wolfhart Pannenberg, *The Apostles' Creed*, London: SCM Press, 1972, p. 18: 'The key-figure of modern atheism was Ludwig Feuerbach . . .'

22 See Karl Barth, *Church Dogmatics*, I/2, translated by G. T. Thompson and H. Knight, Edinburgh: T. and T. Clark, 1956, pp. 5ff. Barth's theological argument was anticipated philosophically by John Ellis in the middle of the eighteenth century in *The Knowledge of Divine Things from Revelation, not from Reason or Nature*, London, 1747.

23 Martin Buber, *Between Man and Man*, translated by R. G. Smith, Boston: Beacon Press, 1955, p. 147.

24 Cf. G. F. Seiler, *Biblical Hermeneutics*, translated by W. Wright, London: Wesley and Davids, 1835, p. 35, for distinctions between 'anthropopoiesis', 'anthropopathy' and 'anthropomorphism'. I use the term 'anthropomorphism', as is now generally the case, to refer to all three.

25 Even a revelation by God must be in terms of the human realm of experience and understanding if it is to be apprehensible and communicable to others. Otherwise it will signify nothing.

26 Quoted from Clement of Alexandria in Jaeger, *Theology of the Early Greek Philosophers*, p. 42.

27 Cf. C. S. Peirce who holds that even descriptions in the natural sciences are anthropomorphic: 'Every scientific explanation of a natural phenomenon is a hypothesis that there really is something in nature to which human reason is analogous; and that it really is so all the successes of science in its applications to human convenience are witnesses . . . In the light of the successes of science to my mind there is a degree of baseness in denying our birthright as children of God and in shamefacedly slinking away from anthropomorphic conceptions of the universe', 'Principles of philosophy', in C. Hartshorne and P. Weiss (eds.), *Collected Papers of Charles Sanders Peirce*, Cambridge: Harvard University Press, 1931, volume I, para. 316, pp. 158f; cf. 'Pragmatism' in ibid., volume V, paras. 46f, 121, 212, 636f, and especially 516: 'I do not believe that man can have the idea of any cause or agency so stupendous that there is any more adequate way of conceiving it than as vaguely like a man.'

28 Feuerbach, *Essence of Christianity*, p. xxxvii; cf. p. 25.

29 Cf. Leibniz, *Monadology*, para. 9. Nicholas of Cusa stated the principle thus: 'There cannot be several things exactly the same, for in that case there would not be several things but the same thing itself. Therefore all things both agree with and differ from one another', *De Venatione Sapientiae*, para. 23; cf. *De Docta Ignorantia*, III, 1, for another statement of the principle.

30 When, for example, electrons are described as particles, the description may be valuable for certain purposes, but it is not to be held to convey the essence of what it is to be an electron.

31 See Paul Tillich, 'Reply to interpretation and criticism' in C. W. Kegley and R. W. Bretall (eds.), *The Theology of Paul Tillich*, New York: Macmillan, 1952, p. 334. If it is not so delimited symbolic usage becomes 'all-embracing and therefore meaningless'.

32 Paul Tillich, *Systematic Theology*, 3 vols., London: Nisbet, 1953, 1957, 1964, volume I, p. 265.

33 See I. T. Ramsey, *Religious Language*, London: SCM Press, 1957, pp. 61ff.

34 Ibid., p. 49. In *Models and Mystery*, Oxford: Oxford University Press, 1964, pp. 60f, I. T. Ramsey holds that the presence of qualifiers in religious discourse is essential since they declare 'the inadequacy of all models' used to describe God, witness that theological words are grounded in what is 'permanent mystery', and point to 'cosmic disclosure' as the only way in which 'the topic of any and every theological utterance' may be perceived.

35 Feuerbach, *Essence of Christianity*, p. 214.

36 See I. T. Ramsey, *Christian Discourse*, Oxford: Oxford University Press, 1965, p. 80.

37 Cf. Rudolf Otto, *The Idea of the Holy*, translated by J. W. Harvey, 2nd edition, Oxford: Oxford University Press, 1950, where Otto describes this experience as analogous to a complex of the experiences of shuddering awe, overpoweringness, creatureliness and profaneness before the wholly other.

38 Martin Buber, *I and Thou*, translated by R. Gregor Smith, Edinburgh: T. and T. Clark, 1937, pp. 78, 80f.

39 It also avoids problems about the identity of what is experienced which trouble the views advanced by Otto and Buber.

40 Charles Hartshorne, *A Natural Theology for Our Time*, La Salle, Ill.: Open Court, 1967, p. 3; cf. p. 4.

41 Cf. ibid., pp. 8ff: only one whose love is all-embracing is properly to be loved with the whole of one's being.

42 Ibid., p. 16.

43 See David A. Pailin, *God and the Processes of Reality: Foundations of a Credible Theism*, London: Routledge, 1989, pp. 66f, for an introductory exposition of Hartshorne's position; cf. chapter 2, note 25, for Hartshorne's major works.

44 Anselm defines God formally as 'that than which a greater cannot be conceived' (*Proslogion*, chapter 2). Hartshorne argues that this does not entail that God has an absolute maximum of value, for this is an incoherent notion, albeit one that has bedevilled theological understanding – including Anselm's – for centuries. The correct analysis of divine perfection is in terms of a dual transcendence according to which the divine is unsurpassable by any other, but surpassable by later states of Godself: 'The transcendent is eternally, independently, and maximally good and aware of whatever is true, but the concrete beauty, the intensity, harmony and richness, of the divine life can reach no final maximum . . . God is absolute and immutable ethically but open to increase aesthetically', Charles Hartshorne, *Creative Synthesis and Philosophic Method*, London: SCM Press, 1970, p. 243, cf. pp. 227–43; *A Natural Theology for Our Time*, pp. 17ff, 71ff.

45 Feuerbach, *Essence of Christianity*, p. xxxvii.

46 Hartshorne also argues that, in the unique case of God, the predicates which are to be attributed a priori to God define 'just one divine individual' since only one being 'could in any world have unrestricted scope for interaction'. Consequently, while Strawson makes a valid point when he holds that predicates in principle have more than one possible application (see P. F. Strawson, *Individuals*, London: Methuen, 1964, p. 99n), consideration of the implications of the combination of those predicates, which together descriptively define the essential characteristics of God, a priori show that in combination they can only be truly affirmed of one being. On the other hand, those predicates which describe the material character of the divine, even though they are subject to special 'qualifiers', are only meaningful because they have

more than one application, i.e., apply in appropriately different but
significantly similar ways both to the human and to the divine.

47 Helen Oppenheimer puts the problem facing the theologian at this
   point thus: 'Is the living God of the Bible no more than an intolerably
   crude piece of anthropomorphism, so that there remains only a choice
   between atheism and the affirmation of some kind of "ground of being"
   which is in no proper sense personal?', *Incarnation and Immanence*,
   London: Hodder and Stoughton, 1973, p. 33.

48 Cf. Ezra 5.5: 'the elders . . . were under God's watchful eye.'

49 Cf. the problems which Kant gets into when he suggests that God knows
   things by intuition as noumena, whereas we can only know them by
   thought as phenomena: *Critique of Pure Reason*, translated by N. K.
   Smith, London: Macmillan, 1933, pp. 89f; Immanuel Kant, *Critique
   of Practical Reason*, translated by T. K. Abbott, London: Longmans,
   1909, pp. 235f. A similar development can be seen in the way that talk
   about 'the hand of God' is successively refined to avoid unacceptable
   connotations. Modification of the notion of 'God's hand' through
   'God's agency' and 'God's will' to an idea of 'God's consequent will'
   finally leaves no significant understanding of God as a responsible
   agent. (The notion of the consequent will of God attempts to maintain
   that whatever happens contingently happens nevertheless according to
   God's will: cf. William Ockham, *Predestination, God's Foreknowledge
   and Future Contingents*, translated with introduction by M. M. Adams
   and N. Kretzmann, New York: Appleton-Century-Crofts, 1969.)

50 This is the significance of the threat to theology which A. Flew describes
   as 'the death by a thousand qualifications' in his paper 'Theology and
   falsification' reprinted in A. Flew and A. MacIntyre (eds.), *New Essays
   in Philosophical Theology*, London: SCM Press, 1955, p. 99. While
   there is much to be said for I. T. Ramsey's response that theological
   models live 'by a thousand enrichments' rather than die 'by a thousand
   qualifications' (*Models and Mystery*, p. 60), this 'life' can only be theologically significant if the various models and their qualifiers 'disclose'
   something that is in some way significantly apprehensible.

51 Cf. the reference to Strawson in note 46, above.

52 He holds that this is because 'the infirmities of our nature do not permit
   us to reach any ideas, which in the least correspond to the ineffable
   sublimity of the divine attributes'.

53 David Hume, *Dialogues Concerning Natural Religion*, edited by N. K.
   Smith, Oxford: Clarendon Press, 1935, pp. 194 (cf. 193f), 195, 197.
   The term 'atheist' is here, of course, used in the pre-Huxley sense
   which includes and predominantly expresses what would now be distinguished from 'atheism' as 'agnosticism'.

54 It is contradictory, for example, to state both that God wills and that
   God's eternal mode of being involves a total simultaneity of all events,
   or both that God creates and is absolutely unchanging. If such joint

claims can only be held to be mutually consistent (and so potentially meaningful) at the cost of their terms losing their normal content, they may be apparently saved only by being rendered unable to communicate anything. Confusions of this kind often arise in theology because people pay 'metaphysical compliments' to God and, then, fall into the trap of regarding these prima facie appropriate remarks as unqualified descriptions of the divine nature.

55 I. M. Crombie, 'Theology and falsification' in Flew and MacIntyre (eds.), *New Essays in Philosophical Theology*, pp. 122f: 'knowing that the truth is not literally that which our parables represent, knowing therefore that now we see in a glass darkly, but trusting, because we trust the [revelatory] source of the parables'; cf. I. M. Crombie, 'The possibility of theological statements' in B. Mitchell (ed.), *Faith and Logic*, London: George Allen and Unwin, 1957, p. 70.

56 Ramsey, *Models and Mystery*, p. 60; cf. *Religious Language*, pp. 49ff.

57 For example, the wave and corpuscular descriptions of light were defended as complementary descriptions by demonstrating that they were required by different ways of examining and understanding light.

58 See A. N. Whitehead, *Religion in the Making*, Cambridge: Cambridge University Press, 1926, pp. 40, 60.

59 See John Baillie, *The Sense of the Presence of God*, Oxford: Oxford University Press, 1962, p. 89: faith is 'an awareness of the divine Presence itself, however hidden behind the veils of sense'. Baillie points out, nevertheless, that such a 'sense' is 'not on all fours with the senses by means of which we apprehend the external world'.

60 John Baillie, *Our Knowledge of God*, London: Oxford University Press, 1939, p. 181.

61 Cf. Baillie, *The Sense of the Presence of God*, p. 65.

62 They are interpretations that are also far from self-evidently required by the nature of the experiences.

63 Anselm, *Proslogion*, chapter 15.

64 Tillich, *Systematic Theology*, Volume I, p. 191. In making such remarks Tillich is profoundly influenced by the work of F. W. J. Schelling.

65 In the next chapter we shall consider further the implications of this triple ultimacy, which is part of the definitive connotation of the notion of God, for theological understanding.

66 F. D. E. Schleiermacher, *Speeches on Religion*, translated by J. Oman, New York: Harper Brothers, 1958, p. 36: 'the immediate consciousness of the universal existence of all finite things, in and through the Infinite, and of all temporal things in and through the Eternal.' A more sober treatment is found in Hartshorne's discussion of God as 'cosmic wholeness' or 'the all-inclusive reality' in *A Natural Theology for Our Time*, pp. 7ff.

67 Langdon Gilkey, *Naming the Whirlwind: The Renewal of God-Language*, Indianapolis: Bobbs-Merrill, 1969, p. 306.

68 See chapter 5 for a discussion of the character and significance of religious experience.

69 Although this factor is particularly influential in the case of self-consciously intellectual people, it is not without significance in all human beings so far as they typically ask questions about the meaning, purpose and value of existence, including their own.

70 See chapter 4 on God as actualizing regulative ideas, and chapter 8 on God as the completion of understanding, for further discussions of the points made here.

71 Cf. Schubert M. Ogden, 'The strange witness of unbelief,' in *The Reality of God*, London: SCM Press, 1967, pp. 120–43; cf. also chapter 7 for more on this.

72 Cf. Søren Kierkegaard, *Concluding Unscientific Postscript*, translated by D. F. Swenson and W. Lowrie, Princeton: Princeton University Press, 1941, pp. 107ff, 183.

73 They are directly provided so far as they are a priori in human beings; they are indirectly provided if they are cultural products, and as such they are open to development.

74 These characteristics are required for the concept of God to meet the three formative factors (a sense of transcendence, the quest for ultimate intelligibility and the hope for goodness) which we have discussed already. In part they correspond to the 'qualifiers' which I. T. Ramsey sees as indicating the cosmic quality of material descriptions of God.

75 In comparison to human beings, birds, for example, have higher modes of instinctive behaviour, computers are able to calculate faster, and some insects seem to be more successful at co-operative activity.

76 This may be criticized in principle as an unjustified use of the anthropic prejudice but, in practice, it does not seem possible for us to conceive of a mode of being which is genuinely superior to the self-aware, purposive, value-appreciative, rationally critical and agential mode of being which human beings consider to be characteristically theirs.

77 Barth, 'An introductory essay' in Feuerbach, *The Essence of Christianity*, p. xv.

78 Cf. G. F. Woods, *Theological Explanation*, Welwyn: Nisbet, 1958, pp. 87ff, 147ff, 160ff, for a study of acts of explanation by analogy with our experience of personal being and, especially, for the way in which causal explanations are considered to be satisfied when they reach a personal 'I did it'. Psychologists who are not content with such an end-point and want to explain why people acted as they did by reference to anterior factors may methodologically prevent themselves from reaching any finally satisfying explanation. In theology the parallel case to this is seen in the intellectualist or rationalist view of God, whereas those who are content with an 'I did it' type of explanation as final are more likely to entertain voluntarist views of God's activity.

79 F. R. Tennant, *Philosophical Theology*, Cambridge: Cambridge University Press, 1928 volume II, pp. 113f.
80 Anselm, *Proslogion*, chapters 5ff.
81 In the case of personal relations, for example, the capacity to be 'moved' by the wants and desires of others, and to share in their feelings, appears to be superior to the absence of such a capacity. Perfection in a friend or a teacher accordingly requires total and responsive awareness rather than compete impassibility. It should be noted, furthermore, that Anselm's own faith and the form in which the *Proslogion* is cast implies a personal, reciprocal relationship with God that would be illusory if God were totally impassible.
82 Cf. the implications of Anselm's prayer in *Proslogion*, chapter 1.
83 See Karl Barth, *Anselm: Fides Quaerens Intellectum*, London: SCM Press, 1960. The common view, followed by Barth, is that Anselm's method is one of 'credo ut intelligam'. It may be, however, that this remark reflects Anselm's attempt to mislead potential critics of his rationalist approach after Lanfranc's expression of unhappiness with the *Monologion*: cf. D. A. Pailin, ' "Credo ut intelligam" as the method of theology and of its verification,' in *Die Wirkungsgeschichte Anselms von Canterbury, Analecta Anselmiana*, Frankfurt-on-Main: Minerva, 1975, volume IV, part 1.
84 Thomas Aquinas, *Summa Theologiae*, Ia, 9, 1, Reply, London: Eyre and Spottiswoode, 1964, volume II (translated by T. McDermott), p. 127.
85 Although all creatures are related to God, 'being related to creatures is not a reality in God'. It is only said 'about him because of the real relation in creatures' who change because of God. It does not express 'any change in him': ibid., Ia, 13, 7, Reply, in volume III, p. 75; cf. Ia, 6, 2, Reply 1; Ia, 14, 15; Ia, 28, 1, Reply 3; Ia, 28, 4.
86 Cf. David A. Pailin, 'Christian and Atheist? An introductory attempt to understand the theology of the "death of God" ', *London Quarterly and Holborn Review*, October 1967, pp. 273–304; 'A Christian Possibility of proclaiming the "death of God" ', *The Church Quarterly*, 1, 3, January 1969, pp. 216–32.
87 Some of the points of the theology of humour are anticipated in Reinhold Niebuhr, 'Humour and faith' in *Discerning the Signs of the Times*, London: SCM Press, 1946, pp. 99f. Whereas, however, Niebuhr sees the humour of 'the incongruities of our existence' as 'a prelude to faith' (p. 99, cf. p. 115), the theology of humour may be correct in preferring to see humour as an expression of faith. It is only those who confidently trust in God who can laugh and not despair at the pretensions and failures of human being. It may thus reflect trust in the ultimate rather than merely express 'our sense of the meaninglessness of life' (p. 102). For theological studies which contain motifs of the theology of play and of humour, cf. Harvey Cox, *The Feast of Fools*, Cambridge Mass:

Harvard University Press, 1969; *The Seduction of the Spirit*, London: Wildwood House, 1974; David L. Miller, *Gods and Games: Towards a Theology of Play*, New York: World Publishing Company, 1970; Sam Keen, *To a Dancing God*, New York: Harper and Row, 1970, and London: Collins, 1971; and J. Moltmann, *Theology and Joy*, London: SCM Press, 1973.

88 A similar pattern can be seen in Christian theology in the way that descriptions of the Jesus of history and of the Christ of faith have persistently been conditioned by current values.

89 Marx, 'Theses on Feuerbach' in Marx and Engels, *On Religion*, p. 70.

90 Such a position has been urged by Don Cupitt: cf. *Taking Leave of God*, London: SCM Press, 1980, p. 69, where, rejecting an objective realist view of God, he asserts that 'Belief in the God of Christian faith is an expression of allegiance to a particular set of values, and experience of the God of Christian faith is experience of the impact of those values in one's life'.

91 Cf. Karl Barth, *Protestant Theology in the Nineteenth Century*, London: SCM Press, 1972, p. 534.

92 Wolfhart Pannenberg, *Basic Questions in Theology*, 3 vols., London: SCM Press, 1970, 1971, 1973, volume II, pp. 189f: 'Theology has to learn after Feuerbach that it can no longer mouth the word "God" without offering any explanation; that it can no longer speak as if the meaning of this word were self-evident; that it cannot pursue theology "from above", as Barth says, if it does not want to fall into the hopeless and, what is more, self-inflicted isolation of a higher glossolalia, and lead the whole church into this blind alley.'

93 E. Troeltsch, *The Absoluteness of Christianity*, London: SCM Press, 1972, p. 123.

94 Cf. Pannenberg, *Basic Questions*, volume II, pp. 98f.

95 This is the fallacy of regarding something as discredited because its origins are considered to be discreditable.

96 In practice it seems impossible to determine the origin of theistic belief. Theories about its origin are best appreciated as speculations derived from current interpretations of the nature of religion.

97 Cf. Basil Mitchell, *The Justification of Religious Belief*, London: Macmillan, 1973; and also articles referred to in chapter 1, note 3.

98 Pannenberg, *Basic Questions*, volume II, p. 191; cf. pp. 22ff; *The Apostles' Creed*, London: SCM Press, 1972, pp. 24f. For Pannenberg 'the structure of human existence' presupposes 'a mystery of reality transcending its finitude', only through relation to which can people find 'the fulfilment' of their own being: *Basic Questions*, volume II p. 103; cf. pp. 245f; cf. also the views of Rahner, H. Richard Niebuhr, Ogden and Küng mentioned in chapter 9, notes 3–6.

99 Cf. Pannenberg, *Basic Questions*, volume II, pp. 101ff.

100 Peter L. Berger, *A Rumour of Angels*, Harmondsworth: Penguin Books, 1971, pp. 63ff.

101 Cf. Peter L. Berger and Thomas Luckman, *The Social Construction of Reality*, Harmondsworth: Penguin Books, 1971.

102 As for claims that 'God' is a reification of social structures or the personification of psychic forces, the problem for theism is to show that, while such analyses may discern what some theistic statements have at least partially expressed, theistic understanding makes more sense of reality as a whole than non-theistic attempts at understanding, and can reasonably be held to reflect what is ultimately the case. The solution of this problem too is a task for theistic verification. Thereby it indicates the validity of theistic understanding of some talk about God.

4   God as actualizing regulative ideas

1 Anselm, *Monologion*, chapters 3f, 80, in *Anselm of Canterbury*, edited and translated by J. Hopkins and H. W. Richardson, London: SCM Press, 1974, pp. 8,10, 85.

2 Anselm, *Proslogion*, chapter 2.

3 Ibid., chapter 15. Anselm's argument for this conclusion is that if we can envisage something, we can also think, at least in principle, of something superior to what we have thought of. In the *Monologion*, in comparison, he had affirmed the possibility of indirect descriptions of God, in order to overcome the threat to God-talk presented by the recognition of the incomprehensibility and ineffability of what is 'higher than all other things': *Monologion*, chapters 64f.

4 It is a pity that studies of Anselm's attempts to prove the existence of God from the concept of God have deflected attention from the significance of this concept for the nature of theistic understanding: cf. David A. Pailin, 'Some comments on Hartshorne's presentation of the ontological argument', *Religious Studies*, 4, 1968, pp. 103–22, and 'An introductory survey of Charles Hartshorne's work on the ontological argument' in *Wirkungsgeschichte Anselms von Canterbury, Analecta Anselmiana*, Frankfurt-on-Main: Minerva, volume I, pp. 195–221.

5 Cf. Charles Hartshorne's argument in 'Grounds for believing in God's existence' in Leroy S. Rouner (ed.), *Meaning, Truth and God*, Notre Dame: University of Notre Dame Press, 1982, pp. 17ff.

6 As contrasted with the divine actuality according to Hartshorne's 'dipolar' distinction between them.

7 God is thus what is ontologically, valuatively and rationally ultimate. A few attempts have been made to put forward a notion of a finite God, for example, by J. S. Mill and E. S. Brightman. Such a notion is unsatisfactory where the finitude is held to be the result of God encountering structures which are ultimately independent of the div-

ine, and impose restrictions upon the divine contrary to the divine will: cf. J. S. Mill, 'Theism' in *Three Essays on Religion*, London: Longmans, Green, Reader and Dyer, 1874, p. 180. It is religiously unsatisfactory because a being so conceived cannot be the object of unreserved worship, and philosophically unsatisfactory because such a being is not the final, all-embracing ultimate on which all is grounded. On the other hand, it is important to recognize that in other respects it is legitimate and even necessary to consider God as limited by the divine nature and being as God. Otherwise the divine would not be identifiable even by God. It is, furthermore, theistically appropriate to perceive that the determinateness of the divine (e.g., that God's existence is necessary and not contingent, that God is loving and not hateful or apathetic, that God is all-inclusively and not merely partially aware, that God seeks aesthetic enrichment and not uniformity), and the creative decisions of the divine (whether this is to be thought of as the result of God choosing to create this cosmic order rather than some other one, or as following necessarily from the creatively loving nature of the divine), involve appropriate notions of divine limitation and so of divine finitude. To put it another way, a God who is infinite in all respects could neither be known to be anything nor even be self-aware of Godself as having any identifiable characteristics and purposes: 'To be an actual thing is to be limited' (A. N. Whitehead, *Religion in the Making*, Cambridge: Cambridge University Press, 1926, p. 135; cf. p. 138: 'The limitation of God is his goodness'). In addition, to hold that God is, for example, all-inclusively aware implies that while potentially the divine awareness is infinite (since whatever is knowable is known by God), in practice the actuality of the divine awareness is finite, since its awareness of what there is now in reality is limited to what there is now in reality to be known. It is a mistake, therefore, to hold that a proper appreciation of divine ultimacy requires the rejection of all possible interpretations of the notion of a finite God.

8 Paul Tillich, *Systematic Theology*, 3 vols., London: Nisbet, 1953, 1957, 1964, volume I, p. 236.

9 A. E. Taylor, *The Mind of Plato*, Ann Arbor: University of Michigan Press, 1960, p. 58: the 'Good' thus acts as 'at once the source of knowledge and illumination to the knowing mind, and the source of reality and being to the objects of its knowledge'. It is according to the patterns of the 'forms' that the Creator–God of Plato's *Timaeus* fashions the world.

10 Plato, *Republic*, 508f, translation by H. D. P. Lee, Harmondsworth: Penguin Books, 1955, p. 273: 'It is the cause of knowledge and truth, and you will be right to think of it as being itself known, and yet as being something other than, and even higher than, knowledge and truth . . . The Good, therefore, may be said to be the source not only of the objects of knowledge, but also of their existence and reality; yet

it is not itself identical with reality, but is beyond reality and superior to it in dignity and power.'

11 Cf. Aristotle, *Nichomachean Ethics*, Book I, chapter 6.

12 Cf. Aristotle, *Metaphysics*, Book Lambda, chapter 7. As theistic thought influenced by these ideas has found to its loss, what Aristotle considered to be necessary to complete his system of understanding is not necessarily intrinsically coherent as a description of a real entity, let alone a way to describe the God of theism.

13 Cf. what Aristotle says 'must' be so in ibid., chapter 8. This 'must-ness' reflects what is needed to complete the system. There is, however, no intrinsic reason for preferring what is so needed to the intellectual incompleteness of an infinite regression as a description of the nature of reality, unless it is presupposed that reality is rational in a way that makes sense to human understanding. This presupposition, however, begs the question.

14 See ibid., Book Alpha the Less, chapter 1: 'there is nothing which explains their being what they are, for it is they that explain the being of other things.'

15 R. Descartes, *Philosophical Works*, translated by E. S. Haldane and G. R. T. Ross, Cambridge: Cambridge University Press, 1911, volume I, p. 102; cf. p. 158; p. 104.

16 Ibid., volume I, p. 172: 'I recognise it to be impossible that He should ever deceive me; for . . . the desire to deceive without doubt testifies to malice or feebleness, and accordingly cannot be found in God. In the next place I experience in myself a certain capacity for judging which I have doubtless received from God, like all the other things I possess; and as He could not desire to deceive me, it is clear that He has not given me a faculty that will lead me to err if I use it aright.'

17 It is interesting to note that in his *Principles of Philosophy*, after making the claim that 'since God is no deceiver, the faculty of knowledge that He has given us cannot be fallacious', Descartes' doubts reappear. He thus concludes this 'Principle' by stating that 'even if this truth could not be rationally demonstrated, we are by nature so disposed to give our assent to things that we clearly perceive, that we cannot possibly doubt of their truth' (volume I, p. 236). This qualified remark, rather than Descartes' general position, is the position of modern secular thought (and also underlies current 'post-modernist' attacks on reason so far as they – somewhat self-contradictingly – attempt to show that their criticisms of enlightenment reason are rationally justified): we have to trust our understanding because it is all we have. In his references to God to justify his epistemological views Descartes belongs to an earlier world of thought. It is with Locke that we find without qualification the modern view of the unquestioned trustworthiness of reason, and of the trustworthiness of God as intellectually acceptable only if it is justified by autonomous reason.

18 Leibniz, *The Monadology and Other Philosophical Writings*, translated by R. Latta, Oxford: Oxford University Press, 1898, p. 415; cf. pp. 235ff, 339f.

19 See ibid., pp. 241, 343. God, for Leibniz, is the origin of all possibilities as well as of all actualities, and the perfection of the divine determines what are actualized.

20 Ibid., p. 263; cf. pp. 246, 333f. In this way Leibniz meets a fundamental epistemological difficulty with his position. In the *Monadology* reality is held to be composed of monads which, as simple substances, are 'windowless'. Leibniz solves the resulting problem of how they influence each other by holding that they do not interact directly but only ideally 'through the mediation of God'. They are united as parts of a single, coherent universe in 'a pre-established harmony' effected by the perfect and creative agency of God. This co-ordinates their individual activities and makes each of them, although windowless, cohere with all the others as part of a single universe. Leibniz's solution to this problem, however, poses another fundamental problem – namely that of the possible freedom of individuals to choose how they will act.

21 G. W. F. Hegel, *Philosophy of Mind*, translated from *The Encyclopaedia of the Philosophical Sciences* by W. Wallace, Oxford: Oxford University Press, p. 7: the exposition of this identification is described as 'the ultimate purpose of all education and all philosophy: it was the point to which turned the impulse of all religion and science: and it is this impulse that must explain the history of the world'.

22 G. W. F. Hegel, *Lectures on the Philosophy of Religion*, translated by E. B. Speirs and J. B. Sanderson, London: Kegan Paul, Trench, Trubner and Co., 1895, volume I, p. 90: 'the absolutely True, the Universal in and for itself, the All-comprehending, All-containing, that from which everything derives subsistence'; cf. pp. 92, 94f.

23 See ibid., volume III, pp. 18ff.

24 See ibid., volume II, p. 328.

25 Cf. G. W. F. Hegel, *The Phenomenology of Mind*, translated by J. B. Baillie, London: Swan Sonnenschein, 1910, volume 2, pp. 787ff, 794.

26 For example, religious notions about God's self-knowledge are interpreted in terms of God's coming to 'self-consciousness in man, and man's knowledge of God'. The content of these claims, however, is held to be directly expressed in philosophical assertions about 'the self-thinking Idea, the truth aware of itself': Hegel, *Philosophy of Mind*, pp. 176, 196; cf. p. 58; cf. *Philosophy of Religion*, volume II, p. 347.

27 Any metaphysical appreciation of the ultimate character of reality that is held to be valid must be compatible with, if not actually incorporated into, theistic understanding if the latter is to be credible.

28 See Hegel, *Phenomenology of Mind*, volume II, pp. 54f.

29 F. Engels, 'Ludwig Feuerbach and the end of classical German philoso-

phy' in K. Marx and F. Engels, *On Religion*, Moscow: Foreign Languages Publishing House, 1957, pp. 216f: 'the revolutionary character of the Hegelian philosophy' is based on its view of truth as not simply a static given waiting to be discovered, but as belonging to 'the process of cognition itself . . . which mounts from lower to ever higher levels of knowledge without ever reaching, by discovering so-called absolute truth, a point at which it can proceed no further . . .'

30 A. N. Whitehead, *Modes of Thought*, Cambridge: Cambridge University Press, 1938, pp. 75, 109f; cf. pp. 139ff; cf. *Essays in Science and Philosophy*, New York: Greenwood Press, 1968, p. 90.

31 A. N. Whitehead, *Adventures of Ideas*, Cambridge: Cambridge University Press, 1933, p. 342. The divine activity is persuasive, not coercive (cf. ibid., p. 215), as well as universal. Because, however, language arises from our concern with 'the prominent facts' which are readily distinguishable (ibid., p. 209), it is difficult to perceive the universal, inescapable and secure states of affairs which belong to everything and are the object of metaphysical enquiry. Consequently, it is not surprising that it is hard to discern the divine grounding of the processes of reality in 'the metaphysical first principles'. While they constitute the divine being, they cannot be detected by a process of discrimination which distinguishes states where they are present from those where they are not, for 'they can never fail of exemplification' (*Process and Reality: An Essay in Cosmology*, corrected edition edited by D. R. Griffin and D. W. Sherburne, New York: The Free Press, 1978, p. 3).

32 In *Process and Reality*, for example, Whitehead speaks of God as 'the outcome of creativity', and of 'every actual entity, including God', as 'a creature transcended by the creativity which it qualifies' (p. 88). Creativity is described as the 'ultimate' and God as 'its primordial non-temporal accident' (p. 7). In the final chapter Whitehead states that 'God is not to be treated as an exception to all metaphysical principles' but as 'their chief exemplification' (p. 343). Both God and the world 'are in the grip of the ultimate metaphysical ground, the creative advance into novelty' (p. 349).

33 A. N. Whitehead, *Science and the Modern World*, Cambridge: Cambridge University Press, 1927, pp. 221ff.

34 When Whitehead speaks of a creative act of 'unfettered conceptual valuation' as 'only possible once in the universe' (*Process and Reality*, p. 247), he is not speaking of an initial creative decision whereby God decided the ultimate metaphysical principles, but of the only (theoretical) point at which a creative decision would not be affected by the objective immortality of previous creative choices and actions as preserved in the consequent nature of God and contributing to (and as such 'fettering' to some extent) all future choices. If the creative activity of God is everlasting, with no beginning as well as no end, the point is theoretical since each actual divine valuation has predecessors.

35 Whitehead, *Process and Reality*, p. 344: God's activity 'presupposes the *general* metaphysical character of creative advance of which it is the primordial exemplification'. Consequently, while God is held to establish 'the categoreal decisions', God does so by exemplifying them in the divine being: cf. David A. Pailin, *God and the Processes of Reality: Foundations of a Credible Theism*, London: Routledge, 1989, pp. 127ff.

36 Although there are differences of approach between the process philosophies of Whitehead (influenced by his interests in the natural sciences) and Hartshorne (reflecting the tradition of rationalist a priori thought), their views on the ultimate have much fundamentally in common: cf. Pailin, *God and the Processes of Reality*: pp. 42, 46ff, 57ff.

37 Charles Hartshorne, *A Natural Theology for Our Time*, La Salle, Ill.: Open Court, 1967, p. 32: 'divinity is not religiously conceived as a mere illustration of first principles but as somehow *the* first principles, the correlate of every interest and every meaning.'

38 Charles Hartshorne, *Creative Synthesis and Philosophic Method*, London: SCM Press, 1970, p. 41; cf. p. 23.

39 See R. B. Braithwaite, 'An empiricist's view of the nature of religious belief,' reprinted in I. T. Ramsey (ed.), *Christian Ethics and Contemporary Philosophy*, London: SCM Press, 1960.

40 See John Wisdom, 'Gods' in *Proceedings of the Aristotelian Society*, London: Harrison and Sons, 1944–5, volume XLV; Paul van Buren, *The Secular Meaning of the Gospel*, London: SCM Press, 1963; Donald D. Evans, *The Logic of Self-Involvement*, London: SCM Press, 1963; W. D. Hudson, *A Philosophical Approach to Religion*, London: Macmillan, 1974, pp. 13–25.

41 Gordon D. Kaufman, *An Essay on Theological Method*, Missoula: Scholars Press for American Academy of Religion, 1975, p. 15. In view, however, of his more recent comment that 'belief in God's existing over against us' is not necessarily required for 'God's functioning as a center of orientation and devotion' (*The Theological Imagination: Constructing the Concept of God*, Philadelphia: Westminster Press, 1981, p. 37), it is debatable how far his understanding of theology requires God to be a reality.

42 See I. T. Ramsey, 'Miracles, an exercise in logical mapwork' reprinted in *The Miracles and the Resurrection*, London: SPCK, 1964.

43 See B. Lonergan, *Method in Theology*, London: Darton, Longman and Todd, 1971, pp. 101ff; *Philosophy of God, and Theology*, London: Darton, Longman and Todd, 1973, pp. 52ff. The question of God thus reflects our questioning of the significance of the basic questions which orientate our thought.

44 See Wolfhart Pannenberg, *Basic Questions in Theology*, 3 vols., London: SCM Press, 1970, 1971, 1973, volume II, pp. 232f.

45 See J. Moltmann, *Theology of Hope*, London: SCM Press, 1967; *Hope and Planning*, London: SCM Press, 1971.

46 See Schubert M. Ogden, *The Reality of God*, London: SCM Press, 1967, pp. 120ff.

47 See P. F. Strawson, *The Bounds of Sense*, London: Methuen, 1966, p. 36.

48 A. C. Ewing, *A Short Commentary on Kant's Critique of Pure Reason*, London: Methuen, 1938, pp. 260–2. By an 'ideal' Kant means 'the idea, not merely *in concreto*, but *in individuo*, that is, as an individual thing, determinable or even determined by the idea alone'. The 'ideal' is thus said to serve as 'the *archetype*' which provides us with theoretical but absolute standards for our critical judgement of things: I. Kant, *The Critique of Pure Reason*, translated by N. K. Smith, London: Macmillan, 1933, pp. 485ff (B596ff).

49 Kant, *Critique of Pure Reason*, pp. 551f (B700f); *Prolegomena to Any Future Metaphysics*, translated by P. G. Lucas, Manchester: Manchester University Press, 1953, pp. 93ff (paras. 43f): on p. 92 (para. 41), he sees the distinction of ideas from concepts as a major contribution of the first *Critique*.

50 See Kant, *Critique of Pure Reason*, pp. 209f (B220), pp. 328ff (B399ff), 551 (B700), 557ff (B710ff); *Prolegomena*, pp. 97ff (paras. 46ff).

51 See Kant, *Critique of Pure Reason*, pp. 515 (B644), 511 (B700); *Prolegomena*, pp. 102f (para. 50). Within the negative form of the cosmological idea it is possible to distinguish further between the principle of perfect homogeneity and the principle of permanent divisibility. The former is the principle of science as it seeks a single, all-embracing genus in which fundamental properties are united and from which the diversity of things 'can be derived through repeated determinations'. The latter represents the opposite principle. It is the principle of science as it unceasingly distinguishes between the objects of its study, seeing itself as under 'the obligation of seeking under every discoverable species for subspecies, and under every difference for yet smaller differences' (*Critique of Pure Reason*, pp. 538ff [B680ff]). A third negative version of the cosmological idea, a corollary of the first but perhaps deserving separate recognition, is the view that since no possible knowledge of nature is able to satisfy reason, nature itself cannot be regarded as 'sufficient in itself'. All understanding of it consequently always points beyond itself (*Prolegomena*, p. 131 [para. 60]).'

52 See Kant, *Critique of Pure Reason*, pp. 450f (B537f), 515 (B644), 551 (B700), 558f (B712f). Other forms of it are the idea of pure substances, since these are needed to explain natural processes although empirically no substance is absolutely pure (see p. 534 [B673f]), and the idea of a fundamental power which is manifested in the various specific powers observed to operate in the world (see pp. 536f [B677]). The

latter seems to be what currently excites physicists to attempt to identify a 'grand unified theory'.

53 See ibid., pp. 648f (B854).

54 In terms of nature this is expressed as the idea of an unknown 'substratum' which gives 'unity, order and purposiveness' to the world (ibid., p. 566 [B725]): See I. Kant, *Critique of Judgement*, translated by J. H. Bernard, New York: Hafner, 1951, pp. 265ff [paras. 79ff], 286ff [paras. 85f]). As for history, Kant sees the idea of purpose, in spite of explicit reservations, as serving 'as a guiding thread for presenting as a system . . . what would otherwise be a planless conglomeration of human actions' (Immanuel Kant, 'Idea for a universal history' in L. W. Beck (ed.), *Kant on History*, Indianapolis: Bobbs-Merrill, 1963, p. 24).

55 See Kant, *Critique of Pure Reason*, pp. 638f (B837ff); I. Kant, *Critique of Practical Reason*, translated by T. K. Abbot, London: Longmans, 1909, pp. 230ff. In the case of morality Kant holds that if we ought (i.e., are morally obliged) to seek this *summum bonum*, it must be possible for us to attain it. Otherwise no moral imperative can be attached to it. The possibility of such attainment, however, requires him to postulate not only that we are morally free, but also that we shall have endless existence and that our degree of happiness will be determined by God. In this respect God is the individuation of the idea of 'the most perfect moral will, united with supreme blessedness' (*Critique of Pure Reason*, p. 639 [B838ff]; cf. *Critique of Practical Reason*, pp. 218ff). In the essay 'The end of all things' Kant describes discussions of the Last Judgement as 'playing' with 'Ideas which reason itself creates' (Beck, *Kant on History*, p. 75). In the *Critique of Pure Reason*, p. 486 (B597) he also speaks of 'virtue, and therewith human wisdom in its complete purity' as ideas. The *summum bonum* is thus not the only expression of the idea of the moral reason.

56 See Immanuel Kant, 'An old question raised again' in Beck, *Kant on History*, p. 150; *Critique of Pure Reason*, p. 312 (B373).

57 See Kant, *Critique of Pure Reason*, p. 488 (B599f); *Prolegomena*, p. 114 (para. 55).

58 Kant attempts to overcome the problem of the non-compossibility of certain attributes by holding, in this respect, that not all predicates are to be attributed to the *ens realissimum* but, where a pair of predicates are contradictory, only 'that which belongs to being absolutely'. Although this seems to undermine the claim that the *ens realissimum* is an all-embracing idea, it allows Kant to treat it as an ideal, that is, an individual object, which is 'the supreme and complete material condition of the possibility of all that exists' (*Critique of Pure Reason*, pp. 490f [B603f]).

59 See ibid., pp. 492 (B606f); 497 (B614).

60 Ibid., p. 495 (B611): 'This ideal of the *ens realissimum* . . . is first

realised, that is, made into an object, then *hypostatised*, and finally, by
the natural progress of reason towards the completion of unity, is . . .
personified.'

61 Cf. Immanuel Kant, *Lectures on Ethics*, translated by L. Infield, New
York: Harper and Row, 1963, p. 85: 'the concept of God is an Idea
which we must regard as the limiting concept of reason and as the
totality of all derivative concepts.'

62 See Kant, *Critique of Pure Reason*, p. 495 (B612).

63 'A reason which gives a reason without requiring one': W. Wallace,
Kant, Edinburgh: Blackwood, 1882, p. 181.

64 See Kant, *Critique of Pure Reason*, p. 486 (B596ff).

65 Ibid., p. 486 (B597).

66 See ibid., p. 492 (B607): 'These terms are not, however, to be taken as
signifying the objective relation of an actual object to other things, but
of an *idea to concepts*. We are left entirely without knowledge as to the
existence of a being of such outstanding pre-eminence.' Cf. pp. 528f
(B664ff).

67 See ibid., p. 495 (B611f), 513ff (B640ff), 517f (647f), 533f (B671ff), 550
(B699).

68 When Kant discusses 'the ideal of the supreme being', he is careful to
point out that it refers to 'nothing but' that regulative principle which
requires us to consider the world '*as if* it originated from an all-sufficient
necessary cause'. On the basis of this ideal we consider that there is an
essential unity in the world, but we cannot hold that the ideal itself
refers to 'an existence necessary in itself': ibid., p. 517 (B647); cf.
pp. 556f (B609f), 649 (B854).

69 Kant, *Prolegomena*, p. 114 (para. 55); cf. pp. 91f (para. 40), 129f
(para. 59).

70 In relation to the idea of a supreme being, for instance, Kant holds that
its nature as being absolutely necessary in relation to the world shows
that it cannot refer to an actual individual: 'the concept of necessity'
only applies to thought and cannot be 'hypostatised as a material condition of existence', *Critique of Pure Reason*, p. 518 (B648); cf.
pp. 514f (B643). Kant's claim that necessity cannot be a quality of
existence is the principle behind J. N. Findlay's argument, 'Can God's
existence be disproved' in A. Flew and A. MacIntyre (eds.), *New
Essays in Philosophical Theology*, London: SCM Press, 1955, pp. 47ff.
Findlay later modified the argument on the grounds that Hartshorne
had shown that a coherent notion of 'necessary existence' was possible:
see J. N. Findlay, 'Reflections on necessary existence' in W. L. Reese
and E. Freeman (eds.), *Process and Divinity*, La Salle, Ill.: Open
Court, 1964, pp. 515ff.

71 See Kant, *Critique of Pure Reason*, pp. 485f (B596ff); *Prolegomena*,
pp. 102ff (paras. 50ff), 120 (para. 57): 'The transcendental ideas . . .
can never be realised.'

72 Kant, *Critique of Pure Reason*, p. 533 (B644); cf. pp. 565f (B724f); *Prolegomena*, pp. 96f (para. 45), 115f (para. 56).

73 See Kant, *Critique of Pure Reason*, p. 533 (B672).

74 As R. C. S. Walker points out, the fact that to 'establish that certain things must obtain, if we are to have experience', does not show that their obtaining is 'due to us: it may just be a fortunate fact about the world': *Kant*, London: Routledge and Kegan Paul, 1978, p. 12.

75 Cf. Kant, *Critique of Pure Reason*, p. 481 (B589f).

76 Ibid., p. 531 (B669); cf. p. 518 (B648).

77 Cf. ibid., p. 555 (B707); cf. Kant, *Prolegomena*, pp. 122f (para. 57), 125ff (para. 58), 129f (para. 59).

78 See Kant, *Critique of Pure Reason*, p. 649 (B854f); see also Kant's assertion in his essay 'What is orientation in thinking?' (printed in Immanuel Kant, *Critique of Practical Reason and Other Writings in Moral Philosophy*, translated by L. W. Beck, Chicago: University of Chicago Press, 1949, pp. 293ff) that just as 'the concept of a First Being as the supreme intelligence and the highest good' is needed by our reason to give a basis to the limitation of all other things, so 'the presupposition' of its existence is needed to give a comprehensible ground for the contingency and order of things. These needs provide 'a sufficient subjective ground for assuming such an author'. On this basis we can interpret Kant's claim that in the first *Critique* he denies 'knowledge, in order to make room for *faith*' (*Critique of Pure Reason*, p. 29 [Bxxx]) as supporting the contention in his *Lectures on Ethics* that 'religion is based on faith alone . . . but [faith] is justified in postulating its content as a necessary hypothesis' (p. 88). Van A. Harvey has an interesting discussion of Nietzsche's challenge to Kant's views of the significance of regulative ideas and Kant's faith in the trustworthiness of reason in 'Nietzsche and the Kantian paradigm of faith' in P. E. Devenish and G. L. Goodwin (eds.), *Witness and Existence*, Chicago and London: University of Chicago Press, 1989, pp. 140–61.

79 Kant, *Critique of Pure Reason*, p. 513 (B640f); cf. p. 531 (B669f).

80 Kant, *Prolegomena*, pp. 119ff (para. 57).

81 C. C. J. Webb points to this characteristic of religion when he speaks of our awareness of God as 'the form of experience in which we divine the coincidence of that which would satisfy the demand of our reason for an object free from all contradiction and unintelligibility with that concrete reality of which we inevitably find our standard in our consciousness of self': *The Historical Element in Religion*, London: George Allen and Unwin, 1935, p. 94.

82 This may be in the form either of a beginningless sequence of cosmic processes or an initial cosmic explosion which was the start of things: in either case, however, the being of whatever happens to be is finally inexplicable and meaningless.

83 The regulative idea of a temporally first cause of all the processes of

reality (and hence of an absolutely first moment of reality) may, for example, be regarded as incompatible with a theism which holds that God, as the essentially creative ground of all things, is without beginning and without end. Such an incompatibility, however, does not entail that the idea is necessarily or in all respects invalid as a guiding principle within the domain of the empirical investigations of the natural sciences.

84 The regulative idea of the centrality of the earth which underlies and directs Ptolemaic astronomy is now regarded as mistaken. Theists are under no obligation to show that such erroneous ideas can be and are incorporated into their understanding of God.

85 For example, such ideas as those of a point in mathematics or a perfectly efficient engine in engineering do not require to be incorporated into theistic understanding as part of the essential reality of the divine.

86 This suggests that it is fallacious to try to make an absolute distinction between religious understanding and other ways of understanding on the grounds that religion deals with 'why' things are as they are, whereas other ways of understanding deal with the 'whats' and 'hows' of reality. From the point of view of theological understanding such distinctions are superficial. In the end the questions of 'what', 'how' and 'why' all lead to the common question of what is ultimate and so to the question of God.

87 Cf. Hartshorne, 'Grounds for believing in God's existence' in Rouner, *Meaning, Truth and God*, p. 20: 'as for the idea of a merely chaotic world, I find that a confused notion. Any world in which the theistic or any other question could arise would have an order . . . Some order or other is a presupposition of inquiry and of all thinking.' My point in this paragraph is not to contradict what Hartshorne maintains, but to indicate that the order which Hartshorne sees as presupposed in our thought is not something which is directly experienced, although reflection on their character may indicate that it is a common presupposition of experience and thought.

88 This view of reality is reflected in Bertrand Russell's comment that while 'the word "universe" is a handy word in some connections', he does not consider that 'it stands for anything that has a meaning'. Thus he holds that there is no meaning in questions about the existence 'of the whole universe': 'The existence of God, a debate between Bertrand Russell and Father F. C. Copleston, SJ' in Bertrand Russell, *Why I am not a Christian and Other Essays*, London: George Allen and Unwin, 1975,

89 It is similarly trivial to say that the items of my experience are linked together because I am aware of them.

90 So far as this kind of argument is significant, it is probably best seen not as a neat inference of the reality of God from the unity of the world, nor of the unity of the world from the reality of God, but as a reciprocal argument in which each insight informs and supports the other in seek-

ing to establish an overall understanding that requires both. Kaufman in *Essay on Theological Method*, pp. 45ff, analyses the construction of theological concepts in terms of three moments: the concept of the world, the concept of God which relativizes and humanizes the world, and the reformulation of the concept of the world in the light of the concept of God. It is important to note, however, that these three moments mutually interact. They are to be regarded as only logically separable and not as distinct successive steps (cf. p. 61). The position suggested here is that in practice the notions of God and of the universe emerge reciprocally.

91 From the perspective of the observer the most probable conclusion may well be that of H. A. L. Fisher who confesses that while others 'have discerned in history a plot, a rhythm, a predetermined pattern', as a historian he finds 'these harmonies are concealed' from him: 'I can only see one emergency following upon another as wave follows upon wave': *A History of Europe*, London: Edward Arnold, 1936, p. v.

92 While, however, theistic investigations into reality presuppose that it has a meaning, apparent successes in the investigations may be regarded as helping to justify the entertainment of the idea. In the end, as in the case of the discernment of the unity of that world, presuppositions, experience and reflection reciprocally interact to inform and reinforce each other.

93 Cf. the admirable quality of life displayed by Camus's heroes as they refuse to be cowed by the final pointlessness of human actions.

94 Cf. Schubert Ogden's argument that only belief in God as one who is totally aware can justify the individual's inalienable confidence in the importance of living and of the values concretely expressed by personal activity. He criticizes atheistic existentialism as incoherent because its 'atheism' denies the possibility of justifying that confidence and hence of the existentialist demand to live. Only on a theistic basis can that confidence and demand make sense: see 'The strange witness of unbelief' in *The Reality of God*, pp. 120ff. Ogden points out, however, that such a theistic basis cannot be provided by a traditional doctrine of God which ascribes impassibility and timeless eternity to the divine (for such a view entails that the divine must be unaware of temporal activities as such). To affirm coherently that human lives have significance for God requires the adoption of a doctrine of God such as is presented by Hartshorne's dipolar panentheism: cf. Pailin, *God and the Processes of Reality*, pp. 208ff.

95 Cf. David A. Pailin, 'The ground of faith', *The Expository Times*, June 1977, pp. 269ff; for the notion of metaphysics as story, cf. D. A. Pailin, 'Narrative, story and the interpretation of metaphysics' in George R. Lucas (ed.), *Hegel and Whitehead: Contemporary Perspectives on Systematic Philosophy*, Albany: State University of New York Press, 1986, pp. 268–84.

96 This does not directly entail a correspondence theory of truth, for it is not immediate reference to the state of the object that is the standard of truth, but the actual state of the object as perceived by God. Since the standard of truth is provided by God's perception, it can in certain respects be held to be subjective. On the other hand, since theism presupposes that God's awareness is perfect, it also holds that what God perceives is what actually is the case, and so in effect is an objective standard. In theistic understanding, therefore, subjective and objective views of truth come together: cf. Pannenberg, *Basic Questions in Theology*, volume II, pp. 1–27.

97 The concept of God's ontological ultimacy, for example, conditions our understanding by presupposing that the divine being is the ground of all else. At the same time our understanding of this aspect of the divine is conditioned by our perception, even if mainly negative and confused, of what it is to be self-existent, uncaused, the final point for any chain of causes, and the point behind or beyond which it is necessarily impossible to go both in practice and in thought.

98 For example, as has been noted, we cannot argue straightforwardly that the world has a rational creator because it has a rational structure, if the view that it has a rational structure is itself a presupposition of our thought or the product of presupposing that it has a rational creator.

99 If, for instance, it is true that I am now wearing a pair of cuff-links, it will always be true that at this time I wore a pair of cuff-links and this cannot be contradicted by anything else that has been or will be.

100 Cf. Hartshorne, 'Why there cannot be empirical proofs', *A Natural Theology for Our Time*, chapter 3, for a discussion of this point.

101 Hence Antony Flew's use of the falsification principle to challenge statements about God's existence is logically mistaken because it treats statements about God's existence as if they have the logical character of statements about contingent facts, whereas they are statements about what is necessarily real: see 'Theology and falsification', in Flew and MacIntyre, *New Essays in Philosophical Theology*, p. 99.

102 Whitehead, *Process and Reality*, p. 4.

103 Although those who want to restrict the concept of 'necessity' to logical relationships may jib at the usage, it seems reasonable to hold that the claims about God which we are considering express what is necessarily the case. It is, therefore, both true a priori of all reality and significant for all reality as determining its fundamental character.

104 Cf. Whitehead, *Science and the Modern World*, pp. 221f, on God as 'the ultimate limitation'. The universal quality of some theological judgements is also seen in the doctrine of *creatio ex nihilo*, where this doctrine draws out the unconditionedness as well as the ultimacy of the divine act, and in those analyses of the ontological argument which stress the 'necessary' character of God's existence.

105 Although it is logically impossible to hold that the same being is both
incapable of action and acts, and is both incapable of response and
responds, this has not prevented theologians from attempting to do
the impossible. Sometimes they have tried to cover the incoherences
by reference to 'paradox' or to 'the incomprehensibility of God'.
Hartshorne's analysis of dipolarity in relation to the concept of God
indicates how many of the basic problems may be solved.

106 Whatever else may be expressed by the notion of God's actual creativity, in some sense or other it must include the idea of bringing about
what would not otherwise be. This, at root, is what it is to 'create'.
Although the antecedents and limits of the creativity may differ enor-
mously according to the nature of the creator, all creativity involves
the production of something and hence change, at least from possibility
to actuality. Consequently it involves change for the creator: not only
does it alter the environment and its possibilities in which concrete
creative activity can occur, so far as the creator is acting consciously
and purposively it also alters the creator's awareness of what is actual.

107 Cf. W. Donald Hudson, *A Philosophical Approach to Religion*,
London: Macmillan, 1974, p. 16: 'the concept of God is the *constitutive*
concept of religious belief' in that it 'determines what in religious belief
constitutes (a) an *explanation* and (b) an *experience*'. In this respect
'belief in God' is said to be not a kind of directly testable hypothesis
but 'a commitment' to a particular, i.e., theistic, way of interpreting
experience.

108 It should be noted, however, that not all forms of moral prescriptivism
regard the determination of moral rules to be an ultimately arbitrary
matter. R. M. Hare, for example, meets the problem by arguing that
proper moral judgements are marked by being completely universaliz-
able: see *The Language of Morals*, Oxford: Oxford University Press,
1964, III, 11, 5; *Freedom and Reason*, Oxford: Oxford University Press,
1965.

109 According to W. G. Maclagan the word 'God' may refer to more
than morality but, so far as our 'consciousness of moral demand' is
concerned, it 'can mean nothing different from "moral law" '. Moral
values are thus neither independent of nor dependent upon God: they
express part of the intrinsic reality of the divine: *The Theological Fron-
tier of Ethics*, London: George Allen and Unwin, 1961, pp. 81f.
Maclagan is accordingly worried about the attribution of a personal
mode of being to God because, among other things, of the danger that
it will lead to the view that moral values are derived from God's will:
see pp. 170ff.

110 B. F. Porter, *Deity and Morality*, London: George Allen and Unwin,
1968, pp. 151f, 157.

111 Immanuel Kant, *Foundations of the Metaphysics of Morals*, translated
by L. W. Beck, Indianapolis: Bobbs-Merrill, 1959, pp. 46f.

112 D. Z. Phillips and H. O. Mounce, for example, argue that 'moral concepts are not functional': 'One can see what is to count as a good knife by asking what a knife is *for*, but can one see the point of generosity in the same way? To ask what generosity is *for* is simply to vulgarise the concept; it is like thinking that "It is more blessed to give than to receive" is some kind of policy.' Consequently, they conclude that it is a radical mistake to hold that the nature of goodness may be demonstrated 'by appeal to evidence' in ways which 'operate *independently* of the various moral opinions people hold'. This response makes moral values their own value: 'On morality's having a point' reprinted in W. D. Hudson (ed.), *The Is-Ought Question*, London: Macmillan, 1969, p. 233.

113 For some it may be at the vulgar level of wine, women and song or the rumbustious banqueting of martial heroes in Valhalla. C. D. Broad is reported to have suggested that for some spiritualists heaven seems to be 'like a perpetual bump-supper at a Welsh university' (quoted in A. J. Ayer, *Part of my Life*, London: Collins, 1977, p. 118). For others it may be more like the delight found in listening to a piece of music or in being enthralled by a work of art.

114 Francis Xavier suggests this view of the true end of being in the lines ('Deus ego amo Te', translated by Edward Caswall, *The Methodist Hymn-Book*, London: Methodist Publishing House, 1933, no. 446),

My God, I love Thee – not because
I hope for heaven thereby . . .

for this love is not a means to heaven. It is heaven.

115 Whitehead, *Adventures of Ideas*, p. 342.

116 In Christianity, for example, the moral guidelines in the Sermon on the Mount are to be seen as indicating the form of life which leads to 'blessedness', where 'blessedness' is that state of being which is intrinsically and ultimately satisfying.

117 Whitehead, *Religion in the Making*, pp. 87, 91. The implications of a theology which sees beauty in Whiteheadian terms as the ultimate value is explored in William D. Dean, *Coming To: A Theology of Beauty*, Philadelphia: Westminster Press, 1972.

118 When Whitehead states that God's 'conceptual actuality at once exemplifies and establishes the categoreal conditions' (*Process and Reality*, p. 344), the use of the term 'establishes' does not mean that God creates or produces the ultimate metaphysical principles, but rather that they exist or are instantiated in the divine being. It is as such that God may properly be said to exemplify them.

119 What Whitehead says about the divine side of the God-world relationship applies to the principles, namely, that they 'lie beyond the accidents of will' (and of understanding, we might add), since they are 'founded upon the necessities of the nature of God': *Adventures of*

Ideas, p. 215; cf. also A. C. Ewing, *Value and Reality*, London: George Allen and Unwin, 1973, pp. 203f, for a similar view of God from a different philosophical background.

120 Cf. Whitehead, *Adventures of Ideas*, p. 198.

121 The notion of God's ultimacy in being, when expressed in terms of the 'uncaused cause', may accordingly be held to be a product of the principle of rationality which holds that everything is explicable, and not a product of reflection on the nature of being as such.

122 The case of the attribution of simplicity to God seems to be one where the attribution is most likely to be a product of our desire for intellectual completeness. Although the notion seems unclear and to create problems for the appreciation of God's other attributes, it is attributed to God in an attempt to make sense of God's infinity (as unlimitedness) and of God's self-existence as always wholly actual. It is questionable, however, whether the divine infinity should be treated in this way rather than as a recognition that God cannot be perceived as a whole. There are, furthermore, good reasons for holding that divine existence must not be understood to exclude all forms of potentiality: any such exclusion prevents the attribution of personal modes of intentionality, responsiveness and activity to the divine.

123 Cf. Anselm, *Proslogion*, chapters 1, 5, 8.

124 Cf. Aristotle, *Metaphysics*, Book Delta, chapter 16, 1021b; cf. Book Lambda, chapter 7, 1072b.

125 Anselm, *Cur Deus Homo*, chapter 12, in *St Anselm: Basic Writings*, translated by S. N. Deane, La Salle, Ill.: Open Court, 1962, p. 203.

126 Anselm here does not challenge the legitimacy of attributing compassion to God as a quality in God.

127 Peter Abelard, *Exposition of the Epistle to the Romans* in *A Scholastic Miscellany, Anselm to Ockham*, edited and translated by E. R. Fairweather, London: SCM Press, 1956, pp. 279, 283.

128 The variety of subcultures in Victorian Britain, however, should not be overlooked.

129 See J. McLeod Campbell, *The Nature of the Atonement*, London: Macmillan, 1869, p. 346.

130 See R. W. Dale, *The Atonement*, London: Hodder and Stoughton, 1876, pp. 391f.

131 Cf. T. E. Hulme's remark that 'there are certain doctrines which for a particular period seem not doctrines, but inevitable categories of the human mind. Men do not look on them merely as correct opinion, for . . . they are never really conscious of them at all. They do not see them, but other things *through* them': *Speculations*, edited by H. Read, London: Kegan Paul, Trench, Trubner and Co., 1924, pp. 50f. Cf. also A. Richardson, *History Sacred and Profane*, London: SCM Press, 1964, pp. 52, 107ff, on the way in which an historian's interpretation of history expresses a myth or ideology which is generally unconsciously

regarded as the unquestionable way to understand the evidence. As is pointed out by sociological investigations of understanding, all our thought is partly determined by such myths, ideologies or 'plausibility structures': cf. P. L. Berger, *A Rumour of Angels*, Harmondsworth: Penguin, 1970, pp. 50ff.

132 Cf. Tillich, *Systematic Theology*, volume I, pp. 264ff, on the way in which 'the segment of finite reality' used to make concrete assertions about God is both 'affirmed and negated' as it is used symbolically of God.

133 I. T. Ramsey, *Christian Discourse*, Oxford: Oxford University Press, 1965, p. 71; cf. also *Religious Language*, London: SCM Press, 1957, *Models and Mystery*, Oxford: Oxford University Press, 1964, and *Models for Divine Activity*, London: SCM Press, 1973, for other expressions of Ramsey's views on this issue. The quotation from White-head is from *Science and the Modern World*, p. 238.

134 Kant, *Critique of Pure Reason*, p. 533 (B672). As noted earlier, how-ever, Kant wavers at times on this point. Occasionally he merely holds that descriptions of the *ens realissimum* may refer to an actual entity but can never be known so to refer.

135 It is, however, advanced as the goal of 'the spiritual life' by Don Cupitt, *Taking Leave of God*, London: SCM Press, 1980, pp. 10, etc. Whatever his interest in religion and the spiritual life, such comments indicate that Cupitt should not want to be classed as a theist.

136 Cf. Kant, *Critique of Pure Reason*, p. 491 (B605), where Kant speaks of 'the representation of the sum of all reality' as that which, 'as regards its transcendental content', both 'comprehends all predicates *under itself*' and 'also contains them *within itself*'.

137 No actual being, for instance, can be *both* wholly loving *and* wholly impassible, *both* creative *and* unchanging, *both* living *and* absolutely complete in every respect (or, in more classical terms, *both* having potentialities *and* being *actus purus*).

138 Because of this incompatibility Anselm is mistaken when he holds that God, as the greatest conceivable, can be coherently regarded as an actual being which lacks no good quality whatsoever: *Proslogion*, chap-ter 5. If we consider what may be regarded as better to have than not to have, we find that to have one quality (say, compassion) prevents us having another quality (say, in this case, bliss), although both qualities seem to be better to have than to lack. Furthermore, the notion of having (and so enjoying) all possible actualizable experiences of value is incoherent once it is accepted that at least part of reality is in process and, therefore, that future events will actualize further experiences of value.

139 Cf. chapter 2, note 25.

140 If, for example, we accept that one of the regulative roles of God is that of ontological ultimacy, this means that God is to be thought of as

the ground of whatever ontological order happens to obtain. This does not require God actually to be the ground of any particular possible order nor, *a fortiori*, of any particular possible object. If, furthermore, it is justifiable to consider that in creating God makes primordial creative decisions, then in creating God must be held to have the freedom to choose to actualize one among several possible orders. What God cannot choose to actualize, however, is an order which is not dependent on Godself. Consequently, while whatever becomes actual may be partly dependent on God's personal choice, nothing at all can become actual which is not dependent on God as its ground.

141 Cf. Baruch Spinoza, *Ethics*, Part v, propositions xvii and xix, in translation by A. Boyle, London: Dent, 1959, pp. 210f. Even though he is convinced that God's existence is demonstrable, Spinoza holds that our love of God must recognize that God 'is free from passions' and so 'loves no one nor hates any one'. Accordingly 'he who loves God cannot endeavour to bring it about that God should love him in return.' What Spinoza does here is to find some religious significance in theology's traditional doctrine of the impassibility of God, but it is at the cost of rendering the divine utterly unresponsive.

142 H. Vaihinger, *The Philosophy of 'As If'*, translated by C. K. Ogden, London: Kegan Paul, Trench, Trubner and Co., 1924, p. 272.

143 Ibid., pp. 124, 264.

144 A. Camus, *The Rebel*, translated by A. Bower, Harmondsworth: Penguin Books, 1971, p. 265: in his view rebellion is to be seen as the 'origin of form, source of real life' and so as what 'keeps us always erect in the savage formless movement of history'.

145 Cf. Pailin, 'The ground of faith', pp. 269ff.

146 According to H. L. Mansel, we can never attain valid '*speculative* knowledge' of the nature of ultimate reality but, through revelation, are given '*regulative* ideas of the Deity, which are sufficient to guide our practice'. These tell us 'not what God is in Himself, but how He wills that we should think of Him': *The Limits of Religious Thought*, Oxford, 1858, pp. 126f.

147 Pannenberg, *Basic Questions*, volume II, p. 233.

148 L. Feuerbach, *The Essence of Christianity*, translated by G. Eliot, New York: Harper and Brothers, 1957, pp. 21f. The treatment of Jesus Christ as the manifestation of the divine nature illustrates how people fashion their understanding of God – or of the character of the divine self-revelation – in accordance with their principles.

5 *Theology and religious experience*

1 Isaac Newton, *Philosophiae Naturalis Principia Mathematica*, 2nd edition, London, 1713, Scholium Generale.

2 Martin Buber, *I and Thou*, translated by R. Gregor Smith, Edinburgh: T. and T. Clark, 1937, p. 81.

3 R. G. Collingwood suggests that while philosophy in general seeks to discover the principles implicit in 'everyday experience', the task of theology is to make 'explicit certain principles which are implicitly, but never explicitly, present in religious consciousness': *Speculum Mentis*, Oxford: Clarendon Press, 1924, p. 85n; cf. pp. 118f. Collingwood changed his mind on the question of the implicitness or explicitness of these principles: cf. ibid., p. 108n.

4 Ibid., pp. 118f; cf. pp. 148ff.

5 Michael Novak finds 'the experience of nothingness' in that nihilism which regards the structure of every experience as 'put into' it by 'culture and the self'. To develop the view that individuals contribute to what they experience to the point where all the significance in their experiences is held to be contributed by them is to finish up, according to Novak, 'near the borderline of insanity': See 'The experience of nothingness' in Norbert O. Schedler (ed.), *Philosophy of Religion: Contemporary Perspectives*, New York: Collier Macmillan, 1974, p. 26. There is no need, however, for such a despairing development: we can accept that a factor contributes to a situation without having to hold that it is the sole contributor to it.

6 John Macquarrie, *Principles of Christian Theology*, London: SCM Press, 1966, pp. 5ff.

7 Marghanita Laski's study of the subject shows that it covers a number of distinguishable states, not all of which need be present for a particular experience to be described as ecstatic: *Ecstasy, A Study of Some Secular and Religious Experiences*, London: The Cresset Press, 1961; see pp. 41ff, for attempts to determine the defining characteristics of ecstacy.

8 Plotinus describes such an experience when he writes that, when we contemplate the dynamically indivisible One, 'we attain the end of our desires and find rest. Then it is that, all discord past, we dance an inspired dance around it. In this dance the soul looks upon the source of Life, the source of the Intelligence, the origin of Being, the cause of the Good, the root of the Soul': *The Enneads*, VI, 9, quoted from *The Essential Plotinus*, translated by E. M. O'Brien, New York: Mentor, 1964, p. 84.

9 It is a feeling which is expressed at the close of T. S. Eliot's 'Little Gidding' in *Four Quartets*, London: Faber and Faber, 1969, p. 59.

10 A. N. Whitehead, *Religion in the Making*, Cambridge: Cambridge University Press, 1926, pp. 109f; cf. H. D. Lewis, *Our Experience of God*, London: George Allen and Unwin, 1959, p. 114, where religious experience is described as a situation in which we are 'more than usually perceptive of certain things in our present environment and responsive

to them'. In this state we are, according to Lewis, especially conscious of the 'unity in things' which follows from their 'transcendent source'.

11 John Baillie, *The Sense of the Presence of God*, Oxford: Oxford University Press, 1962, pp. 73, 89; cf. p. 259; cf. also John Hick, *Faith and Knowledge*, New York: Cornell University Press, 1957, p. 129: the believers' 'apprehension of the divine presence' is 'within' their 'human experience' as 'a mediated meeting with the living God' (p. 115 in 2nd revised edition, London: Macmillan, 1967).

12 John Baillie, *Our Knowledge of God*, Oxford: Oxford University Press, 1939, p. 181; *Sense of the Presence of God*, p. 89.

13 See Buber, *I and Thou*, pp. 76, 80f.

14 See ibid., p. 82. When apparently third-person descriptions of God are given, they are to be understood as names and metaphors for the 'Thou' who is only knowable as the one who is encountered: cf. ibid., pp. 75, 116. It is arguable, therefore, that when Buber seems to give third-person statements about God, they are not to be understood as statements about God, but rather as statements which indicate the proper character of God-talk.

15 Cf. R. W. Hepburn, *Christianity and Paradox*, London: Watts, 1966, pp. 24ff; Macquarrie, *Principles of Christian Theology*, p. 84.

16 Gabriel Marcel, *Being and Having*, London: Collins, 1965, p. 184: for Marcel the pure state of religious experience is not of specific qualities but of utterly uncharacterizable, bare Being.

17 Paul Tillich, *Biblical Religion and the Search for Ultimate Reality*, London: Nisbet, 1955, pp. 82f.

18 F. D. E. Schleiermacher, *On Religion: Speeches to Its Cultured Despisers*, translated by John Oman, New York: Harper and Brothers, 1958, pp. 36, 50. He points out that the feeling that all 'our being and living is a being and living in and through God' is to be distinguished from what he defines as 'knowledge'.

19 F. D. E. Schleiermacher, *The Christian Faith*, Edinburgh: T. and T. Clark, 1928, pp. 16f; cf. pp. 6ff.

20 Because of the way in which his position is expressed, critics, especially from the Barthian side, have maintained that for Schleiermacher religious experience has primarily a subjective reference. It is an immediate self-consciousness. In it individuals become aware of their contingent status and develop the notion of God as a way to understand the grounds of this status. It is arguable, however, that Schleiermacher's use of the notion of 'feeling' shows that it has for him also a kind of cognitive objective reference.

21 Such an 'objective' understanding of the nature of religious experience as a feeling of dependence is also found in H. D. Lewis's view that religion begins with the realization that all existence depends upon 'some absolute or unconditioned being' which is only knowable directly

in an 'intuition of its unconditioned nature as the source of all other reality': *Our Experience of God*, p. 107; cf. pp. 107ff, 110ff.

22 Rudolf Otto, *The Idea of the Holy*, translated by J. W. Harvey, 2nd edition, Oxford: Oxford University Press, 1950, p. 7.

23 Sam Keen, for example, sees the holy in terms of what is experienced as giving 'unity, depth, density, dignity, meaning, and value' to life: *To A Dancing God*, London: Collins, 1971, p. 99.

24 Immanuel Kant, *Religion within the Limits of Reason Alone*, translated by T. M. Green and H. H. Hudson, New York: Harper, 1960, p. 142; cf. also Hastings Rashdall, *The Theory of Good and Evil*, London: Oxford University Press, 1924, volume II, p. 298; *The Idea of Atonement in Christian Theology*, London: Macmillan, 1919, p. 468.

25 H. H. Farmer, *The World and God*, London: Nisbet, 1936, p. 25: the living awareness of God is an awareness both of 'unconditional demand' and of 'ultimate or final succour'. The two modes of awareness are not separable, however, in religious experience: 'they are given in and through one another.'

26 Cf. Romans 6.15; 7.14ff.

27 John Wesley, Sermon on 'The spirit of bondage and adoption' in *The Works of the Rev. John Wesley*, London: T. Cordeux, 1820, volume 7, p. 129.

28 See M. Buber, *Eclipse of God*, New York: Harper, 1952, pp. 23, 66f, 128f: the references are to papers initially given in 1951; William Hamilton, *The New Essence of Christianity*, London: Darton, Longman and Todd, 1966, p. 63.

29 Cf. Peter Berger's five 'signals of transcendence' within 'the domain of our "natural" reality' which appear to point beyond it – the propensity for order, the capacity to play, the strength of hope, the sense of moral outrage, and the ability to laugh: *A Rumour of Angels*, Harmondsworth: Penguin Books, 1971, pp. 70–92. Abraham Maslow lists twenty-five characteristics of what he calls 'peak experiences' and which may be given religious significance: see 'Religion and peak experiences' in Schedler, *Philosophy of Religion: Contemporary Perspectives*, pp. 535ff. D. D. Evans, 'Differences between scientific and religious assertions' in I. G. Barbour (ed.), *Science and Religion, New Perspectives on the Dialogue*, London: SCM Press, 1968, pp. 105ff, includes 'radical despair' and 'indignant compassion' among the 'depth-experiences' that are religiously significant. In another work Barbour includes in a list of seven types of experience which 'have been most prominent in religion' (although not necessarily requiring 'any particular religious interpretation'), 'awe and reverence', 'mystical union', 'moral obligation', 'reorientation and reconciliation', 'interpersonal relationships', 'key historical events' and 'order and creativity in the world': *Myths, Models and Paradigms*, London: SCM Press, 1974, pp. 53ff; cf. pp. 119ff.

30 In *The Remaking of Christian Doctrine*, London: SCM Press, 1974, Maurice F. Wiles sometimes seems to find in his 'experience' as a Christian a ground for upholding less radical conclusions than a thoroughgoing application of his criteria of 'coherence' and 'economy' might lead his readers to expect. In spite of the apparent rationalism of his work which scares orthodox (and obscurantist?) critics, in practice he offers a theology informed by inner convictions about the character of the Christian faith. Such a position could be defended as recognizing that 'the reasons of the heart' are at times a surer guide to wisdom than the cleverness of slick intellects and the stubbornness of closed traditionalists.

31 Rashdall, *The Idea of Atonement*, p. 467.

32 Atkinson Lee, *Groundwork of the Philosophy of Religion*, London: Duckworth, 1946, p. 15.

33 Atkinson Lee, 'Religious experience' in J. Scott Lidgett and B. H. Reed (eds.), *Methodism in the Modern World*, London: Epworth Press, 1929, p. 120.

34 See J. H. Newman, *An Essay in Aid of a Grammar of Assent*, London: Burns and Oates, 1870: edited by I. T. Ker, Oxford: Oxford University Press, 1985, pp. 31ff; Lewis, *Our Experience of God*, p. 110.

35 Faced with contemporary claims that belief in God is no longer possible, Harvey Cox maintains that the problem is basically not an intellectual one. The heart of the problem lies in experience: 'religious language including the word "God" will make sense again only when the lost experiences to which such words point become a felt part of the human reality': *The Feast of Fools*, New York: Harper and Row, 1970, p. 28; cf. pp. 165f.

36 Cf. Daya Krishna, 'Religious experience, language and truth' in S. Hook (ed.), *Religious Experience and Truth*, London: Oliver and Boyd, 1962, pp. 231f, 240, where he protests at the way in which most discussions of the intellectual problems of religion seem to be 'characterized by a singular unconcern with religious experience'. Without such experience philosophical discussions 'hang in the air'.

37 Cf. E. Troeltsch, *Protestantism and Progress*, translated by W. Montgomery, London: Williams and Norgate, 1912, pp. 187–205, where Troeltsch suggests that a development occurs in theological understanding from Luther's concern for assurance of salvation to Protestant theology's present concern with religious experience. Barth's reaction against this development as exemplified in Liberal Protestantism was not as total as he perhaps wished to maintain. His massive dogmatic system is itself a product of reflection on revelation as given to human beings – and so, in effect, as experienced by them – even though Barth wants to stress the predominance of the divine revealer in the grasp, as well as in the giving of revelation.

38 In this respect, critical studies of the phenomenology of prayer might be

illuminating since here many believers expect to enter into a reciprocal relationship with God.

39 Theological understanding is especially open to such challenges because it holds that its fundamental claims about God are universal in their scope. What is thus true of God must be compatible with all actual and all possible states. So far as these claims have material content, it is not surprising that experience often raises queries about them.

40 W. E. Hocking, *The Meaning of God in Human Experience*, New Haven: Yale University Press, 1963, p. 31. Hocking refers to knowledge and human relations: 'knowledge, for example, is an infinite quest in the order of nature . . . but the religious soul knows *now* . . . Human brotherhood is also an infinite problem . . . but in religion men are already brothers and experience their brotherhood in the moment of common worship.'

41 E.g., Wolfhart Pannenberg, *Basic Questions in Theology*, 3 vols., London: SCM Press, 1970, 1971, 1973, volume II, p. 232; cf. p. 26.

42 Cf. Kant, *Critique of Pure Reason* p. 93 (B75): 'Thoughts without content are empty, intuitions without concepts are blind.'

43 Even in such a case, it is hard to describe the process of apprehension in an experience, since the very act of saying what it is that I am trying to apprehend as my experience – a feeling of unease – presupposes and expresses an apprehension of it. I do not just have raw awarenesses which I then interpret. I hear, see, touch and feel things. I do not, therefore, ask myself, 'What am I aware of?', but 'What am I hearing, or seeing, or touching, or feeling?' In the initial act of becoming conscious that I am aware of something, I classify it as something that is heard, or seen, or touched, or felt.

44 Paul Feyerabend, *Against Method, Outline of an Anarchistic Theory of Knowledge*, London: NLB, 1975, p. 168.

45 Cf. Jacob J. Ross, *The Appeal to the Given*, London: George Allen and Unwin, 1970.

46 Sometimes, for example, we find ourselves vaguely aware of distinctions which our language is too coarse to express. Two shades of crimson, for instance, may be perceived to differ but we cannot express the difference between them.

47 L. Wittgenstein, *Philosophical Investigations*, translated by G. E. M. Anscombe, Oxford: Basil Blackwell, 1963, I, 381, 384, pp. 117f: to the question, 'How do I know that this colour is red?', he replies, 'It would be an answer to say: "I have learnt English." ' A little later he states, 'You learned the *concept* "pain" when you learned language'; cf. II, xi, p. 226.

48 When, therefore, theologians consider that their contemporaries have no notion of 'transcendence' in their culture, they should not assume that their task in relation to such people is to provide a secular, non-transcendental interpretation of religion. Their primary task may be to

challenge this culture and to remedy its inadequacy by introducing into it a sense of transcendence. The failure to criticize the adequacy of the culture into which they seek to interpret the Christian faith has been a defect in many of the radical theologies of the past thirty years.

49 Cf. Wittgenstein, *Philosophical Investigations*, II, xi, p. 194.

50 D. Stanbury (ed.), *A Narrative of the Voyage of the Beagle*, London: Folio Society, 1977, pp. 286f; Charles Darwin, *The Voyage of the Beagle*, London: Dent, 1906, pp. 363, 382. It is interesting that, on p. 452, Darwin's report of an incident in Australia omits certain theological musings about the creator which are recorded in his diary: cf. Stanbury, *Narrative*, p. 337.

51 W. Blake, 'The Everlasting Gospel', II.13f, in John Sampson (ed.), *The Poetical Works of William Blake*, London: Oxford University Press, 1913, p. 147.

52 F. A. Worsley, *Shackleton's Boat Journey*, London: Folio Society, 1974, p. 142.

53 Not all the models, however, have come from social relationships. One dominant model in the history of atonement doctrine is that of sacrifice, a model which was taken from existing religious practices. It was, however, a religious model whose significance had then to be interpreted. Otherwise the theory could hardly be regarded as a way of understanding the atonement: it would simply report that God, for unperceivable reasons, required a sacrifice as a necessary condition of salvation, and that it had been provided. What generally happened with this theory was that the religious notion of sacrifice was itself interpreted by reference to some social model – for example, by analogy with the social practice of presenting costly gifts to manifest love, or to secure appeasement, or to win reconciliation.

54 Frank Kermode, *The Sense of an Ending*, Oxford: Oxford University Press, 1968, p. 112.

55 Another way in which forms of understanding dominant in a culture affect atonement theology is through the apprehension of the nature of the situation from which people need to be saved, and of the consequent state of salvation. If, for example, the pre-salvation state is apprehended as one of guilt, then salvation will be seen as a matter of securing forgiveness; whereas, if it is seen as one of ignorance, salvation becomes a matter of education; or as one of degeneration, then a matter of restoration. In such ways, theories of atonement and views of the state of salvation are conditioned to some extent by the models used to understand the state from which people need to be saved.

56 See studies like M. F. Wiles, *The Making of Christian Doctrine*, Cambridge: Cambridge University Press, 1967, and *Working Papers in Doctrine*, London: SCM Press, 1976; and the papers by Wiles and Frances Young in John Hick (ed.), *The Myth of God Incarnate*, London: SCM Press, 1977. The furore stirred up by such works indi-

cates how many supposed theologians are still largely unaware of the way in which theological understanding, including both the doctrines which they have inherited and their understanding of them, is con- ditioned by the presuppositions of a past culture. In the past century theologians like Hatch, Harnack and Bultmann have had to struggle against obscurantist criticisms from those who apparently want their faith, belief and theology to be as supra-cultural as they assume God to be. In the end it is such obscurantists who deny God, for they want to absolutize the God of their thought. The 'cultural relativizers' whom they condemn recognize that human beings are not God, and that theological understanding is the product of attempts to discern the divine in ways conditioned by the current human situation!

57 Eadmer, *The Life of St Anselm*, edited and translated by R. W. Southern, London: Nelson, 1962, pp. 4f.

58 At one extreme there is 'the methodist convert' who scorns 'the mere sky-blue healthy-minded moralist', whereas at the other is the person who feels aversion to 'what seems to him the diseased subjectivism of the Methodist': W. James, *The Varieties of Religious Experience*, London: Longmans, Green and Co., 1952, pp. 164; cf. pp. 79f, 355.

59 See ibid., p. 477: 'a "god of battles" must be allowed to be the god for one kind of person, a god of peace and heaven and home, the god for another . . . If we are peevish and jealous, destruction of the self must be an element in our religion; why need it be one if we are good and sympathetic from the outset?' The way in which theological under- standing is conditioned by notions of salvation is discussed in chapter 7.

60 Otto holds that the only way in which something resembling a descrip- tion of the holy can be given without begging the question is by pointing to various other kinds of experience in the hope of evoking thereby a disclosure of what is meant by the 'holy'. In the end, however, 'it is a purely *a priori* category' which refers to 'an original and underivable capacity of the mind': *The Idea of the Holy*, pp. 112f.

61 L. Wittgenstein, *Tractatus Logico-Philosophicus*, translated by D. F. Pears and B. F. McGuiness, London: Routledge and Kegan Paul, 1961, p. 151, sections 6.522 and 7. Although the immediate context of the last remark by Wittgenstein indicates that he is primarily referring to the paradoxical status of his claims in the *Tractatus*, the wider context of this passage is a discussion of ethical, religious and mystical percep- tions of the meaning of life.

62 Thomas McPherson, 'Religion as the inexpressible' in A. Flew and A. MacIntyre (eds.), *New Essays in Philosophical Theology*, London: SCM Press, 1955, pp. 133, 140f, 142.

63 See *The Cloud of Unknowing*, translated by C. Wolters, Harmonds- worth: Penguin Books, 1961, pp. 58f.

64 Collingwood, *Speculum Mentis*, pp. 148f; cf. pp. 126ff, 145ff, 155ff.

65 As Collingwood puts it in ibid., p. 150: 'The young theologian thinks

that religion has a kernel of literal truth which . . . he will in time bring to light. But religion, as Goethe said of nature, has neither kernel nor husk; and those who are bent on peeling it will some day exemplify the parable of the onion.'

66 Although theological concepts without the correlative percepts of religious experience might not be utterly empty, they would nevertheless only constitute a formal and arid intellectual system.

67 Newman, *Grammar of Assent*, pp. 196f.

68 Ibid., p. 189.

69 The tragedy of martyrdom is compounded by the fact that the persecutors feel as certain about the error of the position which they condemn as their victims feel certain of its truth.

70 John Wesley, Sermon on 'The witness of the spirit' in *Works*, volume 7, p. 140.

71 Hume and Freud understand such experiences as the product of human attempts to cope with threatening forces by personifying them, Feuerbach as the projection of human ideals, and Nietzsche as stories invented to give comfort.

72 From some points of view, however, the identification of the experience as 'religious', rather than the identification of religious experience as 'theistic', is the way that the problem should be posed: cf. Collingwood, *Speculum Mentis*, p. 121: 'God and religion are thus correlative.' For Collingwood, ibid., p. 20, religion, as opposed to aesthetic feeling, is essentially directed towards a real object who is the 'ground and source of our own being' and 'the proper object of adoration'.

73 Lewis, *Our Experience of God*, pp. 110, 112. Although it is arguable that by 'God' Lewis may only mean that 'totally mysterious reality', the introduction of the word 'God' into the description will generally be understood in practice to carry with it a host of theistic connotations.

74 When, for instance, D. D. Evans suggests that there can be both theistic and atheistic descriptions of 'depth-experiences', it is important to recognize that the atheistic description, by omitting a theistic reference, may be as biased as a theistic one which includes it. The atheists' viewpoint may lead them to fail to see what is there just as much as the theists' may lead them to 'see' what is not there: cf. Evans, 'Differences between scientific and religious assertions' in Barbour, *Science and Religion, New Perspectives*.

75 Collingwood, *Speculum Mentis*, p. 130, maintains that religion is not expressed in literal statements but by 'symbolic imagery' which has 'a texture of metaphor through and through'. Whether or not this is true of all religious statements, it does describe the language used in connection with much religious experience, and particularly with those experiences which seem most significant to those having them.

76 See II Corinthians, 12.2ff.

77 Cf., for example, St John of the Cross quoted in James, *Varieties of Religious Experience*, pp. 398ff.

78 What James says of mystical states is generally true of many forms of religious experience: 'when well developed' they 'usually are . . . absolutely authoritative over the individual to whom they come', ibid., p. 414. People having such experiences take them to be perceptions of their actual situation in relation to that which is ultimate. James, however, also asserts that these experiences 'have the right to be binding'. The question of the cognitive status of such experiences is the question of whether they do have this right.

79 Cf. Hepburn, *Christianity and Paradox*, chapters 3 and 4; Macquarrie, *Principles of Christian Theology*, pp. 84f.

80 James, *Varieties of Religious Experience*, pp. 63, 72. They are more convincing to those who have them, according to James, than the conclusions of logical demonstrations.

81 Otto, *The Idea of the Holy*, p. 10; cf. p. 11, where he holds that 'the feeling of a "numinous" *object* objectively given must be posited as a primary immediate datum of consciousness'.

82 Pannenberg, *Basic Questions in Theology*, volume II, pp. 99–104; cf. volume II, pp. 190ff, 245. Pannenberg refers to Troeltsch's unsuccessful attempt to answer the question of the truth of religious experience by reference to religious psychology.

83 Ibid., p. 190.

84 It is amusing to contemplate what would have happened if Eli had given Samuel a different frame of reference for dealing with his experience of a voice in the night, for instance, by suggesting that it was his sons playing tricks, or a dream, or a demon. Would Samuel then have heard the Lord?: cf. I Samuel 3.1ff.

85 When H. H. Farmer writes of 'the religious man's living awareness of God as personal', it is the being 'religious' that may be the condition of having the awareness: *The World and God*, London: Nisbet, 1936, p. 25. It is interesting in this respect to note that John Baillie, who is clearly convinced of 'the sense of the presence of God', reports that his experience that he was ' "not my own" but one under authority' came from 'the spiritual climate' of his home: *Our Knowledge of God*, p. 182; cf. *Invitation to Pilgrimage*, Harmondsworth: Penguin Books, 1960, pp. 47f.

86 F. R. Tennant holds that it is only after we have shown the reasonableness of belief in God by other arguments that we can 'reasonably interpret numinous or religious experience in terms of the theistic concept and world-view: on the way back, so to say, as distinguished from the way out': *Philosophical Theology*, Cambridge: Cambridge University Press, 1928, volume I, p. 311; cf. Hepburn, *Christianity and Paradox*, p. 55.

87 Karl Heim suggests that the basic assumptions of our thought are

received because they are accompanied by 'a quite unique and indestructible feeling, the "feeling of conviction", the "feeling of assent",
the "feeling of certainty" ': 'Certainty' in J. Pelikan (ed.), *Twentieth
Century Theology in the Making*, London: Collins, 1970, volume II,
p. 55. It is the feeling which leads us to say these assumptions 'must'
be true or are 'self-evidently' true.

88 It is interesting to note, however, that many hymns seem to be asking
for such experiences rather than confidently affirming the enjoyment
of them. Perhaps actual 'experiences' of God have not been as common
as has been supposed.

89 D. Bonhoeffer, *Letters and Papers from Prison*, enlarged edition,
edited by E. Bethge, London: SCM Press, 1971, p. 360: letter of
16 July 1944; cf. letters of 29 May and 8 June.

90 Buber, *I and Thou*, p. 99: he regards the anguish as resulting from the
fact that 'we are not always there' to be aware of God, not from the
absence of God, or the will of God; *The Eclipse of God*, pp. 66, 23.

91 Hamilton, *New Essence of Christianity*, p. 63.

92 Harvey Cox does not accept that there is no experience of God. He
states, for instance, that 'we meet God at those places in life where we
come up against that which is not pliable and disposable, at those hard
edges where we are both stopped and challenged to move ahead': *The
Secular City*, London: SCM Press, 1965, p. 262.

93 Gabriel Vahanian, *Wait Without Idols*, New York: Brazillier, 1964,
p. 33; cf. pp. 41ff. On p. 43, Vahanian quotes Weber's remark that
the modern soul is 'religiös unmusikalisch'.

94 Hamilton develops Bonhoeffer's claim that it is not the power of God
but 'God's powerlessness and suffering' that helps humanity to fulfil
God's purposes for it: cf. Bonhoeffer, *Letters and Papers from Prison*,
p. 361, letter of 16 July 1944.

95 See Buber, *Eclipse of God*, p. 129.

96 Vahanian, *Wait Without Idols*, p. 231.

6   *Theology and the apprehension of revelation*

1 John Macquarrie, *Principles of Christian Theology*, London: SCM
Press, 1966, pp. 6, 75, 77.

2 See William Whewell, *The Philosophy of the Inductive Sciences*,
London: Parker, 1847, volume II, pp. 383f, 386.

3 See I. T. Ramsey, *Models and Mystery*, Oxford: Oxford University
Press, 1964, and *Religion and Science: Conflict and Synthesis*, London:
SPCK, 1964. Eadmer, *The Life of St Anselm*, edited and translated by
R. W. Southern, London: Nelson, 1962, p. 30, gives an example of
this type of disclosure situation: after seeking for some time 'a single
argument' which would demonstrate both the existence and nature of
God, the answer came to Anselm suddenly 'one night during matins'

when he perceived that the proper definition of 'God' would provide the self-evident basis of the argument; the *Proslogion* was the result: cf. Anselm, *Proslogion*, preface.

4 If researchers, whether in pharmacology or in philosophy of religion, are said to have an 'inspired' idea, what is usually meant is that the idea was most unexpected and highly fruitful, not that they have been given divine aid in reaching that idea.

5 The case of Anselm is interesting in that Eadmer states that the disclosure of the desired insight was a situation in which 'the grace of God illuminated his [*sc.* Anselm's] heart, the whole matter became clear to his mind . . .' (*Life of St Anselm*, p. 30). Anselm himself is more restrained: 'So, one day . . . in the very conflict of my thoughts, the proof of which I had despaired offered itself' (*Proslogion*, preface). What is described, in spite of the religious trappings included by Eadmer, is a natural event – the perception of an illuminating insight or the clue to the solution of a problem, whose significance does not depend on its having been revealed but on its verifiable truth. In Anselm's case, in spite of the misleading indication of his 'credo ut intelligam', the basis of the argument in *Proslogion* is the self-evident truth and implications of the definition of 'God', and not the source of the insight that this is how 'God' is to be defined.

6 See Aquinas, *Summa Theologiae*, ia, 1, 1, Reply.

7 Other theologians have agreed with Aquinas that revelation is essential for salvation because of the limitations of human reason. Thomas Halyburton, for example, asserts this in a volume attacking Herbert of Cherbury and others entitled *Natural Religion Insufficient and Revealed Necessary to Man's Happiness In His Present State* (first published in 1714). According to the subtitle the work shows 'the weakness' of the deists' assertion of 'the sufficiency of Nature's Light to eternal happiness'. This was a basic charge levelled by defenders of the necessity of revelation against those urging the significance of rational reflection and natural theology (whose radical members were commonly dubbed 'deist') in the faith–reason controversies from Herbert of Cherbury to Paley.

8 John Locke, *Essay Concerning Human Understanding*, London, 1690, Book iv, chapter 18, para. 7.

9 Aquinas, *Summa Theologiae*, ia, 1, 1, Reply, London: Eyre and Spottiswoode, 1964, volume i (translated by T. Gilby), p. 7.

10 See ibid., ia, 1, 2, Reply; ia, 1, 5, Reply. According to Aquinas, revelation has greater certainty than other ways of knowledge because the latter depend on 'the natural light of human reason which can make mistakes', whereas the former reflects 'divine knowledge which cannot falter'. This comment shows that Aquinas is only a qualified apologist for human reason in theological understanding.

11 Even Samuel Clarke, whose Boyle Lectures for 1704 put forward an a

priori natural theology in opposition to Locke's empiricism, asserts in the series for the following year that revelation is needed to rescue people from 'their universal corruption and degeneracy': *A Discourse Concerning the Being and Attributes of God . . .*, 8th edition, London, 1732, p. 306.

12 For a classic statement of this, cf. Locke's chapter, 'Of faith and reason and their distinct provinces' in *Essay Concerning Human Understanding*, Book IV, chapter 18.

13 This position is baldly asserted by Ockham in his investigation of God's foreknowledge: he holds that it must be accepted that God knows 'all future contingents', although philosophical argument proves it to be false, because this is what is stated by the Bible and the saints (and so is a revealed truth): see William Ockham, *Philosophical Writings*, edited by P. Boehner, London: Nelson, 1957, pp. 133f.

14 See ibid., pp. 125f.

15 John Ellis, *The Knowledge of Divine Things from Revelation, not from Reason or Nature*, London, 1747, pp. 3, 438; cf. pp. 130f; cf. also *Some Brief Considerations upon Mr Locke's Hypothesis*, London, 1743; and *An Enquiry, Whence Cometh Wisdom and Understanding to Man?*, London, 1757.

16 H. L. Mansel, *The Limits of Religious Thought*, Oxford, 1858, pp. 126f.

17 Karl Barth, *The Epistle to the Romans*, translated by E. C. Hoskyns, Oxford: Oxford University Press, 1933, p. 37.

18 Karl Barth, *Church Dogmatics*, I/1, 'The doctrine of the Word of God', translated by G. T. Thomson, Edinburgh: T. and T. Clark, 1936, p. 25; cf. pp. 12, 15.

19 Thomas F. Torrance, *Theological Science*, Oxford: Oxford University Press, 1969, pp. 29, 31ff.

20 C. Issawi (ed. and trans.), *An Arab Philosophy of History, Selections from the Prolegomena of Ibn Kaldun of Tunis (1332–1406)*, London: John Murray, 1950, pp. 173f; see also his view of what mystics can privately understand, pp. 175ff. B. Spinoza, *Theologico-Political Treatise* in *Chief Works of Spinoza*, translated by R. H. M. Elwes, New York: Dover, 1951, volume I, p. 13ff, has a similar view.

21 Muslims have argued for the primacy of Arabic, and some Jews and Christians for that of Hebrew in grasping God's revelation.

22 Thus, according to one of his critics, Locke allows the possibility that 'God can open and enable our Faculties to discern new Objects, hitherto unseen and unknown to the mortal Mind, from which they would collect new simple ideas': Ellis, *Some Brief Considerations*, p. 45.

23 Locke, *Essay Concerning Human Understanding*, Book IV, chapter 18, para. 3.

24 This range may also be understood to include what people might naturally come to understand as their experience and thought develop, but it is regarded as limited at any particular time to their existing patterns

of understanding. God, for instance, could be held to give a revelation whose meaning would only be properly grasped after human experience and understanding had matured, in the sense that the correct significance of symbols given at one time would only be perceived at a later time. This could be one way of understanding the ongoing revelatory value of the story of Jesus in Christian thought.

25 Feuerbach and Freud have both pointed out that how people view God develops in step with the maturing of their self-appreciation and their personal relationships with others, especially with their father.

26 See Peter Browne, *The Procedure, Extent and Limits of Human Understanding*, 3rd edition, London, 1737, p. 472.

27 Browne thus states that in this way the 'Notions' which are '*Natural*, and *Easy*, and *Familiar*' to us are used 'to *Represent* and *Stand For* those immaterial heavenly Things, of whose real Nature and Properties we can otherwise obtain no Notion or Idea': ibid., p. 199; cf. pp. 29ff, 196ff.

28 Ibid., p. 136; cf. pp. 132ff, 473ff. Browne is concerned to distinguish between analogy, which he sees as providing exact information, and metaphors, which provide further illustrations of what is already basically known analogically, cf. pp. 135f; cf. also Peter Browne, *Things Divine and Supernatural Conceived by Analogy with Things Natural and Human*, London, 1733, pp. 1ff.

29 Cf. Humphrey Palmer, *Analogy, A Study of Qualification and Argument in Theology*, London: Macmillan, 1973, for difficulties with the notion of analogy; Charles M. Wood, *Theory and Understanding*, Missoula: Scholars Press for American Academy for Religion, 1975, pp. 99ff, 137ff, 158ff, and *The Formation of Christian Understanding*, Philadelphia: Westminster Press, 1981, pp. 58ff, on understanding as involving application.

30 Paul Tillich, *Systematic Theology*, London: Nisbet, 1957, volume ii, pp. 8, 10.

31 C. W. Kegley and R. W. Bretall (eds.), *The Theology of Paul Tillich*, New York: Macmillan, 1952, p. 334.

32 In Paul Tillich, *The Protestant Era*, translated by John Luther Adams, Chicago: Chicago University Press, 1948; (English edition, London: Nisbet, 1951), talk about God is said to unite 'a symbolic and a non-symbolic element'; in *Systematic Theology*, 1951, volume i, 'the statement that God is being-itself is a non-symbolic statement'; in *Systematic Theology*, volume ii (1957), the 'assertion about God which is not symbolic' is 'the statement that everything we say about God is symbolic'; in *The Dynamics of Faith*, New York: Harper Torchbooks, 1958, 'God is the symbol for what concerns us ultimately . . . God is the symbol for God', because 'symbolic language alone is able to express the ultimate'. Tillich thus changes his mind about how to meet the principle expressed

in Urban's criticism and finally leaves the significance of 'symbolic' usage as he employs the notion somewhat unclear.

33 Tillich, *Systematic Theology*, volume I, p. 121.

34 Mansel, *Limits of Religious Thought*, p. 47.

35 Ibid., p. 127. In a footnote on p. 362, Mansel points to the difference between Kant's view of 'regulative' ideas and his own. A similar view had been put forward by Richard Whately. He argues that what is revealed in Scripture is not speculative knowledge, but knowledge of 'the *relations* between God and man, and of the practical truths thence resulting'. Supposedly revealed doctrines are to be interpreted as directions about conduct and, therefore, as essentially 'relative' to the human situation before God: *Essays on Some of the Difficulties in the Writings of St Paul*, London, 1833, p. 236; cf. pp. 138ff; cf. also George Berkeley, *Alciphron: or, the Minute Philosopher*, Dialogue 7, para. 11, in *The Works of George Berkeley, D. D.*, edited by G. N. Wright, London: Thomas Tegg, 1843, volume I, p. 504.

36 I. M. Crombie, 'Theology and falsification' in A. Flew and A. MacIntyre (eds.), *New Essays in Philosophical Theology*, London: SCM Press, 1955, p. 124; cf. I. M. Crombie, 'The possibility of theological statements' in Basil Mitchell (ed.), *Faith and Logic*, London: George Allen and Unwin, 1957, pp. 31ff.

37 Mansel, *Limits of Religious Thought*, p. 261.

38 Crombie, 'Theology and falsification' in Flew and MacIntyre, *New Essays in Philosophical Theology*, p. 123.

39 Karl Barth, *The Humanity of God*, London: Collins, 1967, p. 87; cf. p. 53, where he states that theology is the attempt 'to see, to understand, and to put into language the intercourse of God with man in which there comes about intercourse of man with God. It means that theology will deal with the word and act of the grace of God and the word and act of the human gratitude challenged, awakened, and nourished through it'.

40 Ibid., p. 9; cf. pp. 23f; cf. Newton's comment quoted at the beginning of chapter 5.

41 Karl Barth, *Dogmatics in Outline*, translated by G. T. Thomson, London: SCM Press, 1949, pp. 24, 32.

42 See Barth, *Church Dogmatics*, I/1, pp. 11f, 176f; I/2, p. 719: 'The decisive point is that in scriptural exegesis Scripture itself as a witness to revelation must have unconditional precedence of all the evidence of our own being and becoming, our own thoughts and endeavours, hope and suffering, of all the evidence of intellect and senses, of all axioms and theorems, which we inherit and as such bear with us;' cf. I/2, p. 816; III/3, p. 404.

43 See ibid., I/2, pp. 203, 242, 244, 258.

44 Ibid., I/1, pp. 51f.

45 Barth asserts that God is not limited to language as a means of com-

munication. As he vividly puts it, God may speak and people may be brought by the Spirit to hear the divine word to them 'through Russian communism or a flute concerto, a blossoming shrub or a dead dog': ibid., I/1, p. 60.

46 The surprising implication of the Barthian position, in view of Barth's extensive expositions of the Christian revelation, is that, since the grasp of God's 'Word' depends on God and not on any human words, nothing Barth has written can communicate the 'Word' unless God chooses to use it.

47 It is likely that a label cannot function without having some understood connection with information about what it labels. As P. F. Strawson, *Individuals*, London: Methuen, 1964, p. 20, puts it in terms of proper names: 'it is no good using a name for a particular unless one knows who or what is referred to by the use of the name. A name is worthless without a backing of descriptions which can be produced on demand to explain its application.'

48 Cf. Strawson, *Individuals*, p. 99n (mentioned in chapter 3, note 46 above). When applied to theological understanding, this principle implies that if theists can make sense of monotheism, they cannot also hold that God is intrinsically and absolutely 'utterly other'. On the other hand, it does not imply that they can hold that God exists only if the concepts they use to describe God could be applied to more than one God, i.e., that monotheism only makes sense if polytheism also does (though the former may be true and the latter false). In the case of God, what the principle requires is that, in some appropriate way, the different predicates used of 'God' have also appropriate attribution to other entities. The combination of them (e.g., 'highest' and 'good', or 'first' and 'cause', or 'supreme' and 'ruler'), however, may only properly be predicated of one entity. In this way, the significance of God-talk and the uniqueness of its referent are seen to be compatible with each other.

49 Wolfhart Pannenberg, *Basic Questions in Theology*, 3 vols., London: SCM Press, 1970, 1971, 1973, volume II, p. 68.

50 Ibid., pp. 192, 194f.

51 Ibid., p. 205; cf. the understandings of theology offered by Feuerbach, Freud and Braun.

52 Cf. Barth's thunder against any form of religious apologetics: 'no divinity which NEEDS ANYTHING, any human propaganda (Acts XVII, 24, 26), – can be God': *The Epistle to the Romans*, p. 36.

53 Pannenberg, *Basic Questions* volume II, p. 207.

54 Ibid., pp. 227, 232; cf. pp. 104, 233.

55 Cf. also Barth, *The Epistle to the Romans*, p. 36: 'God is the unknown God . . . Therefore the power of God can be detected neither in the world of nature nor in the souls of men.'

56 Cf. Pannenberg who holds that God's nature can be disclosed to some

extent by revelation, namely, so far as it stands in relation to human existence.

57 See Rudolf Bultmann, 'The concept of revelation in the New Testament' in *Existence and Faith*, translated and edited by Schubert M. Ogden, London: Hodder and Stoughton, 1961, pp. 85, 87.

58 Ibid., p. 88.

59 Ibid., p. 86; cf. pp. 90f; cf. Rudolf Bultmann, 'Church and teaching in the New Testament' in *Faith and Understanding*, edited by R. W. Funk, translated by L. P. Smith, London: SCM Press, 1969, pp. 209f: '*Understanding* is achieved in decision, in obedience . . . God's revelation is primarily an event, not a communication of knowledge. But the event is a basis for both a knowledge and a teaching, since it makes possible a new self-understanding.' What is discerned in revelation is thus not the nature of God but the nature and situation of human being.

60 See Bultmann, 'The problem of "natural theology" ' in ibid., p. 323: unbelief can discover the question of authentic existence but refuses to recognize the only basis of its answer.

61 Bultmann, 'What does it mean to speak of God?' in ibid., p. 53; cf. pp. 55ff, 63.

62 Macquarrie, *Principles of Christian Theology*, p. 7; cf. p. 86. In the passage cited Macquarrie speaks of a revelation 'granted to the founder' of the community of faith. The use of the preposition 'to' seems odd in the case of Christianity, unless the apostles are taken to be the 'founders' of that faith. If, as is more likely, Jesus is held to be the founder of Christianity, Christians would usually speak of their primordial revelation being *by* or *through* Jesus, rather than as an experience which happened to Jesus. This is not to rule out the possibility that Jesus did have some revelatory experiences (at his baptism, for example), but to point out that such experiences, while contributing to the full understanding of Jesus as the Christ, do not constitute what Christians consider to be the Christian revelation. Although Christians have traditionally been prepared to speak of revelatory insights being granted to Moses, Isaiah and Paul, and some might be prepared to talk of revelation being given to religious leaders outside their tradition of faith, such as Gotama Buddha and Muhammad, Christians would typically place Jesus in a different category, seeing him as giving (or being) rather than as receiving the primordial revelation. This view of Jesus raises interesting questions about his self-consciousness. On the one hand, if what Jesus revealed was the result of what God directly made known to him (cf. John 4.34; 8.28), then it seems that the consequent Christological understanding of Jesus must be subordinationist. On the other hand, if Jesus revealed God directly since his nature is to be identified with that of God (cf. John 10.30; 14.9), then it seems that the consequent Christology should be monophysite. On either understanding, therefore, consideration of Jesus' own self-conscious-

ness and his knowledge of God's nature and will seems to produce a Christological heresy! The only way to save orthodox Christology seems to be to divorce it from questions of Jesus' self-consciousness – Was he aware of himself as having received a revelation from God or of himself as being the revelation of God? – but to do this raises a further problem in that it makes the foundation of the Christian faith not the life of Jesus but the recognition of that life as a revelation of God. The founder of Christianity thus turns out to be the insight of the members of the community who came to this recognition. This conclusion is eminently defensible but it will probably seem surprising to those who entertain what they regard as the general ('traditional' or 'orthodox') self-understanding of Christianity.

63 Ibid., p. 6; cf. pp. 75, 85.

64 Ibid., p. 85.

65 Cf. ibid., pp. 86ff, where Macquarrie describes the 'moods' that may be involved in revelatory experiences, and argues that this characteristic does not undermine the trustworthiness of the resulting awareness (cf. p. 90).

66 See R. G. Collingwood, *An Autobiography*, Oxford: Oxford University Press, 1970, p. 31: 'you cannot find out what a man means by simply studying his spoken or written statements . . . In order to find out his meaning you must also know what the question was (a question in his own mind, and presumed by him to be in yours) to which the thing he has said or written was meant as an answer'; cf. p. 33.

67 Cf. Tillich, *Systematic Theology*, volume I, p. 123.

68 Cf. Barth, *Church Dogmatics*, II/2, pp. 52f.

69 Critics of the revelation which Muhammad claimed to have been given to him have pointed out that at some points the supposed revelations provide suspiciously convenient solutions to particular predicaments in which Muhammad found himself.

70 In 1645 Peter Sterry criticized the House of Commons for using 'humane wit and reason' to debate and to decide about 'the great affairs' of state. The grounds for his condemnation of their attempts to sort out their problems by using their understanding is Paul's confession that he 'consulted not with flesh and blood' after what happened to him on the Damascus road: *The Spirit Convincing of Sinne*, London, 1646, p. 19.

71 What, for example, are Christians today to make of Jesus' instructions to the disciples recorded in Matthew 10.9f? Were those orders confined to the mission then or do they still have significance for missionaries in the different conditions of modern travel, and, if so, what significance? On a larger and deeper scale, what is the relationship between the style of life lived by Jesus and that which one of his followers should adopt today in an urban setting?

72 For example, by leading the Israelites by pillar of cloud and fire.

73 On the 'open-textured' character of language, see F. Waismann, 'Verifiability' reprinted in A. G. N. Flew (ed.), *Logic and Language*, first series, Oxford: Blackwell, 1955, pp. 119ff; and L. Wittgenstein on 'family resemblances' in *Philosophical Investigations*, translated by G. E. M. Anscombe, Oxford: Basil Blackwell, 1958, 1:66ff, pp. 31ff. George Steiner speaks of language as 'slippery, ambiguous, altering' with 'subconscious or traditional reflexes', and finds its untidiness and multivalency as crucial to its value: *After Babel*, Oxford: Oxford University Press, 1975, p. 203.

74 R. G. Collingwood, *An Essay on Philosophical Method*, Oxford: Clarendon Press, 1933, p. 216: we may thus find that a once unintelligible book becomes intelligible when we return to it 'ripened by several years' of experience.

75 Cf. Steiner, *After Babel*, p. 250: in reply to those who question in principle the possibility of translation, to take a primary task in all reading, Steiner responds that a defence of translation 'has the immense advantage of abundant, vulgar fact'.

76 Take, for instance, the law recorded in Exodus 23.19. Granted that it is a word from God, is it simply to be obeyed literally (no goat to be stewed in its own mother's milk), or is it an order against stewing goat in any (goat's) milk, or is it a way of banning gratuitous cruelty, or is it a ban on consuming meat and milk in the same meal – no steak and ice-cream for lunch?

77 Barth, 'The gift of freedom' in *The Humanity of God*, p. 91.

78 Barth, *Church Dogmatics*, III/3, p. 404: in discussing the need to accept Scriptural references to angels, Barth states that, 'if we try to find angels both in the Bible and elsewhere, we shall only see hazy pictures. Our philosophy will spoil our theology, and our theology our philosophy'; cf. pp. 272ff, 404ff.

79 Barth's early theological work was powerfully influenced by the sense of crisis for civilization found in and after the 1914–18 War. When he found the word 'krisis' in the Bible, he interpreted it in terms of his understanding of contemporary civilization. In the lecture, 'The humanity of God', given in 1956, he recognizes that he later needed to change what he had said in order to meet a different situation: see *The Humanity of God*, pp. 33ff, and especially p. 63, where he holds that theology cannot be carried on in a 'private lighthouse' but only in a community.

80 Cf. Macquarrie, *Principles of Christian Theology*, p. 6; cf. pp. 84ff, 95f; cf. also Barth, *Church Dogmatics*, I/1, p. 60, quoted in note 45, above.

81 Macquarrie, *Principles of Christian Theology*, p. 80: Macquarrie prefers the final form of expression; cf. also Pannenberg, *Basic Questions*, volume II, p. 104.

82 Cf. Leonard Hodgson, *For Faith and Freedom*, Oxford: Basil

Blackwell, 1957, volume II, p. 7, for an amusing story about a student who so interpreted two Gospel reports that Jesus emerged as apparently recognizing class distinctions.

83 It might be held to be implied, for instance, by Jesus' decision to go to Jerusalem, his apparent awareness of his likely fate and the absence of any attempts to escape.

84 Cf. David A. Pailin, 'Lessing's ditch revisited' in R. H. Preston (ed.), *Theology and Change*, London: SCM Press, 1975, pp. 78–103; *Groundwork of Philosophy of Religion*, London: Epworth Press, 1986, pp. 98ff; *God and the Processes of Reality, Foundations of a Credible Theism*, London: Routledge, 1989, pp. 185ff; Gordon E. Michalson, *Lessing's 'Ugly Ditch': A Study of Theology and History*, University Park and London: Pennsylvania State University Press, 1985, for further discussions of some of the issues involved.

85 Karl Rahner, *Foundations of Christian Faith*, translated by W. V. Dych, New York: Seabury Press, 1978, pp. 86f, 174f.

86 Ibid., p. 280: 'Jesus . . . is the historical presence of this final and unsurpassable word of God's self-disclosure: this is his claim and he is vindicated in this claim by the resurrection.'

87 Cf. Romans 1.4; Wolfhart Pannenberg, *Jesus – God and Man*, translated by L. L. Wilkins and D. A. Priebe, London: SCM Press, 1968.

88 Cf. Kendrick Grobel, 'Revelation and resurrection' in J. M. Robinson and J. B. Cobb (eds.), *Theology as History*, New York: Harper and Row, 1967, pp. 155ff, especially p. 175.

89 Hans Küng, *On Being a Christian*, translated by E. Quinn, London: Collins, 1977, p. 379; cf. pp. 361ff.

90 Maurice F. Wiles, *The Remaking of Christian Doctrine*, London: SCM Press, 1974, p. 38. As Wiles says, this view 'is not deistic in the most strongly pejorative sense, in that it allows for a continuing relationship of God to the world as source of existence and giver of purpose to the whole. It is deistic in so far as it refrains from claiming any effective causation on the part of God in relation to particular occurrences'; cf. also Wiles, *God's Action in the World*, London: SCM Press, 1986, and 'In what contexts does it make sense to say "God acts in history"?' in P. E. Devenish and G. L. Goodwin (eds.), *Witness and Existence*, Chicago and London: University of Chicago Press, 1989, pp. 190ff.

91 Cf. A. N. Whitehead, *Religion in the Making*, Cambridge: Cambridge University Press, 1926, p. 21: 'Hence religion bases itself primarily upon a small selection from the common experiences of the race . . . But on its other side, religion claims that its concepts, though derived primarily from special experiences, are yet of universal validity, to be applied by faith to the ordering of all experience. Rational religion . . . arises from that which is special, and extends it to what is general'; and p. 110: 'Religion starts from the generalization of final truths first perceived as exemplified in particular instances.'

92 Cf. Matthew 10.34; Luke 12.49; Matthew 10.39; 19.27ff.
93 Samuel T. Coleridge, *Confessions of an Inquiring Spirit*, edited by H.
   St J. Hart, London: Adam and Charles Black, 1956, pp. 42f; cf. p. 80.
94 Pannenberg, *Basic Questions* volume II, p. 104.
95 See B. Spinoza, *Theologico-Political Treatise* in *The Chief Works of
   Benedict de Spinoza*, translated with an introduction by R. H. M.
   Elwes, New York: Dover Publications, 1955, volume I, p. 30.
96 See John 16.12f.
97 Cf. G. E. Lessing, 'The education of the human race' in *Lessing's
   Theological Writings*, translated and edited by H. Chadwick, London:
   Adam and Charles Black, 1956, pp. 82ff.

7   Theology and human need

1 R. Sibs [Sibbes], *The Returning Backslider*, 3rd edition, London, 1950,
   pp. 169f, 196f.
2 *Memorials of Edwin Hatch, D.D.*, edited by his brother (Samuel C.
   Hatch), London: Hodder and Stoughton, 1890, pp. 255f; cf. p. 291,
   where Hatch holds that Stoicism was 'insufficient' because it 'appealed
   only to the intellect'. It did not present an 'ethical impulse' and 'a
   consolation for suffering'. It was 'the Cross of Christ' which provided
   the 'spiritual power' which Stoicism lacked.
3 G. Van Der Leeuw, *Religion in Essence and Manifestation*, London:
   George Allen and Unwin, 1964, pp. 679, 681f.
4 Ludwig Feuerbach, *The Essence of Faith According to Luther*, translated by M. Cherno, New York: Harper and Row, 1967, p. 54. Feuerbach quotes Luther's assertion that, 'The works and divine services of
   all peoples testify to the fact that to be a God is nothing but to do
   good to man . . . However wrong they are in regard to the person of
   God . . . they expect all good and help from Him' (pp. 51f). Luther's
   belief is that God is 'good and beneficent' towards humanity (p. 64).
5 See Paul Tillich, *The Courage to Be*, London: Collins, 1962, pp. 49f,
   167f.
6 Wolfhart Pannenberg, *Basic Questions in Theology*, 3 vols., London:
   SCM Press, 1970, 1971, 1973, volume II, p. 232; cf. pp. 214f, 233.
7 Harvey Cox, *The Seduction of the Spirit*, London: Wildwood House,
   1974, p. 153; cf. p. 311.
8 See James H. Cone, *Black Theology and Black Power*, New York:
   Seabury Press, 1969; *God of the Oppressed*, New York: Seabury Press,
   1975.
9 See Mary Daly, *Beyond God the Father: Toward a Philosophy of
   Women's Liberation*, Boston: Beacon Press, 1974; Rosemary Radford
   Ruether, *To Change the World: Christology and Cultural Criticism*,
   London: SCM Press, 1981, p. 53. From a different background Ignacio
   Castuera argues that a concept of God needs to be developed which

combines 'the best elements of masculinity and femininity', in order to counter the prejudices of Latin American machismo: 'The theology and practice of liberation in the Mexican American context', *Perkins Journal*, Autumn 1975, pp. 6f.

10 Cf. '. . . the *guise* in which Transcendence appears varies with the mode of life's deficiency. Those who suffer from bondage and confinement see it as promising liberation and expansion. Those who suffer from darkness look to it for light. To those who groan under the weight of death and transitoriness it intimates eternity. To those who are restless it betokens peace': Huston Smith, 'The reach and grasp: transcendence today', in Norbert O. Schedler (ed.), *Philosophy of Religion: Contemporary Perspectives*, New York: Collier Macmillan, 1974, p. 545.

11 Feuerbach, *The Essence of Faith according to Luther*, pp. 51, 54.

12 Those who imply in their protests about nuclear armaments that God's purposes will be wholly frustrated if humanity is destroyed should consider whether they are attaching to God their anthropocentric vision. In the end the destruction of this planet is only the end of one planet circling one of billions of stars – and it will eventually be destroyed cosmically, if not earlier, by developments in the solar system.

13 Søren Kierkegaard, *The Sickness unto Death*, translated by W. Lowrie, New York: Doubleday, 1955, p. 216.

14 The story of Noah shows that it is possible to think of God as being prepared to wipe out a creation which has gone awry in order to start again. May not God be thought of as capable of doing the same with individuals who cease to be creatively fruitful and so cease to contribute to the enrichment of the divine reality as it embraces them?

15 A canonical saying of Jesus can be offered in support of this view: Matthew 10.31.

16 Gordon D. Kaufman, *An Essay on Theological Method*, Missoula: Scholars Press for American Academy of Religion, 1975, pp. 51f; cf. pp. 48ff.

17 Gordon D. Kaufman, *The Theological Imagination: Constructing the Concept of God*, Philadelphia: Westminster Press, 1981, pp. 182f, 189.

18 Satanism and other forms of devil worship are also to be found, but these practices usually seem to be perverse forms of, and parasitic upon, beliefs in a supreme and benevolent God.

19 Cf. Hatch's understanding of religious concerns referred to earlier.

20 E. Troeltsch, *Protestantism and Progress*, translated by W. Montgomery, London: Williams and Norgate, 1912, p. 197: whereas Luther had no doubts about God's existence but wondered whether he was one of the saved, modern people wonder if there is a God, but regard it as 'beyond question that to be once certain of the being of God' is to 'have found the meaning and goal of life, salvation and grace'.

21 F. Engels, 'L. Feuerbach and the end of classical German philosophy'

in K. Marx and F. Engels, *On Religion*, Moscow: Foreign Languages Publishing House, 1957, p. 262.

22 Cox, *Seduction of the Spirit*, pp. 6off.

23 For example, primitive people's concerns about the forces of physical nature are still echoed in modern city-dwellers' worship at harvest and in prayers for those who suffer.

24 Paul Tillich, *The Dynamics of Faith*, New York: Harper Torchbooks, 1958, p. 43; cf. *Systematic Theology*, 3 vols., London: Nisbet, 1953, 1957, 1964, volume I, pp. 266f.

25 See Tillich, *The Courage to Be*, p. 63; cf. pp. 48ff, 63ff.

26 H. A. Williams, 'Theology and self-awareness' in A. R. Vidler (ed.), *Soundings: Essays Concerning Christian Understanding*, Cambridge: Cambridge University Press, 1962, p. 80.

27 For many of them the basic worry is not one of dying, but one of not dying soon enough to avoid senility.

28 Many, however, do feel guilt in a social sense and express it in healthy concerns for social justice, ecological protection, the rights of minorities and care for the disadvantaged.

29 See Colossians 1.16; 2.15.

30 John Wesley, sermon on 'Salvation by faith' in *The Works of the Rev. John Wesley*, London: T. Cordeux, 1820, volume VII, p. 10; sermon on 'Justification by faith' in ibid., p. 67.

31 Cf. the attempt by Grobel to translate the Pauline '*dikaiosune*' (δικαιοσυνη) by the old word 'rightwise' in his translation of Rudolf Bultmann, *Theology of the New Testament*, London: SCM Press, 1952, volume I, p. 253n.

32 Karl Barth, *The Epistle to the Romans*, translated by E. C. Hoskyns, Oxford: Oxford University Press, 1933, p. 1; cf. p. 10. The reference to 'the Eternal Spirit' in the Bible echoes, at least superficially, the 'timeless truths' of Liberal Protestantism against which Barth reacted!

33 See Rudolf Bultmann, 'Bultmann replies to his critics' in H. W. Bartsch, (ed.), *Kerygma and Myth*, translated by R. H. Fuller, London: SPCK, 1964, volume I, pp. 192ff; *Jesus Christ and Mythology*, New York: Scribners, 1958, pp. 52ff. For some the controversial aspect of Bultmann's hermeneutical position is his claim that Heidegger's existentialist conceptuality, somewhat modified, provides the most adequate way for his contemporaries to grasp the New Testament's view of the human predicament and the Gospel's answer.

34 Some theologians argue that this acceptance of death is only an appearance. In their view people are so afraid of death that they try to avoid acknowledging its existence as much as possible. This interpretation of the widespread curtailment of funerary rites may, however, be the result of an attempt to maintain that death must be still a problem for people because it was for their predecessors. The case may thus

depend on the principle of a universal human nature, and it is this
principle which is under question.

35 Cf. Pannenberg, *Basic Questions*, volume II, p. 213.

36 The confusion which results from a failure to recognize that people of
different cultures can be really different is illustrated by two sentences
in Stephen N. Ezeanya's paper, 'God, spirits and the spirit world' in
K. Dickson and P. Ellingworth (eds.), *Biblical Revelation and African
Beliefs*, London: Lutterworth, 1969, p. 31: '. . . human nature remains
essentially the same throughout the world and throughout the ages and
is destined to fulfilment in the one God of all the earth. In exercising
her divine mission of teaching all nations, the Church must preach to
all the people in the language they will understand: the Church must
try to adapt herself to different environments.' The church will be
most likely to succeed in the task outlined in the second sentence if it
abandons the unnecessary assumption of a universal common humanity
stated (as apparently self-evident) in the first. To say that people of
different cultures are essentially different is not to devalue any, but to
avoid the misleading implications of presupposed uniformity.

37 This does not mean that the end justifies any kind of means, but that a
need is not morally justified as a need unless it is necessary for a morally
justified end.

38 For example, if the expression and appreciation of aesthetic creativity
are held to be the self-justifying goals of being, and if salvation is
perceived as that which releases people from whatever restrains their
creativity and enjoyment, then such goals as content (the lazy person's
view of bliss) and unsurpassable perfection (where nothing more can
be achieved) will be recognized to be in some respects the antithesis of
what is truly desirable.

39 Barth, *The Epistle to the Romans*, p. 383; cf. pp. 8, 36ff, 80, 282;
Church Dogmatics, I/I, Edinburgh, T. and T. Clark, 1936–69, pp. 224f.

40 Rudolf Bultmann, *Faith and Understanding*, edited by R. W. Frank,
translated by L. P. Smith, London: SCM Press, 1969, p. 47; cf. p. 317:
'The revelation brings to actuality the questionableness in which human
existence, with its natural self-understanding, always stands.'

41 See also ibid., pp. 314ff; Rudolf Bultmann, *Essays Philosophical and
Theological*, translated by J. C. C. Greig, London: SCM Press, 1955,
pp. 94ff.

42 Tillich, *Systematic Theology*, volume I, p. 8.

43 Ibid., pp. 68f. In volume II, pp. 14ff, Tillich summarizes his position
under the heading, 'Independence and interdependence of existential
questions and theological answers'. In view of Tillich's stress on the
interdependence of the two in his method of correlation, his position
is misrepresented by Pannenberg when, with references to volume II,
pp. 14f, the latter classes Tillich with Barth and Bultmann as holding
that the question depends upon the answer: see *Basic Questions*,

volume II, p. 214. In contrast to what Pannenberg describes as Tillich's position, Tillich states on p. 15 that 'it is equally wrong to derive the question implied in human existence from the revelatory answer. This is impossible because the revelatory answer is meaningless if there is no question to which it is the answer. Man cannot receive an answer to a question he has not asked'.

44 Ibid., volume I, pp. 70f. In seeking to take account of as many different forms of contemporary culture as possible, Tillich mentions philosophy, poetry, drama, the novel, therapeutic psychology and sociology.

45 Ibid., volume I, p. 8.

46 Cf. Pannenberg, *Basic Questions*, volume II, p. 224: 'the question is always framed in relation to a projection of its answer. Insofar as a question is a genuine question and asks about something, it already anticipates a possible answer.'

47 Cf. Psalm 59. Some religions carry these views to the point of having institutionalized procedures for complaining to God when the people's expectations are not met and, in the context of worship, instruct the deity to perform better in future according to the needs of the worshippers: cf. William James, *The Varieties of Religious Experience*, London: Longmans, Green and Co., 1952, p. 497, where he quotes Leuba on the ways in which people 'use' their deity.

48 An example is provided by C. Lalive d'Epinay, *Haven of the Masses*, London: Lutterworth, 1969, where it is argued that the paternalistic structure and close community life of Chilean pentecostalist groups may be understood as an attempt to recreate the hacienda form of society in an urban setting.

49 One of the reasons for the decline of religious faith in modern Western society may well be that many people have come to consider that God does not offer real salvation from the concrete problems of life. God, rather, is a solution to pseudo-problems that arise because of religious belief (such as the problem of sin), and a pseudo-solution to authentic problems of human being. Prayer to God for aid is thus a tacit admission that the real helpers – doctors, counsellors, scientists, technologists, friends – have not yet found a solution but hope remains.

50 Cf. *Memorials of Edwin Hatch*, pp. 255f, 291, referred to earlier.

51 Just as people may have experiences of what is not their actual state (e.g., they may feel that someone loathes them when this is not actually the case), so they may fail to experience what is their actual state in relation to God's saving activity. The fact that people do not feel forgiven does not show that they are not forgiven. This further complicates attempts to determine the reference and status of claims about salvation, because it shows the ambiguous nature of the evidence of experience. There is no way of avoiding this ambiguity by holding that God makes known the character of salvation, for the apprehension of

what God 'makes known' can be illusory or biased because of the desire for salvation.

52 See Romans 3.24; 11.6; Ephesians 2.5, 8.

53 This does not imply that God must be thought of as acting in the same way in each situation. Presumably the saving activity is appropriate to what is needed to fulfil the divine will for persons in each situation. What it does imply is that if theistic faith is true, it is arguable that there is no situation in which God is not savingly involved.

54 One important exception, as our earlier discussion of his views indicated, is Gordon D. Kaufman.

55 Edward, Lord Herbert of Cherbury, *The Antient Religion of the Gentiles*, translated by W. Lewis, London, 1705, pp. 44ff; cf., pp. 318ff; cf. Herbert of Cherbury, *De Veritate*, translated by M. H. Carré, Bristol: Bristol University Press, 1937, chapter 9.

56 [Matthew Tindal], *Christianity as Old as the Creation, or, The Gospel, a Republication of the Religion of Nature*, London, 1731, p. 10.

57 See ibid., p. 4.

58 David Hume, *The Natural History of Religion*, edited by H. E. Root, London: A. and C. Black, 1956, p. 52.

59 Friedrich Nietzsche, *The Twilight of the Idols and the Anti-Christ*, translated by R. J. Hollingdale, Harmondsworth: Penguin Books, 1968, pp. 53f; cf. p. 45: God is 'the enemy of life' since 'the saint in whom God takes pleasure is the ideal castrate'.

60 Such criticisms are not only found in attacks on theism. Patrick Masterson argues that 'the story of the development of contemporary atheism is . . . a progressive repudiation not only of a theistic absolute but also of every secular substitute such as the absolute spirit of Hegel, the social absolute of Feuerbach and Marx, or the scientific absolutism of Positivism': *Atheism and Alienation*, Dublin: Gill and Macmillan, 1971, p. x. All this is done in the name of human subjectivity. The rejected ideologies are rejected because they are incompatible with the flourishing and fulfilment of people as free individuals.

61 See John Oman, *Grace and Personality*, London: Collins, 1960, pp. 24ff, 77.

62 D. Bonhoeffer, *Letters and Papers from Prison*, enlarged edition, edited by E. Bethge, London: SCM Press, 1971, pp. 360f; letter of 16 July 1944.

63 Harvey Cox, *The Secular City*, London: SCM Press, 1965, p. 255.

64 Cf. Schubert M. Ogden's arguments in *The Reality of God*, London: SCM Press, 1967, pp. 120ff, 140ff.

65 William A. Beardslee, *A House for Hope*, Philadelphia: Westminster Press, 1972, pp. 74, 172.

66 John Hick, 'The Copernican Revolution in theology' in *God and the Universe of Faiths*, London: Collins, 1977, pp. 120, 122, 131.

67 See 'The new map of the universe of faiths' in ibid., p. 139. The strength

of the opposition to Hick's suggestion seems to reflect to some extent a failure within Christian thought to work out thoroughly the implications of its monotheistic understanding of the divine, and of its claim that the nature of the divine is primarily one of saving love.

68 Cf. Frances Young's statements that 'christological expositions are parasitic upon definitions and concepts of salvation', and 'christological formulations derive from a sense of having experienced God's promised salvation (however interpreted) in and through Jesus Christ': 'A cloud of witnesses' in John Hick (ed.), *The Myth of God Incarnate*, London: SCM Press, 1977, pp. 13, 19.

69 Cf. Schubert, M. Ogden, *Christ Without Myth*, London: Collins, 1962, pp. 143ff, 154ff; John B. Cobb, Jr., *Christ in a Pluralistic Age*, Philadelphia: Westminster Press, 1975, for studies of how God's saving activity may be normatively revealed in Jesus, but not restricted in its effectiveness to the Christian tradition.

70 The substantial attack of science on religion is probably a psychological one along these lines. The sciences as such may not disprove religion, nor even be interested in religion, but their advances undermine religious belief by suggesting that theistic faith is unnecessary for practical purposes, and that these purposes are the only ones that are important.

71 Cf. Sigmund Freud, *The Future of an Illusion*, translated by W. D. Robson-Scott, edited by J. Strachey, London: Hogarth Press, 1962, p. 52, for a classical statement of this point of view: 'our science is no illusion. But an illusion it would be to suppose that what science cannot give us we can get elsewhere.' For Freud religion is not merely an illusion – a fulfilment of 'the oldest, strongest and most urgent wishes of mankind' (p. 26); it is a delusion which provides no real help to humanity today.

72 Pannenberg, *Basic Questions*, volume II, p. 233.

73 See the provocative study of Sartre's position by Ogden, 'The strange witness of unbelief' in *The Reality of God*, pp. 120ff.

74 Augustine, *Confessions*, book I, chapter I.

75 Matthew 4.4.

8 Theology and the completion of understanding

1 Thomas Stackhouse, *Compleat Body of Speculative and Practical Divinity*, 3rd edition, London, 1743, pp. 751f.

2 Cf. Aquinas, *Summa Theologiae*, I, I, 5, London: Eyre and Spottiswoode, 1964, volume I, (translated by T. Gilby), Aquinas' first argument for the supremacy of Christian theology is on the grounds of its certainty as coming not 'from the natural light of human reason which can make mistakes', but from 'the light of divine knowledge which cannot falter'. This argument fails to convince because what God

reveals and what is humanly apprehended as revelation may not coincide.

3. Cf. ibid. Aquinas puts it that 'sacred doctrine' is supreme because it 'leads to heights the reason cannot climb', and because its aim is that 'eternal happiness' which is 'the final end governing' all activity.

4 Whitehead, *Religion in the Making*, p. 37; cf. pp. 21, 37ff, 47ff.

5 This does not imply that 'God' as theistically understood is the only such orientation-point available to thought. The notions of 'the Absolute' and of 'Matter' have similar functions for idealist and materialist ways of understanding.

6 Bertrand Russell, *Why I Am Not a Christian and Other Essays*, London: George Allen and Unwin, 1975, pp. 138f.

7 Gordon D. Kaufman, *An Essay on Theological Method*, Missoula: Scholars Press for American Academy of Religion, 1975, pp. 28f.

8 See M. Durrant, *The Logical Status of 'God'*, London: Macmillan, 1973, for a discussion of the various roles of the term 'God'.

9 Cf. Hartshorne, *The Logic of Perfection*, pp. 126, 131: in the end 'the theistic question' is not just 'the most important question': it is 'the sole question'; p. 297: 'God' stands for 'the soul of significance in general'; Hans Küng, *On Being a Christian*, translated by E. Quinn, London: Collins, 1977, p. 295: God is 'the most real reality, active in all reality' which provides 'a final point of reference, a unity, value and meaning'; Kaufman, *Essay on Theological Method*, pp. 14f: 'God' is 'the key term in a complex of meaning which is intended to grasp all experience and reality'. It presents 'the ultimate point of reference' as 'personal or agential in character'.

10 Although 'God' is the 'object of investigation' as that personal entity which theology is concerned to understand, Kaufman, ibid., pp. 21ff, points out that theologians do not study a given object 'God' in the way that physicists and biologists study given objects. On the other hand, while the concept of God may be most adequately understood as a construct of the theologians' imagination (cf. ibid., pp. 26ff), it does not follow that this construct is not an attempt to apprehend an actual reality.

11 Whatever intellectual ideal may be enshrined in the doctrine of the simplicity of God, the nature of the divine as apprehended is inescapably complex and puzzling because of its function in thought: cf. A. N. Whitehead, *Religion in the Making*, Cambridge: Cambridge University Press, 1926, pp. 64ff.

12 Cf. Paul Feyerabend, *Against Method: Outline of an Anarchistic Theory of Knowledge*, London: NLB, 1975, for a lively examination of the reasonableness of the rejection of Galileo's empirical approach. Galileo himself shared certain of his rationalist opponents' dogmas – such as that movements in the heavens must be uniform and circular. The preference for empirical observations over rational principles took a

long time to become established: cf. R. Hookyaas, *Religion and the Rise of Modern Science*, Edinburgh: Scottish Academic Press, 1973, pp. 35ff.

13 [John Hutchinson], *Moses's Principia*, London, 1724, pp. 1f; cf. also J. B. Sumner, *A Treatise on the Records of the Creation and on the Moral Attributes of the Creator*, London, 1833, volume I, p. xiii: 'Where Reason, however, leaves us, Revelation takes us up: and furnishes us with a record of the creation, preserved by the wisdom, and authenticated by the power, of the Creator . . .'

14 Cf. Kaufman, *Essay on Theological Method*, pp. 19ff. This would still be the case if the reasoning involved in the ontological argument were valid and its premise, the definition of God, acceptable. Since the presupposition of the ultimate rationality of reality may be challenged, it would be necessary to show that the conclusions of the argument agree with what observation indicates about the nature of reality. Charles Hartshorne, for example, considers that in the end the ontological argument only shows that we are faced with the disjunction: either God exists or reality is ultimately irrational (or, as he puts it, positivism is true): see *Anselm's Discovery*, La Salle, Ill.: Open Court, 1965, pp. 53ff, 95ff. The only solution to this disjunction is by determining which alternative fits reality.

15 The way in which the notion of being 'rationally appropriate' is controversial is illustrated by the argument about the plot of land in John Wisdom, 'Gods' reprinted in A. Flew (ed.), *Logic and Language*, first series, Oxford: Basil Blackwell, 1955, pp. 192ff, and in the parable of the partisan and the stranger in Basil Mitchell's contribution to the 'Theology and falsification' debate, reprinted in A. Flew and A. MacIntyre (eds.), *New Essays in Philosophical Theology*, London: SCM Press, 1955, pp. 104f.

16 Even though it should not be forgotten that theology is concerned with understanding reality as it will become, as well as with reality as it now exists, claims about the purposes of the creator for the future will only be credible if they significantly accord with what we now find to be the case.

17 The interaction may also happen in the reverse direction as when a theological insight into the nature of God opens up a fruitful way of making sense of the world: cf. Kaufman's view of the third moment of theological construction in *Essay on Theological Method*, pp. 56ff.

18 'Meaningfulness' is accordingly a possible component of what is understood rather than something separate from it. Talk of the 'meaning' of an object or an event refers to the purposes which gave rise to it, and the significance which it has for other objects and events. It is thus particularly concerned with identifying relational aspects of the object of understanding.

19 This includes the 'answer' to our question which is in the form of reflec-

tion that shows that what we are asking is unanswerable and so is an illegitimate question.

20 Even those who seek to show that there is no final coherence about the structure of reality want to have the satisfaction of understanding it as an intelligible case of randomness!

21 Attempts to show that something is intrinsically random may be regarded as a limiting case of this rule, for they are attempts to show that there is no regular pattern applicable to the object of the enquiry, and hence that it is internally coherent as a case of randomness.

22 Cf. how a behaviourist psychiatrist, a Tridentine Roman Catholic, a Marxist sociologist, a pentecostalist anthropologist and a Methodist historian are likely to make sense of the Hussite movement even though they refer to the same body of evidence.

23 Cf. John Macquarrie, *Principles of Christian Theology*, London: SCM Press, 1966, p. 32: 'wherever there is understanding, there is also interpretation.'

24 On the significance of stories for understanding, cf. D. A. Pailin, 'Narrative, story and the interpretation of metaphysics' in George R. Lucas (ed.), *Hegel and Whitehead: Contemporary Perspectives on Systematic Philosophy*, Albany: State University of New York Press, 1986, pp. 268–84; and in theological understanding, cf. Harvey Cox, *The Seduction of the Spirit*, London: Wildwood House, 1974, pp. 9ff, 91ff; Sam Keen, *To a Dancing God*, London: Collins, 1971, pp. 82ff.

25 Cf. J. H. Poincaré, *Dernières Pensées*, Paris: Flamarion, 1913, pp.237f, where he suggests that while science 'makes us go towards unity' as it shows increasingly 'the solidarity' and 'harmony' of the universe, it leaves us with the question whether 'this harmony is real', or appears because 'our intelligence has such a need'. If it is the latter, it is 'a scientific postulate'.

26 As Kierkegaard pointed out to the Hegelians, total understanding is not attainable in the case of what may not yet be totally determined; cf. also Frank Kermode, *The Sense of an Ending*, Oxford: Oxford University Press, 1967, on the way in which we may unwarrantably impose completion on stories, especially when they lead up to the present.

27 Theism has, of course, the initial problem of showing that it is the correct way to understand the ultimate structure of things. All that is being suggested here is that once theism is granted, the intelligibility of reality follows from it.

28 In this respect Hans Küng may require too much when he holds that 'the modern understanding of God must start out from a coherent understanding of reality: God in this world and this world in God': *On Being a Christian*, p. 295. Such a coherent understanding may not be available even at the end of any currently possible process of theological understanding, let alone at its start.

29 Cf. Leszek Kolakowski, *Religion*, Glasgow: Fontana, 1982, p. 70. Kolakowski makes the point in relation to the argument from contingency, but it applies to all such arguments in natural theology. Arguments for atheism which point to 'evidence' that the cosmos is a chaotic and unintelligible collection of items may similarly beg the question by presupposing that there is no God and so no fundamental unity in their apprehension of that 'evidence'.

30 F. C. Copleston, 'The existence of God, a debate between Bertrand Russell and Father F. C. Copleston SJ' in Russell, *Why I Am Not a Christian*, pp. 137ff.

31 If, for example, we seek to understand why, among the properties of a triangle, the sum of its internal angles is 180°, we cannot go beyond explaining what is meant by 'triangle', 'angle', 'sum' and 'degree'. There is nothing further that can be explained.

32 Cf. what A. N. Whitehead speaks of as 'the ontological principle', namely that 'actual entities are the only *reasons*; so that to search for a *reason* is to search for one or more actual entities': *Process and Reality: An Essay in Cosmology*, corrected edition edited by D. R. Griffin and D. W. Sherburne, New York: The Free Press, 1978, p. 24; cf. p. 19.

33 See Whitehead, *Religion in the Making*, p. 60.

34 Whitehead, *Science and the Modern World*, p. 115.

35 F. W. J. Schelling, *Of Human Freedom*, translated by J. Gutmann, Chicago: Open Court, 1936, p. 87.

36 Paul Tillich, *Systematic Theology*, 3 vols., London: Nisbet, 1953, 1957, 1964, volume I, pp. 191, 227; cf. Paul Tillich, *Perspectives on Nineteenth and Twentieth Century Protestant Theology*, edited by C. E. Braaten, London: SCM Press, 1967, p. 142.

37 Tillich, *Systematic Theology*, volume II, pp. 8, 12.

38 Aquinas, *Summa Theologiae*, I, 3, 4.

39 Ibid., I, 3, 1–2 and 6–7.

40 Ibid., I, 2, 3; cf. also Aquinas, *De Ente et Essentia*, 5, in *Concerning Being and Essence*, translated and edited by George G. Leckie, New York: Appleton-Century-Crofts, 1937, pp. 16ff.

41 Charles Hartshorne, *Aquinas to Whitehead: Seven Centuries of Metaphysics of Religion*, Milwaukee: Marquette University Publications, 1976, pp. 2, 9.

42 Hartshorne, *Anselm's Discovery*, pp. 71, 67, 81f; cf. p. 58.

43 See chapter 4 on how regulative ideas condition the concept of God.

44 Cf. Aquinas, *Summa Theologiae*, I, 4, 2.

45 Cf. Whitehead, *Religion in the Making*, pp. 87, 90ff, 101ff, 110ff, 138ff.

46 Ibid., p. 87.

47 Cf. Charles Hartshorne, *A Natural Theology for our Time*, La Salle, Ill.: Open Court, 1967, chapter 3.

48 According to Karl Popper the method of the natural sciences is to be

seen and practised as one in which the investigator primarily seeks to falsify hypotheses: see *The Logic of Scientific Discovery*, London: Hutchinson, 1959, p. 14; *Conjectures and Refutations*, London: Routledge and Kegan Paul, 1974, pp. 36f.

49 Henry Cole, *Popular Geology Subversive of Divine Revelation!*, London: Hatchard, 1834, p. v. This preface incorporates a letter published in *The Times* on 2 February 1834.

50 Philip Gosse suggested that God put the fossils into the rocks in order to test the faith of the geologists. Although this theory now appears quite implausible, it is interesting to note that methodologically Gosse might claim to satisfy the principle of Ockham's razor better than the geologists, since he offers a simpler explanation of the origin of the fossils! To claim that Gosse errs because 'God' is not to be used to explain anything is to take up a principle which would lead to a secularist understanding of everything. The refutation of Gosse's theory must be along the lines that it is theologically unsatisfactory to make out that God is a deceiver, and that the standard scientific theory of fossils fits in with a huge amount of other scientific understanding. Those who use Ockham's razor must make sure that they take account of the whole case. On discussing this point Raymond Plant pointed out that the logical problem posed by the need to refute Gosse's theory is acute in the case of brain–mind controversies.

51 While it is easy to be critical of theologians who rush to adopt the latest ideas to expound their views, if theologians are to show that theism is a credible basis for understanding and practice, they must show that it makes sense of the reality which people consider to exist. It was, then, not inappropriate that William Derham took up the recently developed theory of gravity to illustrate the providence of God since, as he puts it, the theory 'hath great Reason and Probability on its Side': *Astro-Theology*, 7th edition, London, 1738, p. 142; cf. pp. 141–6. The equivalent situation today is when relativity theory is applied to the doctrine of God: cf. Hartshorne, *A Natural Theology for Our Time*, pp. 93ff, and Paul Fitzgerald, 'Relativity physics and the God of process philosophy', *Process Studies*, 2, 4, Winter 1972, pp. 251ff.

52 John Stuart Mill, *A System of Logic, Ratiocinative and Inductive*, London and New York: George Routledge and Sons, n.d., Book III, chapter 5, para. 2; cf. paras. 7f, pp. 205ff; Book VI, chapter 2, pp. 504ff.

53 Ibid., Book II, chapter 5, para. 2, p. 196.

54 Similarly, the fact that the natural sciences explain events only by reference to physically quantifiable forces is not a result of its having been discovered that only such forces exist. It is because those forces are the only ones open to the methods of investigation used in the natural sciences.

55 Cf. Aquinas, *Summa Theologiae*, I, 65–74, for examples of the

problems found in the records. When, for instance, he recognizes problems with the statements about the appearance of plants, he does not question the accuracy of the various reports, but finds a way of interpreting them so that the conflict disappears – in one case following Augustine in suggesting that the first account describes the constitution of plants 'in their causes' but not 'in act', while the second relates their actual propagation by God, cf. I, 69, 2, Reply.

56 Origen is a notable exception. Although paying tribute to the enlightening power of what Moses wrote, he asserts that no 'man of intelligence' will accept that there were days before the sun existed. He also describes literal acceptance of the story of the Garden of Eden as 'silly': *On First Principles*, Book III, chapter 5 and Book IV, chapter 3. Such views, however, were relatively rare before the Enlightenment and not generally acceptable by self-consciously orthodox believers before this century.

57 George Gleig, *Directions for the Study of Theology*, London, 1827, pp. 97f.

58 Cf. Psalm 8.3f.

59 Isaiah 55.8 would be literally correct in that case except that if the claim be true, it would follow that we cannot even properly understand who is the 'Lord' whose 'word' reports this incomprehensibility to us.

60 F. R. Tennant, *Philosophical Theology*, Cambridge: Cambridge University Press, 1928, volume II, p. 80.

61 Cf. Whitehead's remark that 'the purpose of God is the attainment of value in the temporal world' (*Religion in the Making*, p. 87), and his understanding of the fundamental character of the divine creative activity (cf. pp. 100ff).

62 See Tennant, *Philosophical Theology*, volume II, p. 125. The reason for this is that explanation is in terms of what is experienced, 'whereas creation is the activity through which experients and what is experienced by them come to be. The notion of creation, consequently, is not derivable from experience', but is an 'unanalysable and unassimilable' ultimate notion.

63 John Stuart Mill, 'Nature' in *Three Essays on Religion*, London: Longmans, Green, Reader and Dyer, 1874, p. 28. This essay had been written between 1850 and 1858: cf. p. vii.

64 Alfred, Lord Tennyson, 'In Memoriam', LIV and LV, in *Poems of Tennyson, 1830–1870*, London: Humphrey Milford, Oxford University Press, 1912, pp. 392f.

65 David Hume, *Dialogues Concerning Natural Religion*, edited by N. K. Smith, Oxford: Clarendon Press, 1935, part V.

66 Whitehead, *Religion in the Making*, pp. 82f.

67 Ibid., p. 139.

68 Cf. the way in which claims about natural religion were attacked in the seventeenth and eighteenth centuries by reference to observations of

'heathen' cultures: David A. Pailin, *Attitudes to Other Religions: Comparative Religion in Seventeenth- and Eighteenth-Century Britain*, Manchester: Manchester University Press, 1984, pp. 25ff.

69 From the Decalogue's rejection of other gods and the Shahada's affirmation of monotheism to Kraemer's assertion of the 'intolerant' and 'offensive exclusivism' of Christianity as 'the ultimate truth', other religious faiths have been regarded as strange errors with little to contribute to understanding beside that of illustrating human mistakes: cf. Hendrik Kraemer, *Religion and the Christian Faith*, London: Lutterworth Press, 1956, p. 373; cf. pp. 304f, where he acknowledges evidence of God's concern for those outside the biblical revelation, but holds that that revelation is 'the sole *religio vera*'.

70 Cf. the militaristic symbolism in an ordination sermon for two missionaries: 'The ultimate conquest and possession of all the heathen lands is certain . . . "The strong man armed" is to be ejected as a cruel usurper. Unnumbered millions of captives are to be set free. Jerusalem and the holy city are to be rescued from the hands of the infidels': Heman Humphrey, *The Promised Land, A Sermon Delivered at Goshen (Conn.)*, Boston: Armstrong, 1819, pp. 10f.

71 Cf. the presuppositions implied in the title of J. N. Farquhar's study of the relation of Christianity to Hinduism, *The Crown of Hinduism*, (Oxford: Oxford University Press, 1913), in spite of its being for its time a liberal work of Christian apologetic. John Hick makes an interesting analysis of traditional religious views when he writes of the 'Ptolemaic' approach: in its place he calls for a 'Copernican revolution'; see *God and the Universe of Faiths*, Glasgow: Collins, 1977, pp. 120ff.

72 The question of the truth of beliefs is complicated by the problem of determining their root significance in view of the cultural relativity of their self-understanding. Cf. John Hick's suggestions about what might have happened to Christianity's understanding of Jesus as the Christ, if it had initially developed in an Indian culture rather than in the Graeco-Roman culture: 'Jesus and the world religions' in John Hick (ed.), *The Myth of God Incarnate*, London: SCM Press, 1977, p. 176.

73 Both the word and the study of 'hermeneutics' are not new: John Conr. Dannhauer published his *Hermeneutica sacra, sive methodus exponendarum sacrarum literarum* (Argentorati) in 1654, while the English equivalent appears in Samuel Davidson's *Sacred Hermeneutics Developed and Applied*, Edinburgh: Thomas Clark, 1843.

74 Cf. Aquinas, *Summa Theologiae*, I, I, 10. Aquinas also argues that as its author is God, the same biblical text can have several senses – literal, allegorical, moral and analogical. As W. Cantwell Smith points out, Muslims have an even stronger doctrine of scripture than Christians, for they regard the text of the Koran in a way that is similar to the Christian attitude to Christ: *Questions of Religious Truth*, London: Gollancz, 1967, p. 40n.

75 Cf. the argument that the Bible as canon is to be seen as having a primarily negative role in that it is the touchstone for determining what is not acceptable as a possible Christian position; cf. Charles M. Wood, 'The aim of theology', *Perkins Journal*, 31, 3, Spring 1978, p. 25: Scripture's 'function as canon is not to supply all our ideas but to enable us to judge their adequacy, their likelihood of usefulness within the language and life of faith'; see also his *The Formation of Christian Understanding*, Philadelphia: Westminster Press, 1981.

76 Cf. Macquarrie, *Principles of Christian Theology*, p. 9; Maurice F. Wiles, *What is Theology?*, Oxford: Oxford University Press, 1976, pp. 14, 33f.

77 Schubert M. Ogden, 'What is theology?' in *On Theology*, San Francisco: Harper and Row, 1986, p. 10. In an earlier version of this paper published in *The Journal of Religion*, 52, January 1972 (and reprinted in *Perkins Journal*, 26, 2, Winter 1973), Ogden described 'the primary test' as that of 'agreement with the witness of Scripture'.

78 It is arguable, however, that in doing this theologians have continued to use the Bible as the kind of document that biblical scholarship has shown it not to be, while at the same time professing to accept the general correctness of that scholarship. In this respect Barth has a more integrated attitude when he divorces God's word to humanity from the biblical means through which it is heard: see *The Word of God and The Word of Man*, translated by D. Horton, New York: Harper and Row, 1957, pp. 60f. The implication of this passage is that for faith's hearing biblical scholarship, whatever its validity as scholarship, is a satanic tempter; cf. also Wood's distinction between 'scripture' and 'canon' in *The Formation of Christian Understanding*, pp. 86ff.

79 George Steiner, *After Babel*, Oxford: Oxford University Press, 1975, p. 250.

80 H. G. Gadamer's thesis is that 'the thing which hermeneutics teaches us is to see through the dogmatism of asserting an opposition and separation between the ongoing, natural "tradition" and the reflective appropriation of it'. The understander must be seen 'in relationship to the hermeneutical situation and the constant operativeness of history in his own consciousness': *Philosophical Hermeneutics*, translated and edited by D. E. Linge, Berkeley, Los Angeles and London: University of California Press, 1977, p. 28.

81 E. D. Hirsch, *The Aims of Interpretation*, Chicago: University of Chicago Press, 1976, pp. 39f, describes Gadamer as wanting to 'vitalize the inscrutable texts of the past by distorting them to our own perspectives', on the grounds that 'the perspective-ridden meanings of the past are irremediably alien to us'; cf. also p. 49.

82 See Paul Ricoeur, *Interpretation Theory: Discourse and the Surplus of Meaning*, Fort Worth: Texas Christian University Press, 1976, p. 79. Here he is largely in agreement with Hirsch; cf. p. 78.

83 See ibid., pp. 87f, 93, 100.

84 The continuing saga of the quest for the historical Jesus, however, sometimes looks like the modern version of the medieval quest for the holy grail.

85 Cf. Voltaire, *Philosophical Dictionary*, translated and edited by P. Gay, New York: Harcourt, Brace and World, 1962, p. 207; R. W. Dale, *Christian Doctrine*, London, 1895, pp. 306f; John Henry Newman, *The Arians of the Fourth Century*, 5th edition, Pickering and Co., London, 1883, pp. 389–92, speaks of members of the Council of Constantinople in 381 as 'turbulent' and moved by 'pride and jealousy', 'inflamed with resentment', and having to have 'their insulted patriotism' appeased. Edward Gibbon is much less reserved about what happened: see *The Decline and Fall of the Roman Empire*, edited by J. B. Bury, London: Methuen, 1897, volume III, p. 149.

86 Cf. J. F. Bethune-Baker, *An Introduction to the Early History of Christian Doctrine*, London: Methuen, 1903, pp. 283f; Gibbon, *Decline and Fall*, volume V, p. 122.

87 John Henry Newman, *On Consulting the Faithful in Matters of Doctrine*, edited by J. Coulson, London: Geoffrey Chapman, 1961, pp. 39, 77; for the evidence cited by Newman, cf. pp. 77ff.

88 Henry Edward [Manning], Second Cardinal Archbishop of Westminster, *The Grounds of Faith*, London: Burns and Oates, n.d., p. 34.

89 Jan Walgrave, *Unfolding Revelation*, London: Hutchinson, 1972, p. 281.

90 Donald A. Schon, *Invention and the Evolution of Ideas*, London: Tavistock, 1967, cf. pp. 65, 68. (This work was first published in 1963 as *Displacement of Concepts*.)

91 See I. T. Ramsey, *Religious Language*, London: SCM Press, 1957; *Models and Mystery*, Oxford: Oxford University Press, 1964; I. G. Barbour, *Myths, Models and Paradigms*, London: SCM Press, 1974; for the role of models in thought in general, cf. T. Shanin (ed.), *The Rules of the Game*, London: Tavistock, 1972.

92 Cf., for example, Edwin Hatch, *The Influence of Greek Ideas and Usages upon the Christian Church* (Hibbert Lectures for 1888), London: Williams and Norgate, 1890, pp. 350ff; Wolfhart Pannenberg, *Basic Questions in Theology*, London: SCM Press, 1970, 1971, 1973, volume II, pp. 119ff.

93 Hatch, *Influence of Greek Ideas*, pp. 2f.

94 Cf. David A. Pailin, *God and the Processes of Reality: Foundations of a Credible Theism*, London: Routledge, 1989, pp. 57–117.

95 Bernard Lonergan, *A Second Collection*, London: Darton, Longman and Todd, 1974, pp. 65f.

96 H. A. Hodges, *Languages, Standpoints and Attitudes*, Oxford: Oxford University Press, 1953, p. 59; cf. p. 58.

97 Cf., however, ibid., p. 62: Hodges dismisses consistency as a criterion.

98 See ibid., p. 64. As Hodges recognizes, this test is not necessarily self-evident: it is only significant for those who are whole-heartedly life-affirming. It would serve as a cross-cultural test only if it could be shown that all people do ultimately seek life-enhancement; cf. also G. D. Kaufman's criterion of 'humanization': *The Theological Imagination: Constructing the Concept of God*, Philadelphia: Westminster Press, 1981, pp. 192–204.

99 F. Engels, 'Ludwig Feuerbach and the end of classical German philosophy' in K. Marx and F. Engels, *On Religion*, Moscow: Foreign Languages Publishing House, 1957, pp. 249, 217.

100 Cf. Rudolf Bultmann, *History and Eschatology*, Edinburgh: Edinburgh University Press, 1957, p. 155.

101 See Karl Britton, *Philosophy and the Meaning of Life*, Cambridge: Cambridge University Press, 1969, pp. 12ff, 187ff.

102 See Bultmann, *History and Eschatology*, pp. 152ff.

103 William D. Dean, *Coming To: A Theology of Beauty*, Philadelphia: Westminster Press, 1972, pp. 153f; cf. also Feyerabend, *Against Method*, pp. 180, 216.

104 Cf. Dean, *Coming To*, pp. 43f.

105 See Harvey Cox, *The Feast of Fools*, Cambridge, Mass.: Harvard University Press, 1969, and New York: Harper and Row, 1970, p. 162; cf. pp. 7ff; cf. his comments on theology as a form of play in *Seduction of the Spirit*, pp. 317ff; cf. also S. Keen, 'Manifesto for a Dionysian theology' reprinted in Norbert O. Schedler, (ed.), *Philosophy of Religion, Contemporary Perspectives*, New York: Collier Macmillan, 1974, p. 526.

106 José Míguez Bonino, *Revolutionary Theology Comes of Age*, London: SPCK, 1975, p. 151.

107 Job 2.9.

108 Cf. Hebrews 11.1.

109 See Pannenberg, *Basic Questions*, volume II, p. 232; Jürgen Moltmann, *Hope and Planning*, London: SCM Press, 1971, p. 26.

110 John B. Cobb, Jr., *Christ in a Pluralistic Age*, Philadelphia: Westminster Press, 1975, p. 183.

111 Voltaire, *Philosophical Dictionary*, pp. 480f.

9 Conclusion

1 Rudolf Bultmann, 'New Testament and mythology: the problem of demythologizing the New Testament proclamation' in *New Testament and Mythology and Other Basic Writings*, edited and translated by Schubert M. Ogden, London: SCM Press, 1985, pp. 4f. To recognize the truth of what Bultmann says here, however, does not necessarily imply agreement with his 'demythologized' interpretation of the Christian gospel.

2 I have tried to indicate some possible answers in *God and the Processes of Reality: Foundations of a Credible Theism*, London: Routledge, 1989.
3 Karl Rahner, *Foundations of Christian Faith*, translated by W. V. Dych, New York: Seabury Press, 1978, p. 44. It is a view with which Bernard Lonergan states that he is 'in substantial agreement': *A Second Collection*, edited by W. F. J. Ryan and B. J. Tyrrell, London: Darton, Longman and Todd, 1974, p. 148; cf. pp. 147f: 'all theological questions and answers have to be matched by the transcendental questions and answers that reveal in the human subject the conditions of the possibility of the theological answers . . . His [Rahner's] position is that man is for God, that religion is intrinsic to an authentic humanism, that in theology theocentrism and anthropocentrism coincide.' Cf. also the views of Pannenberg cited in chapter 3, note 98 above.
4 H. Richard Niebuhr, *The Meaning of Revelation*, New York: Macmillan, 1941, pp. 77, 151.
5 Schubert M. Ogden, *The Reality of God*, London: SCM Press, 1967, pp. 44, 47.
6 Hans Küng, *On Being a Christian*, translated by E. Quinn, London: Collins, 1977, pp. 70, 76.

Select bibliography

Anselm. *Monologion, Proslogion, Reply to Gaunilo,* and *Cur Deus Homo*: a convenient collection is in *St Anselm Basic Writings,* edited by S. N. Deane, La Salle, Ill.: Open Court, 1962.

Aquinas, Thomas. *Summa Theologiae,* 60 volumes, London: Eyre and Spottiswoode and New York: McGraw-Hill, 1964.

Arbib, Michael A. and Hesse, Mary B. *The Construction of Reality,* Cambridge: Cambridge University Press, 1986.

Baillie, John. *Our Knowledge of God,* London: Oxford University Press, 1939.

The Sense of the Presence of God, Oxford: Oxford University Press, 1962.

Barbour, I. G. *Myths, Models and Paradigms,* London: SCM Press, 1974.

Barnes, Barry. *Scientific Knowledge and Sociological Theory,* London and Boston: Routledge and Kegan Paul, 1974.

Barth, Karl. *The Epistle to the Romans,* translated by E. C. Hoskyns, Oxford: Oxford University Press, 1933.

Church Dogmatics, I/1–IV/4, Edinburgh: T. and T. Clark, 1936–69.

The Humanity of God, London: Collins, 1967.

Berger, Peter L. *A Rumour of Angels,* Harmondsworth: Penguin Books, 1971.

The Social Reality of Religion, Harmondsworth: Penguin Books, 1973 (published in the USA as *The Sacred Canopy*).

Berger, Peter L. and Luckman, Thomas. *The Social Construction of Reality,* Harmondsworth: Penguin Books, 1971.

Buber, Martin. *I and Thou,* translated by R. Gregor Smith, Edinburgh: T. and T. Clark, 1937.

The Eclipse of God, New York: Harper, 1952.

Bultmann, Rudolf. *Jesus Christ and Mythology,* New York: Scribners, 1958.

Existence and Faith, translated and edited by Schubert M. Ogden, London: Hodder and Stoughton, 1961.

New Testament and Mythology and Other Basic Writings, translated and edited by Schubert M. Ogden, London: SCM Press, 1985.

Cobb, John B., Jr. *Christ in a Pluralistic Age,* Philadelphia: Westminster Press, 1975.

Collingwood, R. G. *An Essay on Philosophical Method*, Oxford: Clarendon Press, 1933.

Cox, Harvey. *The Secular City*, London: SCM Press, 1965.
  Feast of Fools, New York: Harper and Row, 1970.
  The Seduction of the Spirit, London: Wildwood House, 1974.

Cupitt, Don. *Taking Leave of God*, London: SCM Press, 1980.

Dean, William D. *Coming To: A Theology of Beauty*, Philadelphia: Westminster Press, 1972.

Dickson, K. and Ellingworth, P. *Biblical Revelation and African Beliefs*, London: Lutterworth, 1969.

Dillistone, F. W. *The Power of Symbols*, London: SCM Press, 1986.

Durkheim, E. *The Elementary Forms of the Religious Life*, translated by J. W. Swain, London: George Allen and Unwin, 1951.

Evans, R. A., ed. *The Future of Philosophical Theology*, Philadelphia: Westminster Press, 1971.

Ewing, A. C. *Value and Reality*, London: George Allen and Unwin, 1973.

Farley, Edward. *Ecclesial Man: A Social Phenomenology of Faith and Reality*, Philadelphia: Fortress Press, 1975.
  Ecclesial Reflection: An Anatomy of Theological Method, Philadelphia: Fortress Press, 1982.

Farmer, H. H. *The World and God*, London: Nisbet, 1936.

Feuerbach, Ludwig. *The Essence of Christianity*, translated by G. Eliot, New York: Harper and Brothers, 1957.
  Principles of the Philosophy of the Future, translated by M. F. Vogel, Indianapolis: Bobbs-Merrill, 1966.

Feyerabend, Paul. *Against Method: Outline of an Anarchistic Theory of Knowledge*, London: NLB, 1975.

Fichte, J. F. *Attempt at a Critique of All Revelation*, translated by Garrett Green, Cambridge: Cambridge University Press, 1978.

Flew, A. and MacIntyre, A., eds. *New Essays in Philosophical Theology*, London: SCM Press, 1955.

Freud, Sigmund. *Totem and Taboo*, London: Routledge and Kegan Paul, 1960.
  The Future of an Illusion, translated by W. D. Robson-Scott, London: Hogarth Press, 1962.

Gadamer, H. G. *Truth and Method*, Sheed and Ward, 1975.
  Philosophical Hermeneutics, translated and edited by D. E. Linge, Berkeley, Los Angeles and London: University of California Press, 1977.

Gill, Robin. *The Social Context of Theology, A Methodological Enquiry*, London and Oxford: Mowbrays, 1975.
  Theology and Social Structure, London and Oxford: Mowbrays, 1977.

Green, Garrett. *Imagining God: Theology and the Religious Imagination*, Philadelphia: Westminster Press, 1989.

Gunn, Giles. *The Interpretation of Otherness: Literature, Religion and the American Imagination*, New York: Oxford University Press, 1979.

Hartshorne, Charles. *Man's Vision of God and the Logic of Theism*, Chicago: Willet, Clark and Co., 1941.

The Divine Relativity, New Haven: Yale University Press, 1948.

A Natural Theology for Our Time, La Salle, Ill.: Open Court, 1967.

Creative Synthesis and Philosophic Method, London: SCM Press, 1970.

Hartt, Julian N. *Theological Method and Imagination*, New York: Seabury Press, 1977.

Hatch, Edwin. *The Influence of Greek Ideas and Usages upon the Christian Church*, (Hibbert Lectures for 1888), London: Williams and Norgate, 1890.

Hepburn, R. W. *Christianity and Paradox*, London: Watts, 1966.

Hick, John. *Faith and Knowledge*, New York: Cornell University Press, 1957 (2nd revised edition, London: Macmillan, 1967).

God and the Universe of Faiths, London: Collins, 1977.

Hick, John, ed. *The Myth of God Incarnate*, London: SCM Press, 1977.

Hirsch, E. D. *Validity in Interpretation*, New Haven and London: Yale University Press, 1967.

The Aims of Interpretation, Chicago: University of Chicago Press, 1976.

Hocking, W. E. *The Meaning of God in Human Experience*, New Haven: Yale University Press, 1963.

Hodges, H. A. *Languages, Standpoints and Attitudes*, Oxford: Oxford University Press, 1953.

Hume, David. *Dialogues Concerning Natural Religion*, edited by N. K. Smith, Oxford: Clarendon Press, 1935.

The Natural History of Religion, edited by H. E. Root, London: A. and C. Black, 1956.

James, William. *The Varieties of Religious Experience*, London: Longmans, Green and Co., 1952.

Jennings, T. W. *Introduction to Theology: Invitation to Reflection on the Christian Mythos*, London, SPCK, 1977.

Beyond Theism, New York and Oxford: Oxford University Press, 1985.

Kant, Immanuel. *Critique of Practical Reason*, translated by T. K. Abbott, London: Longmans, 1909.

Critique of Pure Reason, translated by N. K. Smith, London: Macmillan, 1933.

Prolegomena to Any Future Metaphysics, translated by P. G. Lucas, Manchester: Manchester University Press, 1953.

Foundations of the Metaphysics of Morals, translated by L. W. Beck, Indianapolis: Bobbs-Merrill, 1959.

Religion Within the Limits of Reason Alone, translated by T. M. Green and H. H. Hudson, New York: Harper, 1960.

Kaufman, Gordon D. *Relativism, Knowledge and Truth*, Chicago: University of Chicago Press, 1960.

An Essay on Theological Method, Missoula: Scholars Press for American Academy of Religion, 1975.

Select bibliography

The Theological Imagination: Constructing the Concept of God, Philadelphia: Westminster Press, 1981.

Kermode, Frank. *The Sense of an Ending*, Oxford: Oxford University Press, 1968.

Kierkegaard, Søren. *Philosophical Fragments*, translated by D. F. Swenson, Princeton: Princeton University Press, 1936.

Concluding Unscientific Postscript, translated by D. F. Swenson and W. Lowrie, Princeton: Princeton University Press, 1941.

Locke, John. *Essay Concerning Human Understanding*, London, 1690.

Lonergan, B. *Method in Theology*, London: Darton, Longman and Todd, 1971.

Macquarrie, John. *Principles of Christian Theology*, London: SCM Press, 1966.

Mansel, H. L. *The Limits of Religious Thought*, Oxford, 1858.

Mascall, E. L. *He Who Is*, London: Green and Co., 1943.

Existence and Analogy, London: Longmans, Green and Co., 1949.

Michalson, Gordon E. *Lessing's 'Ugly Ditch': A Study of Theology and History*, University Park and London: Pennsylvania State University Press, 1985.

Mitchell, Basil, ed. *Faith and Logic*, London: George Allen and Unwin, 1957.

Newman, John Henry. *An Essay in Aid of a Grammar of Assent*, London: Burns and Oates, 1870: edited by I. T. Ker, Oxford: Oxford University Press, 1985.

Nietzsche, Friedrich. *The Portable Nietzsche*, edited by W. Kaufmann, New York: Viking Press, 1954.

Ogden, Schubert M. *Christ Without Myth*, London: Collins, 1962.

The Reality of God, London: SCM Press, 1967.

On Theology, San Fransisco: Harper and Row, 1986.

Otto, Rudolf. *The Idea of the Holy*, translated by J. W. Harvey, 2nd edition, Oxford: Oxford University Press, 1950.

Page, Ruth. *Ambiguity and the Presence of God*, London: SCM Press, 1985.

Pailin, David A. *Groundwork of Philosophy of Religion*, London: Epworth Press, 1986.

God and the Processes of Reality: Foundations of a Credible Theism, London: Routledge, 1989.

Pannenberg, Wolfhart. *Basic Questions in Theology*, 3 volumes, London: SCM Press, 1970, 1971, 1973.

The Apostles' Creed, London: SCM Press, 1972.

Theology and the Philosophy of Science, Darton, Longman and Todd, 1976.

Peacocke, Arthur R. *Creation and the World of Science*, Oxford: Clarendon Press, 1979.

Rahner, Karl. *Foundations of Christian Faith*, translated by W. V. Dych, New York: Seabury Press, 1978.

Ramsey, I. T. *Religious Language*, London: SCM Press, 1957.
Models and Mystery, Oxford: Oxford University Press, 1964.
Christian Discourse, Oxford: Oxford University Press, 1965.
Models for Divine Activity, London: SCM Press, 1973.

Ricoeur, Paul. *Interpretation Theory: Discourse and the Surplus of Meaning*, Fort Worth: Texas Christian University Press, 1976.

Rouner, Leroy, S., ed. *Meaning, Truth and God*, Notre Dame: University of Notre Dame Press, 1982.

Ruether, Rosemary Radford. *To Change the World: Christology and Cultural Criticism*, London: SCM Press, 1981.

Schleiermacher, F. D. E. *The Christian Faith*, Edinburgh: T. and T. Clark, 1928.
On Religion. Speeches to Its Cultured Despisers, translated by John Oman, New York: Harper and Brothers, 1958.

Schon, Donald A. *Invention and the Evolution of Ideas*, London: Tavistock, 1967.

Tennant, F. R. *Philosophical Theology*, 2 volumes, Cambridge: Cambridge University Press, 1928.

Tillich, Paul. *Systematic Theology*, 3 volumes, London: Nisbet, 1953, 1957, 1964.
Biblical Religion and the Search for Ultimate Reality, London: Nisbet, 1955.
The Dynamics of Faith, New York: Harper Torchbooks, 1958.
The Courage to Be, London: Collins, 1962.

Torrance, Thomas F. *Theological Science*, Oxford: Oxford University Press, 1969.

Toulmin, Stephen. *The Uses of Argument*, Cambridge: Cambridge University Press, 1958.
Human Understanding, Oxford: Clarendon Press, 1972.

Tracy, David. *The Analogical Imagination: Christian Theology and the Culture of Pluralism*, London: SCM Press, 1981.
Pluralism and Ambiguity, London: SCM Press, 1988.

Vaihinger, E. *The Philosophy of 'As If'*, translated by C. K. Ogden, London: Kegan Paul, Trench, Trubner and Co., 1924.

Van Der Leeuw, G. *Religion in Essence and Manifestation*, London: George Allen and Unwin, 1964.

Vidler, A. R., ed. *Soundings: Essays Concerning Christian Understanding*, Cambridge: Cambridge University Press, 1962.

Whitehead, A. N. *Religion in the Making*, Cambridge: Cambridge University Press, 1926.
Science and the Modern World, Cambridge: Cambridge University Press, 1927.
Adventures of Ideas, Cambridge: Cambridge University Press, 1933.

Select bibliography

Process and Reality: An Essay in Cosmology, corrected edition edited by D. R. Griffin and D. W. Sherburne, New York: The Free Press, 1978.

Wiles, M. F. *The Remaking of Christian Doctrine*, London: SCM Press, 1974.

Wittgenstein, L. *Philosophical Investigations*, translated by G. E. M. Anscombe, Oxford: Basil Blackwell, 1958.

Wood, Charles M. *The Formation of Christian Understanding*, Philadelphia: Westminster Press, 1981.

Woods, G. F. *Theological Explanation*, Welwyn: Nisbet, 1958.

Index

Abelard, 32, 77
adoration, 65–6, 82
aesthetic values, 73–4, 179, 182
analogical knowledge of God, 120, 123, 252
Anselm, 10, 11, 20, 26, 32, 42, 46–7, 55–6, 76–7, 101–2, 137, 143, 159, 202, 204, 211, 212, 216, 220, 222, 238, 249–50, 253
anthropomorphism, 34–42, 49, 214, 215
a priori truths, 74, 79
Aquinas, T., 26, 29, 47, 171–2, 212, 220, 250, 270–1, 272
Aristotle, 57, 172, 224
Arnold, M., 13–14, 205–6
atheism, 13, 15, 54, 67, 168, 208, 247, 264
atonement theory, 22, 77–8, 99–101, 133, 245
auditions of the divine, 90–1, 101–2, 132
Augustine, 84, 161, 271
authorities for faith and belief, status of, 185–6
Ayer, A. J., 15

Baillie, J. B., 24, 88, 205, 218
Barbour, I. G., 188, 242
Barth, K., 5, 15, 16, 29, 33, 45, 47, 50, 116, 122–4, 131, 146, 148, 187, 201, 202, 212, 214, 243, 253–4, 257, 261, 273
Bartholomew, D., 206
Beardsley, W., 157
beatific vision, 73
beauty as self-justifying, 73–4
Being, experience of, 88
belief and actions, 10
  consistency of, 10–11
  cultural relativity of, 188–9
  nature of, 10–11
  realist reference of, 11–17

relation to faith, 10–11
and theology, 17–20
Belshazzar, 90
Berger, P., 43, 54, 242
Berkeley, G., 20, 24
Bernadette Soubirous, 90
Bible, 138, 183–4, 185, 253, 272–3
biology, 180f.
bishops, authority of, 185–6
Blake, W., 98
Bonhoeffer, D., 110–11, 157, 187, 249
Bonino, J. M., 193
Book of Common Prayer, 11
Braithwaite, R. B., 10, 60, 189, 203–4
Britton, K., 192
Broad, C. D., 236
Browne, P., 24, 120, 252
Buber, M., 34, 38, 86, 88, 90, 92, 110, 111, 241
Buddhist, 12
Bultmann, R., 26, 125–6, 147, 149, 188, 192, 198, 255, 261, 275
Buri, F., 189
Butler, J., 137

Calvin, J., 137
causal nexus, 176–7
Camus, A., 82, 239
certainty, 8
  sense of, 105, 109–10, 249
Christ, see Jesus Christ
Christianity, 2, 12, 156, 158, 183, 189, 192, 272
Christology, 101, 255–6, 265, 272
church, authority of, 185–6
Cicero, 31
Clarke, S., 250–1
Cleanthes, 31
Cloud of Unknowing, 103–4
Cobb, J. B, 16, 189, 194
Cole, H., 175–6
Coleridge, S. T., 138

283

Index

Galileo, 266–7
Genesis, creation stories in, 178
genetic fallacy, 52
geology, 180
Gibbon, E., 274
Gilkey, L., 43
Gleig, G., 178
God, as absent, 90, 110–12, 249
  anthropomorphic view of, 34, 39,
    45–6, 49, 54
  arguments for the existence of, 169
  as author of revelation, 123, 130–1
  as aware of all, 39–40, 67–8, 157,
    211, 223, 234
  as basis of coherence and purpose of
    all, 15, 43, 44–5, 50, 53–4, 56–60,
    64, 66–9, 78, 80, 87–8, 112, 158,
    161–2, 164, 168–73, 174, 178, 189,
    224, 235
  as basis of understanding, 7, 44–5,
    70–1, 163–4, 169–73, 266
  as benevolent, 143–4, 155–6, 181,
    252
  and the character of reality, 93,
    165–6, 173, 174–5, 186
  concept of, its origin and
    development, 31–3, 34, 42–8, 52,
    55, 71, 75–8, 80–1, 158–9, 171–2,
    213, 233–5, 270
  concept of, as construct, 42–6, 53,
    143–4, 207, 213–4, 266
  as creative, 13, 45, 58–9, 68, 79–80,
    164, 165, 171–2, 173–82, 196, 206,
    225, 226, 231–2, 234–5, 236, 239,
    270–1
  cultural relativity of concept of,
    44–5, 54, 76–8, 173, 186–7, 246
  definition of, 2, 21, 27, 38, 42, 55,
    143–4, 159–60, 222
  as determinate, 223
  dipolar view of, 26, 38–9, 71, 81,
    189–90, 235
  divine knowledge, 25, 211, 225
  as *ens realissimum*, 62, 81
  eternity of, 20, 25, 76, 157
  experience of, 41–2, 88, 92–3, 98–9,
    105–12, 120, 205, 231, 241–2
  as finite, 222–3
  as future, 30, 161, 194
  goal of, 59, 74, 157, 174, 271
  as goal of understanding, 164, 171,
    173
  and good, 72, 223–4
  goodness of, 72–4
  and history, 93, 131–8
  and hope, 193–4

  as human invention, 31–2, 34, 49–54
  identity of, 36–9, 159, 216, 223
  as impassible, 10, 11, 26, 46, 48,
    75–6, 82, 157, 204, 211, 220, 239
  as inapprehensible, 35, 40, 63,
    103–5, 116
  knowledge of, 5, 13, 23, 119–26,
    131–2, 187
  known by revelation, 116–18, 122–4,
    134
  language of, xi, 5, 12, 16, 31–54,
    78–80, 88, 103–5, 120–1, 123–5,
    172, 196, 205, 215, 216, 222, 226,
    254
  as limit, 6, 13, 59, 64, 69–71, 74,
    169–70, 230, 234
  as living, 29, 117–18
  mercy of, 11
  necessity of, 70, 74, 239
  non-realist view of, 10, 12, 50, 60,
    81–2, 221
  not an object, 41, 86, 111–12, 164,
    172, 230, 266
  as omnipotent, 32
  as other, 35, 38–9, 40–1, 112, 120,
    125–6, 254
  perfection of, 11, 20, 25, 27, 39, 47,
    55, 57–8, 76, 143, 173, 216, 224
  as personal, 13–14, 21, 43, 45–6, 81,
    83, 107, 112, 117–18, 217
  as projection of the human, 31–54,
    196, 213, 214, 219
  as puzzling, 69, 104, 266
  qualities of, 14, 26–7, 37–42, 71, 74,
    77, 204, 214, 217–18
  realist view of, 9–17, 50–4, 56, 58,
    60, 63, 80–4, 108–9. 142. 164
  as regulative, 64–6, 69–85, 196
  as regulative idea, 62, 64–9, 231
  as saving, 22, 140–6, 147, 149–50,
    152–62, 263–4
  simplicity of, 237
  as suffering, 48
  as Thou, 88, 92
  as ultimate, 9, 21, 43–4, 50, 55–85,
    143, 163–4, 170, 171–2, 222–3,
    226–7, 232
  as uncaused, 70–71, 75, 234–5
  as unchanging, 26, 216, 220
  as without beginning and end, 174
  and the world, 14, 47, 134, 154–8,
    165, 169–73, 174–82, 186, 258,
    270–1
Gosse, P., 270
Gotama, 129, 255
Grobel, K., 261

Gunton, C., 201

Halyburton, T., 250
Hamilton, Sir W., 24, 116
Hamilton, W., 28, 90, 110–11
Hare, R., 203, 235
Harnack, A., 27, 137, 188
Hartshorne, C., 20, 26, 27, 38, 56,
    59–60, 81, 143, 172, 189, 207, 209,
    211, 216, 218, 227, 232, 233, 267
Harvey, V. A., 231
Hatch, E., 27, 140, 188, 259
Hegel, G. W. F., 24, 44, 58, 225
Heidegger, M., 128, 261
Herbert of Cherbury, E., 20, 155–6
hermeneutics and theology, 183–4,
    257, 272–3
heuristic fictions, 82, 100
Hick, J., 157–8, 197, 264–5, 272
Hirsch, E. D., 184, 273
historical events and revelation, 131–8
historical judgements and theology,
    184–6, 237–8
history, unit and purpose of, 67, 233
Hobbes, T., 31, 52, 152
Hocking, W. E., 93, 244
Hodges, H. A., 190–1, 275
Hodgson, L., 257–8
Holbach, P. H. D., Baron, 15
holy, experience of the, 89, 106, 246
hope, theology as, 220
Hudson, W. D., 60, 235
Hulme, T. E., 237
human being, based on God, 53, 60,
    84, 108–9, 124–5, 142, 147, 161,
    199–200, 203, 233, 260, 262–3, 276
    fulfilment of, 147–8, 260
    future directivity of, 29, 108, 203
    nature of, 146–7, 161–2, 182–3, 262
    needs of, 140–2, 144–52, 160–2
    and religion, 33
    value of, 14, 43, 53, 60, 67, 142–3,
        199, 261, 264
human self-understanding, 6, 7, 149
Hume, D., 24, 31, 40, 52, 141, 156,
    175, 179, 181, 207
humour, theology as, 220
Humphrey, H., 272
Husserl, E., 95
Hutchinson, J., 165, 267

I as subject, 61
ideal, 228
ideal utilitarianism, 74
immortality, 18, 204

incarnation, 26, 48, 101, 132–5, 142,
    160, 255–6, 265
inspiration, 250
intelligibility, 166–7, 168
    see understanding
interpretation of texts, 183–4
intrinsic value, 73–4
Islam, 2

James, W., 102, 107, 246, 248, 263
Jenkins, D., 197
Jennings, T. W., 24
Jesus Christ, 5, 22, 25, 26, 31, 32, 48,
    77–8, 82, 94, 99, 101, 103, 129,
    132–5, 146, 160, 185, 192, 194,
    213, 221, 239, 255–6, 258, 265,
    272, 274
    cultural relativity of portraits of,
        137–8
Joan of Arc, 90
Job, 29, 50
John of the Cross, 106
Judaism, 2

Kaldun, Ibn, 118
Kant, I., 1, 4, 20, 24, 60–4, 72, 80, 89,
    94, 201, 217, 228–31, 244
Kaufman, G. D., 21, 24, 60, 143–4,
    164, 189, 210, 227, 233
Keen, S., 89, 242
Kermode, F., 100, 268
Kierkegaard, S., 24, 44, 142, 203, 207,
    268
Kolakowski, L., 269
Kraemer, H., 272
Küng, H., 16, 135, 197, 199, 208, 268

La Mettrie, J. O. de, 15, 175
language, and experience, 96, 106,
    118–19, 244, 247
    for God, xi, 5, 12, 16, 31–54, 78–80,
        88, 103–5, 120–1, 123–5, 251
    historical relativity of, 130–1
    open-textured, 130
Laski, M., 99, 106, 240
Lee, A., 91
Leibniz, G. W., 20, 36, 58, 225
Lessing, G. E., 134
Lewis, H. D., 92, 106, 240–1, 247
Liberal Protestantism, 47, 92
Locke, J., 6, 24, 115, 116, 118, 224,
    251
Lonergan, B., 60, 276
Lucretius, 31, 213
Luther, M., 92, 137, 141, 142, 259, 260

Index

MacKinnon, D. M., 212
Maclagan, W. G., 72, 235
Macquarrie, J., 87, 113, 126–8, 132, 189, 208, 255, 268
Manning, H. E., 186
Mansel, H. L., 24, 84, 116, 121–2, 239, 253
Marcel, G., 88
Marx, K., 32, 49
Mascall, E. L., 204–5, 211
Maslow, A., 242
McLeod Campbell, J., 77
McPherson, T., 103
meaning of life, 16
  of statements, 256
  of objects and events, 267
metaphysics, 1, 10, 20, 21, 58–9, 68, 70, 131, 134, 164, 167–8, 201
Mill, J. S., 15, 176, 181
mind, 61
miracle, 5, 134
models, 37–8, 41, 78–9, 99–100, 167, 188, 215
Moltmann, J., 60, 194
monism, 14, 87
Monod, J., 206
monotheism compared to polytheism, 156
Moore, G. E., 104
moral experience, 89
morality, 13, 235–6
  and God, 71–3, 229, 235, 264
  value of, 73–4
Moses, 90, 129, 136, 255, 271
Mounce, H. O., 236
Muhammad, 129, 255, 256
Muslim, 12

naturalistic fallacy, 72
natural science, see science
necessity, 74, 79, 230, 234
Newman, F., 102
Newman, J. H., 92, 105, 185, 203, 274
Newton, I., 86, 175
Nicholas of Cusa, 215
Niebuhr, H. R., 199
Nietzsche, F., 11, 15, 31, 124, 156, 247
Nineham, D., 197
non-compossibility of values, 80–1, 238
Novak, M., 240
numinous, sense of the 51, 89

Ockham, William of, 116, 251
Ogden, S. M., 11, 16, 18, 60, 161, 183–4, 199, 205, 209, 210, 233
Oman, J., 157, 203

ontological argument, 83, 267
ontological principle, 269
operators, 37
Oppenheimer, H., 217
Origen, 271
other faiths, 183, 264–5, 271–2
Otto, R., 38, 43, 51, 89, 98, 103, 104, 108, 216

Paley, W., 175
Pannenberg, W., 30, 33, 53, 60, 84, 94, 108, 124–6, 134, 141, 161, 194, 201, 203, 221, 248, 254–5, 262–3
pantheism, 14
parables, 41, 121, 218
Paul, 106, 146, 154, 255
Peacocke, A. R., 206
Peirce, C. S., 215
perfection, 47, 76
personal influences on understanding, 102–3
personal, notions of God as, see God, as personal
persons, knowledge of, 52–3
Phillips, D. Z., 204, 236
philosophy, 17–8, 140, 240
Plant, R., 270
Plato, 57, 223–4
plausibility structures, 190
Plotinus, 240
Poincaré, J. H., 286
Popper, K., 93, 269–70
Porter, B. F., 72
praise, 65–6
prayer, 10–1, 25, 204
projection, concept of God as, 31–54

qualifiers, 37, 49, 217
quantum theory, 176–7
queen of the sciences, theology as, 6, 163, 194

Rahner, K., 16, 134–5, 200, 276
Ramsey, I. T., 37, 41, 49, 60, 78–9, 114, 127–8, 188, 215, 217
rational reflection, contributions to theology of, 19–20
Rashdall, H., 91
Ray, J., 175
realist reference of faith and belief, 11–17
reality, as basically theistic, 83–4, 169–73
  as meaningful, 67, 82, 195–6
  as processive, 29–30, 58–9

287

Index

Sibs [Sibbes], R., 140
sin, 77, 89, 145–6
Smith, H., 260
Smith, J., 184
Smith, W. C., 272
social basis of concept of God, 32–3
Spinoza, B., 20, 138, 239
Stackhouse, T., 163
Statius, 31
Steiner, G., 184, 257
Sterry, P., 256
Stoicism, 259
story, notion of, 110, 167–8, 195
Strawson, P. F., 61, 201, 216, 254
sufficient reason, principle of, 58
Swinburne, R., 16
symbolic talk of God, 36–7, 41, 104,
    119–21, 145, 252–3

Teilhard de Chardin, P., 137
Tennant, F. R., 24, 45, 179, 189, 248,
    271
Tennyson, A., 181
Teresa, 106
texts, interpretation of, 183–4
The-anthropology, 123
theism, compared to metaphysics,
    167–9
  defining characteristics of, 2, 10,
    13–4, 222
  realistic reference of, 11–17, 49–54,
    186–7
  see God
theistic ethics, 74
theologian, 194, 246–7
theology, and anthropology, 183, 199
  and anthropomorphic notions, 35–42
  and Bible, 273
  and the character of the world, 165,
    169, 193–4
  as comic, 48
  complex nature of, 20, 198
  credibility of, 3–4, 165
  criteria of, 4, 143–4, 183–4, 209
  as culturally relative, 47–9, 187–8,
    246
  data for, 19, 21–2, 113, 135, 149,
    163, 250, 253, 267, 269
  as dependent upon grace, 122–3, 253
  as descriptive, 3, 19–21
  development of, 18, 198–9
  future-reference of, 29–30, 93,
    193–4, 244
  and hermeneutics, 183–4
  and history, 132–4, 184–6
  and hope, 193–4

human basis of, 5–6, 202
and the humanities, 182–6
as immune from external criticism, 3
as influenced by tradition, 17–18,
    246
interpretation of non-experience of
    God, 111–12
its limits, 1
and metaphysics, 21, 131, 251, 257
method of, 4, 21–2, 131, 165–6
method of correlation, 150–1, 262–3
as mode of understanding, 1, 2, 3,
    4–7, 121–2, 195–6
natural and revealed, 135, 250, 267,
    269
nature of, 1, 17–22, 116, 121–6, 131,
    143–4, 158–9, 197–200, 221, 253
as object of study, 6–7
primary source of, 113
as queen of the sciences, 6–7, 163,
    194, 265
and reason, 22, 23–8, 115–16, 201,
    202
as regulative knowledge, 121–2, 253
relation to a believing community,
    17–20, 208
relation to faith and belief, 17–20,
    208, 210
as relational 86, 122
relativity of, 186–90, 191–2, 198
and religious experience, 86–112
and revelation, 113–39, 163, 265–6
as revisionary, 3, 18–21
and scientific thought, 165, 174–82,
    265
significance of, 6
structures of, 190–2
as sui generis, 3
superiority of, 163–4, 265–6
tentativeness of, 28–30, 191–2
truth-claims of, 27–8, 29, 49–54,
    115–16, 143–4, 193–4, 209
as way of understanding reality,
    163–94, 196–7
Thomas Aquinas, see Aquinas, T.
Tillich, P., 8, 36, 41, 42, 88–9, 120–1,
    141, 145, 150–1, 152, 171, 172,
    252–3, 262–3
time, 20, 25
Tindal, M., 156
Torrance, T. F., 5, 23, 50, 116–17
tradition, 7–18
Troeltsch, E., 51, 144, 201, 243, 248,
    260
truth-claims, 4, 15–16, 27–8, 49–54, 68,

69–70, 105, 110, 115–16, 135, 233, 234, 275

understanding, choice of structures of, 190–2
  completion in God, 58, 83, 173, 236
  credibility of, 4, 57, 68–9, 109–10
  cultural relativity of, 46–7, 52–3, 97–102, 166–9, 186–7, 201
  depends on questions and models available, 66, 167–8, 173
  desire for, 43
  and experience, 109, 112
  limited to what is intelligible, 166–7, 231
  as mode of intepretation, 167, 268
  nature of, 4–6, 52–3, 59, 60–4, 71, 114–15, 165, 171, 186–7, 192, 267–9
  personal relativity of, 102
  presuppositions of, 66–9, 78, 237
  of reality as a whole, 44–6, 167–8
  scientific and theological, 176–7, 267
  structures of, 44, 84, 173, 188, 189–90
  as ultimately satisfying, 170–1
  ultimate unity of ways of, 67–8, 164
  see also God, as basis of coherence and purpose of all; God, as basis of understanding
universe, notion of the, 66–7, 232
universal character of some claims about God, 70
Unmoved Mover, 57
Urban, W. M., 36, 37, 120, 253

Vahanian, G., 110, 111, 249
Vaihinger, H., 82
value, intrinsic, 73–4
value-judgements and God, 72–3

van Buren, P., 60, 189
Van Der Leeuw, G., 6, 141
verification, 69–70, 93
Vidler, A., 28
visions, 90f, 101f, 106, 132
Voltaire, 194

Walgrave, J., 186–7
Walker, R. C. S., 231
Ward, K., 16
Watts, I., 180
Webb, C. C. J., 231
Wesley, C., 90, 94
Wesley, J., 90, 91, 92, 105, 137, 146
Whately, R., 253
Whewell, W., 114
Whitehead, A. N., 12, 14, 20, 59, 70, 74, 79, 88, 163–4, 171, 181–2, 210, 223, 226–7, 234, 236, 258, 269, 271
Wiles, M. F., 135, 197, 243, 258
Williams, H. A., 145
Wisdom, J. O., 16, 60
Wittgenstein, L., 3, 12, 24, 96, 103
world, coherence of, 15, 43–4, 56–7, 62, 64, 66–7, 164, 268, 269
  creation of, 178–82
  extent of, 178–9
  goal of, 15, 179, 182, 193–4
  goodness of, 43–4
  nature of, 44, 175, 176–7
  significance of, 179–80
  understanding of, 165–6, 169–73, 175–82, 232, 234, 268, 269
  see God, as creative
Wood, C. M., 273
Woods, G. F., 219
worship, object of, 27, 38, 65–6, 82

Xavier, F., 235
Xenophanes, 31, 35